'A collection of Fritz Kratochwil's essays is self-recommending – his standing as one of the most interesting and challenging of contemporary scholars of International Political Theory is incontestable. The particular merit of this collection is that it contains a number of less well-known and difficult to find pieces as well as some of his most famous contributions to the field. This is a book that deserves a very wide audience.'

Chris Brown *Professor of International Relations,*
London School of Economics, UK

'Nobody has done more to expand the scope of IR theory and to explore how politics is enabled and sustained by social order, and how order in turn rests on principles of justice. These essays bring together some of Fritz's outstanding essays on these subjects and should be read by anyone with a serious interest in IR theory.'
Richard Ned Lebow *James O. Freedman Presidential Professor at Dartmouth College,*
US and Centennial Professor at the London School of Economics, UK

The Puzzles of Politics

Friedrich Kratochwil is the author of the classic book *Rules, Norms and Decisions* (1989), which introduced constructivism to international relations and has had a profound and significant impact on the discipline.

The Puzzles of Politics brings together for the first time a collection of his key essays to explain his approach to international relations and how his thinking has developed over the last 30 years. It addresses topical themes and issues central to his work including sovereignty, law, epistemology, boundaries, global governance and world society.

The book includes a framing introduction written for this volume in which Kratochwil provides an intellectual biography providing context as well as an introduction to his work.

This important volume will be of very strong interest to students and scholars of international relations, political theory and law.

Friedrich Kratochwil is presently Professor of International Relations at the European University Institute in Florence, Italy, and visiting scholar at Kyung Hee University, Seoul, Korea. After receiving his Ph.D. from Princeton he taught in the US at Maryland, Columbia and Penn, before returning to the LMU in Munich, Germany. He has been the editor of the *European Journal of International Relations* and member of the editorial boards of several journals, including the *Journal of International Relations of the Asia-Pacific*, *International Studies Quarterly*, *International Organization*, *World Politics*, *Review of International Studies*, and the *Journal of International Relations and Development*.

The New International Relations

Edited by Richard Little, *University of Bristol*, Iver B. Neumann, *Norwegian Institute of International Affairs (NUPI), Norway* and Jutta Weldes, *University of Bristol*.

The field of international relations has changed dramatically in recent years. This new series will cover the major issues that have emerged and reflect the latest academic thinking in this particular dynamic area.

International Law, Rights and Politics
Developments in Eastern Europe and the CIS
Rein Mullerson

The Logic of Internationalism
Coercion and accommodation
Kjell Goldmann

Russia and the Idea of Europe
A study in identity and international relations
Iver B. Neumann

The Future of International Relations
Masters in the making?
Edited by Iver B. Neumann and Ole Wæver

Constructing the World Polity
Essays on international institutionalization
John Gerard Ruggie

Realism in International Relations and International Political Economy
The continuing story of a death foretold
Stefano Guzzini

International Relations, Political Theory and the Problem of Order
Beyond international relations theory?
N.J. Rengger

War, Peace and World Orders in European History
Edited by Anja V. Hartmann and Beatrice Heuser

European Integration and National Identity
The challenge of the Nordic states
Edited by Lene Hansen and Ole Wæver

Shadow Globalization, Ethnic Conflicts and New Wars
A political economy of intra-state war
Dietrich Jung

Contemporary Security Analysis and Copenhagen Peace Research
Edited by Stefano Guzzini and Dietrich Jung

Hegemony & History
Adam Watson

Territorial Conflicts in World Society
Modern systems theory,
international relations and conflict
studies
Edited by Stephan Stetter

**Ontological Security in International
Relations**
Self-identity and the IR State
Brent J. Steele

**The International Politics of Judicial
Intervention**
Creating a more *just* order
Andrea Birdsall

**Pragmatism in International
Relations**
*Edited by Harry Bauer and
Elisabetta Brighi*

Civilization and Empire
China and Japan's encounter
with European international
society
Shogo Suzuki

Transforming World Politics
From empire to multiple worlds
*Anna M. Agathangelou and
L.H.M. Ling*

The Politics of Becoming European
A study of Polish and Baltic
post-Cold War security
imaginaries
Maria Mälksoo

Social Power in International Politics
Peter Van Ham

International Relations and Identity
A dialogical approach
Xavier Guillaume

The Puzzles of Politics

Inquiries into the genesis and transformation of international relations

Friedrich Kratochwil

Routledge
Taylor & Francis Group

LONDON AND NEW YORK

First published 2011
by Routledge
2 Park Square, Milton Park, Abingdon, Oxon OX14 4RN

Simultaneously published in the USA and Canada
by Routledge
270 Madison Avenue, New York, NY 10016

*Routledge is an imprint of the Taylor & Francis Group,
an informa business*

The right of Friedrich Kratochwil to be identified as author of this
work has been asserted by him in accordance with sections 77 and 78
of the Copyright, Designs and Patents Act 1988.

Typeset in Times by
RefineCatch Limited, Bungay, Suffolk
Printed and bound in Great Britain by
TJ International Ltd, Padstow, Cornwall

British Library Cataloguing in Publication Data
A catalogue record for this book is available from the British Library

Library of Congress Cataloging-in-Publication Data
Kratochwil, Friedrich V.
   The puzzles of politics : inquiries into the genesis and transformation
of international relations / Friedrich Kratochwil.
      p. cm.—(The new international relations)
   Includes bibliographical references and index.
   1. International relations.   I. Title.
   JZ1242.K73 2010
   327.1—dc22   2010007266

ISBN: 978–0–415–58101–1 (hbk)
ISBN: 978–0–415–58102–8 (pbk)
ISBN: 978–0–203–84511–0 (ebk)

Contents

Acknowledgements

The publishers would like to thank the following publishers for permission to reprint their material:

Princeton Institute for International and Regional Studies for "The Humean conception of international relations", Center of International Studies, Princeton University, World Order Studies Program, Occasional Paper No. 3, June 1981.

MIT Press for "On the notion of interest in international relations", *International Organization*, Vol. 36 (Winter 1982): 1–30.

Springer Science and Business Media for "Sovereignty, property, and propriety: the generative grammar of modernity", English version of the article "Souverinitaet und Moderne" in Festschjrift fuer Beate Kohler-Koch, edited by Markus Jachtenfuchs, Michelle Knodt, *Regieren in Internationalen Institutionen* (Opladen, Ger.: Leske und Budrich, 2002): 29–52.

School of International Affairs, Columbia University for "Thrasymmachos revisited: On the relevance of norms and the study of law for international relations", *Journal of International Affairs* (Winter, 1983): 343–56.

European Journal of International Law for "The limits of contract", *European Journal of International Law*, Vol. 5 (1994): 465–91.

Hart Publishing Ltd for "Has the 'rule of law' become a 'rule of lawyers'?", in Gianluigi Palombella, Neil Walker (eds.), *Relocating the Rule of Law* (Oxford: Hart Publishing, 2009): 171–96.

Sage Publications Ltd for "Constructing a new orthodoxy? Wendt's 'social theory of international politics' and the constructivist challenge", *Millennium*, Vol. 29, No. 1 (2000): 73–101.

Sage Publications Ltd for "History, action and identity: Revisiting the 'second great debate' and assessing its importance for social theory", *European Journal of International Relations*, vol. 12, No. 1 (2006): 5–29.

Cengage Learning Services Limited for "Ten points to ponder about pragmatism: Some critical reflections on knowledge generation in the social sciences", in Harry Bauer, Elisabetta Brighi (eds.), *Pragmatism in International Relations* (London: Routledge, 2009): 11–25.

Cambridge University Press for "Of systems and boundaries: An inquiry into the formation of the state system", *World Politics*, Vol. 39, No. 1 (1986): 27–52. Copyright © 1986 Trustees of Princeton University.

Millennium Publishing Group for "The politics of place and origin: An enquiry into the changing boundaries of representation and legitimacy", *International Relations of the Asia Pacific*, Vol. 1 (2001): 143–65.

Liverpool University Press for "Global governance and the emergence of 'world society'", in Nathalie Karagiannis, Peter Wagner (eds.), *Varieties of World Making: Beyond Globalization* (Liverpool: Liverpool University Press, 2007): 266–83.

Every effort has been made to contact copyright holders for their permission to reprint material in this book. The publishers would be grateful to hear from any copyright holder who is not here acknowledged and will undertake to rectify any errors or omissions in future editions of this book.

Preface

When I entered the discipline at the end of the 1980s, it was only tenuously linked to the other social sciences, and only patchily linked to the study of international law. Since then, numerous links have been forged between the three, and for that we may largely thank the emergence of constructivism. For many, constructivism has come to mean the thin American constructivism which studies the importance of ideas in processes of socialisation. Among the contenders, we find a variant that is steeped in the broad tradition of classics, continental philosophy and legal theorising. This variant was spearheaded by Fritz Kratochwil and Nick Onuf.

Fritz has put his mark on the discipline in three ways. First, by publishing *On Rules, Politics and Knowledge* in 1989. Secondly, by contributing a series of articles, the most central of which are collected here. And thirdly, by being the polyhistor to whom the rest of us would turn for inspiration and advice. At every ISA, Fritz, his former students and sundry hangers-on would make up a peripatetic *Stammtisch*, an untranslatable German term meaning a group of people meeting to discuss something at regular intervals as well as the table itself. For Fritz may love his ancient Greeks and know many languages, but there is no doubt about his nationality. In the German tradition, his students seem to think about him not only as a supervisor for a doctoral project, but as a *Doktorvater* ("doctor father") for life. And in the German tradition, his pedagogical methods would strike most British people as, shall we say, unorthodox. I recall a panel in San Diego where Fritz served as discussant. The first paper was on Hedley Bull's approach to international relations which the author apparently misinterpreted. The author, who in Kratochwil's opinion, had badly misrepresented Bull's position, was told, "and if he had been here, I am certain he would have grabbed hold of anything he could lay his hand on and clobbered you over the head with it, repeatedly". I was the co-author of the next paper. Fritz noted that we found interesting consuls were new to the IR gaze, and opined that: "You say that no one has looked as this topic before. Well, as I say to my PhD students when they make that point: There may be a reason for that."

The very same scholarly take-no-prisoners ethos shines out of the autobiographical essay that opens the book. We are then treated to three perspectival essays, three legal essays, three epistemological essays and three categorising essays. Taken together, they demonstrate what a philosophically and socially informed constructivism looks like.

Iver B. Neumann

1 A Wanderer between two worlds

An attempt at an intellectual biography

Where to begin?

The task of providing the reader with a brief intellectual biography is challenging for several reasons, especially at this stage of my life. But all of them actually boil down to the problem inherent in any biographical attempt, i.e. in the making out of the contingencies and accidents of one's journeys some more encompassing narrative that gives every detail its place shows its role in the developments that are being traced. This makes it necessary to chose a proper beginning, or perhaps put better, one needs to select a decisive break that organises the "before" and "after" and lets us follow through to the present. Such a move imposes thereby the perspective of an all-knowing narrator whose perceptions might be at odds with the actual twists and turns of the ongoing process of life, but which tries to make sense out of the contingent and seemingly unrelated elements. Given the story line, things and events attain by hindsight an importance and coherence they hardly had when they occurred. Different from the "first inklings" or "antecedents" that play such a role later, both the "inklings" and the various attempts at dealing with the contingencies of life were in "real time" little more than the effort to deal with the buzzing, blooming confusion of the world.

In a rather generous and sympathetic appraisal of my work Richard Falk has recently argued that I had "always been a Humean", and that he remembers me as one graduate student at Princeton who did not have to engage with lengthy soul-searching that is usually part of a graduate career.[1] True, by the time I met Richard and he had become my dissertation mentor I was well on my way to defining my approach to politics that – admittedly – was rather removed from the dominant "isms", be it realism, liberalism, or (at that time still) Marxism. Robert Gilpin had encouraged me during my seminars to follow up on the issue of "conventions", which seemed promising to him, but coming from a "realist" his suggestion left me somewhat puzzled at first. Actual help could have been available just a few buildings down College Walk since David Lewis was – if I remember correctly – at that time still in the philosophy department at Princeton. Unfortunately, I never met him and only later discovered his work which took off from Hume. Rather, it was Richard Falk who (in a long talk several months after the dissertation defense) twisted my arm and encouraged me to draw out the implications on signaling, on the emergence of custom, and of "unspoken rules" which develop through interaction, all of which had been the topic of my dissertation (which dealt with the emergence of the Cold War and attempts of détente).[2] What was needed was a much more integrated statement of a research program that could be built on such a conventionalist approach.

It is here that Hume became so important for me since following up on some of his ideas allowed me to integrate such issues as "salience", the emergence of conventions, and the need for a "public entrepreneur" procuring public goods, but also the question of "emotions" and the extension of "sympathy" to others, of "interest" (that which is "in-between us" rather than a mere preference), of the role of language in social life, and of the "constructed character" of the social world and its inevitable "historicity". Suddenly international law, particularly the discussions on custom or on "soft law" and a strategic analysis *à la* Schelling – with its emphasis on salience – showed some surprising elective affinities that could be brought together. The attention to history, so well justified by Bull and the British school, also seemed to fit with a focus on practical reason and the "classical approach" that took seriously the "particular" in politics. Rather than becoming enthralled by some grand "theory" and "science" that was based on an understanding of classical "physics that never was", as Toulmin remarked later, there was much work to be done to give greater stringency to an approach that traditionally oriented itself on "prudence" rather than "theory" and which only in law had been worked out somehow. In short, all these elements seemed to define a research program of considerable scope and of heuristic power. Later my encounter with Berger and Luckmann's work on the *Construction of Social Reality*, my deeper engagement with Austin's and Searle's language philosophy and with Luhmann's often rather obscure sociology prepared the way for the "constructivist" approach with which I became later identified.

Even from this rather sketchy account it becomes clear that Richard Falk's perception that I always had been a Humean was in a way fitting, but it also needed some correction. True, at the dissertation stage, when our meetings and discussions became frequent and covered a lot of ground, and following that, the one year I was at the Center for International Studies where both the *Humean Perspective* and *The notion of interest* were written, my approach had remained essentially in place for some time. What Falk's interpretation underplays, though, is the years of graduate studies in the States, first at Georgetown and later at Princeton, that had provided me not only with a solid grounding in the discipline – I had entered graduate school without having ever taken a course on international politics – but also with an astonishing amount of food for thought that forced me to go back to and re-think what I had learned before.

Thus, I actually learned more about the "German tradition" in sociology (Weber, Marx, Schuetz, and Simmel) and history (Dehio, Hintze, and Meinecke) from Professors Allers (Georgetown) and Gilpin (Princeton) than from my teachers at the University of Munich. Richard Falk's anti-formalist approach to law, although policy oriented – and here we did not always see eye to eye – was tremendously important for me breaking the sterile mode of a Kelseonian conception of law. It also impelled me to read some of the classics such as de Vitoria, Grotius, Vattell, or Savigny. Oran Young's year long tutorial on the "Philosophy of the Social Sciences" at Princeton – which was an extensive course on both "scope and method" of political science (with occasional excursions to economics and sociology) – forced me not only to engage fully with the "scientific" study of politics but also to re-think some of the arguments that I had encountered in Germany, which later were referred to as the *Positivismusstreit* (which had pitted the Frankfurt School against logical positivists). So, if in a way I had hoped in 1967 to escape my past by "leaving town" and going to America, I quickly had to realise that such an escape was not viable. Nevertheless, I also quickly noticed that without such a sudden departure from the "old world" and its strictures, the new engagement with these debates and sources would not have been possible.

To that extent, the years in the US between 1967, when I arrived, and 1974, when I left Princeton for a job at Maryland (while 1969 I spent as an assistant at the Technical University back in Munich before returning to the States), were truly formative. They thus provide the justification for treating them in the sense of the all-knowing narrator as the crucial turning point that establishes the "before" and "after" and endows these categories with meaning.

The before

If I had to name the influences that most strongly shaped my early life, they were certainly not ideas but the brutal circumstances of the post-war period. Being a refugee from the former Czechoslovakia and expelled again by Austria – which had in time discovered that it had nothing to do with the Third Reich – we landed in the American occupation zone in Germany in a little village in Bavaria near Augsburg. My father, a lawyer by training, had found a job in a saw mill, while my grandfather went back to his trade and produced brushes in a "cottage" industry. My function was mainly to be a worry to my parents as I had contracted tuberculosis. With no antibiotics available, all one could do was to wait and pray. Even staying with my family had become a problem, since a couple – well connected with the military government – wanted to adopt me, alleging that my parents could not care for me. Later, also, school officials objected to admitting me to school because of the dangers of infection. Needless to say, it was not a happy childhood and our precarious situation in Germany was reinforced by the general anxieties which were induced by the increasing chilliness of the Cold War manifesting itself in the Berlin Blockade, the Korean War, and the division of Europe.

These events and the hyper-politisation they engendered belong to my first recollections. I remember vividly the long debates that took place within my family as those parts of the family who were in Czechoslovakia and those who had been expelled to the German "Eastern zone" became increasingly unreachable. Even for me as a pre-school toddler the Marshall and Schuman plans, the debates about Western integration spearheaded by the much-admired Adenauer, and even the landing at Inchon (that turned the tide in Korea) became quite naturally part of my vocabulary. Living with politics and "history" was also powerfully reinforced by my grandfather and the many tales he told me from his life. He had been a POW in WWI, and having been captured rather early in the war he and some thirty Czech and Austrian soldiers had been put in a camp in the far Eastern part of Siberia. Yet, just before the Russian Revolution this group dared a breakout. They succeeded and embarked on a march "home", to the newly emerged Czechoslovakia. The journey took five and a half years and followed – with some significant deviations occasioned by the circumstances of the Russian civil war – more or less the trans-Siberian railroad. The group took on odd jobs, traded salt that they had acquired in the southern steppes, fought for the "reds" or "whites" as circumstances commanded, or just hid in the forests and tried to live off of the land. Eighteen of them, among them my grandfather, finally made it back to Moravia. Listening to these tales it is hardly surprising that names like Vladivostok, Irkutsk, Alma Ata, or Omsk were familiar to me long before I could locate them on the small globe which my grandpa bought me when I entered school.

Materially things were looking up only by the mid-fifties when we had moved to Munich where my father found a civil service position and I had entered the Gymnasium (classical language branch). With hindsight I must say that I had some very remarkable teachers during my high school years in virtually all fields, ranging from classical languages to the sciences (the school proudly counted Max Planck and Werner Heisenberg to its alumni). Above all, what I took from there as the most valuable "good forever" (so to speak the Thucydidean *ktema eis aei*) was: the respect for the "word". This meant first of all the close attention to the text and what is said (instead of constru-ing some meanings through "free translations" or fanciful imputations of meaning). Perhaps my persistent uneasiness with "grand theories" derives from these early experiences of disciplining one's imagination in order to understand what "the other" has to say. They also are a reminder that "grand schemes" turn out to be mostly trivial or untrue, as things seldom fit neatly together, all "elegant" representations notwithstanding. But second, respect for the word also meant the respect for the *logos* and for its critical potential as can be found in the early Platonic dialogues. There Socrates subjects some of the most "obvious" common sense concepts to scathing criticism while also showing the nihilist implications of "universal" suspicion and criticism for criticism's sake, as exemplified by the sophists. Third, the respect for the "word" also entailed the respect for language that makes us human and special among all "gregarious animals" as Aristotle so beautifully elaborates in his *Politics* by making a crucial distinction between *phone* (voice) and *logos* (concept/reason). At the time, the most important implication of this argument for me was that the attempts of utilitarians to reduce everything to a calculus of pain and pleasure had to end up in a platitudinous social theory, unless one reintroduced – entirely inconsistent with the liberal program – again "higher" and "lower" pleasures *à la* Mill. Thus, long before I became a "constructivist" I had learned from Aristotle that the human world is not "natural" but that it is based on commonly accepted concepts without, however, thereby becoming arbitrary or meaningless!

Finally, there was the realization of the historical rootedness of our concepts and their semantics, most tragically exemplified by the case of Germany. Indeed, much of the traditional political language had become unusable due to its taintedness by the Nazi ideology. Establishing a basis for understanding in the absence of a general trust in a "common sense" and the good judgment of one's interlocutors is difficult indeed. Perhaps this explains how for my generation the issue of "understanding" (now containing also dimensions other than the old epistemological controversies to which they could be related) has become such a preoccupation.

Yet, one had not only to watch out for "old" usages of some compromised concepts in the political discourses; one had also to be aware that similarly disastrous political projects could be pursued under an "antifascist" or "reformist" cover that could justify the worst crimes of the "proletarian revolutions" be they Stalin's purges or Mao's later antics. Germany, having distanced itself throughout the modern era from the West and its traditions and having insisted instead on a *Sonderweg* by taking pride in its high "culture" – as opposed to the "mere civilization" of the French or Anglo-Saxon world – seemed ill prepared for developing a *Streitkultur* (mode of dealing with controversy) that allowed for disagreements and cooperation. The tedious tendency to make out of everything a question of *Weltanschauung*, and of not only dismissing other arguments but to frequently consider them as issuing from ill will or treachery, did not ease communications across political differences. Frequently this tendency also led to instrumentalizing the past instead of facing the German catastrophe in a candid and honest fashion.

I liked going to school, I was doing well, and I acquired a quite good general education, despite the fact that my extracurricular activities, ranging from music to sports, often took more of my time than my school work. My passion, though, was politics. I edited the school newspaper (and twice won the award for the best paper in the state), joined the European Federalists, and later, at the University, the Christian Democratic Students Organization and soon served on the staff of a member of parliament while taking courses and seminars in ancient history, philosophy, and political science.

My *Studienbuch* of the LMU in Munich (i.e. the academic record of the lectures and seminars which the student had to keep and that s/he was supposed to submit to the examining board after some 4 or 5 years) shows a vast array of subjects. There are courses and seminars on Plato, Aristotle, Kant, and Hegel but also courses on numismatics, on "historical sources" and the supplementary sciences of historiography, on the social teachings of the Christian Churches, on Weber and the *Erklären/Verstehen* controversy, on Heidegger and Kierkegaard, on the Contractarians, on Epistemology, on Aesthetics, on Thomas and the transcendental notions in scholastic philosophy, on the Greek colonies in Sicily, on Cesar and the end of the Roman Republic, on Hellenism, on Wittgenstein, on the Glorious Revolution, on Soviet politics, on Sources of Nazi politics, on the Codex Hammurabi and the Gilgamesh epic, on West European Party systems, on the German Constitutional Court, on modern logic, on the Florentine Humanists, on Descartes and his opponents, on the Federalist papers, on Thucydides and Greek historiography, on Roman Inscriptions, Napoleon and his time, on political systems in comparative perspective, on the 19th century French novel, on Rome from Augustus to Commodus, on the German Reformation, on the sources of Herodotus, on Hesiod and Homer, on the history of Roman Law, on the Exegesis of the Codex Justinianus, and on the European Powers and Imperialism. In addition, one also finds a workshop on the new production of Tannhäuser at the opera house, a seminar on Augustine's Confessions, a Seminar on Giambattista Vico, on selected topics of electoral politics, on Rousseau's political writings, on European integration, on Arendt's work on Totalitarianism and so on . . .

Obviously the record shows far flung interests but no sharp focus. In the meantime, I had begun with the preliminary draft of a dissertation but on the whole I felt ill-prepared for an examination . . . in what? According to the guidelines, I could try in all three fields, history, philosophy or political science, as I had fulfilled all requirements. But the stultifying atmosphere in many of the university institutes at Munich, the lack of sensible curricula, the more or less benign neglect of the students who were left to fend for themselves – all justified in terms of academic freedom – did not help. Particularly problematic was the situation at the institute of political science where the strangest orthodoxy (allegedly based on Plato and Aristotle) was dispensed as the only "*true episteme politike*". All other ideas were simply treated as "gnostic derailments", (probably in order to dispose of them more quickly before the "thought police" formed at the *Lehrstuhl* by some zealot acolytes). After having been fortunate enough to enjoy a high-school education that was entirely anti-authoritarian (although never making such claims), I now had to face the music at the university. Needless to say, I did not like the tune.

Thus, the conjuncture of my dissatisfaction with the German university – not being helped by some parts of what later has been euphemistically called the "student movement" but which Habermas more appropriately characterised at the time as "red Fascism" – my personal problems in a relationship, changing career aspirations, and a rather problematic encounter with my then "mentor" concerning my dissertation on St. Augustine's conception of community (of course "gnostic to the core") culminated one day in a snap decision to apply for a Fulbright scholarship. I had to go through two interviews, while it helped that I had been selected by the Adenauer foundation as one of their "hopefuls" the year before. Being lucky enough to get one of the few full tuition and stipend scholarships, I left in late August 1967 by a steamer from Bremen to New York.

In September, fresh from the boat, I enrolled in Nick Onuf's first class that he taught at Georgetown after coming from Hopkins graduate school. After 18 months (and some unnerving fights with US immigration) I received my MA. I had lacked the funding for the last 6 months as budget cuts had eliminated the funding for my second year. Since I was a student, I could not work, but since I did not work I could not show sufficient funds, a perfect Catch 22. Finally I was able to fox this problem with the help of my later wife, a linguist and former Argentinean Fulbright student, by obtaining a special visa for teaching at the Defense Language Institute as an instructor for German.

The after

To my never-ending chagrin, my graduate advisor at Princeton forced me one year earlier than usual to leave the intellectually exciting and rather happy world of the Graduate College since I had gotten two job offers shortly after having passed my generals and the defence of my dissertation prospectus. I had been hired by the University of Maryland at Baltimore County, a place with high aspirations and little funds. Of course over-eager deans and neurotic university presidents – one of them had to be stopped by a state trooper when he tried to abscond with the furniture of his office after he had been fired – wanted to make this university (hardly more than a glorified college) the "flagship" of the university system. Of course such plans paid little attention to what was possible under the best of circumstances. Hopes of being in the league of Harvard, Yale, and Princeton were also voiced. My ironic remark that a "Harvard on the Patapsco" (a little creek running through the Campus) did not have the same ring than a "Harvard at the Charles River" was noticed and not forgotten.

The next year after having passed my first year of probation I was told that yes, I had fulfilled all the requirements, but that I would be out of a job. When I retorted that this was against the contract, I was simply told by the academic vice-president: "So? Just sue me!" The background of this travesty was that a faction in the department, who had wanted my position to be an American politics slot but who had lost out previously, had been "getting together" with some administrators who had overheard my remark and had considered it "negative". To that extent, the result was one of those endearing qualities of academic life that seems to be truly universal. As Henry Kissinger so aptly remarked, "what makes academic politics so vicious is the smallness of the stakes".

In any case, after the usual blood-letting I had the job back but had of course to put all my efforts into writing my way out of there. A year at the Princeton Center of International Studies came in handy, as did a fellowship from the Humboldt Foundation. Having gotten the fellowship on the basis of a proposal for writing a book on international organisation, I came to realize that antecedent to questions of organisational forms and of the design of organisation, the norms that structure our expectations and that constitute our institutions need to be investigated first. So I chucked my proposal and began the work on what would later become my *Rules Norms and Decisions*. When in 1980 Columbia offered me an eight year contract on a non-tenure line I took it despite a tenure offer from Maryland. After all, what can be the incentive of having "tenure in hell", as I told my chairman in Baltimore?

My time at Columbia was strange but highly interesting. It was strange since I was one of 25 or 30 junior faculty members facing 30 or so senior professors. Most of us knew that at best we could hope for a "soft bounce" after our time was up. This increased anxiety and perhaps productivity but not necessarily mental health, a precious commodity in New York in any case. I, not even having the prospect of being considered for further employ-ment when one of the grants that financed my line ran out, did my best to accommodate to being the lowest form of life on the academic food chain. Yet, it was not all bad since people left me alone. Oscar Schachter, Louis Henkin, and Bruce Ackerman in Law showed interest in my work. David Baldwin, a powerful conceptual analyst from whose writings I had profited, joined the department soon, and in John Ruggie I met a kindred spirit.

The article on which Ruggie and I collaborated emerged from some odd circumstances. John had researched the IO literature and made the pitch that not organisations but the way of organising, i.e. organisation in the collective singular, should be the proper focus for analysis. In this way inter-national organisation would not be just a sub-field of IR but an analytical focus that could revive IR theory and could integrate the regime debate into the mainstream. I had just come back from an interview at the Graduate Institute at Geneva where I had outlined why the study of norms cannot be dealt with by the traditional positivist methods. (Of course, the talk had flown like a lead balloon, since my unorthodox approach seemed to have disturbed even the historians, while the lawyers argued that what I said was hardly new to them, and the political scientists, mostly number-crunchers, felt uncomfortable.)

Thus, Ruggie and I decided to try to bring these two pieces together. John offered to write a first draft sharpening the distinction of ontology and epis-temology. I went over it. We agreed on a second draft. John found the catchy title and off it went to *International Organization*. From there the apocryphal story goes that the article got rejected by both reviewers but that Peter Katzenstein, the then editor, took a chance. He asked us to make only minor changes which we gladly did. After publication, though, there was a near avalanche of – let's say "highly critical" – mail. One author even claimed that it was "people like us" who preached "relativism" – apparently irked by our emphasis on the term "inter-subjective" which for him abolishes IR theorising as an "objective" science – and who had made Hitler possible!!!

Some of my colleagues in the political science department at Columbia must indeed have thought that I was simply weird as I got interested in norms when détente was clearly on the decline. Besides, some new fangled "constructivism" was unlikely to challenge the ruling positivist orthodoxy which had bolted logical positivism, instrumentalism, and the paradigms of Kuhn together, making it appear as if they fitted hand in glove. So why not join the "profession" and haul with the wolves?

An amusing quip of one of my colleagues who taught in the morning the "bombs for breakfast" course in the same room in which I had my lecture on international law in the afternoon was indicative of the mood at that time. Apparently he had developed some proprietary interest in "his" lecture hall where he for years had taught foreign policy and national security. No wonder that he must have felt somewhat odd when this young upstart was now to teach international law in his hallowed rooms. In seeing me march towards the class room he jokingly called over to me: "Remember Fritz, if it does not move, maim, stink or kill, it is not IR!"

All these differences did not impair serious intellectual discussion at the lunch table – which Bob Jervis got together virtually every day – at Zbig Brzezinski's institute on International Change that brought in, weekly, interesting people from academia and politics, or at the high powered legal theory workshop where I encountered many of the leading intellectuals from Charles Taylor to Dworkin, Habermas, and others. In addition, some of the most interesting discussions we had occurred at the graduate-student run seminars at Columbia, where Simone Chambers was frequently the *spiritus rector*, or at the joint seminar between Columbia and Princeton that Daniel Deudney had organised.

It was these seminars that I most sorely missed when I moved to Penn in 1988, and the graduate students both at Princeton and Columbia also disappeared taking on jobs all over the place. My years at Penn were largely characterised by administrative work. When I arrived the department had just gotten out of receivership, and with promises from the Dean and President we all hoped to be able to successfully rebuild the place. Two new colleagues came with me. So being a good citizen I served for six years on the personnel committee and waded through hundreds of job applications since we had every year more than two or three searches. To make a long story short: after initial successes an incompetent dean stayed long enough to do considerable damage. He finally left, becoming a university president somewhere else, but he was drummed out of town a few years later, as the same pattern repeated itself there. Despite these burdens, I managed to get several articles out, two co-authored with doctoral students and published in *International Organization*, one on medieval politics, and one on transformative change. A reader on international organisation along the lines of Ruggie's suggestions followed.

Penn nevertheless provided me with one of the greatest challenges as a teacher. I went twice with the summer program "Penn at Seoul" to Korea and taught students at Seoul National and at Kyung Hee universities. Being confronted with an entirely different culture was an eye-opener, much like the difficulty of finding a way to reach students whose English was largely not "functional" enough to rely on traditional lecturing or even discussions (given the cultural and language inhibitions).

My return to Germany in 1995 was motivated by more or less personal reasons. My father had died and my mother was getting on in age. I had always felt somewhat guilty since the lion's share of my Fulbright and of my doctoral fellowships had been paid by the German taxpayer. Although I had to show in writing that German authorities did not need my services when I asked for a permanent resident visa in the US back in 1974 – such a letter was actually written by one of my former professors at Munich who had meanwhile become the minister of education – this gambit did not take care of the nagging feeling that I ought to give something back. When jobs opened up at the German universities after the reunification and when a professor of law in Munich, who was familiar with my writings, encouraged me to apply at the LMU I did so. It seemed the time there was ripe for some reforms and both the rector and the minister of education asked me to submit some reform proposals for the institute of political science when I, after much infighting, was finally offered the position.

As no good deed shall go unpunished, reality soon caught up with me. The tip-off was when I appeared before the rector with a reform proposal for the institute and for the curriculum. He was totally surprised to see me, as I should have understood that tasking me with such proposals was for show only. He looked briefly at the papers, actually liked the idea of instruction in English for the doctoral courses and put them aside without discussion, promising to hand them to the legal department. Three months later I got the news from the university lawyers: unfortunately one could not proceed with any of the reforms, as they were not in conformity with the existing rules! Meanwhile a majority of the colleagues – a.k.a. the notorious "Gang of Four" – had rounded up the wagons and was firing from behind the lines against the "American" who wanted to ruin the good German university. Business as usual!

A big grant from the *VW Stiftung* for the establishment of an interdisciplinary program in philosophy, law, and political science created some much needed space for thought in an otherwise untenable situation. With the collaboration of Bruno Simma (now judge at the ICJ) and Wilhelm Vossenkuhl (from philosophy), a doctoral program of considerable power emerged, as evidenced by the success of the graduates: one teaching at Oxford, one being an editor in Chief of a newspaper, one being an associate professor in Mexico, another in Ecuador, one finishing his habilitation, another working at a public policy institute, and so on.

With the move to the European University Institute in 2003 I escaped the milieu of damages that otherwise would have taken their toll. But despite the conducive environment at Fiesole, working on my magnum opus on *Praxis* has been delayed again and again. Being a mentor to some 18 doctoral students does take its time despite the easy teaching load. At least some of the programmatic statements concerning my "pragmatic turn" have meanwhile been published showing my increasing disillusionment with the "theory" debates in the field and reinforcing also my former objections against "grand theory". The article with my former student Joerg Friedrichs that appears this year in *International Organization* will provide some sketches of future projects. Otherwise, I just have to say that while it might be true that Florence is a hardship post, someone has to do it! Where else could a "Wanderer between two worlds", between Europe and America, and between the classics and the moderns find a better place for doing his job? But then again, are the moves between these two worlds still sufficient for understanding the transformative changes of our times? I often wonder.

Notes

1 Richard Falk, Foreword to *On Rules, Politics and Knowledge* (Festschrift für Friedrich Kratochwil) ed. by Oliver Kessler, Rodney Hall, Cecilia Lynch and Nicholas Onuf (New York: Palgrave, forthcoming).
2 See my *International Order and Foreign Policy* (Boulder: Westview, 1978).

The present collection of essays brings together a variety of articles written over the years. It is organised according to classical topics, such as I-Defining the Approach, II-Writings on International Law and III-Writings on Epistemology. Only the fourth section, Drawing Boundaries, seems to fall out of this classical division. It tries to make the "constructivist" point though that the drawing of boundaries is not only constitutive of the fields but also demonstrates how the latter change through the ways in which we make distinctions and include, alter, or exclude certain practices. I gratefully acknowledge the research help of Hannes Peltonen, Helena Carapiço and Guilherme Vasconcelos Vilaça.

Part I
Defining the approach

2   The Humean perspective on international relations

I

In this essay I want to argue that the theory-building in international relations is particularly well served by adopting a "Humean" perspective. Such
a perspective would enable us not only to create a research programme[1] (or
approach) that would allow for the systematic inquiry into some normative
problems [. . .]; it would also aid in the development of criteria for judging
competing approaches to international politics. Finally, the adoption of a
Humean perspective seems to hold out the prospect of providing an integrative framework for various types of analysis that are currently carried out
separately and in a nearly *ad hoc*[2] fashion.

[. . .]

In developing these thoughts more fully, my argument will proceed as
follows. First, I will try to show that the research programme of realism[3] established international relations not only as an autonomous discipline, but
informed most alternative modes of analysis. It can be shown that most
behavioural,[4] as well as normative approaches (which developed in opposition
to some of the conclusions of realism) were informed by the same problem-set[5]
that realism had selected as constituting the field of inquiry.

Second, in trying to assess the explanatory power of various approaches,
purely formal criteria such as consistency of the logical structure, clear definition of terms, and so forth, are necessary but not sufficient yardsticks in
judging a theoretical effort. They have to be supplemented by a critical reflection upon the fruitfulness of the problem-set itself;[6] otherwise such important
aspects as relevance (and, conversely, triviality) cannot be adequately dealt
with. For all these reasons, I will argue that the Humean perspective leads to a
particularly instructive reflection on the dominant realist problem-set.[7]

Third, if we establish a competing problem-set, we can show not only that
realism is a special case of the Humean "puzzle", but also that new lines
of research – such as modern power analysis[8] and some theoretical efforts
of the interdependence literature[9] – can be integrated into a larger whole. In
addition, new questions concerning the establishment and maintenance of
international order can be asked in a more extensive fashion.[10]

These considerations provide the plan for the present paper. Section II consists of a critical examination of realism and its problem-set. . . . In the third section the Humean perspective, which has as its central feature the investigation of order in social life, is introduced. This framework, in turn, provides us with a transcendental critique of the Hobbesian model of international relations analysis – whether realist, behaviouralist, or reformist. Finally, in Section IV, I shall outline a Humean research programme in greater detail and show how various research enterprises that are at present carried out in an *ad hoc* fashion may be understood as resulting from a coherent theoretical effort.

II

Since politics is present whether or not a science of politics exists, the task of such a science has to be the explication of a set of actions which we call "political".[11] It is here that realism suggests a criterion of demarcation that allegedly sets political actions apart from those of an economic, moral, or legal nature, and thus creates the proper field of study. Having established the autonomy of the political sphere, and in view of "the ubiquity of the power struggle in all social relations and all levels of social organisations", the political realist does "not find it surprising that international politics is of necessity power politics".[12] Thus, the "main signpost that helps political realism find its way through the landscape of international politics is the concept of interest in terms of power". Morgenthau compares realist thinking along these lines to the inquiry of the economist who thinks in terms of "interest defined as wealth" and the lawyer who thinks of "the conformity of action with legal norms".[13]

A great deal of criticism that has been levelled at these sweeping statements does not need to be repeated here. There are two points, however, that deserve a brief discussion: first, the universality of the struggle for power that allegedly defines the political sphere, and second, the somewhat ambiguous concept of "interest". Both could have occasioned a fundamental criticism of realist thinking and its definition of the political/international problem-set. The reasons why this did not occur, and why the analogy between political and economic man was widely accepted, are among the most surprising features of the debate between the realists and their critics.

Concerning the first point, even the most casual observer of political theory must have noticed that people who reflect upon political practices have spent a good deal of time, treasure, and blood on such "trifles" as the question of the "good life", the problem of "legitimacy", and safeguards against "political man" as a power maximizer. But such counter-factuals could be considered as examples of "wrong consciousness" were it not for the notion of "interest": its explication casts serious doubt upon the possibility of regarding power maximisation as a defining characteristic of politics. Faced with political man, Plato (in the first book of the *Republic*), tries to demonstrate that the reckless pursuit of power may not be in the "interest" of the stronger, since interest calculations involve many factors well beyond the hoarding of power (resources) suggested by the maximisation principle.[14] Considerations such as the possible reaction of the masses weaken the explanatory power of the maximisation model considerably.[15] The explication of the notion of interest thus serves as a starting point for Socrates' more normatively oriented inquiry into politics, conceived as "a praise of justice for its own sake".[16]

Interestingly enough, it is the notion of "interest" that served, nearly two thousand years later, as a key concept in an inquiry into international politics by Pufendorf.[17] That this is not a temporary derailment of analysis, but intrinsic to the reason-of-state tradition is evidenced by Metternich's distinction between interests and mere preferences of the actors.

> *Politics* is the science of the vital interests of States in its widest meaning. Since, however, an isolated state no longer exists, and is found only in the annals of the heathen world . . . we must always view the *society* of states as the essential condition of the modern world. . . . The great axioms of political science proceed from the knowledge of the true political interests of *all states*; it is upon these general interests that rests the guarantee of their existence. . . . What characterizes the modern world and distinguishes it from the ancient is the tendency of states to draw near each other and to form a kind of social body based on the same principle as human society. . . . In the most ancient world isolation and the practice of the most absolute selfishness without other restraint than that of prudence was the sum of politics. . . . Modern society on the other hand exhibits the application of the principle of solidarity and of the balance of power between states. . . . The establishing of international relations, on the basis of reciprocity under the guarantee of respect for acquired rights, . . . constitutes in our time the essence of politics.[18]

It is perhaps telling that these lines of inquiry were not followed more systematically. That fact is all the more surprising because realism is built upon two contradictory assumptions: the struggle for power (derived from a Hobbesian image of international politics) and the notion of diplomacy, which requires an accepted set of rules. Thus the reputation of realism as a generally hawkish stance is explicable more in terms of the policy imperatives of the cold war and fascination with the technological dimensions of the new weapons systems – so easily (and mistakenly) identified with "power"[19] – than with any intrinsic interventionist bent of this Janus-faced theory.

Furthermore, the destruction of a universe of discourse concerning normative conceptions of order – by the double attack of a statist philosophy (Hegel) and totalitarian ideologies – seemed to deny the possibility of a sensible discussion of such matters. After all, classical political theory, so concerned with man's political nature, had viewed the international realm as not being susceptible to rational ordering. Violence and the latent possibility of war was taken for granted and often served as a justification for particular militaristic institutions in a "good" polity.[20] When a speculation about order of more encompassing scope arose in the classical tradition, it did so in the context of the cosmic polity of the Stoics[21] and their concomitant elaboration of natural law, or it occurred in the justification of an ecumenic empire, whether of the Roman or the medieval kind.[22]

In both cases, however, international (or better, inter-unit) politics had to be transformed into a domestic model of politics – either imperial or, at best, federative.[23]

It was this poverty of normative political thought, and the lack of iso-morphism of any proposed normative model with the actual international game, that led to the rapid adoption of the realist problem-set for the analysis of international politics, despite its obvious shortcomings. [. . .]

Other approaches competed with realism – for instance, more or less sophisticated historical analyses,[24] as well as various psychological theories.[25] With regard to the latter, the UNESCO argument comes to mind: war starts in the minds of men,[26] and therefore the investigation of psychological states such as tension, authoritarianism, and so forth, will provide us with a theory of international conflict/peace. But the lack of a clearly formulated framework for inquiry, the many inferential leaps resulting from an *ad hoc* theorizing of the neo-Baconian fact hunt, and the therapeutic bent of many research approaches assuming conflict to be a characteristic of "sick" minds, hardly provided a challenge to the apparent parsimony and explanatory power of realist assumptions.[27]

A more principled criticism of the realist approach emerged, however, when attention turned away from power as the *means* of politics, and toward the *goals* of foreign policy. The essays of Arnold Wolfers are a good example.[28] Beginning with a classificatory scheme of foreign policy goals, Wolfers tried to elaborate on the implications of various goals for the analysis of world politics.[29] In his article, "The Actors in World Politics", Wolfers investigated the preconditions of state action according to the maxims of power politics. Instead of accepting the "universality of the power struggle" as an adequate theoretical assumption for the analysis of international relations, Wolfers showed that environmental factors are crucial in creating the presumptions of power politics,[30] and he likened the decisions of actors to the "compulsion" people experience in a burning house.

> Imagine a number of individuals, varying widely in their predispositions who find themselves inside a house on fire. It would be perfectly realistic to expect that these individuals, with rare exceptions, would feel com-pelled to run toward the exit. . . . Surely there is no need to analyze the individual decisions. . . .[31]

The moral of this analogy is clear: as nations are increasingly drawn to the pole of "compulsion", their behavior is likely to correspond to the deductions made from the "state as actor" model, which is based on the assumption of power maximisation. This observation, leading to restriction of the validity of the realist claim, has epistemological as well as moral implications. If all states behaved exactly alike, then it would be difficult to blame any one of them for aggression, breach of trust, and so forth. Indeed, the elaboration of these implications by the German school of *Realpolitik*, from Ratzenhofer to Riezler,[32] clearly foreshadows the breakdown of the European state system and its conventions of the pre-1914 era. Still, the fact that Morgenthau devoted a whole chapter to international morality (see his discussion of the moral standards of sovereigns, in contrast to his debunking of the conception of international morality in modern times) shows a certain awareness of the restricted applicability of the realist assumptions to international political analysis.[33] However, the necessary steps in correcting the flawed frame-work were not taken.

A significant expansion of the theoretical problem-set resulted only after the assumptions underlying the realist research program were modified. Instead of being based on the universalist assertion of the ubiquity of power struggle, the new systems approach recognised the influence of the particular structure of the international environment upon the choices of the various decision makers.[34] Thus differentiated from *homo oeconomicus* (who is forced to maximise profit as he makes his decisions *independently* from any other actor), the "political man" is mainly concerned with the puzzle of strategic interaction: *interdependent* decision making. The investigation of particular structures of the international environment significantly expands the research program by showing that behavioral maxims for political action are not universal, but system-specific. Nevertheless, the old mould of realism has not been broken. [. . .]

It is also important to note that even the behavioural movement[35] in international relations has by and large accepted the framework provided by the realist problem-set. The theoretical discussion during the next few years was, on the one hand, concerned with the testing of hypotheses concerning the stability or instability of various systems differentiated by the number of poles,[36] and on the other hand, with the operationalisation and measurement of power.[37] However, even the latter projects were clearly rooted in the same theoretical concerns. Whatever the disagreements between the behaviourists and the realists might have been, the guiding notion that power defines the autonomy of the political sphere – as measured wealth defines economics – was accepted by both. Furthermore, there was no disagreement on the point that the distribution of power throughout the system (polarisation) determines the structure and thereby informs the political choices of the actors. In practice, this meant that the realist research program had been modified and expanded but not superseded, despite some serious theoretical problems.

An attempt to question exactly this implicit set of assumptions was made relatively late by Oran Young,[38] and at approximately the same time by Stanley Hoffmann.[39]

Young's point of departure is to propose an alternative to the polarity model of politics by emphasizing the dynamics of international systems instead of their structural properties. By focusing on the policy process, Young advances a model that depicts the "patterns of political interests and relationships of power" in their similarities and differences "as between the global arena and various regional arenas and as between the different regional arenas themselves".[40] . . . The somewhat obscure conception of discontinuity is an important step toward recognising that, for purposes of political analysis, the distribution of power within the system may not be a useful way of conceptualising international interactions. The patterns of influence may differ from subsystem to subsystem. In practice, the concept of discontinuity foreshadows the notion that power is not an all-purpose currency within the international system, and that the great powers may well encounter substantial difficulties in translating their power potential into patterns of effective influence over policy outcomes,[41] depending upon particular features of the interaction process.[42] Although still articulated in the *language* of the old research programme, Young's article raises the fundamental issue of whether power, when conceived along the lines of wealth, can serve as an organising concept for an international research program. . . .

Hoffmann's argument in *Gulliver's Troubles* is similar. He also approaches the international system not as one simple distribution of power. Rather, he argues that – depending on the *issue area* – the international system has to be represented by different polarity models.[43] This approach, in turn, casts some doubt upon the behavioural maxims by which the realist programme claimed empirical relevance. It is now easily conceivable that the maximisation of power on one issue may be counterproductive for the attainment of goals in other issue areas, thus impairing the constitutive function of power in creating an autonomous field of study.

Clearly, the limitations of the realist programme have now come to the fore, and a reorientation of theorizing not only requires new research on the boundaries of the old programme, but also a critical, transcendental reflection upon the central concept of realism: power and the analogy between power maximisation and the accumulation of wealth. . . . In the next section, I shall show that a Humean perspective provides such an opportunity for reflection, as well as a new beginning for research.

III

The fact that Hume's work[44] can serve as an instrument for the transcendental reflection upon the power-politics model is perhaps not surprising: it was one of Hume's objectives to show the deficiencies of Hobbes's speculation on the preconditions of social order. The connection between a theory of political order and international relations is by no means accidental, since international reality serves for Hobbes as the justification of the analytical construction of a "state of nature":

But though there had never been any time wherein particular men were in a condition of warre one against another; yet at all times, Kings and Persons of Soveraigne authority, because of their independency are in continuall jealousies and in the state and posture of Gladiators; having their weapons pointing and their eyes fixed on one another; that is, their Forts, Garrisons, and Guns upon the Frontiers of their Kingdomes; and contual Spyes upon their neighbours; which is a posture of war.

. . . For Warre consisteth not in Battel onely or the act of fighting; but in a tract of time wherein the Will to contend by Battel is sufficiently known; and therefore the notion of Time is to be considered in the nature of Warre. . . . So the nature of Warre consisteth not in actual fighting, but in the known disposition thereto, during all the time there is no assurance to the contrary. All other time is peace.

So this Warre of every man against every man this is also consequent: that nothing can be Unjust. The notions of Right and Wrong, Justice and Injustice have there no place. When there is no common power there is no law: where no law no Injustice. . . . Justice and Injustice are none of the faculties neither of the Body nor Mind. . . . They are Qualities that relate to men in Society, not in Solitude.[45]

Opposition to Hobbes's conceptualisation eventually came about because his emphasis on force, as the constitutive factor of order, resulted from his extremely pessimistic view of human nature:

If a covenant be made wherein neither of the parties perform presently but trust one another it is the condition of meer nature . . . upon any reasonable suspicion it is Voyd. But if there be a common Power to stay over them both with right and force sufficient to compell performance it is not Voyd. For he that performed first has no assurance the other will perform after, because the bonds of words are too weak to bridle men's ambition, anger and other Passions without the fear of some coercive Power. . . . But in civill estate where there is a power set up to constrain those that would otherwise violate their faith that fear is no more reasonable; and for that cause he which by the Covenant is to perform first is obliged to do so.[46]

The result is the famous dilemma: if, in the state of nature, contracts without sanctions are not binding, then no social contract can come about in the first place. Apparently Hobbes's exclusive reliance on force was logically untenable and, as modern research shows, empirically inaccurate.[47] Emphasis on the legitimate use of force, even on the part of convinced command theorists, also demonstrates that the instruments of coercion cannot serve as the sole criterion of law. Norms that structure expectations operate in cases where no need for enforcement arises; as a matter of fact, we usually speak of "anomie"[48] when enforcement action surpasses a limit considered normal. Norms work through socialisation; ideally, they define certain alternatives in a given situation as illegal, thereby limiting the set of possible choices of an actor. Thus, in the search for an equivalent of force that would explain not only the continued existence of a political order but its very establishment, Hume advanced the argument that conventions arising out of interactions which prove mutually beneficial can structure expectations and thus allow the participants to overcome the posed dilemma:

> This convention is not of the nature of a promise; for even promises themselves arise from human conventions. It is only a general sense of common interest. ... When this common sense of interest is mutually expressed and known to both, it produces a suitable resolution and behavior. And this may properly enough be called a convention or agreement betwixt us though without the interposition of a promise, since the actions of each of us have a reference to those of the other and are performed upon the supposition that something is to be performed on the other part ... this experience assures us ... that the sense of interest has become common to all our fellows and gives us a confidence of the future regularity of their conduct; and it is only on the expectation of this that our moderation and abstinence are founded. In like manner are languages gradually established by human convention, without any promise. In like manner do gold and silver become the common measure of exchange and are esteemed sufficient payment for what is of a hundred times their value.[49]

It is obvious that this perspective on order is of particular interest for international politics, as it allows for a theory of order in a decentralised authority structure instead of making the centralisation of effective and accepted power the prerequisite for order. According to Hume, "rules of justice" are not "entirely suspended among political societies" and "alliances and treaties are every day made ... which would only be so much waste of parchment if they were not found by experience to have some influence and authority".[50]

The advantage of this particular problem-set for the analysis of international politics goes far beyond the conventional argument of isomorphism, as it suggests new avenues for investigation. By focusing on the problem of conventions arising out of interaction, the subject of order can now be addressed in a fundamentally different way and – as I will show – in a more comprehensive fashion.

To make this point somewhat clearer, it will be necessary to step back once more in order to fully understand the Hobbesian tradition. Hobbes also started from the phenomenon of order and took the availability of superior force as its precondition, or source. This precondition in turn defines the rudimentary research program of realism. Intrinsic to such a programme is the argument that only through the institutionalisation of a sovereign can the degeneration of conflict, in a world of self-interested actors that is character-ised by scarcity, be prevented.[51] Although in the state of nature, conflict over scarce objects must change into a struggle for power (since power becomes the means of attaining everything else),[52] the institutionalisation of a "com-mon power" superior to the actors inhibits their resort to violence and thus saves people from the condition of a "solitary, poor, brutish, nasty, and short form of life".[53]

From these brief remarks it should be obvious that Hobbes's argument is somewhat more complicated than the explanation of conflict in terms of inherent aggressiveness or individual pathology; consequently, the emphasis on certain forms of restraint can be considered part of a realist theory. Morgenthau's argument about the characteristics of the political arena for-cing actors to maximise power while emphasising at the same time the notion of diplomatic give-and-take[54] demonstrates how the paradox of the Hobbesian problem-set is quite logically translated into a conceptually ambiguous research programme.

This type of paradox is common not only among realists, but also among advocates of world government.[55] By explaining war as being caused by the absence of institutional safeguards of a *particular kind* – i.e., governmental structures – world government advocates envisage a more benign inter-national environment after the creation of a super-Leviathan that prevents competition from degenerating into a struggle for power. Actually, Hobbes himself perceived that this type of analogous reasoning was inadequate for the illumination of international politics. In a passage that is often overlooked, Hobbes tried to show that neither the negative incentive (fear of violent death) nor the inducements of more "commodious living" and the hope to "attain it by industry" (leading people out of the state of nature) are compel-lingly present in international life.[56] But beyond the question of the common misinterpretation of a theory for the analysis of international relations – a problem of interest mainly to the historian of political thought concerned with keeping the historical record straight[57] – lies a more fundamental problem with Hobbes's analysis of order.

It is here that the Humean perspective provides valuable insights, since its problem-set concerning the conditions of order results in a wider research program. If order depends upon the mutual compatibility of expectation which facilitates the coordination of choices in a non-violent fashion, then the struggle for power is a possible but not a necessary result of the international condition. It will occur when the lack of commonly accepted conventions does not prevent the degeneration of a conflict of interest into a power strug-gle.[58] This perspective shares the Hobbesian view that order is an artefact rather than a naturally given condition – whose ontological underpinnings need to be discovered – as the classical tradition from Plato to Aquinas main-tained.[59] But the Humean perspective is also substantially different from the Hobbesian construct. It is historical; it is concerned with the importance of perception and the embodiment of experiences in rules. Such rules serve as guides for inferences when actors face unstructured choice situations.[60]

Order is not conformity with external compellence, but rather a minimum agreement on the limits of the pursuit of conflict. It can therefore not be identified with any particular distribution of values at a given time, nor is it directly informed by any specification of the conditions of the "good life".[61] It is simply a minimal consensus on the preconditions of "social coexistence", in Hedley Bull's words.[62] Accordingly, we speak of order if three conditions are met: first, resort to violence is restricted; second, actors work on the presumption that promises will be kept; and third, there are accepted ways of securing the stability of possessions.[63]

The foregoing may sound rather uninspiring to those who demand from a theory of politics a vision of the future or a goal of history from which the ultimate meaning of human existence can be derived.[64] Indeed, human aspirations translated into political action will always be more encompassing than any theory that may develop in the explication of political action.[65] Relevant to theories as explanatory devices is the specification of the factors that one has to take into account in explicating phenomena, and their derivation from the assumptions of the problem-set.

Here the Humean perspective leads to a distinct set of puzzles and shows its heuristic fruitfulness. As mentioned earlier, Hume likened the establishment of conventions to the genesis of language and to commodities such as gold or silver attaining the status of a medium of exchange. This "money" then becomes "the common measure . . . esteemed sufficient payment for what is of a hundred times their value".[66] In applying this concept to our problem of politics, we may say that, as "economic man" depends upon the creation of "money" in order to become a useful heuristic construct, so "political man" would presuppose the existence of "power" serving the same function. Such scholars as Catlin, Parsons, Deutsch, and Singer indeed tried to go that route in the development of power analysis.[67] The difference between behaviouralism and traditional realism tended to focus on the possibility or impossibility, and the various types, of measurement rather than on the more fundamental question of whether this analogy was really sensible. True, when pressed, behaviouralists usually fell back on the old argument that power is quantifiable, but "more imperfectly so" than money.[68] But theorists often talked about measuring force as the backing of power in the same way that gold allegedly backs money. Thus, power analysis was quickly reduced to the more manageable analysis of military capabilities, *en vogue* among military contingency planners. Indeed, the notion of "political man" amassing power resources had been suggested by Hobbes.

Nevertheless, this analogy produces a type of reasoning that is seriously misleading. To argue that power is like money except for the difference in measurability is to argue "that the problem of measuring power is very much like the problem of purchasing power in an economy without money" – i.e., precisely the situation which "invention of money was supposed to overcome".[69]

Furthermore, Parsons' analogy of force playing a role similar to that of gold as a backing of currency[70] is simply mistaken, as Hume's discussion clearly shows: it is not the intrinsic value of these commodities, but rather the social convention of measuring every other commodity in terms of them, that makes gold or silver "money".

Applied to our discussion of power and the difficulty of its measurement, this means that it is not the technical difficulty of measuring power (despite all attempts to provide some esoteric techniques for doing so) – but rather the absence of a *social convention* to express political values in terms of a generalised means of exchange and value – that inhibits the scientific study (behaviouralism) of the autonomous field of politics (realism). Although there seems to be no intrinsic difficulty with the idea that people could agree on such a generalised means of exchange,[71] it nevertheless remains true that no such widespread consensus for the expression of values in terms of a given medium of exchange exists in politics. Such difficulties are not unknown in economics: friendship, love, and so forth supposedly have no price because of the understandable reluctance of people to measure them as commodities. Similarly, in economics, the problem of the "holy cow" is well known to students of development. Such phenomena, however, are sufficiently peripheral to the main concerns of economic theorists so that they do not impede their analysis. Political exchanges, on the other hand, seem to be largely of a different kind: they are tied to particular contexts and are narrowly circumscribed in scope and domain. Thus, for example, the political power of a senator does not (or at least should not) entitle that power holder to be exempt from a traffic ticket or criminal prosecution, even when apprehended by a "powerless" citizen.

In short, a general-purpose currency for exercising general political purchasing power cannot be found. Before we lament this fact, we must realise that the analysis of politics must follow the explication of the practice in question, and furthermore, that the possibility of a limited government crucially depends upon such a lack of a medium of exchange.[72]

Conversely we may say – and this is of particular interest to the specialist in international relations – *that if* conditions arose which led to the establishment of a social convention allowing for the measuring of political values in terms of one yardstick, then realism would provide a relatively good fit. Thus, we could argue that during the balance-of-power period, statesmen actually tried to establish and to depend upon the existence of such conventions. In this context, it is interesting that the measurement unit of power in various compensation formulas circulated at the Congress of Vienna in 1815 was the number of subjects rather than of soldiers, as later capability analysis would have suggested.[73] The calculation of equilibrium was predicated upon the agreement that "subjects" are a proper way of viewing the balance of power. This, in turn, was possible only by tying the notion of "balance" to the conventions of the pre-Napoleonic era, when shifts in the power distribution did not result from internal mobilization but from territorial changes. A stable technology as well as an agreement on the legitimate goals of policy – so rudely upset by Napoleon's unprecedented use of artillery as well as the *levée en masse* – made the rational calculation of power possible.

The criticism that realism is little more than a restatement of the classical teachings of the balance-of-power period, dressed up as universal theory and falsely linked to a Hobbesian framework, is not new or particularly Humean. It has been stated particularly well by systems theorists. However, the Humean perspective goes somewhat further than the traditional argument of systemic factors leading to a particular set of rules that moderate conflict. In addition to the question of how the distribution of power influences the nature of the political game by increasing or decreasing the polarities, two further routes of investigation are suggested: international systems change when new answers are found to the additional questions, "What *can* the units do to each other?" (i.e., the breakdown of the old convention that makes power somewhat calculable), and "What do the units *want* to do to each other?" (i.e., the question of legitimacy).[74]

This idea is further elaborated by two more theoretically oriented efforts which can be seen as growing out of the Humean critique of the analogy of power and money that underlies the realist framework: Keohane and Nye's work on *Power and Interdependence*,[75] and Baldwin's power analysis.[76]

[. . .]

The fact that Hoffmann, Keohane and Nye, and Baldwin spell out these extremely important points without linking them to an overarching and conceptually elaborated set of concerns is hardly surprising. "Theorising" as an activity can be concomitant to the "normal" research activity even when the old problem-set is increasingly under attack. The usefulness of theoretical structures with wider scope, however, lies in the integration of otherwise disparate research enterprises and in their heuristic power, thus providing structure and rigor for further analyses.

IV

In this (admittedly sketchy) fourth section, I will attempt to show that the Humean perspective is not only able to integrate several important types of contemporary analysis, but also to stimulate new research in areas that have been neglected up to now. More rigorous inquiries will naturally be forthcoming only after a more coherent set of questions derived from the Humean perspective has been developed. Nevertheless, the following ideas warrant further investigation and are part of the new research programme.

There is, first of all, the inquiry into the nature and function of rules or conventions that guide political behaviour.[77]

This subject has important epistemological repercussions upon the study of international relations. The investigation of rules can solve some of the puzzles of systems theory. Systems are now classified most appropriately by the different conventions that guide behaviour rather than by the distribution

of resources (often naively identified with power), or by patterns of alignment (polarities).[78] Furthermore, the explanation appropriate for international relations is "structural" in one of Waltz's senses.[79] Nevertheless, we
need not make the heroic (and, historically speaking, false) assumption that
"the balance of power is simply a theory about the outcome of units'
behavior under conditions of anarchy".[80]

The ambiguities of Waltz's treatment of structure is paralleled by Hume's
remarks in the essay, "Of the Balance of Power." On the one hand, Hume
too, sees in the idea of a balance of power a natural dictate of reason –
operating, so to speak, automatically whenever a multiplicity of actors interact; on the other hand, he notes that such precepts of reason have not been
followed by many states. The history of the Roman Empire is an example:

> It must be noted that the Romans never met with any such general com-
> bination of confederacy against them as might naturally have been
> expected for the rapid conquests and declared ambition: but were
> allowed peaceably to subdue their neighbors, one after another, till they
> extended their dominion over the whole known world. Not to mention
> the fabulous history of their Italic wars, there was upon Hannibal's inva-
> sion of the Roman state, a remarkable crisis which ought to have called
> up the attention of all civilized nations. . . .
>
> The Rhodian and Achean republics are much celebrated by ancient
> historians for their wisdom and their sound policy; yet both of them
> assisted the Romans in their wars against Philip and Antiochus. And what
> might be esteemed still a stronger proof that this maxim was not generally
> known in those ages, no ancient author has remarked the imprudence of
> these measures, nor has even blamed that absurd treaty above mentioned,
> made by Philip with the Carthagenians.[81]

Thus, it is surely misleading to look only at outcomes, and only at military
coalitions at that, without seeing the larger picture of which such patterns are
a part. After all, nobody would seriously contend that it is not worth knowing
whether a man was killed accidentally or by premeditation despite the fact
that the result remains the same. Thus, motives and reasons *do* matter; they
must be part of the explanation despite Waltz's somewhat contorted attempts
to avoid them. (Instead of motives and rules, "structural givens" are invoked
as the "explanans".)[82] Moreover, Waltz disregards his own call to carry out a
Copernican revolution in international relations by explaining the pertinent
phenomena on the level of the system rather than the unit: he quickly resorts
to socialisation in addition to competition as an explanatory variable.[83] This
obvious inconsistency points to an underlying difficulty of international relations research that may be more serious than is usually assumed. If it is true
that structure influences behaviour only insofar as the various actors have
been socialised into a given structure, then an explication of a particular
phenomenon in terms of the underlying rules is no longer strictly falsifiable.

That is so because, as Wittgenstein reminds us, the grammar of rules also entails the counterfactual case of making a mistake.[84] Thus, the whole advocacy of a science of international relations (or politics in general) along the lines of the hypothetical-deductive model may be misleading. That is surely a disturbing result for a structuralist like Waltz, who wields the allegedly sharp scalpel of science.[85] Perhaps Lakatos's substitution of Popper's criterion of refutability for that of fruitfulness has more far-reaching implications for the study of politics than is commonly realized.[86]

Whatever the answers to these questions are, it is clear that – given the nature of rules or conventions as "inference guidance devices"[87] – a concern with perceptions and the defining of situations must be a primary research task of the Humean programme.[88] Thus, aside from the bargaining theory's elaboration on threats[89] and their effects upon decision making, the study of inducements[90] and strategies leading to perceptual shifts should constitute a complementary focus of interest.

In this context, the logic of the Humean perspective goes further than Hume himself suggested. The process of rule generation, with which Hume explicitly dealt, mainly concerned coordination situations. The example of two men learning to coordinate their efforts in order to propel a boat through water clearly covers the situation of a "game of coordination".[91] As their respective activity of rowing generates mutual expectations about future behavior, a convention comes into existence. This evolution of a norm that guides behaviour has important implications for the puzzling concept of custom in international law, as Nicholas Onuf has shown.[92]

Custom is based not solely on repetition or the development of a habit. This position is in tune with otherwise somewhat oracular statements by the International Court of Justice on this subject in the cases of Asylum and North Sea Continental Shelf.[93] It is also in congruence with common experience: individual and collective habits do not create obligations.[94]

> Conventions create tangible and reciprocal expectations from which the makers of such conventions deduce equally tangible obligations. Gone is the need to infer specific obligations from a general will to be ruled by law. . . . Parties to an order need not be told that they ought to behave as they always have. They will for the most part behave that way anyway. They do so because of an individualistic imperative and not a social one. Should they fail to recognize such an imperative individually, then others will respond, as their needs dictate, and either have the imperiled convention honored or its terms adjusted. . . . The inherently conservative nature of law and order is thus acknowledged but so are orderly progresses of change and growth.
>
> Another virtue of Hume's position is its avoidance of a narrow construction of any society's principal conventionally fixed sources of order. Conventions are not just sources of rights and obligations, but also the symbols to express or identify things, relations, ideas or values. Language and economy thus join as conventional sources of order.[95]

This leads us to the next step: starting with Hume's observation of the function of common interest for the creation of order, a variety of research tasks can be identified. They would include the work on negotiations[96] and on arbitration schemes, as well as more philosophically oriented approaches that try to clarify the language games of the national interest (perhaps along the lines of the debate on public or common interest).[97] In this context, it is significant that the concept of "interest of princes", which later became the "national interest", appeared originally in the writings of international lawyers like Pufendorf; its definition satisfies the conditions for a serious discourse on "the public interest".[98] Similarly, in the absence of a political theory of international life, a clarification of issues concerning the notions of justice, equality, personal and corporate responsibility, and justifications for the resort to violence are of the utmost relevance; they deserve to be explicated by a science of politics.[99]

Furthermore, in view of the interest in human rights and the ascriptions of entitlements not only to individuals but also to aggregates, a clarification of the often competing claims at various levels of aggregation (individual versus group, group versus state, etc.) is of particular importance for a coherent "world order" approach.[100]

If the foregoing examples primarily explain the process of rule generation under conditions that are susceptible to formalisation as a game of coordination, other rule-creating processes will have to be investigated. Thus, many social situations exhibit features in which the actors have cooperative as well as antagonistic interests, as the large literature on the prisoners' dilemma shows. My attempts to illuminate the generation of rules under such conditions through the constraints imposed by iterative bargaining and perceptual shifts fall into this category.[101]

Although the emergence of conventions under conditions of the prisoners' dilemma do not seem to have been part of Hume's main concern, some of his remarks are suggestive in relation to the problem of collective goods.[102] An example is his discussion of the lack of incentives for a large group of individuals to provide for the draining of a collectively held meadow.[103] The problem of the "political entrepreneur", a formalization of Hume's "magistrates", can be seen as a preliminary answer.[104]

The concept of the political entrepreneur – the "hegemon"[105] of international relations – raises a further question that is perhaps susceptible to analysis in terms of a situation in which the created rule (the "regimes" of the present) distributes values *unequally* (e.g., between regime maker and regime takers).[106] The investigation of regime changes under these conditions will, I suspect, be substantially different from the other two situations. Thus, recent attempts to formulate a general theory of regime creation and change may be in need of further conceptual differentiation. Precisely because rules and their concomitant "rights" are not neutral, Oran Young's suggestions deserve further attention:

It would be of great value to identify alternative systems of rights and rules for the international polity as precisely as possible and then to ask questions: Which actors would be advantaged or disadvantaged by the introduction of specific rights and rules, and what mechanisms would produce these results? Although we would not reach decisive conclusions about the relative desirability of alternative systems of rights and rules, we would be more likely to understand the preference orderings of various actors in the international polity with respect to alternative systems.[107]

Also, it becomes clear that even in the "anarchy" of international politics, a particularly efficient way of getting one's way is not through the amassing of power or even of resources, but through influencing the creation of rules. The recent bargaining at the UNCLOS III conference concerning the regulations according to which the "enterprise" of the U.N. is supposed to exploit the deep sea bed is a good and perhaps a decisive test case for prospective major changes in resource distribution. Thus, distributional changes can result from the adoption of new rules, despite the weakness of the Third World's participants when judged in terms of the traditional attributes of power.[108]

Finally, the above remarks imply that within the Humean perspective, a revision of the "structural theory of imperialism"[109] may lead to some interesting avenues for research. Although Galtung seems to believe that inequality in the distribution of resources as measured against an equalitarian ideal is an indicator of imperialism, the presence of inequality hardly makes a convincing case for the existence of an exploitative system. The inequality of distribution represented by the Gaussian curve is rather common in nature and society; and thus, inequality is not always a phenomenon in need of further theoretical labour. Moreover, if we accept the argument that the gap between the rich and the poor is a decisive indicator of imperialism, we also have to accept that a depression in the industrialized world would have to be taken as proof of the demise of imperialism.[110]

Although such violations of common sense make it easy to dismiss the theory of imperialism *in toto*, this position eliminates important theoretical and normative concerns. Thus, even if we accept the view that absolute equality is a utopian goal, departures above and beyond the "normal distribution" or its logical derivatives remain to be explained.[111] Since sharp deviations from a normality thus defined can no longer be defended as the natural result of a *laissez faire* system, they have to be explained in terms of (structural?) causes. This argument not only casts doubt upon the ability of the contractarian conceptions embodied in the theory of "justice as fairness" to provide relevant insights to the problem of international order,[112] but also suggests justifications for regulatory interventions while at the same time limiting their scope.[113] Thus, if the term "international organisation" is understood in its widest and perhaps most appropriate meaning, the organisation of international life and not the description of institutional analysis of this or that particular bureaucracy represents its field of study. The object, therefore, is to cast the net wider than has been customary in this area of international relations, a task that is helped by the Humean perspective. Instead of simply focusing on state actors and their bargaining, and adding on – as an after-thought – the marginal impact of international organizations in such an arena, the focus on conventions and various allocation mechanisms enlarges the agenda of international organization and frees it from the fetters of purely institutional descriptive analysis.[114]

Although most of these suggestions are tentative at the moment, there seems to be justification in hoping that a research programme that is informed by a Humean perspective will not only revitalise the theoretical discussion in international relations research, but will significantly enlarge the set of questions that can be investigated in a methodologically rigorous fashion.

Notes

1 I use "perspective" to denote the fact that the consideration of a set of phenom-ena from a particular angle creates a certain "vision" which is then elaborated in an interrelated set of concepts, assumptions, and variables that define a conceptual framework, or approach. The reason why I prefer to emphasize the programmatic character of the conceptual framework rather than the logical status of its inter-related propositions is that no good "theory" can be found in the social sciences in terms of the logical requirements of the deductive explanatory scheme, and that therefore the criterion of "fruitfulness" of the entire research programme, rather than the refutation of a singular theoretical proposition, represents an appropriate criterion for the choice of competing frameworks. To that extent, I follow the reformulation of the Popperian demarcation criterion.

   On the question of "fruitfulness", see, for example, Carl G. Hempel, "The Theoretician's Dilemma", in Hempel, *Aspects of Scientific Explanation* (New York: Free Press, 1965), 173–226.

   On Lakatos's reformulation of the Popperian position, see Imre Lakatos, "Falsi-fication and the Methodology of Scientific Research Programmes", in Imre Lakatos and Alan Musgrave, eds., *Criticism and the Growth of Knowledge* (Cambridge: Cambridge University Press, 1970), 91–197.

2 On the dangers of *ad hoc* theorizing, see, i.e., Karl Popper, *The Logic of Scientific Discovery*, Part I (New York: Harper & Row, 1968).

3 I take Hans J. Morgenthau's "Six Principles of Political Realism", as contained (with slight variations) in the various editions of his *Politics Among Nations*, 5th ed. (New York: Knopf, 1975), as a statement of the realist approach. One of the argu-ments is that the realist programme, by incorporating some contradictory assump-tions (and thereby failing on the level of theoretical rigour), nevertheless provided a research programme for various forms of inquiry linked to a Hobbesian vision.

4 On the question of behaviourism versus traditionalism, see, i.e., Klaus Knorr and James N. Rosenau, (eds.), *Contending Approaches to International Politics* (Princeton: Princeton University Press, 1969).

5 The idea that a research programme is defined in terms of a set of puzzles is taken from Kuhn. See Thomas S. Kuhn, The Structure of Scientific Revolutions (Chicago: Chicago University Press, 1962). However, I do not want to imply that such programs originate only after the definition of a paradigm. Although that might apply to the true sciences, it does not necessarily follow that a set of

problems defining a research programme can only emerge from a paradigmatic revolution. For that reason, I chose the term "problem-set", indicating, logically speaking, a looser assortment of interesting questions that define a research programme.

6 On the question of fruitfulness, see fn. 1.

7 Something like a Kantian transcendental reflection is intended here. Instead of asking, "What is power politics?" (which is Morgenthau's famous guide post), the transcendental reflection would ask: "What are the *conditions of the possibility* for a power-politics analysis?"

8 See, i.e., David A. Baldwin, "Power Analysis and World Politics: New Trends versus Old Tendencies", *World Politics* XXXI (January 1979), 161–94.

9 See, i.e., Rober O. Keohane and Joseph S. Nye, *Power and Interdependence* (Boston: Little, Brown, 1977).

10 On the question of international order from a Humean perspective, see Hedley Bull, *The Anarchical Society* (New York: Columbia University Press, 1977), and Friedrich V. Kratochwil, *International Order and Foreign Policy* (Boulder, Colorado: Westview Press, 1978).

11 For an interesting discussion of finding some core terms for politics rather than defining politics in terms of class properties exhibited by all political events or actions, see Fred Frohock, "The Structure of Politics", *American Political Science Review*, Vol. 72 (September 1978), 859–71.

12 Morgenthau (fn. 3), 38.

13 Morgenthau (fn. 3), Principles 2 and 6, pp. 5 and 14.

14 Plato, *Republic*, 338 c–d; for the stronger case that the true ruler has the interests of his subjects at heart, see *Republic*, 342–43.

15 The power of a theory refers here to the ratio between the explanation of a set of events and the number of assumptions from which the explanation is derived. Obviously, the larger this ratio is, the more parsimonious the theory, and the more powerful the explanation.

16 Plato, *Republic*, 367 d–e.

17 See, i.e., Pufendorf's distinction between "imaginary" interests – i.e., mere indications of preferences – and "real" interests: Samuel Pufendorf, *An Introduction to the History of the Principal Kingdoms and States of Europe*, English transl. (London, 1702), Preface, p. v.

18 Prince Metternich, *Memoirs*, I (Paris: 1880–84), 30, as quoted in Edward Gulick, *Europe's Classical Balance of Power* (New York: Norton, 1967), 32.

19 For the shortcomings of a "military capability" analysis as compared to the more complicated "power" assessment, see Klaus Knorr, *The Power of Nations* (New York: Basic Books, 1975), chap. 1.

20 See, i.e., the problem of "Spartanism" underlying many of Plato's educational concerns as exemplified in the second book of the *Republic*.

21 For a short discussion of the concept of "cosmic polity", see George Sabine, *A History of Political Theory*, 3rd ed. (New York: Holt, Rinehart & Winston, 1961), chaps. 2 and 8.

22 For the latter kind, see Dante's proposal in *De Monarchia*, transl. by Herbert Schneider, 2d rev. ed. (New York: Liberal Arts Press, 1957).

23 See i.e., Kant's proposals. For a discussion of the Kantian "international relations" theory, see Francis Hinsley, *Power and the Pursuit of Peace* (Cambridge: Cambridge University Press, 1963). See also Rousseau's objections to the peace plan of the Abbe St. Pierre: "The State of War", in C. E. Vaughan, ed., *Rousseau's Political Writings* (Cambridge: Harvard University Press, 1915).

24 Richard Snyder and Glenn Paige, "The United States Decision to Resist Aggression in Korea: The Application of an Analytical Scheme", *Administrative Science Quarterly*, III (December 1958), 341–78.

25 For a useful collection of some social psychological contributions to international relations see Herbert Kelman, *International Behavior* (New York: Holt, 1965).

26 For a discussion of the shortcomings of such approaches, see Kenneth Waltz, *Man, the State and War* (New York: Columbia University Press, 1963), chap. 3.

27 For a critique of the serious shortcomings of a naive psychologism, see Robert Jervis, *Perception and Misperception in International Politics* (Princeton: Princeton University Press, 1976).

28 Arnold Wolfers, *Discord and Collaboration* (Baltimore: The Johns Hopkins University Press, 1962), chaps. 2, 5, and 6.

29 *Ibid.*, chaps. 5 and 6.

30 *Ibid.*, chap. 1.

31 *Ibid.*, 13ff.

32 Gustav Ratzenhofer, *Wesen und Zweck der Politik* (Leipzig: Brockhaus, 1893); Kurt Riezler, *Tagebücher* (ed.), Karl Erdman (Göttingen: Vanderhoek and Ruprecht, 1972).

33 Morgenthau (fn. 3), chap. 16.

34 See, i.e., Morton Kaplan: *System and Process in International Relations* (New York: John Wiley, 1957).

35 Since behaviouralism was more a mood than a clear-cut alternative programme, this should not be too surprising. After all, there were as many differences of great epistemological import as there was disagreement with the traditional agenda. For an assessment of the behavioural mood, see Heinz Eulau, *Behaviorism in Political Science* (New York: Atherton Press, 1969). For the debate within the confines of the "new scientists", often (falsely) identified with behaviouralism, see, i.e., the exchange between Oran R. Young and Bruce Russett, "Professor Russett: Industrious Taylor to a Naked Emperor", *World Politics*, XXI (April 1969, 486–511); Bruce Russett, "The Young Science of International Politics", *World Politics*, XXII (October 1969), 87–94; also Robert Jervis, "The Costs of the Quantitative Study of International Relations", and Robert C. North, "Research Pluralism and the International Elephant", in Knorr and Rosenau (fn. 4), 177–217 and 218–42 respectively.

36 For a good discussion of the literature concerned with the problem of "poles", or polarities of the international system, see Joseph Nogee, "Polarity and Ambiguous Concept", *Orbis*, XVIII (Winter 1978), 1193–1224. See also Karl W. Deutsch and J. David Singer, "Multipolar Power Systems and International Stability", *World Politics*, XVI (April 1964), 390–406; Richard Rosecrance, "Bipolarity, Multipolarity, and the Future" reprinted in James Rosenau, (ed.), *International Politics and Foreign Policy*, rev. ed. (New York: Free Press, 1969), chap. 30; Wolfram Hanrieder, "The International System: Bipolar or Multibloc?" *Journal of Conflict Resolution*, IX (September 1965), 299–308; Kenneth Waltz, "The Stability of a Bipolar World", *Daedalus*, Vol. 93 (Summer 1964), 881–909; Steven Spiegel, *Dominance and Diversity: The International Hierarchy* (Boston: Little, Brown, 1972).

37 Examples of the "measurement of power" literature (capability analysis) are, i.e., Katherine and A.F.K. Organski, *Population and World Power* (New York: Knopf, 1961); Ray S. Cline, *World Power Assessment* (Washington, D.C.: Georgetown Center for Strategic Studies, 1975).

38 Young, "Political Discontinuities in the International System", *World Politics*, XX (April 1968), 369–92.

39 Stanley Hoffmann, *Gulliver's Troubles* (New York: McGraw-Hill, 1968), and "International Organizations and the International System", *International Organization*, XXIV (Summer 1970), 389–414.

40 Young (fn. 38), 370.

41 For an attempt to distinguish three conceptions of power depending upon the

ability to control resources, actors, or outcomes, see Jeffrey A. Hart, "Three Approaches to the Measurement of Power in International Relations", *International Organization*, XXX (Spring 1976), 397–401.

42 For an example of a strict modelling exercise that recognises the multidimensionality problem of power, see Hayward Alker, "On Political Capabilities in a Schedule Sense", in Hayward Alker, Karl Deutsch, and Antoine Stoetzel, (eds.), *Mathematical Approaches to Politics* (San Francisco: Jossey Bass, 1973), 307–73.

43 Hoffmann (fn. 39), chap. 2.

44 Several treatises are accessible in various anthologies such as Henry Aiken, (ed.), *David Hume's Moral and Political Philosophy* (Darien, Conn.: Hafner, 1970).

45 Thomas Hobbes, *Leviathan*, chap. 13.

46 *Ibid.*

47 See, i.e., Michael Barkun, *Law Without Sanction* (New Haven: Yale University Press, 1968).

48 For an elaboration of the concept of anomie, see Emile Durkheim, *Suicide* (Glencoe, Ill.: Free Press, 1952).

49 Hume, *Treatise on Human Nature*, Book III of "Morals", in Aiken (fn. 44), 59–60.

50 Hume, *Enquiry Concerning the Principles of Morals*, Sec. IV, *ibid.*, 202.

51 For the Hobbesian roots of the "rational action model" see Talcott Parsons, *The Structure of Social Action* (New York: Free Press, 1968), I, chaps. 2 and 3.

52 Hobbes, *Leviathan*, chap. 11: "restless desire of power after power, that ceaseth only in death."

53 *Ibid.*, chap. 13.

54 For an argument that the notion of "interest" is a conception that *limits* aspirations, see Kratochwil, "On the Notion of Interest in International Relations" (forthcoming).

55 For a thorough discussion of this approach, see Inis Claude, *Power and International Relations* (New York: Random House, 1962).

56 Hobbes, *Leviathan*, chap. 13.

57 On the difference between political thought, political theory, and the role of particular "traditions" in theorizing, see Leo Strauss, *What is Political Philosophy?* (Glencoe, Ill.: Free Press, 1959).

58 For an attempt to conceptualise the degeneration of conflict into such a struggle, see Kratochwil (fn. 10), chap. 2.

59 For a statement maintaining the speculation on unity of order provided by the classical tradition, see the essay by Eric Voegelin, "What is Political Reality?" in Voegelin, *Anamnesis*, trans. by Gerhart Niemeyer (Notre Dame, Ind.: Notre Dame University Press, 1978).

60 For an instructive inquiry into the workings of rules in decision-making situations, see Gidon Gottlieb, *The Logic of Choice* (London: Allen & Unwin, 1968).

61 For a discussion of the problems resulting from attempts to specify the conditions for the "good life", see Stanley Hoffmann, "Report of the Conference on Conditions of World Order", *Daedalus*, Vol. 95 (Spring 1966), 455–78.

62 Hedley Bull, "Order and Justice in International Society", *Political Studies*, XIX (September 1971), 268–83.

63 I would like to modify Bull's argument slightly concerning the security of possessions. This stipulation could easily be misconstrued as the necessity of guaranteeing a particular distribution of values. But as Rousseau has shown, the right to possession is based on the social acceptance of a claim. Thus, it is not the effective possession or utilisation of a value that is protected by the social order. Rather, protection of possessions means that *arbitrary* changes of the rules which govern the enjoyment of property by the individual are enjoined. It is entirely conceivable that vast rearrangements in the distribution of values can occur without a breakdown of social order; on the other hand, relatively few but obviously

"criminal" violations of the rules governing possessions might result in such a breakdown. After all, not even Locke, who tried to argue for a "natural right" of property antedating the civil society, objected in principle to the idea of taxation. For a further short discussion of this problem, see section IV.

64 I have in mind the millenarian movements. For a treatment of the "politics" of such movements, see Eric Voegelin, *Wissenschaft, Politik und Gnosis* (Munich: Koesel, 1959). For a more historically oriented account concerning medieval *millenarian sectarianism*, see Norman Cohn, *The Pursuit of the Millennium* (New York: Oxford University Press, 1970). For an interesting treatment of Marx's intellectual development along these lines, see Robert C. Tucker, *Philosophy and Myth in Karl Marx* (Cambridge: Cambridge University Press, 1972).

65 In this context, see Hannah Arendt's remarks about "political action" versus "behavior" in *The Human Condition* (Chicago: Chicago University Press, 1958); also *On Revolution* (New York: Viking Press, 1963).

66 Aiken (fn. 44), 59–60.

67 G. E. Catlin, *The Science and Method of Politics* (New York: Knopf, 1927); Talcott Parsons, "The Political Aspects of Social Structure and Process" in David Easton, (ed.), *Varieties of Political Theory* (Englewood Cliffs, N.J.: Prentice-Hall, 1966); Karl Deutsch, *The Nerves of Government* (New York: Free Press, 1963), 120 ff; J. David Singer, "Internation Influence, a Formal Model," *American Political Science Review*, Vol. 57 (June 1963), 420–30.

68 Deutsch (fn. 67), 120.

69 David A. Baldwin, "Money and Power", *Journal of Politics*, XXXIII (August 1971), 578–614.

70 Parsons (fn. 67).

71 Baldwin somewhat facetiously mentions that cavemen may have had less difficulty with estimating power than with assessing the "price" of all other commodities in terms of money (fn. 69), 595.

72 For a further investigation into the problems of political exchanges and the safeguards for preventing a "general currency" of politics through the development of different means of exchange like votes, vouchers, etc., see James Coleman, "Political Money," *American Political Science Review*, Vol. 64 (December 1970), 1074–87.

73 See the various circulated proposals reproduced in Edward Gulick, Europe's Classical Balance of Power (New York: Norton, 1967), 249–51.

74 See Stanley Hoffmann, "International Systems and International Law", reprinted in Richard Falk and Saul Mendlovitz, (eds.), *The Strategy of World Order*, II, *International Law* (New York: World Law Fund, 1966), 136–66.

75 Keohane and Nye (fn. 9).

76 Baldwin (fn. 62).

77 Aside from the works by Bull (fn. 69) and Kratochwil (fn. 10), the focus on rules has been a well-defined approach to international law. See, for instance, William D. Coplin, "International Law and Assumptions about the State System", *World Politics*, XVII (July 1965), 615–34, and Richard A. Falk, "New Approaches to the Study of International Law", *American Journal of International Law*, Vol. 61 (April 1967), 477–95. For an imaginative application of this general approach to the problem of reprisals, see Nicholas G. Onuf, *Reprisals: Rituals, Rules, Rationales*, Center of International Studies, Princeton University, Research Monograph No. 42 (Princeton, 1974). For the epistemological implications, see Michael Barkun and Wesley Gould, *International Law and the Social Sciences* (Princeton: Princeton University Press, 1970).

78 For an attempt to give more precision to the notions of "poles" and "polarisation", see George Modelski, *World Power Concentrations, Typology, Data, Explanatory Frameworks* (Morristown, N.J.: General Learning Press, 1974).

79 Kenneth Waltz, *Theory of International Politics* (Reading, Mass.: Addison Wesley, 1979), esp. chaps. 4 and 5.
80 *Ibid.*, 57.
81 David Hume, "Of the Balance of Power", in Frederick Watkins, ed., *Hume's Theory of Politics* (New York: Thomas Nelson and Sons, 1951), 185–93, at 187–88.
82 Waltz (fn. 79), 5.
83 *Ibid.*, 74.
84 On this point, see K. T. Fann, *Wittgenstein's Concept of Philosophy* (Berkeley: University of California Press, 1969).
   On the problem of explaining by means of "rules", see Alfred Schuetz, "The Social World and the Theory of Social Action", *Social Research*, XXVII (Summer 1960), 203–23, and S. E. Benn and R. S. Peters, *The Principles of Political Thought* (New York: Free Press, 1965), chap. 9.
85 For a critique of Waltz's position, see Morton Kaplan, *Towards Professionalism in International Theory* (New York: Free Press, 1979).
86 Lakatos (fn. 1).
87 This notion of inference guidance by rules is elaborated in Gottlieb (fn. 60).
88 Robert Jervis's work, *Perception and Misperception in International Politics* (Princeton: Princeton University Press, 1976), is clearly relevant to this research task. See also the discussion by Jack Snyder, "Rationality at the Brink", *World Politics*, XXX (April 1978), 345–65, and John Steinbruner, *The Cybernetic Theory of Decision* (Princeton: Princeton University Press, 1974). Less convincing is Irving Janis, *Victims of Groupthink* (Boston: Houghton Mifflin, 1972).
89 On the role of threats, see Thomas Schelling, *The Strategy of Conflict* (Cambridge: Harvard University Press, 1960), chap. 2.
90 This postulate is in tune with the conclusions drawn by Alexander George and Richard Smoke in their study of the theory and practice of deterrence in the postwar era. See especially chap. 21 of George and Smoke, *Deterrence in American Foreign Policy* (New York: Columbia University Press, 1974).
91 On this point, see David K. Lewis, *Convention* (Cambridge: Harvard University Press, 1969), chap. 1.
92 N. Onuf, (ed.), *Law-Making in the Global Community* (Chapel Hill: University of North Carolina Press, 1982).
93 For excerpts of the I.C.J. judgements, see Louis Henkin and others, *International Law: Cases and Materials* (Minneapolis: West Publishing Co., 1980), 53, 59, 89, 366.
94 On the distinction between habits and norms, see H.L.A. Hart, *The Concept of Law* (New York: Oxford University Press, 1961), 84ff.
95 Onuf. (fn. 92).
96 Thus, what Iklé calls "innovative bargaining" would need further clarification. See Fred Iklé, *How Nations Negotiate* (New York: Harper & Row, 1964); also Richard Walton and Robert McKersie, *A Behavioral Theory of Labor Negotiations* (New York: McGraw-Hill, 1965). For the most comprehensive recent work on bargaining and decision making, see Glenn Snyder and Paul Diesing, *Conflict Among Nations* (Princeton: Princeton University Press, 1977).
97 See Kratochwil (fn. 54).
98 Richard Flathman, *The Public Interest* (New York: John Wiley, 1966).
99 See, i.e., the discussion by Robert Amdur on the implications of a Rawlsian conception of justice for international relations: "Rawls' Theory of Justice: Domestic and International Perspectives", *World Politics*, XXIX (April 1977), 438–61. For some critical reflections on this topic, see fn. 112 below.
100 For an attempt to contrast the world-order approach informed by the values of the World Order Models Project with the dominant thinking concerning

international relations, see Robert C. Johansen, *The National Interest and the Human Interest* (Princeton: Princeton University Press, 1980), chap. 1.

101 Kratochwil (fn. 10).

102 For the basic ideas underlying the debate on collective goods, see Mancur Olson, *The Logic of Collective Action* (Cambridge: Harvard University Press, 1965).

103 Hume, *Treatise on Human Nature*, Book III of "Morals", sec. VII, in Aiken (fn. 44).

104 Norman Frohlich, Joe A. Oppenheimer, and Oran R. Young, *Political Leadership and Collective Goods* (Princeton: Princeton University Press, 1971).

105 On this point, see Robert Gilpin's discussion of "hegemonic power" in *U.S. Power and the Multinational Corporation* (New York: Basic Books, 1975).

106 Stephen Krasner, "U.S. Commercial and Monetary Policy", *International Organization*, XXXI (Autumn 1977), 635–71.

107 Oran R. Young, "Anarchy and Social Choice: Reflections on the International Polity", *World Politics*, XXX (January 1978) 241–63, at 261.

108 On the issues remaining to be solved by the 9th session of UNCLOS III, see Bernard Oxman, "The Third Conference on the Law of the Sea (The eighth session)" *American Journal of International Law*, Vol. 74 (No. 1, 1980), 1–47.

109 Johan Galtung, "A Structural Theory of Imperialism", *Journal of Peace Research*, VIII (No. 2, 1971), 81–117.

110 This point has been made by Robert Jervis; see also Waltz (fn. 79), 35n.

111 For an interesting argument that the log transformation rather than the normal bell-shaped curve represents a normal distribution, see Jeffrey A. Hart and Nicholas Onuf, "The Distribution of State Power" (Princeton University: Center of International Studies, 1977), mimeo, 5–6.

112 Because Rawls's theory depends on the initial assumption of radical equality between the contracting parties, its implications are far less convincing for international relations than for domestic purposes.

113 The case for regulatory interventions is brought out in Oscar Schachter, *Sharing the World's Resources* (New York: Columbia University Press, 1977).

114 For a theoretical treatment of a much wider field of "international organization", see John Ruggie, "Collective Goods and the Future International Collaboration", *American Political Science Review*, Vol. 66 (September 1972), 874–94. See also Ernst B. Haas, "Why Collaborate? Issue-Linkage and International Regimes", *World Politics*, XXXII (April 1980), 357–405.

3 On the notion of "interest" in international relations

As the decline of America's position in the world becomes obvious to the observer of international reality, the re-examination of our national interest does not seem to need special justification. [. . .] But the concept of the national interest, celebrated by its champions as "the main signpost that helps political realism through the landscape of international politics",[1] proves elusive. Scholars who try to clarify the concept also appear to be at a loss, since the conflicting demands made in the name of the national interest clearly defy a substantive definition of its content.[2] Three strategies come to mind, by which the scientist of our day might deal with this embarrassment.

There is first the notion of denying the relevance of such a concept for any sensible inquiry on the grounds that the concept is a myth – a meaningless phrase or at best an indication of subjective preferences[3] – which excludes the possibility of the term's having an intersubjective content. But to abandon the concept would probably cause embarrassment, since the notion of the national interest is part of our political reality and is integral to our discourse on public affairs. We cannot eliminate with impunity the part of political reality for which the term stands.

[. . .] As a second strategy we therefore might deal with the problem in terms of false consciousness or ideology. Oddly enough, in this respect the Marxist position is similar to the radical liberal one, holding that particular interests masquerade as the national interest while in some miraculous manner the interest of groups (liberal version)[4] or the proletarian class interest (Marxist deviation)[5] is accepted as a given.

Third, there is the possibility of arguing for further empirical study, in the hope of discovering some yet-unperceived pattern in terms of which the divergent claims embodying the "true" national interest can be viewed or categorised. Thus "the best and perhaps the only available procedure may be to take the official definition and the policy output as the basis for our understanding".[6] Such an inventory of the national interest arguments might not lead to a clarification of the issues. What can be learned, however, from such nuggets of wisdom as Mahan's advocacy of a large navy in order to defend not only the US homeland but "our just national interests, whatever they be and wherever they are"?[7] Is not the determination of the "whatever" and "wherever" at issue?

[. . .] How is one to proceed?

In this article I base my argument on two theses and four corollaries.

My *first thesis* is that conventional attempts to define the true meaning of the national interest by delineating a common core of underlying phenomena are essentially mistaken since such an enterprise assumes that the notion of interest functions as a descriptive term (label) within the political discourse. Classification schemes that imply a common underlying dimension or property among a class of events or objects are not helpful, however, for the illumination of the function of terms that are used in a normative fashion for evaluating, criticising, or justifying action. Here meaning cannot be reduced to a commonality; rather, it is disclosed by the usage of the term in specific contexts, satisfying certain criteria. Thus normative terms follow a logic different from that of descriptive definitions, which distinguish according to species, genus, family, etc., by means of various taxa. This logic, or, to use a term from language philosophy, "grammar", is often misunderstood when it is measured against the requirements of the descriptive classification: normative terms allegedly do not exhibit any clear referent and are therefore assumed to be solely indicators of personal preferences. However, much of their alleged arbitrariness can be eliminated when a distinction between the "commendatory" and "descriptive" meanings of a normative term is made.[8] While the first is unchanging – giving rise to mistaken attempts to construe, i.e., an underlying dimension for all "good" things in which the objects or actions participate to varying degrees[9] – the second is field-dependent, which is to say that it provides reasons by virtue of which we justify the application of the normative term. This conceptual distinction implies that particular attention has to be paid to the reasons supplied in the descriptive meaning; criteria will have to be specified that the reasons must satisfy.

My *second thesis* is that the function of the term national interest is best analysed by following the explication of a similar and (as will be shown) interrelated term, the public interest.

These two theses, indebted more to language philosophy than to prevalent positivistic inquiries into politics, have some far-reaching corollaries.

First corollary: if the theses are correct, then the proper use of the term national interest in justifying political action could be specified and possible misuses [. . .] could be disclosed.

Second corollary: aside from normative implications, such a perspective should also be heuristically fruitful for the investigation of the origins and demise of the European state system and its conventions. In this context it is particularly interesting to investigate the relationship between the public interest and the national interest. The two notions came into existence simultaneously, since the concept of the "interest of the prince" made necessary a clarification of both the internal and the external dimensions of this interest. Thus while the public interest, or more often the common weal (*salus publica*), fortified or defended a policy against internal challenges, the notion of the national interest was used in advancing the goals of foreign policy.

Implicit in this notion was the recognition not only that political action was constrained by an international system but that the failure or success of a policy could crucially depend on its compatibility with certain "rules of the game", which served as a common framework for all sovereigns and allowed decision makers to pursue conflicting goals without falling into a totally unregulated struggle. Thus I hope to show that within the reason of state tradition, theorists and statesmen alike clearly distinguished interest from preference. A decisive test for my assertions will be whether changes of the system are preceded (or at least paralleled) by decisive shifts of meaning in key concepts of the political discourse.

This leads to my third corollary: that my proposed perspective provides an approach that competes with Waltzian systemic analysis[10] concerned with structure in terms of the distribution of capabilities, and with Kaplan's systems approach.[11] In addition, I claim that some of the puzzles of both approaches and at least some of their controversial points can be understood better from the vantage point I outline below. In my approach the unit of analysis is neither the structure nor the actor. It is, rather, the norms that serve to guide and justify the making as well as the explanation of decisions.

[. . .]

In the next section I summarise the considerations relevant to an investigation of the national interest. I use the criteria developed by the public interest debate as exemplified in the work of Flathman,[12] Held,[13] Barry,[14] Hare,[15] and others. In Section II, the works of several writers of the *raison d'état* school are considered. My goal is not to give a complete account of the history of political thought, as this has been done to a certain extent – though with an underlying Hegelian conception of intellectual history – in Meinecke's work on *Staatsräson*.[16] Rather, it is to show that the thoughts of de Rohan, Pufendorf, Frederick the Great, Rousset, and Metternich to a large extent satisfy the conditions I have specified for a reasoned public interest argument. Furthermore, I argue that by the second half of the nineteenth century there had occurred a remarkable shift in the meaning of the national interest. The term was increasingly interpreted merely as an indication of the preferences of decision makers, preferences that were increasingly conceived in social-Darwinistic terms. Thus, long before the actual breakdown of the European state system in World War I, the nature of the game had fundamentally changed.

Section III provides a short summary and addresses some of the more recent controversies concerning structural explanations of world politics.

I

What do we mean when we say that something is in my interest? On the most general level we could argue that we want to indicate some preference, wish, or want. Reflection, however, soon discloses that the grammar of interest does not coincide with the usage of preference and want, since we can think of cases in which it makes sense to distinguish carefully something wanted or desired – like sitting down in a snowstorm due to exhaustion – from the interest involved – not doing so because of the danger of freezing to death. Thus, even on the simplest level, the interest argument requires some giving of reasons, a justification that goes beyond the mere indication of likes and dislikes.

Similarly, when we argue that something is in the public interest we do not want solely to state that something happens to please our fancy, but that something is to be preferred and ought to be chosen because certain reasons can be marshalled to support this claim when challenged. We are forced to go beyond idiosyncratic preferences and argue on the basis of intersubjective grounds that can be adduced for backing a claim. This feature is of decisive importance, as Flathman points out: "[T]he validity of reasons depends on rules of inference and the existence of evidence not upon purely personal . . . preference. This means that reasons provide grounds upon which agreement can be reached despite differences of the latter kind."[17] If this is true, the term public interest functions to justify claims and demands, and obliges members of a public to defer to such a decision even if they regard it as being contrary to their own preferences. This naturally does not prove that the public interest *has* to be incompatible with personal preferences; in certain situations they might coincide. It does show, however, that the reasons offered in defence of a public interest claim have to be substantially different from indications of personal preference; it also disposes of the argument that the public interest *cannot* be used in any way other than in conveying idiosyncrasies.

There remains the difficulty of ascertaining the public interest in a concrete case, as different claims can be backed up by a variety of reasons. Thus the problem of deciding between competing reasons merely pushes the dilemma one step further back. Obviously one needs criteria to weigh evidence offered in support of public interest claims. This might not enable us to decide once and for all the real public interest, but it provides the conditions for assessing public interest claims. Unless we make an essentialist argument parallel to the platonic theory in which, for example, goodness can be defined in terms of the participation[18] of various things and actions in the essence of the idea of good, we must be satisfied with the conclusion that the public interest does not coincide with any single value. Therefore, taxonomic definitions of good as well as of the public interest, based on the identification of a common property among a class of objects or events, are founded on mistaken assumptions. Indeed, the analogy of the functioning of the term good proves to be instructive in this respect. "Good", as Hare reminds us,[19] is used in a way that makes possible the distinction of two functions of the term. First, there is the commendatory function, which stays the same despite a great variety of meanings conveyed by the second function, the descriptive meaning.[20] It is the descriptive meaning, however, that supplies the reasons in virtue of which we call something good; and to that extent, the commendatory meaning of good is, like the claim of the public interest, restricted by the appropriateness of the reasons supplied in the descriptive meaning.

The focus on reasons as the validating principle in public interest claims makes it clearer that the public interest need not be merely an interest all members of the public have in common, as Barry argues.[21]

[. . .]

This leads us back to the criteria that the descriptive meaning of the public interest has to satisfy in order to establish a justifiable claim. There is first the logical requirement of generalization ("universalizability"), which states that "what is right (or wrong) for one actor must be right (or wrong) for any actor in similar circumstances".[22] Although this principle is purely formal (in that it does not provide a substantive answer to value questions), it stipulates a logical requirement that any substantive answer has to meet, thereby ruling out capricious exemptions. But might not the stipulation "similar persons similarly situated" relax the requirement of true universality to one of permissible classifications under certain circumstances?

In other words, what seems to be required is that the individual making a public interest claim "is not obligated to find common ground with an entire population: but it is his (or her) duty to test the classifications he proposes in the light of this principle".[23] However, arguing that, for example, a particular policy is right and justifiable in terms of the public interest forms a claim larger than prescribing a particular standard solution to a class of problems, even if we are willing to impose it impartially. This becomes clear when we

> consider the case of assigning punishments according to the classification "all those who have committed murder in the first degree". . . . If we agree to this and we treat all persons the same we have satisfied the demands of one part of the principle. But the application of the principle also presupposes an answer to the question "Is it right (or wrong) to treat X (who has committed murder in the first degree) in manner Y?" This depends upon the consequences of so treating him. Universalizability is relevant in that it teaches that if Y is right for X it must be right for A, B, C, and D, if they are similar persons similarly situated. But universalizing alone cannot determine whether the consequences are good or bad, the policy right or wrong.[24]

Thus a public interest claim has to satisfy another formal requirement, that of considering the consequences, which involves us in the arduous task of providing data for assessing the impact of various policies upon community values. This requirement clarifies the public interest in its descriptive meaning in two ways. First, it imposes the burden of proof upon the claimant to demonstrate how a particular policy furthers a given value. But beyond this condition of instrumental rationality, the "principle of consequences" makes it necessary to specify all affected values and to assess the relative costs of a policy (given that competing values are often at stake). While the enumeration of affected values does not involve the question of how to assess a particular proposal, the collection of relevant data becomes possible only after the specification of values. This disposes, on one hand, of a good deal of empty political rhetoric, as the invocation even of widely shared values does not by itself legitimize a particular policy. On the other hand, the presentation of facts becomes relevant and persuasive only when they concern the anticipated effects of a policy on community values, and when that relationship is tested in terms of the formal principles enumerated.

Flathman illustrates this point by means of the debate concerning the construction of an expressway, facilitating traffic flow but disturbing established neighbourhoods.

> An investigation presupposes criteria of relevance and principles of judgment.
>
> But it is equally the case that the values, taken alone, will not provide a basis for a decision concerning the merits of the proposal. For the question is not whether fast and safe traffic flow or preservation of family neighborhoods is in the public interest. The question is whether building *this* expressway is in the public interest. . . . Before a decision can be made as to whether building *this* expressway would be in the public interest, we must know whether (or to what extent) this expressway would in fact contribute to a safe and speedy flow of traffic, disrupt neighborhood life, raise or lower taxes. Detailed studies would have to be made. . . .[25]

Provided these conditions are met, we can say that the descriptive meaning of the public interest has been established: disagreement has not necessarily been eliminated, as it is very unlikely that only one policy will survive the tests required by the public interest discourse. To that extent, a certain arbitrariness in the final choice remains. But this arbitrariness, based on different judgements about valid reasons in support of value choices or about the assessment of the reliability of certain facts or contextual factors, is fundamentally different from the unelaborated randomness of "I like" or "I prefer". Indeed, the frequent phenomenon that more than one proposal satisfies the elaborated principles is one of the reasons that authoritative decisions have to be made on behalf of the public. Furthermore, it demonstrates that the political discourse – in which the public interest is a key term – revolves largely around justifiable and non-justifiable decisions and not simply around "incorrect" and "correct" (logically compelling) solutions. But to say that authority plays an important role in establishing the descriptive meaning of the public interest is not to imply that the public interest is simply identifiable with "what the decision maker says the public interest is". After all, the legitimacy of the public authority, and its resultant ability to make binding decisions, depends crucially upon perceptions that its decisions *are* in the public interest.

Those who focus solely on decision outcomes and fail to inquire into the grounds on which decisions are based misunderstand the problem, as do those who argue that, since the term does not provide for a definable content once and for all, it is useless in a science of politics. It is because the term public interest has a commendatory function that it aids in our deliberation for choosing policies and serves as a yardstick of criticism. To maintain that nothing is worth knowing which does not yield unequivocal results, through either experiment or logical entailment, is to misconstrue the problem of politics. [. . .] The next section shows that the logic of the term national interest can be analysed in a similar fashion and that new insights into the preconditions of order in international relations can thereby be gained.

II

How relevant are these considerations for our explication of the concept of the national interest? A first point is readily apparent: like the public interest, the term national interest seems to be a general commendatory concept used for judging and selecting policies for a particular public. Thus, our remarks about the primary meaning of the term are directly relevant. It is when we try to establish the descriptive meaning that we face new difficulties. In order to show this in a systematic fashion we take one step back and clarify a concept that, until now, has been treated as axiomatic: the "public".

We said that, for a public interest claim to be sensible, some sort of validating system must exist. This does not necessarily mean an established authority structure that makes the final determination of descriptive meaning – in that, we risk another platonic fallacy.[26] Rather, we said, there must be an established discourse within which a public interest claim can be located and tested through the specification of criteria. These criteria consist of two principles and one substantive moral rule. The principles have been called the principle of generalisation and the principle of consequences; the moral rule is, "Serve community values unless doing so violates the formal principles".[27] It is clear that such a validating system would be totally indeterminate if the term community remained unspecified. In other words, differing from general moral precepts that assume true universality, the public interest has as a determining feature the distinction between "ins" and "outs" through the stipulation of a public or community. A classical passage sheds light on the link between the public interest and the existence of an identifiable community: Thucydides' description of the revolution in Corcyra, where the disintegration of the community is paralleled by a change in meaning in certain key words of the political discourse.

> . . . [I]n every state there was a fight between the champions of democracy who wished to call in the Athenians and the champions of oligarchy who did the same for the Spartans. In times of peace neither side had the excuse or the willingness to call in the two great powers, but when

the war was on, and the prospects good for damaging the opposing party while strengthening one's own thereby, invitations to foreign powers were made without [due] consideration by those who wished to change the government. . . . The leading men in the various states each heading a party with a specious slogan, one allegedly being in favor of democracy and equality of the people, the other professing to adhere to the rule of the best elements, actually played booty with the public interests they so loudly professed. In their frenzy to compete with each other and to outdo each other they dared the most awful deeds! In their acts of vengeance they went to even greater lengths, not setting any limits in justice or the interest of the state but only in the capriciousness of the moment. . . .

To put an end to this one could neither depend upon a promise nor an oath. . . . All parties considering in their calculations the hopelessness of a permanent state of affairs were more intent upon self-defense than capable of trust. . . .

Indeed men too often take upon themselves in the prosecution of their revenge to set an example of doing away with those general laws to which all alike can look for salvation in adversity, instead of allowing them to subsist against the day of danger when their aid may be required.[28]

Several points deserve further attention. The first is Thucydides' observation that slogans of the public interest become hollow phrases in the face of treason (the abolition of the value in maintaining a community). A policy directed against one's own community by denying legitimacy to a part or the whole of the body politic for personal ambitions drives home the point that such public interest considerations are usually taken into account, thereby providing for some restraint and the maintenance of the domestic and international political order. The inability to define a public interest in the face of other powers is thus destructive not only of the state itself but of the minimum order in international relations; the division or the incorporation of the contentious state results.

Second, the Corcyraean example demonstrates that the question of the public interest is transformed into the interest of the state as soon as the question of boundaries dividing various publics comes into focus or the policy that is advanced deals with the relations of the body politic vis-à-vis other bodies. This has important implications for the evaluative criteria proposed for the public interest discourse. Since external policies universalize internally, by definition, the consequences of a given policy as the "citizens become liable for it",[29] the generalization principle provides little guidance in the domestic debate to distinguish genuine from spurious claims on the national interest.

The principle of consequences, on the other hand, attains ominous importance as it introduces a host of considerations concerning the environment of the polity, considerations that impose particularly exacting informational requirements upon the claimant. A theory that tries to come to terms with the resulting complexities gives rise to a systemic conception of inter-unit politics, in which the contingent character of the policies pursued by the various states becomes the dominant theme (as in the teaching of the *raison d'état* school). Rather than identifying the national interest with the decision of the authorised agent of a body politic, the reason of state literature clearly tries to distinguish between decisions and interests (which coincide ideally but not necessarily) as the following passage from the Huguenot de Rohan shows.

> The princes command people, and the Interest commands the princes. The knowledge of this Interest is much more raised above that of Princes' actions, as they themselves are above the People. The Prince may deceive himselfe, his Counsell may be corrupted, but the interest alone can never faile. According as it is well or ill understood, it maketh States to live or die. And as it allwaies aimeth at the augmentation or at least-wise the conservation of a State, so likewise to get thither, it ought to varie according to the times.[30]

The parallels to the conception of the "general will" as aiming at the common advantage, which constitutes one of the most explicit public interest theories, will not be lost on anyone familiar with Rousseau.[31] Although the listing of "augmentation" and "preservation" – the argument of national survival of later days – could be construed as a definition of the national interest, the whole passage makes clear that a specification of a range of consideration to be taken into account, rather than the identification of interest with one factor, establishes the descriptive meaning of the term.

De Rohan's teaching on the interest of the state is particularly instructive when one considers what precepts of conventional wisdom he excludes. There is neither the usual recourse to historical examples and to persuasion that the *salus publica* consists in imitating these great deeds – a problem that played a considerable role in Machiavelli's theory[32] – nor any mention of the *arcana imperii*, those pieces of advice that tried through the observation of human weaknesses and passions to provide guidelines for "successful actions".[33] Furthermore, no dynastic considerations are admitted in this theory of the state since de Rohan, in tune with the Huguenot "politicians",[34] had already warned, in 1621, that the "power of a kingdom rests in the king and his alliances, not his blood-line, but in his Interests".[35] The largely personalistic politics of the feudal period, which often still influenced de Rohan's political actions,[36] is here clearly subordinated to the interest of the state in Richelieu's sense. As a defeated Huguenot after the fall of La Rochelle, de Rohan tries to establish a theory of politics that goes far beyond the original toleration of religious freedom before and under Henri IV. The old tolerance embodied in the Edict of Nantes, based on protection of privileges, religious and other-wise,[37] has now to be supplanted by a new organising concept that will end factionalism at home and the continuous intervention in the domestic affairs by other powers. The definition of a public interest free from feudal remnants and established with the realisation of the systemic constraints within which the French state had to operate, creates a secular ideal of an encompassing community that can be served by individuals irrespective of rank, religion, or lineage.[38] Thus, the state, in its interests, is as much defined by the external pressures resulting from the interactions of the various parts of Christendom (the *res publica Christiana*) as it is by the subordination of internal, particular goals under the imperatives of the common public interest uniting all citizens. Christendom, on the other hand, has lost its imperial connotations and stands now for the frame of reference within which the new game of independent nations takes place.[39] A decision maker following the true interest of his body politic must consequently act in accordance with certain standards rather than choose simply on the impulse of his preferences. Well aware of Richelieu's policies during the Thirty Years War, de Rohan mentions that

> France should make shew to the Protestant Princes and States that all-though shee be of diverse Religion to theirs, yet shee would rather [see] their conversion than their destruction, assuring them that this shall not at all hinder her that shee contribute not of her owne to conserve them, and to aide them freely against all those that would trouble or change any thing in their States and liberties.[40]

This is obviously more than the mere pursuit of temporary advantage so familiar from the interactions of Italian or Greek city states. It is rather an attempt to specify criteria that make possible a principled formulation of policy. That these principles are not deontological, moral precepts[41] but result largely from selfish calculations is obvious. Nevertheless, the need to take others into account and thereby reduce purely idiosyncratic preferences acts as a considerable constraint upon the formulation of policies in the interest of the state.[42] It also provides for a more predictable environment in which foreign policy choices have to be made.

How such strategic calculations attain, over time, the status of "rules of the international game" is perhaps most clearly elaborated in the work of Jean Rousset, an eighteenth-century French refugee in the Netherlands. Rousset tries to demonstrate that irrespective of the merits of French claims to the southern part of the Netherlands, such an acquisition was out of the question within a politics of interest. The *droit de convenance*, as he calls it, prohibited such aggrandizement, as it would upset the general balance of power on the continent.

> The alliances that were concluded among the principal powers of Europe in regards to this matter should have convinced the French court that it is not *in the public interest* [*pas de l'intérêt public*] that she is ruling these rich provinces. I know well that they were once upon a time fiefdoms of the Crown ... But nothing of that sort matters, as the "Droit de convenance" of all Europe is against it. ... [A]ll of Europe will always

oppose an aggrandizement of the French crown at the expense of the Netherlands. In vain will France decry the injustice. Has she not herself on a thousand occasions given the example of the force of the "droit de convenance"? Does she have any other right than that to Brittany, Normandy or Acquitania, Alsace or the French Cômté. . . . The reason for the convention among the principal powers of Europe is easy to see. These provinces are so rich, strategically located [*si bien situées*] . . . that if France, Britain or [even] Holland possessed them, there would be no longer a Balance of Power in Europe. France should therefore give up forever the hope of such a conquest. . . .[43]

This passage is remarkable for two reasons. First, we find again the close logical connection between the public interest discourse and the claims of the interest of state, or national interests, as we did in de Rohan. Second, the justifiability of a national interest claim is clearly tied to a systemic conception of international politics: the states' individual preferences have to be assessed in terms of the repercussions for all. To that extent, we could say, a weaker form of the principle of generalization begins to operate as soon as a system of conventions (*droit de convenance*) comes into existence and decision makers start to think of themselves as members of a (distinct) class of actors. "Through this process they subsume their interests under a larger precept or maxim and thereby begin to transform them into 'claims' which can be legitimately pressed in the public forum".[44]

From a Hobbesian perspective on international reality, this seems indeed strange. Nevertheless, the awareness of the distinctiveness of a European state system and its conventions, which mitigated many of the anarchical features of the international arena, was commonly accepted by reason of state theorists and practitioners alike. No less an exponent of the *raison d'état* than Metternich remarked, in his memoirs,

> *Politics* is the science of the vital interests of States in its widest meaning. Since, however, an isolated state no longer exists, and is found only in the annals of the heathen world . . . we must always view the *society* of states as the essential condition of the modern world. . . . The great axioms of political science proceed from the knowledge of the true political interests of *all states*; it is upon these general interests that rests the guarantee of their existence. . . . The establishing of international relations, on the basis of reciprocity under the guarantee of respect for acquired rights, . . . constitutes in our time the essence of politics.[45]

One might be inclined to dismiss such utterances as ideological stances, were it not for the fact that such theoretical elaborations did in fact tap significant dimensions of the European state practice of the time.[46] After all, Metternich, a "restaurator" of the European order, consciously tried to link his political moves to an established tradition that had contributed to safeguard the minimum conditions of order within the society of nations.[47] True, the establishment of such a minimum order did not provide for the preservation of peace – indeed it not only sanctioned war but made it under certain circumstances a systemic necessity – but it tried to circumscribe war and sanctioned resort to violence for certain accepted interests instead of the more transcendental values that had led to unprecedented savageries in religious wars and the revolutionary adventures of a Napoleon.

By postulating solely secular interests as the proper domain of the international arena, the notion of interest gave rise to certain maxims and conventions that clearly lacked the moral persuasiveness of more transcendental visions. The restraints imposed by the emerging conventions of the state system were human contrivances. They lacked deontological rigor because of their largely utilitarian character, but they were far from useless.[48]

Despite appeals to the "law of nature" or a common heritage, most theorists of the international game recognized that the force of certain conventions regulating state behaviour depended as much upon the maintenance of certain organizational givens as on moral considerations. This explains the fascination of thinkers and statesmen alike with the conception of the balance of power as a guarantor of liberty as well as minimum order.[49] A new theory of order emerged, quite different from either the Hobbesian speculation or a vision based on commonality of purposes. As I have dealt with this subject elsewhere[50] only a few remarks concerning theories of order are necessary. While the imperial order is one based on command ("one-power" world), the interactions of two self-interested equals are likely to result in outcomes to which two-person game theory gives us important clues. Only in a three-power world does "reputation" become an important device for simplifying the complicated calculations of interactions that have no longer a logically compelling solution.[51] The more participants enter the game, the more difficult the task of calculating one's interest becomes, and the greater the role that precedents and rules play.[52] This is the reason why such "cynical" statesmen as Richelieu maintain – and quite seriously so – that reputation, not solely military might, is the most decisive ingredient of a successful policy. Reputation here means not only prestige but a certain amount of trust, sympathy, and assurance among one's peers that one is a bona fide "player".[53] But exactly because reputation and the rules that define the international game attain a certain influence and create presumptions on the part of all participants, they also create incentives to subvert them. This is the tragedy of any regulatory communications system, Jervis reminds us,[54] as it is impossible to devise a system that does not allow for deception.[55] The high costs, however, connected with an all too straightforward violation are clearly brought out in Frederick the Great's "Political Testament" of 1752:

> England and France have been for a century now the ultimate movers in any changes. In case a belligerent sovereign decided to go to war and,

provided both agree on the maintenance of peace, they would offer him their good offices and thus force him to accept this mediation. Once put into operation this system prevents great seizures of territory and makes wars unprofitable except when they are carried out with superior forces and continuous luck. It is inappropriate for us to commence the war anew. A daring stroke such as the seizure of Silesia resembles books which are successful in the original version, but their imitation is lackluster. Through the seizure of Silesia we directed the envy of all Europe toward us. All our neighbors were alarmed by it: there is not one who does not mistrust us. My own life will be too short to put them at ease as it is advantageous to our interests.[56]

But while these reflections spell out the practical implications of too "machiavellian" a policy, Samuel Pufendorf's observations concerning interests in the European state system provide a more theoretical treatment. Pufendorf, like the host of international lawyers after him who assert the validity of norms governing international conduct, had the unenviable task of squaring the circle of the postulates of sovereignty (non-recognition of formal superior authority) and obligation (acceptance of certain normative constraints).[57] The notion of interest serves him as mediating conception. [. . .]

Interests may be divided into an imaginary and real Interests. By the first I understand when a Prince judges the welfare of his state to consist of such things as cannot be performed without disquieting, and being injurious to, a great many other states, and which these are obliged to oppose with all their power; as for example the monarchy of Europe, or the universal monopoly, this being the fuel with which the whole world may be put to flame. The real interest may be subdivided into a perpetual and temporary. The former depends chiefly on the situation and constitution of the country, and the natural inclinations of the people; the latter, on the condition, strength and weakness of the neighboring nations; for as those vary, the Interests also must vary.[58]

Aside from the distinction between the commendatory and descriptive meanings of interest that appears here, Pufendorf points out the limits such a conception of interest imposes upon decision makers, since certain goals can be only inappropriately labelled interests. Furthermore, the maintenance of the system of states is seen as the precondition for the functioning of norms, which become maxims for political action. Here the connection between the balance of power as prescription for state behaviour and *raison d'état* doctrines becomes visible. Minimum order does not automatically result from the interaction of various units in the international arena – the failures of antiquity in checking Roman expansionism were shrewdly pointed out by Frederick the Great[59] – and hence the preservation of liberty and the attainment of minimum order have to be the results of the managerial skill of the main players, as well as of agreement concerning what "the game" was about. Thus Hume, in his short essay on the balance of power, oscillates between two tendencies. On the one hand he sees in the idea of a balance of power a "natural" dictate of reason and, so to speak, an automatic precept that operates whenever a multiplicity of actors interact. On the other hand, he notes that such precepts of reason have *not* been followed by many states, as the history of Rome teaches us.

> It must be noted that the Romans never met with any general combin-
> ation of confederacy against them as might naturally have been expected
> from the rapid conquests and declared ambition: but were allowed
> peaceably to subdue their neighbors, one after another. . . .
> The Rhodian and Achean republics are much celebrated by ancient
> historians for their wisdom and their sound policy: yet both of them
> assisted the Romans in their wars against Philip and Antiochus. And
> what might be esteemed still a stronger proof that this maxim was not
> generally known in those ages, no ancient author has remarked the
> imprudence of these measures. . . .[60]

This passage may suffice to dispense with the idea that the emergence of a balance of power as a guiding notion of politics is a necessary ingredient of a multipolar system. [. . .]

As we have seen, the inability of the Greek city states to conceive of inter-ests other than as pure expansion led to the *pleonechthia* and *hybris* that Thucydides decried so vividly. The result was the eclipse of Greek independ-ence and the intervention of Persia, an outsider rather than a "balancer", as the final arbiter of the system.

The balance of power as understood in the European state system was based on a set of conventions rather than on logical or objective necessity. Only against the background of the conception of interest incorporating into its grammar the role of others did the balance of power make prescriptive sense. Similarly, only against this background is the definition of the interest of the state (and later the nation) in terms of power meaningful. Although the "maximisation of power" principle seems at first a parsimonious explanation for state action comparable to the assumptions underlying *homo oeconomicus* as a revenue-maximiser,[61] there are decisive differences.

Admittedly, certain similarities obtain. The market as the arena of economic interactions creates an ordered allocation of resources through the price mechanism, as does the clash of interests in the international arena. However, the order created by the market is the direct result of the actions of purely self-interested individuals acting *independently* of each other. The mainten-ance of a balance of power, on the other hand, which creates minimum order in the political arena, depends on the conscious management of the *interdependencies* created by the strategic interactions of the players.

Another decisive difference between the political and economic realms is worth mentioning. Maximisation of revenue serves as a powerful explanatory variable as well as a maxim for action of the individual in the market. But it depends crucially on the existence of a social convention called money,[62] on the readiness of all participants to measure purchasable goods and services in terms of one commodity or symbolic yardstick. Furthermore, this means of exchange also has the ability to serve as a store of value so that the stored resource can be converted into purchasing power. True, possession of money or resources does not always imply purchasing power; nevertheless, in economic life such conversions are usually made quite easily as long as there is widespread trust in the currency. The conversion of resources to usable power is substantially more difficult in politics, of course, as Knorr has amply demonstrated.[63] Second, political power differs from economic purchasing power in that it is generally circumscribed in scope and domain. Thus, the usual case in politics is that various goals require different types of resources.[64] The possession of nuclear weapons might be not only useless for the objective of having one of your nationals elected Secretary-General of the United Nations but actually counter-productive, given present international conventions.[65]

This last example demonstrates rather clearly why the balance of power – although rather intuitive as a principle of politics – depends for its empirical and normative significance upon a set of conventions that are far less automatic and readily brought into existence than is sometimes assumed. There must first of all be a method of estimating power, or, rather, resources or capabilities convertible into actual power. In this context it is interesting that, from Talleyrand's attempts to dissuade Napoleon from imperial expansion[66] to the various compensation schemes floated at the Congress of Vienna,[67] such a measure was generally linked to the number of taxpaying inhabitants rather than to purely military capabilities. Naturally such a convention on estimating power was helped by stable technology as well as tacit agreement on legitimate political goals and modes of attaining them. Thus, more than any elaborate arithmetic of power it was the notion of legitimate interests that preserved a predictable environment within which conflicts could be perceived as limited to adjustments in power. That this called for a policy fundamentally different from mere Machiavellianism should be obvious, as Machiavelli's Prince was concerned only with the maintenance of his dominion and the shrewd recognition of opportunities that might lead to his aggrandisement. Fenelon, an eighteenth-century balance-of-power proponent, illustrates the different aims and justifications of a policy concerned with the interests of states in a balance of power system:

> Each nation is obliged to take care to prevent the excessive aggrandizement of each neighbor, for its own security. To prevent the neighbor from becoming too powerful is not to do wrong: it is to protect oneself from slavery and to protect one's other neighbors from it; in a word, it is to

work for liberty, for tranquillity, for the public safety: because the aggrandizement of one nation beyond a certain limit changes the general system of all the nations which have relations with it.[68]

How destructive an obsession with power alone was, for the politics based on the notion of interests of the European state system, has been shown by a contemporary student of the European tradition of international politics. In his too little appreciated article on Bismarck, Kissinger taps the significant shifts in European politics in the second half of the nineteenth century despite the outward appearance of stability that underlay the Bismarckian alliance structure.[69] Bismarck simply ignored the efforts of the European Concert that had mediated the various interests of the players and thus endowed change with the aura of European consensus. Instead, the German chancellor, whom Kissinger calls a white revolutionary, sought security in the manipulation of military alliances.

> Because of his own magnificent grasp of nuances of power relationships, Bismarck saw in his philosophy a doctrine of self-limitation. . . . Because these nuances were not apparent to his successors and imitators, the applications of Bismarck's lesson led to an armament race and a world war. . . . The nemesis of power is that except in the hands of a master, reliance on it is more likely to produce a contest at arms than self-restraint. . . .[70]

But there is a more fundamental reason why, from 1870 on, a slow but inevitable breakdown of the conventions of the European state system took place.

As we saw, inherent in the notion of interest was a weakened form of generalisation; each state pursuing its goals had to think of its role in a larger system. Here Bismarck breaks critically with the accepted tradition. When the Eastern question occupied the European powers in 1876 and Gortschakoff had argued that the Great Powers had a European responsibility, Bismarck noted on the margin of the dispatch, "Anyone who speaks of Europe is mistaken", adding, one line later, "Who is Europe?"[71] In a memorandum dictated on the same occasion, Bismarck continues, "Germany resolutely opposes this insupportable fiction [Europe] . . . I no longer see Europe . . . I would always be happy to be able and useful to *Russian* interests . . . but not at all to the rest of Europe. Officially it is necessary for us earnestly to hold far from us this charlatanism with regard to Europe."[72]

That such utterances were not the occasional martial derailment of an essentially moderate statesman but rather indicate Bismarck's bargaining style is illustrated by his advice to Frederick Wilhelm in connection with the Austro-Prussian alliance in 1854. When an Austrian ultimatum forced a Russian retreat from the lower Danube, raising the spectre of the invocation of the *casus foederis* by Vienna, Bismarck suggested that the promised 200,000 men should not be assembled in Lissa in order to strengthen the

Austrian position but rather in Upper Silesia, thus to be in position "to cross either the Russian or the Austrian borders with equal facility".[73] The rationale for this machiavellian ploy was the recognition that, "with 200,000 men Your Majesty would at this moment become the master of the entire European situation, would be able to dictate the peace and win for Prussia a worthy position in Germany".[74]

This is not yet the exclusivity of pure and unadulterated self-interest that emerges later, when social-Darwinism makes a cult out of struggle – oddly enough, nearly always understood as the socially organized mass killings of modern wars. But it is already a decisive step, from interests defined within a set of conventions to interests conceived of, at best, allowing for *ad hoc* recognition of others through bargaining. Besides, social-Darwinistic over-tones are already detectable. Inveighing against the notion that a science of politics is possible – a notion crucial in the Metternich tradition even if substantially different from our positivistic conceptions – Bismarck stresses patience and the intuitive recognition of the right moment for "the kill" as the most important underlying principle of political action.[75] Otto Pflanze, a perceptive historian of Bismarck's achievement, concludes,

> In the popular biology of Social Darwinism, he [Bismarck] found a better parallel between science and society. His views reflected the revolt of the nineteenth century against the seventeenth and eighteenth centuries, the period of biological discovery against that of astronomy and physics, the age of romanticism against that of rationalism.[76]

Flowing from this was a total disregard of institutional or legal checks, evident in Bismarck's contempt for the Reichstag and the invocation of con-science as the ultimate validator of essentially arbitrary actions. Politics is reduced to manipulation or irrational forces. Instead of an adjustment of interests, through collective legitimisation the cultivation of the military spirit and its manipulation now occupy center stage. It is significant that in his memoirs concerning the notorious Ems telegram Bismarck sees danger only in the lack of proper management of the military spirit he so heartily embraced, not in the militarisation that had taken place in the notion of politics itself.[77]

The glorification of unbridled self-interest as the essence of politics remains one of the sad achievements of the period before World War I. It emerges in perhaps its clearest form in the writings of Riezler[78] and Ratzenhofer[79] in Germany.

The difference between the old politics of interest and the new conception of politics as the struggle for survival is perhaps best characterised by two works that were destined to become of major importance in Anglo-German relations: Sir Eyre Crowe's memorandum of January 1907 and Karl Riezler's treatise on German *Weltpolitik*, significantly called "The Necessity of the Impossible".[80] Although the recognition of a deep-seated conflict of interest is common to both treatises, Crowe's allegedly anti-German memorandum results in a relatively cautious containment policy while Riezler's summation turns to a metaphysical principle in order to justify virtually unlimited expansionism. Crowe's memorandum deals with the structural conflict with Germany on two levels, that of aspirations and that of interest. On both, he advocates a perhaps restrictive but nevertheless not hostile accommodation with German expansion. While sympathetic to "what is best in the German mind", Crowe insists that for a sensible accommodation to occur, "There must be respect for the individualities of other nations, equally valuable coadjutors, in their way, in the work of human progress, equally entitled to full elbow room in which to contribute, in freedom, to the evolution of a higher civiliza-tion".[81] On the level of more tangible interests, Crowe maintains that

> ... it would be neither just nor politic to ignore the claims to a healthy expansion which a vigorous and growing country like Germany has a natural right to assert in the field of legitimate endeavour . . . . It cannot be a good policy for England to thwart such a process of development where it does not directly conflict either with British interests or with those of other nations to which England is bound by solemn treaty obli-gations . . . . Nor is it for British Governments to oppose Germany's building as large a fleet as she might consider necessary or desirable for the defense of her national interest.[82]

Thus even German naval expansion, a clearly sensitive problem for British policy, is in itself not barred but tied to the larger conception of the defence of legitimate interests. When Riezler's views are read in conjunction with this policy memorandum the differences become striking. On the level of aspir-ation he states, "Ideally every nation wants to grow, to expand, to rule and subject [others] without end, wants to become an even more powerful unit, until the Universe has under its rule become one organic unit".[83] On the level of practical policy this meant that, in order to free Germany from the night-mare of alliances, the Reich had to become so powerful that it would have a chance of victory against any possible combination; hence, no limitation of its power could be accepted. "For the sake of freedom in its world policy [*Weltpolitik*] [Germany] must be guarded against any eventuality",[84] Riezler maintained. The idea that the national interest requires validation within a discourse that provides a common frame of reference for the conflicting claims of the participants in the international game has become foreign to this theory of international relations. [. . .]

When, with the outbreak of the First World War, "the political structure crumbled", writes David Calleo,

> power ran amok. Military ambition lost all restraint. . . . Increasingly absent from German calculations was the necessity for leaving other countries some acceptable role and situation in the interests of long-range

peace. . . . It is extraordinary how these ambitions continued to grow right until August 1918. Thoughts of compromise were firmly repulsed as traitorous. Yet all was fantasy. The real war was hopeless. Army leaders presumably knew, but deceived everyone. Even the Kaiser was astonished at the end. Suddenly, the military declared the war lost.[85]

Hybris, so clearly recognised by Thucydides as the enemy of a defensible conception of interest, had triumphed once more.

III

The conception of the national interest as understood in the *raison d'état* tradition was neither a merely honorific label for effective decisions nor simply another name for choices that had been made on essentially arbitrary grounds. The discourse on interests had a discernable logic and the arguments it sustained had to satisfy certain criteria, which turned out to be those of a weakened form of the public interest discourse. The public interest has two forms of relevance for our purposes, one systematic and one historical. The systematic connection is grounded in the recognition that both terms are evaluative and justificatory devices for policies. Consequently both function fundamentally differently from descriptive labels, although only the notion of the public interest has received sufficient attention and thus the normative-descriptive distinction has been elaborated only in that context. The reasons for this are mainly historical.

Both notions developed simultaneously: the public interest was the *internal* while the interest of the prince and later the national interest was the *external* dimension of the reason of state. But the contractualist approach of political theory was better able to clarify the notion of the public interest, because no common compact among states could be found. Thus within the contractualist approach the public interest could be used as a justificatory device against particular interests, be they the old feudal privileges or the *volonté générale* opposed to the *volonté des tous*. When measured against this conceptual apparatus the national interest seemed to lack an identifiable content; the temptation to identify the descriptive meaning of the term with the effective decision of an authorized decision maker was more than tempting. The moral seemed to be clear: the notion of the national interest seemed little more than *kto kogo* (who does it to whom) and indeed, in both Machiavellian and Bismarckian versions such an interpretation seemed appropriate. But such a version of the national interest argument is neither normatively nor historically the only possible, or even the true, one.

For a significant period the notion of interest gave rise to a conception of international politics that was, in Hedley Bull's terms, much closer to an "international society" than to Hobbes's state of nature. It nevertheless remains true that international politics did not result in the establishment of a universal society.

The preceding analysis pointed out significant differences between the public and the national interest. The specified criteria for assessing public interests usually are not sufficient to eliminate all alternatives. Thus a choice by a public authority becomes necessary, to select one of the policies that satisfy the criteria. This point has important implications for the national interest. First, as we saw, the generalisation criterion exists only in a weakened form; and second, given the decentralised authority structure of the international environment, the national interest argument cannot be addressed to a public authority above the bargaining parties. Thus ambiguities often cannot be resolved even with the best of intentions on the part of all or most players. Nevertheless, the discourse on the national interest does not thereby become meaningless. Its guidance, supplied by reasons and debate, depends on the willingness of the parties to be persuaded.

[. . .]

This perspective may seem odd at a time when structural explanations of international politics are not only in fashion but also seem to hold out the promise of a purely positivistic science of politics. [. . .]

From this viewpoint espoused here the hope to provide structuralist explanations is rather futile and indeed, as the sterile discussion about the stability or instability of bipolar, multipolar, and mixed systems showed,[86] even stringently formulated models concerned not with the explanation and prediction of singular actions but with systemic behaviour are indeterminate on this level of abstraction.[87] The result of such attempts is simply that structure means different things at different times, immunising the proposed models from criticisms. Nowhere is this clearer than in Waltz's treatment of structure, which variously refers to the organising principle of international relations ("anarchy" and self-help), differentiation of units and functional specificity, and the distribution of capabilities.[88]

It is obvious that an argument about capability distribution does not tell us very much about a system as long as its "polarities", that is, its alignment patterns, are not specified (quite aside from the known difficulties of a capability analysis).[89] Second, though Waltz maintains that the second meaning of structure, functional specificity, is irrelevant in international relations since states as the units of the system are functionally undifferentiated, the role of the great power seems to suggest the opposite. Important information concerning the functioning of the system is discarded when this level is not taken into consideration. This leads to the concept of anarchy and the explanatory power of self-help.

Even if we agree that the international system is an anarchy, brief reflection discloses that anarchies themselves are mixed. Institutions such as the market, the Nuer lineage system,[90] and medieval feudalism,[91] though all are anarchical, exhibit fundamentally different features that are important in understanding their functioning. My earlier discussion of the differences between the market and the international system made this point by showing the embeddedness of market anarchy in a set of conventions, of which money is the most important.[92] Money makes the measuring, exchanging, and storing of values possible.

The neglect of decisive distinguishing features among anarchical systems might thus lead not to the often invoked "Copernican revolution" but to a research program that is very quickly exhausted. Nowhere does this become clearer than in the discussion of the balance of power, which is for Waltz the natural outcome in an anarchical system. But as Hume pointed out, several systems existed without discovering the balance of power as a principle of systems-management. Given these contrary examples the theory can only be immunized from this decisive criticism by restricting its scope – by maintaining that the balance of power will only emerge under conditions of rationality among actors.

[. . .]

This *problématique* has two repercussions. First, there is a tendency of structuralism à la Waltz to introduce *ad hoc* auxiliary hypotheses, as when the balance of power is derived not only from international anarchy but from a particular socialization of the actors.[93] These two explanations are mutually exclusive as long as all recourse to motivational accounts is declared reductionist and incompatible with systemic explanation. Second, beyond the epistemological problem of *ad hoc* theorising, there is good reason to resist a structuralist research program that starts out as a general theory and quickly restricts its applicability due to lack of fit with the empirical evidence. Instead of leading to more and more interesting problems, such a procedure seems unable to avoid becoming a "degenerative problem shift," in Lakatos's words[94] – it illuminates by lower and lower wattage.

It is obvious why the mode of analysis suggested here holds the promise of being heuristically more fruitful than a structural model based on a rather questionable analogy to the market. Starting from the investigation of interactions, this approach tries to understand the rules underlying particular actions.[95] These rules in turn provide for an intersubjective communications system that fixes the meanings of certain terms and thus structures expectations, limits discretion, and excuses and serves as a normative criterion for the evaluation of political action. Beyond the epistemological dimension, the approach I have outlined, concerned with the logic of state action (exemplified in the notion of interest), should be useful – at least indirectly – for a discourse on world order at a time when the reason of state is under the double attack of moral obtuseness[96] and decreasing empirical relevance. Reflecting on a past tradition and discovering its underlying rationale, this paper is more than a purely historical exercise. It should be read as a prolegomenon to an approach to global politics and world order that, epistemologically as well as morally, will have to embody a new vision of politics.[97]

Notes

1 Hans Morgenthau, *Politics among Nations*, 5th ed. (New York: Knopf, 1978), p. 5.
2 See, for example, the somewhat confused attempt of Joseph Frankel in *National Interest* (London: Pall Mall, 1970), which fails to tell us why a given classification is sensible or fitting.
3 See, for example, Edgar Furniss and Richard Snyder, *An Introduction to American Foreign Policy* (New York: Rinehart, 1955), on p. 5: "The national interest is what the nation, i.e., the decision-maker decides it is."
4 Perhaps most clearly stated in the context of the public interest debate: see David Truman, *The Governmental Process* (New York: Knopf, 1951) and Glendon Schubert, *The Public Interest* (New York: Free Press, 1960).
5 Differing from this traditional Marxist point of view, Isaak Balbus tried to utilise the Marxian distinction of class *an sich* and *für sich* to render objective the notion of interest. Balbus, "The Concept of Interest in Pluralist and Marxian Analysis", *Politics and Society* 1, 2 (1978): 151–79.
6 Fred Sondermann, "The Concept of the National Interest", *Orbis* 21, 1 (1977), p. 132.
7 Quoted in Beard, *Idea of the National Interest*, p. 339.
8 This distinction between commendatory and descriptive meaning is crucial to Hare's language analysis. See R. M. Hare, *The Language of Morals* (Oxford: Oxford University Press, 1952).
9 This is the Platonic fallacy of "essences" embodied in varying degrees in actual objects or actions.
10 See, for example, Kenneth Waltz, *Theory of International Relations* (Reading, Mass: Addison Wesley, 1979).
11 Morton Kaplan, *System and Process in International Relations* (New York: Wiley, 1964). The most recent work on this subject debating Waltz's points is Kaplan, *Towards Professionalism in International Theory* (New York: Free Press, 1979).
12 Richard Flathman, *The Public Interest* (New York: Wiley, 1966).
13 Virginia Held, *The Public Interest and Individual Interests* (New York: Basic Books, 1970).
14 Brian Barry, *Political Argument* (London: Routledge and Kegan Paul, 1965).
15 Hare, *The Language of Morals*.
16 Friedrich Meinecke, *Die Idee der Staatsräson* (Munich and Berlin: R. Oldenburg, 1929).
17 Flathman, *The Public Interest*, p. 43.
18 For a clear statement of the participation theory underlying the classical tradition, see Eric Voegelin, *Anamnesis* (Notre Dame, Ind.: Notre Dame University Press, 1978).
19 Hare, *The Language of Morals*, especially pp. 119ff.
20 Flathman, *The Public Interest*, p. 10.
21 Barry, *Political Argument*, chap. 13.
22 Marcus G. Singer, *Generalization in Ethics* (New York: Knopf, 1960), p. 5.
23 Flathman, *The Public Interest*, p. 42.
24 Ibid.
25 Ibid., p. 70.
26 Plato concluded that public interest and common good are conceptions appropriately employed only by philosopher kings in discussions with other philosopher kings. If it is true that public interest functions to commend and justify public policy, and if only philosopher kings are capable of fully understanding the justifications and commendations, it follows that there would be no occasion to use the concept outside the circle of philosopher kings. Whatever one might think about

the philosophical position that underlies this conclusion, the result is at variance with public interest as employed in our discourse. Flathman, *The Public Interest*, pp. 56ff.

27 Flathman, *The Public Interest*, p. 74.
28 Thucydides, *History of the Peloponnesian War* 2. 10. 82–84.
29 On this point, see Bernard de Jouvenel, *The Pure Theory of Politics* (New Haven: Yale University Press, 1963), particularly chap. 2.
30 Henri Duc de Rohan, *A Treatise of the Interest of the Princes and States of Christendome,* trans. into English by H. H. (Paris, 1640).
31 Jean-Jacques Rousseau, *Du Contrat Social.*
32 See, for example, his preface to the *Discourses.*
33 See, for example, the works of Trajano Boccalini, *Raguaggli di Parnaso* (1612–1613), and *Pietra del Paragone Politico* (1615); both works are reprinted in *Scrittori d' Italia,* 2 vols. (Bari: G. Laterza e figli, 1910 and 1912).
34 See Meinecke, *Staatsräson*, chap. 6.
35 Ibid., p. 233.
36 See Auguste Laugel, *Henry de Rohan* (Paris: Firmin Didot, 1889).
37 On this point, see Meinecke, *Staatsräson*, chap. 6.
38 In this context, it is interesting that de Rohan dedicates his *De L'Interest des Princes et Éstats de la Chrestienté* to Richelieu.
39 See Rohan, *A Treatise*, pp. 1–2.
40 Ibid., pp. 14–15.
41 See, for example, W. Frankena's position: "Prudentialism, of living wholly by the principle of self-love is just not a kind of morality." *Ethics*, 2nd ed. (Englewood Cliffs, N.J.: Prentice Hall, 1973), p. 19.
42 In this context the elimination of sectarian goals is particularly important. See, for example, Frederick the Great's telling and relevant indictment of religious fervor, in "On Diplomatic Negotiations and on Just Causes for War": "Concerning wars of religion I want to say here only that much, i.e. that a ruler should try his utmost to avoid them. Otherwise there is no word hard enough for the criminal misuse which claims for any act the word of justice and equity, which does not feel ashamed of the blasphemy and which tries to hide its striving after power behind the name of the Almighty. It is a sign of the highest order of rascality to intend to deceive the world with such unabashed pretenses. . . ." Gustav B. Voltz, (ed.), *Ausgewählte Werke Friedrichs des Grossen* (Berlin: Reimar Hobbing, 1917), 2:23; see also Frederick's sarcastic remarks in *History of My Time* concerning the Lutheran zealot, Christian VI of Denmark; *Werke* 1:56.
43 Jean Rousset, *Les Intérêts Présents et les Prétensions des Puissances de l'Europe,* 2nd ed. (The Hague: Adrien Moetjens, 1736), 1:533.
44 Flathman, *The Public Interest*, p. 41.
45 As quoted in Edward V. Gulick, *Europe's Classical Balance of Power* (New York: Norton, 1967), p. 32.
46 For a record of the practical implications of such theories, see Gulick's study and Henry Kissinger, *A World Restored* (New York: Grosset and Dunlap, 1964).
47 For a good account of the minimum conditions of order in international politics, see Hedley Bull, *The Anarchical Society* (New York: Columbia University Press, 1977). For the particular conventions in the European "society of nations", see Maurice Kenns-Soper, "The Practice of a States-system", in Michael Donelan, (ed.), *The Reason of States* (London: Allen & Unwin, 1978), pp. 25–45.
48 How much for granted we take the usefulness of conventions was painfully demonstrated by the Iranian crisis, when diplomatic immunity was deliberately violated for the first time since the Boxer rebellion.
49 For a justification on these grounds, see Gulick, *Europe's Classical Balance,* especially chap. 11.

50 See my *International Order and Foreign Policy* (Boulder, Col.: Westview Press, 1978), especially pp. 74–77.

51 Riker's theory of coalitions, sometimes quoted as a possible solution, fails, as its applicability is restricted to n-person, zero-sum games with perfect information. These conditions are hardly isomorphic with international reality. But there is an even more principled reason why Riker's "size principle" leading to "minimum winning coalitions" as developed in Riker, *The Theory of Political Coalitions* (New Haven: Yale University Press, 1962), will generally fail even if the ideal conditions are present. See, on that point, Russel Hardin, "Hollow Victory: The Minimum Winning Coalition", *American Political Science Review* 70 (December 1976): 1202–1214, for the case of legislative coalition formation.

52 This is naturally the reason behind the "focal point solution" by which Thomas Schelling expanded classical game theory. For further treatment, see Schelling, *The Strategy of Conflict* (New York: Oxford University Press, 1963) and *Arms and Influence* (New Haven: Yale University Press, 1965). For an imaginative treatment of "symbolic signposts" and their role in conflict resolution, see Michael Barkun, *Law without Sanctions* (New Haven: Yale University Press, 1968).

53 See, for example, his thoughts on reputation as the first ingredient of a prince's power and the equation of a loss of reputation as a step to "ruin". Armand du Plessis, Cardinal de Richelieu, *Testament Politique*, 8th ed. (Amsterdam: Jansons a Waesberge, 1738), part 2, chap. 9, sections 1 and 2, pp. 64–68.

54 Robert Jervis, *The Logic of Images in International Relations* (Princeton: Princeton University Press, 1970).

55 Indeed, the more conventions attain the status of social facts and inform choices, the greater the incentive to subvert them, as the presumption of all other actors will be that the defecting actor just "made an error".

56 Voltz, *Ausgewählte Werke Friedrichs des Grossen*, 2:66ff.

57 For a classical treatment of this problem, see J. J. Brierley, *The Basis of Obligation in International Law*, ed. by Sir Hersh Lauterpacht (Oxford: Clarendon Press, 1958).

58 Samuel Pufendorf, *An Introduction to the History of the Principal Kingdoms and States of Europe* (London, 1711), preface.

59 Frederick the Great, *Antimachiavell*, in *Werke* 2:21.

60 David Hume, "Of the Balance of Power", in *Hume's Theory of Politics*, ed. by Frederick Watkins (New York: Thomas Nelson, 1951), pp. 187–88.

61 For this analogy, see Morgenthau, *Politics among Nations*, p. 5.

62 For a classical treatment of the money-power analogy and its pitfalls, see David Baldwin, "Money and Power", *Journal of Politics* 33 (1971): 578–614; also James Coleman, "Political Money", *American Political Science Review* 64 (1970): 1074–1087.

63 Klaus Knorr, *The War Potential of Nations* (Princeton: Princeton University Press, 1956).

64 David Baldwin, "Power Analysis and World Politics", *World Politics* 31 (January 1979): 161–95.

65 Ibid., p. 166.

66 Gulick, *Europe's Classical Balance*, pp. 25–26.

67 Ibid., chap. 9.

68 As quoted in Gulick, *Europe's Classical Balance*, p. 50.

69 Henry Kissinger, "The White Revolutionary, Reflections on Bismarck", *Daedalus*, Summer 1968, pp. 888–924.

70 Ibid., pp. 919 and 920.

71 As quoted in R. B. Mowat, *The Concert of Europe* (London: Macmillan, 1930), p. 44.

72 Ibid., p. 45.

73 Otto Pflanze, *Bismarck and the Development of Germany* (Princeton: Princeton University Press, 1963), p. 98.
74 Ibid.
75 Ibid., p. 90.
76 Ibid., p. 89.
77 Cf. Otto von Bismarck, *Erinnerung und Gedanke*, chap. 22, in Bismarck, *Werke in Auswahl*, ed. by Rudolf Buchner (Stuttgart: Kohlhammer, 1975), 2:360–61.
78 Kurt Riezler, *Tagebücher*, ed. by Karl Erdmann (Göttingen: Vanderhoek und Rupprecht, 1972).
79 Gustav Ratzenhofer, *Wesen und Zweck der Politik* (Leipzig: Brockhaus, 1893).
80 Kurt Riezler, *Die Erforderlichkeit des Unmöglichen, Prolegonoma zu einer Theorie der Politik und zu anderen Theorien* (Munich, 1912). In this context it is significant to notice the change in the conception of politics even when compared to the Bismarck era, as Bismarck's famous dictum was that "politics is the art of the possible". Riezler's influence on German foreign policy stems from his position as a close adviser to the Chancellor, Bethmann-Hollweg. Sir Eyre Crowe's memorandum can be found in G. P. Good and Harold Temperly, eds., *British Documents on the Origins of the War, 1898–1914*, 11 vols. (London, 1926–1938), 3:397–420.
81 Good and Temperly, *British Documents* 3:406.
82 Ibid., p. 417.
83 Riezler, *Die Erfordlichkeit*, as quoted in Immanuel Geis, *July 1914* (London: B. T. Batsford, 1967), p. 34.
84 Ibid., p. 35.
85 David Calleo, *The German Problem Reconsidered* (Cambridge: Cambridge University Press, 1979), pp. 48–49.
86 See, for example, Kenneth Waltz, "The Stability of a Bipolar World", *Daedalus* 93 (Summer 1964): 299–308.
87 For this point, see Joseph Nogee, "Polarity: An Ambiguous Concept", *Orbis* 18 (Winter 1978): 1193–1224.
88 Waltz, *Theory of International Relations*, chap. 5.
89 See, for example, Knorr, *The War Potential of Nations*. Naturally, this objection does not seem to hold for Waltz's argument about the stability of the bipolar world as in this case "poles" and "polarities" coincide. Nevertheless, for Waltz's argument to hold, a stable deterrence must be in operation. Since deterrence is a psychological and not a systemic relationship, a purely systemic explanation without recourse to "reductionist" explanations, including motives, purposes, and decision making characteristics of the antagonists, seems impossible. For a critique of deterrence theories along these lines see Alexander George and Richard Smoke, *Deterrence in American Foreign Policy* (New York: Columbia University Press, 1974).
90 See John Middleton and David Tait, eds., *Tribes without Rulers: Studies in African Segmentary Systems* (London: Routledge and Kegan Paul, 1958); Roger D. Masters, "World Politics as a Primitive Political System", *World Politics* 16 (July 1964): 595–619.
91 Gianfranco Poggi, *The Development of the Modern State* (Stanford: Stanford University Press, 1978).
92 On the historical evolution and the political embeddedness of the market, see Karl Polanyi, *The Great Transformation* (Boston: Beacon Press, 1957).
93 Waltz, *Theory of International Relations*, p. 74 on socialisation. Contrast this with the assertion on p. 57 that the "balance of power is simply a theory about the outcome of unit's behavior under conditions of anarchy".
94 See Imre Lakatos, "Falsification and the Methodology of Scientific Research Programmes", in Lakatos and Alan Musgrave, eds., *Criticism and the Growth of Knowledge* (Cambridge: Cambridge University Press, 1970), pp. 91–197.

95 For an elaboration of this approach to international relations, see my forthcoming paper "The Humean Perspective on International Relations", *Princeton University Center of International Studies Occasional Paper no. 9* (Princeton, N.J., 1981).

96 On this point, especially in regard to problems of distributive justice, see Charles Beitz, *Political Theory and International Relations* (Princeton: Princeton University Press, 1979).

97 For the context of political theory and a particular "vision" embodied in it, see Sheldon Wolin, *Politics and Vision* (Boston: Little, Brown, 1960).

4   Sovereignty, property and propriety

The generative grammar of modernity

Introduction

The problem of sovereignty needs no further justification in a time in which the "European project" is being realized, even though not without difficulties but in which we are in dire need of a vocabulary that does justice to the transformative changes brought on by global change. It is therefore fitting to engage in such a reflection in a festschrift for the author who has worked on European Integration and made significant contributions to this debate. But engaging in such a reflection raises the issue of how to approach the problem since the required conceptual analysis seems to transcend the usual theoretical and methodological questions precisely because it is prior to them. Since the social world is not simply "there" but constituted by concepts and the practices to which they give rise, any reflection on the actual practices has to be attentive to the constitutive understandings that underlie the "world of our making".

In this way such an analysis also has always to become "historical" since practices are not simply immutable structures akin to "natural kinds". The resulting "explanation" can obviously not be one of efficient causality but focuses on the (changing) uses of the term and its embeddedness in a semantic field, and on how thereby certain practices are authorized or enjoined. It provides therefore an understanding that shows how things fit and how the social world hangs together, as Ruggie once suggested, and how the changes are part of a generative grammar rather than mere random events.

In this article I want to investigate in this manner the way in which sovereignty and "property" (dominium) emerged and changed over time as the key notions for understanding not only the territorial state and its concomitant "system" – in the European context the term "republic" was often used – but also how the "invention" of the state and the construction of the modern "individual" are connected. This allows us to investigate more closely the "will" *problématique* that plays such a role in sovereignty (and in the "theory" of the fashioning of the individual and his goals) and that stands in tension with the more institutional notion of "property" and "propriety" (as in the case of the individual).

[...]

In order to explicate this thesis I take the following steps. In the next section I examine the *locus classicus* of the sovereignty *problématique* as it emerges from Bodin's notion of the sovereign as a lawgiver. In the second section I show some of the problems that arise out of the construal of the absolute "will" which is no longer constrained by certain laws of nature. In the third section I analyze the notion of "dominium", i.e. the institutionalist version of sovereignty that emerges from the writings of Grotius and some jurisconsults that rely on the private law analogy to Roman real property. Section four is devoted to an investigation of "property". This contractarian thinking not only expands the private law analogy in respect to the development of the public sphere and its relations with such other zones of exclusive jurisdiction, but takes on a life of its own. It transforms not only social relations, but ethics as well, and thereby initiates a particular program of individual self-fashioning which is characteristic of the modern project of individualism. To that extent, the semantic field of sovereignty is adumbrated. It relates to concepts of individualism, anarchy, property, as well as *propriety* and thus systematically connects individual and systemic levels. A short reflection on political language and conceptualisation concludes the paper.

Majestas vs. dominium: the semantics of sovereignty

The *locus classicus* for the modern meaning of the term sovereignty is certainly Bodin's 8th chapter in the first Book of his *Six Books on the Republic*. Sovereignty is one of the few concepts that came out of medieval thinking and its meaning was simply to denote a relationship of sub- and supraordination. As it indicates a hierarchical relationship among at least two positions it did not necessarily mean supremacy so that a person could have several sovereigns. However, in Bodin's theory, sovereignty emerges as supreme law making capacity, a notion that is also foreign to medieval thought. Bodin writes:

> Majestie or Soveraingtie is the most high, absolute and perpetual power over citizens and subjects in a Commonweale: which the Latins call *majestatem*, the Greeks *arche* . . ., the Italians Segnoria and the Hebrews *'elôhîm*. For so it behovest first to define what majestie or Sovereintie is, which neither lawyer nor political philosopher hath yet defined; although it is the principall and most necessarie point for the understanding of the nature of the Commonweale. And foreasmuch as we have before defined a Commonweale to be the right government of many families and of things common among them, with most high and perpetual power: it resteth to be declared, what is to be understood by the name of a most high and perpetual power. We have said that this power ought to be perpetuall, for that it may be, that it is absolute power over the subjects and may be given to one or many for a short or certain time, which expired, they are no more subjects themselves: so that whilst they

are in their puissant authoritie, they cannot call themselves Sovereign princes, seeing that they are but men put in trust, and keepers of the sovereign power, until it shall please the people or the prince that gave it to them to recall it . . . For as they who lend or pawne into another man their goods, remain still the lords and owners thereof: so it is also with them, who give unto others power and authoritie to judge and command, be it for a certain limited time, or so great and long time, as all please them; they themselves neverthelesse continuing still seased of the powers and jurisdiction, which others exercise but by way of loane or borrowing.[1]

This text merits further inquiry into what it says and also about what is left out or put in the background. One of the first things we notice is that the conceptualisation of an absolute and abstract power stands in strange tension with the still classical notion of original rights to rule on the basis of both possession and tradition. To that extent a ruler who derives his title from inheritance is a "true sovereign" while someone who becomes ruler through consent of the nobles or of "the people" is actually no "sovereign" at all.[2] Second, for our modern understanding, the traditional corporatist notion of the state as an association not of individual persons but of "houses" as well as the Aristotelian classification of political regimes, shows that Bodin is still quite far from the modern notion of politics which the contractualists introduce.

Interestingly, Bodin, a Roman lawyer himself, does not root his argument in the classical concepts of Roman public law: potestas and imperium but utilizes instead the notion of *majestas* in order to determine the nature of sovereignty. The latter concept – not a legal one to begin with – is usually only used in the context of God as the supreme law giver and for the aura of the Roman people which thereby command respect. To that extent the term conveys more the reaction of the audience to the encounter with some extraordinary phenomenon rather than a clarification of the awe inspiring phenomenon itself. Bodin analogises this power of the ruler to make laws[3] with the majesty of God giving commands and not being subject to tradition and custom. Therefore Bodin not only begins (or revives) the "command" theory of law so dear to "positivists" of a later period, he also essentially reconceptualizes the notion of the ruler and of the presumptions upon which these commands are based and are entitled to compliance. The power of the king is no longer limited to *pax et justitia*, i.e. in pursuance of the latter goal to give everybody his due (*suum cuique tribuere*) but to make rules that are no longer based on traditional notion of privilege and original entitlement, which was typical for the [. . .] Middle Ages.

It would be far fetched to see in Bodin an unadulterated positivist as for him Natural law and God's commandments are still an important part,[4] even if they are no longer central to his argument. This is the case because, different from medieval thought, their violation does not bring a right of resistance to illegal acts into operation.[5] Furthermore, on the one hand Bodin does not want to accept the limitation of the sovereign will through earlier acts or declarations of the ruler (such as e.g. the reaffirmation of "original" privileges of his nobles). On the other hand he is aware of the problem of an "arbitrary will" that might destroy the foundations of the kingdom. Therefore his theory becomes contradictory as the "paradox of taxation"[6] and his emphasis of the importance of contractual obligations vis-à-vis the subjects demonstrates. Bodin's argument that no prince "has the power to impose taxes[7] on his subjects"[8] is difficult to understand given his "absolutist" stance. On the other hand taxation is one of the earliest and staunchly defended original privileges that provided parliament with its capacities to counteract centralizing tendencies of the crown early on, and later to keep legislative activities of the governments in check.

Two further rather odd characteristics of the text have to be mentioned. First Bodin, despite his respect for the people, obviously has no notion of a *pouvoir constituante*, according to which the legislator could also change the constitutional framework. The laws that make up the "constitution" of the realm (inclusive of the *lex Salica*) are explicitly exempted from the legislative powers of the prince without however lodging them in the "people". Second, he seems to remain a child of his day in viewing the structural principles of political order. They are as far removed from the medieval corporatist notions as they are from those of modernity in which the public order is constituted by the consent of legally equal individuals in a social contract. For Bodin, custom and the existing groups and estates are the elements which have to be moulded into one commonweal. To that extent the constitutional framework does not yet (or looking back to Roman law) simply no longer possess any notion of an abstract public sphere separated from the "possessions" regulated by private law. Thus despite his invocation of Roman law and his emphasis on the legislative "will" it is puzzling that Bodin resorts at crucial points in his argument to notions of "original possession" of the right to rule by the "legitimate" traditional ruler in order to provide the framework for his new conception of sovereignty.

It cannot be the task of this paper to follow all the details of the two strands of argumentation, i.e. that of sovereignty as "will" vs. that of sovereignty as an institution moulded after the model of Roman real property (*dominium*). Nevertheless, a brief sketch is in order. The development of the "will" *problématique* runs from Hobbes' construction of an unlimited sovereign who is authorised by his subjects to exercise his sovereign rights without limitations (save in the residual right of disobedience in case of mortal danger) to Rousseau and Kant and their specification of the "free will" that lends legitimacy to actions and stipulates criteria for the rule of law (Rechtsstaat). Finally the jurisprudence of the 19th century sees in the principle of the "self limitation of the sovereign" a way to reconcile the "supremacy" element inherent in sovereignty on the one hand [. . .] and the existence of a community of states with attendant rights and duties on the other hand.

The other institutional conception of sovereignty, received its most important impulses from Roman private law although it has become clear that there existed a certain elective affinity between this conception and the medieval notion of personal rule. By taking the exclusive possession of a piece of real estate as a template – as Roman law provided for in contradistinction to various use rights, familiar from the Germanic tradition – one can avoid some of the conceptual puzzles that result from the "will" problematic. Because authority and power need not be located in a pyramid of competences whereby the superior has always to be free from the decisions of the inferior until we reach the apex where the sovereign is *"omnibus legibus absolutus"* we can now grasp "sovereignty" as one institution located in a network of various rights and duties that are part and parcel of a particular form of "property". As every law student learns in his first year, "property" is a complicated matter that simply cannot be reduced to "things" and their correct representation in concepts. For example, while I might possess something without owning it and while "possessing" i.e. means literally "sitting" on something, such conceptions are hardly useful for understanding modern forms of property such as e.g. trade marks, patents, or even the "good will" of a firm. Therefore it is better to conceive of property as a bundle of rights that are packed and unpacked differently depending on the particular proprietary form. Furthermore we:

> must realize that a property right is a relation not between an owner and a thing but between the owner and other individuals in reference to a thing . . . The classical view of property as a right over things resolves it into components rights such as *ius utendi, ius disponendi* etc. But the essence of private property is always the right to exclude others.[9]

In other words, we are dealing here with the institutionalisation of power. The generative capacity of the institution of *dominium* consisted in its peculiar way of "bundling" all rights which usually were separable in the customary arrangements of Germanic law. Some examples of the English common law show the difference clearly. Ownership e.g. of a forest in common law did not entitle the holder of the property title to prevent peasants from herding their hogs there or poor people from collecting firewood. As a matter of fact they even had the right of pulling down the dried out branches "by hook and by crook". On the other hand, game was treated entirely differently and illegal hunting was severely punished.

To that extent it is not surprising that important functions which we consider to belong to the "public" domain, such as jurisdictional authority "went with" the land. Maitland,[10] the great historian of the common law could still some 100 years ago argue that the history of the British constitution could be written as an appendix to English property law. But while the bundling and unbundling of rights was different in Roman and Germanic law the connection between institutionalised power – also public power – and property is common to both legal orders. Since Roman law transferred title only with the entire bundle of rights – *usque ad coelum, usque ad inferos* as the Digest say –

all natural resources and even the air column were part of the property and entitled the owner to exclusive use. Parallels to the "territorial" constitution of the international order are not difficult to fathom. Until today it is one of the most important and least controversial principles of international law [. . .] that exclusive ownership over natural resources is an intrinsic part of sovereignty (see GA Resolution on the "Permanent Sovereignty over Natural Resources).[11]

From this brief discussion it becomes clear how the abstract "state" (instead of personal rule) i.e. the exclusive jurisdictional domain could emerge out of this conception of *dominium*, as no other groups or persons could insist on some original privileges or "rights of usage". But it also becomes clear why the actual state practice remained for a long time quasi-feudal, as "sovereignty" went with the land and could be transferred and inherited. Thus the great struggles of the 18th century and its concomitant alliances were by no means dictated alone by balance of power reasons, but the result of various claims to succession. (War of Austrian, Spanish succession etc.)[12] Thus the order established by the Westphalian peace is certainly "territorial" but it is quite different from those structures of anarchy that simply result from the interaction of "like units" as argued by neo-realists. Instead we see a system that comprises more or less "modern" territorial states headed by now firmly established sovereigns, like France and Sweden, perhaps England after the Glorious Revolution, the old Empire and its loose structures and many remnants of the old order such as i.e., the institution of the *Reichsacht* and the famous *ius armorum*. Contrary to the common assertion that here the right of alliances exemplifies the emergence of the "state system", the latter is a right that belonged to the "estates" and was part and parcel of the old right of resistance of the nobles of the realm! The fact that the "estates" of former times become in Krasner's version simply "states" however, does not prove the (neo)realist point but rather betokens a lack of familiarity with the historical record.[13]

The empire, which even Pufendorf found difficult to describe in terms of the *ius publicum Europaeum* and to which he referred as a *monstrum* was also surrounded by some notable exceptions. One example were the "republics". These enter as players into the system although they were neither the old city republics – they represented larger territorial entities – nor did they possess the same dynastic arrangements that structure the relations among most members of the *res publica Christiana*. Finally there were some "outsiders", such as the Ottoman empire which significantly shaped this order by being allied to France and helping it in its struggle to prevent a Hapsburg hegemony. However, it never became a member in the club to which it was only admitted after the Crimean War.

The heterogeneity and longevity of these disparate units remains an unresolved puzzle for a structural systems theory, nor can the eventual "homogeneisation" of the units be explained along the lines of functional necessity a la Hintze[14] or Tilly.[15] Most of the small states disappeared because of nationalism and some – seen from the angle of optimal defense – "dysfunctional" small states such as Luxemburg or Liechtenstein survived despite their lack of military wherewithal. Again, the secular changes of the system can be illuminated by the property analogy. Several stages can be distinguished, as Rodney Hall has shown in his careful study.[16] Three of them are of particular importance.

The first significant change occurred when the "people" rather than the ruler were considered the "sovereign". The "people" were not yet the "nation" – at least not in the European context – but rather the former "subjects" which become in the new assignment of rights "the people" and articulate themselves as the owners of sovereign powers.

The second change, i.e. substitution of the people by the "nation" articulates the project of nationalism. Now not only the consent of the governed is required to bestow legitimacy on the government, but the state as shorthand for the public domain has to be an expression of the nation. This shift ends traditional multi-ethnic empires that usually were united only through the "crown", i.e. the person of the ruler. It also created some of the most virulent problems as no homogenous units emerged but virtually everywhere the "nation state" created minorities and the concomitant problems of transgression against and the protection of them.

The third transformation occurred through the recognition of the principle of self-determination. On the one hand this principle is an expansion of the notion that public power has to be an expression of the peculiar properties of a group even if it has not (yet) the status of a nation. Practically this amounts to some form of autonomy or protection on the basis of some identity features or concerns. [. . .]

Whatever the merits or shortcomings of such speculations may be, a short historical reflection shows that only once worked these principles in tandem i.e. in the case of the USA (and even then only because of the considerable blind spots of the participants). Legitimization of public power, the creation of a "people" through the constitutive act of declaring independence and giving itself a constitution, and the assertion of a particular identity neatly coincided. In the new world the territory was the container that created a people and then a particular form of legitimate government that had strong implications for individual and collective identity formation. After all, most of the immigrants that arrived here – different from the settler aristocracy of the Iberian colonies – had little reason to look back to their countries of origin for inspiration, hope, or a sense of self.[17] It needs no further elaboration that in Europe the historical development was different, leading to serious conflicts, which we need not follow further.

The above considerations also show that together with the principle of self-determination some similar paradoxes appear which we have encountered in the will *problématique*. We should not be surprised by this. Selfhood and the freedom of will form a cluster of problems. These are connected with authenticity which animates the nationalist project as well as the claims for specific cultural rights of sub-national groups. It gives rise to acts of collective self-assertion as in the demand of specific "rights" of indigenous groups for example. But through the line of argument concerning the need of authenticity it also leads to intolerance and a certain aesthetisation of politics. This is because "authenticity" and the glorification of a "will" that is no longer "bound" by conventions or laws rather than the shared understandings that enable us to make binding choices become the criterion of politics. In the section below I do not want to follow this line of thought. Rather I want to return to the problem of "property" and show its place within the project of modernity, i.e. its role in the disciplinary understanding of individualism. This understanding is disciplinary in a double meaning insofar as it determines the bounds of "sense" – of what can be said and understood – and in the sense that this "discipline" also implies a program of self-fashioning, of becoming a certain person.

Power, property and the project of individualism

The above discussion has shown how the concept of dominium was constitutive for the emergence of the territorial state and the European state system, which however retained certain feudal features. This is the case because the conceptual link between the (personal) sovereign and the construal of public power as a function of the "land". To that extent the revolutionary transformation of political thought and of the constitutive norms informing the political practices remained somewhat hidden. Two conceptual interfaces are particularly useful for probing the transformations of political life: the new conceptualisation of public authority and power on the one hand, and the context of individual and society on the other hand. In the former case, authority become an impersonal force that is no longer founded on a social prestige of certain persons, or on a particular notion of the "good life". Rather it results from the "authorization" by all who thus become equal in their status as "subjects". In the latter case the individual no longer experiences himself as part of a group (estate) or society, or as God's creature, which underlies the traditional notion of a "person". He or she is rather an "owner" of his body and his capacities, as already suggested by Locke, and adumbrated by Hobbes. Increasingly even the criteria for assessing actions are removed from conceptions of ways of life and from the necessary virtues[18] in attaining them. It becomes a question of "propriety" i.e. of acting in accordance with the one one calls ones's "own". To that extent the "propriety" as both "property" and of "acting properly" is by no means accidental.[19]

Let us begin with the conception of sovereignty as a new form of impersonally constituted authority, as we encounter it among the contractarians. Here Hobbes can serve as the starting point.[20] Facing the disintegration of estate society and an order that received its legitimacy from ontology, as social order was connected through the Great Chain of Being to these larger world views, Hobbes problem is not only the constitution of some new effective authority. He understands that such a new sovereign can be only effective if he bases his authority on some commonly accepted ground. To that extent the "state of nature" is in a way an "erasing device" whose hypothetical nature is always emphasized by Hobbes. Here the traditional understandings are eliminated, in order to establish a new order on the basis of new but commonly shared presuppositions. After all the Hobbesian sovereign is not only the personification of this public authority which is composed by all individuals who now make one person as on the initial page of the original edition of *Leviathan*. He can play this role only because of the consent and submission of all concerned. He is not only executor but also the "fixer of signs". Thus one of his important obligations is to institute "discipline" again in the sense of what can be said and what is out of bounds.[21] Here definitions abound and penalties are threatened for those acting against these common understandings, in the sense of disciplining those who violate these rules. It is again ownership and "property" which are adduced to explicate the new phenomenon.[22]

> Of Persons Artificiall, some have their words and actions owned by those whom they represent. And the Person is the Actor; and he that owneth his words and actions, is the AUTHOR: In which case the Actor acteth by Authority. For that which in speaking of goods and posses-sions, is called an Owner, and in latine Dominus, in Greek kyrios; speaking of Actions is called Author. And as the Right of possession is called Dominion; so the Right of doing any Action, is called Authority. So that by Authority is always understood a Right of doing any Act: and done by Authority, done by Commission, or Licence from him whose right it is.[23]

The differences to traditional notions of authority could not be greater. Hobbes conception is actually nothing but the fullness of powers inherent in the Roman conception of *imperium*. This power, because it was given to the consuls at war, was much farther reaching than the more specific powers during times of peace when each office has a certain *potestas*. *Auctoritas* originally has no official standing. It denoted the "weight" of an opinion voiced in support of or against a course of action. It derives from the root *augere*, i.e. to increase and signifies thereby the prestige that is lent to an opinion when someone well-respected lends his support to a cause.[24] *Auctoritas* had always to do with practical matters. It was thus different from expertise or theoretical knowledge. [. . .] Only because the contingent nature of any practical decision one needs authority in order to buttress the legiti-macy of a choice. But Hobbes' new "authority" does not imply such a lending of prestige to an action. It is at a minimum *potestas* and probably closer to the *imperium* of Roman times.[25]

This abstract institutionalised power of the sovereign claimed, in a way, absoluteness which, of course was never reachable in actual life. This we have already encounterd above in the context of the will-problematic. The distinction between absolute validity and actual exercise takes care of some difficulties. However, the liberal notion of "limited government" and a sovereign that was only entrusted with this new authority (thereby responsible to and under scrutiny by those who transferred this office to him) reproduced the same difficulty within the sphere of "validity".

One of the early answers was of course the emphasis on subjective rights which were exempted from the public domain and thus form the normal interference by actions of the sovereign. This privatisation of "property" as an area with which the public power had no business of interfering, was perhaps the most revolutionary innovation. Now it made a "private" right suddenly a more powerful "trump" as it could be used even against the public authority, a conception which was rather foreign to Roman legal thought. As a matter of fact, this is probably the most revolutionary implication of the "natural rights" doctrine. In addition, this construal disguised power by making it a "private" matter. Consequently, it increasingly made it illegitimate for the state to participate in the social reproduction. Rather it increasingly transferred those tasks of the material – and later also of the ideal reproduction of social life – to the market.

This change in meaning and of practices no traditional political order, nor even the absolutist state during the mercantilist era, could have even conceived. Similarly, the scope of public authority is similarly transformed. It is diminished and the "state" is simply the provider of public goods which enable the citizens to enjoy their property. "Society" denotes now no longer some common ancestry or the *synoikismos* of certain clans and houses, but the institution where individuals recognize each other as property owners. Their relations are pre-politically construed, since the consensus on property and its protection is antecedent to every political formation that has to "perfect" but not transformed or even reshaped by civil society. Instead of traditional ranks, based on honour and origin, we find now a regulation of the relations between the members of civil society via the relations to the things owned, which allows not only an emancipation of "economic" activity from social relations. Here Aristotle's observations and exclusion of the "chresmatic" mode of production from his "economy" comes to mind as the former was no longer part of the satisfaction of wants but had as an aim simply the acquisition of wealth. In this new conceptualisation, politics becomes increasingly a common concern of what interests us privately and individually and not as something that addresses those concerns that we hold in common.[26] [. . .]

Thus despite the absolute character of public power in terms of claims to validity, the government is increasingly limited and understands its task to be the protection of property, the efficiency of markets and of common defense. Locke puts the matter nearly laconically but very precisely in his *Second Treatise*:

> Political Power I take to be a Right making Laws with Penalties of Death
> . . . for the regulating and Preserving of Property, and of employing the
> force of the Community in the Execution of such Laws, and in the
> defence of the Commonwealth from Foreign Injury, and all this only for
> the Publick Good.[27]

How far-reaching the conceptual change has become is visible in the construction of the individual. He or she is no longer a member of a distinct and
historically constituted community or even group but experiences his or her
singularity as owner of his/her body and faculties of which, of course, labour
becomes the most important in establishing further titles. In the chapter "On
Property" of the Second Discourse Locke establishes this perspective clearly:

> From all which is evident (that) Man (by being being Master of himself,
> and Proprietor of his own Person, and the Actions or Labor of it) had
> still in himself the Great Foundation of Property . . .[28]

This is of course the point where Marx's critique begins. Here, to Marx,
labour increasingly becomes commodified under conditions of the capitalist
mode of production in which the acquisition of wealth – the making of
money – becomes the only goal of the "economy" and thus creates
"alienation", i.e. a situation in which man can no longer determine his own
fate.

This project of modernity of course does not remain unchallenged. The
German political discourse and the concomitant *Polizeywissenschaft*[29] orient
themselves on the older Aristotelian tradition and on the notion of patriarchal rule in which ruler is likened to both God on the one side and to the
good house-father who provides for those around or under him on the other
side. To that extent the arguments resemble more those of Filmer's[30] *Patriarcha*, against which Locke wrote his two treatises, than those of the incipient
liberalism.

But it is nevertheless important to realise that even here among the defend-
ers of the "natural" order among different estates, "property" has become an
outstanding concern. This is quite at odds with the classical tradition where
the rule of the house-father was explicitly distinguished from political rule.
How deeply "property" however influenced the political thinking during that
time can also be seen from the discussion within the "republican" tradition,
probably the dominant mode of political reflection before the ascendancy of
liberalism. The latter had practically undermined all "natural" limits to
acquisitiveness of the "possessive individualists". [. . .]

The *topoi* of the republican reflection extols the virtues of landed property
that is indispensable for the survival of republics.[31] Commerce and the
emergence of a "moneyed" group lead to a decay of manners and to the
ascendancy of private over public interests.[32] In addition, the mobility of
capital dissolves according to Republican thinkers, such as Harrington[33] or

Jefferson, the loyalty to a given place that is the basis of community as a trans-generational ongoing concern and of solidarity.

Perhaps the most explicit treatment of the role of property for the development of society and of man in general we find in Rousseau who criticizes the liberal notions of a "natural right" in property. At the same time he acknowledges the constitutive function of property for human development. It is after all property that leads to the denaturing of man,[34] to the ascendancy of *paraitre* over the natural goodness[35] and to the establishment of "society". However it also leads to the possibility of refashioning oneself as a moral being. Property thus becomes the motor of human development. The interdependence between social order and the formation of a certain type of person is particularly emphasised. Thus the social contract is not simply a "perfection" of civil society and the setting up of a government as a "trust" for preserving the rights and proprietary interests of the individuals. It involves an *aliénation totale* of all claims and the fashioning of the person. The individual learns to substitute morality for inclination, authenticity for appearances.

> The passage from the state of nature to the civil state produces in man a very remarkable change by substituting in his conduct justice for instinct, and by giving his actions the moral quality that they previously lacked. It is only when the voice of duty succeeds physical impulse and law succeeds appetite, that man, who till then had regarded himself, sees that he is obliged to act on other principles, and to consult his reason before listening to his inclination. Although, in this state, he is deprived of many advantages that he derives from nature, he acquires equally great ones in return; his faculties are exercised and developed; his ideas are expanded; his feelings are ennobled; his whole soul is exalted to such a degree that, if the abuses of his new condition did not often degrade him below that from which he has emerged, he ought to bless without ceasing the happy moment that released him from it forever and transform him from a stupid and ignorant animal into an intelligent being and man. . . . Besides the preceeding. We might add to the acquisitions of the civil state moral freedom, which also renders man truly master of himself; for the impulse of mere appetite is slavery, while obedience to a self prescribed law is liberty . . .[36]

To that extent Rousseau's solution to the problems brought on by modernity is not the privatisation of power through the assertion of pre-political property rights, or its mystification though their attribution to the private sphere. Rather it results in a fundamental educational program in which the individual, the family and the community are reformed. Not the pursuit of happiness[37] which consists in the satisfaction of the goals dictated by "passions" but the transformation and cultivation of sentiments is the aim of this educational project. As Nicole Fermon has shown, a new "political economy" attempts to implement this reform program by reviving the family and the public domain as a viable form of social reproduction instead of making the passions and the market the final arbiter.

This sketched account of the main strands of political theory amply demonstrates the crucial importance of notions of property. Not only did it establish the territorial state and the modern international system, it also fundamentally transformed our notions of the person of "society". In this sense the semantic field of sovereignty comprises a far wider field than merely state practice and shows the intimate connection between individuals and social structures. [. . .]

Summary

The present paper attempted three things. [. . .]

First it offered a type of conceptual analysis that is particularly interested in the exploration of the "constitutional" dimension of the social world. In particular, for me, as an international relations specialist, "sovereignty" represents an important element in the establishment of the social order. The explication of this concept and of the practices constituted by it as well as their historical changes are of exemplary importance for our understanding of (inter)-national politics. Locating the inquiry at the symbolic level and focusing on change rather than on the persistence of some allegedly trans-historical structures avoids the danger of submitting to an a-historical approach, be it in terms of the categories utilized or in terms of the "materials" themselves that stay identical despite all surface alterations. At the same time it prevents us from losing the focus of our analysis. Avoiding the former pitfall frees us from some metaphysical assumptions concerning the "ultimate givens" of the world, without preventing a directed inquiry. The institution or institutions that are part of this concept and the practices need not stay the same or have a clearly identifiable trans-historical core, but possess a certain "family resemblance" without necessarily sharing all or several of the same features.

The second goal of this paper was an historical overview of the sovereignty *problématique*. To that extent one of the lines of argument we followed was the root of the institutional account of sovereignty in "property". This analogy had important implications for the analysis of the social world and provided us with several instructive lessons. For example, property is not a simple concept that stands for a thing or "things" in the world but stands for quite distinctive claims, by excluding others or granting them certain uses. Therefore it is the explication of the variability and the various transformations from one version of property to the other, that entitles us to claim to have advanced our understanding. [. . .]

We began our analysis with the examination of the *locus classicus* in the 8th chapter of the first book of Bodin's *Six Books on the Republic*. As we saw in this text, the construction of "absolute" sovereignty is far less clear than later interpretations have made it appear. This was particularly the case in the late 19th century. Then the "new" features of Bodin's thinking were emphasised while many important facets were omitted that show him to be in most respects "still" a child of his time. To that extent the paradox of taxes and the various contradictions between the "absoluteness" of the public power and the still personalistic and corporatist notions of actual rule make it necessary to locate the text within the context. In addition it is necessary to analyse two distinct features of Bodin's speculation on sovereignty: the analogy to a supreme "will" and sovereignty as an institution analogous to "property". Both provided us with two lines of inquiry, although the "will-*problématique*" leading to notions of "self-limitation" were only cursorily treated. [. . .]

In dealing with the issue of changes in the concept of property the argument advanced in two steps. The first step was a further examination of the property analogy via the institution of *dominium* in Roman private law. We could show how the transition from a personalistic rule to the modern territorial conception of an abstract public domain and jurisdictional power was effectuated. It also became clear why throughout the 18th century the states system, despite its territorial constitution, remained still quite "feudal" as the various wars of succession demonstrated. This has important implications for the contemporary discussion of sovereignty, in particular as it addresses the issue of the divergence between institutional form and actual practice. Our analysis suggested that this divergence cannot simply be cast aside without further ado as "organized hypocrisy" that has been at work throughout history.[38] On the contrary, this "slippage" should encourage theoretical innovation which could uncover the kind of "divergence" and its "logic" of development. [. . .]

In the second step of the analysis the metaphor of "property" showed its usefulness in quite a different area, i.e. in that of the constitution of the actor or individual. While it is common in constructivist and post-modern writings to address the agent/structure problem, seldom is such an analysis done in a fashion that actually conveys the co-constitution of the social system and its actors. Either one emphasizes the fact that actors can change the system, as a well known argument in IR so nicely says: "anarchy is what states make of it",[39] or one privileges the system by pointing to the "constraints" imposed by the structures on the decisions of the actors. I think part of the contemporary discussion is somewhat misleading as it is beholden to the old causal thinking in that one (either system or actor) has to come "before" the other, thus creating the familiar chicken and egg dilemma. Without wanting to claim that I can overcome this dilemma – as no dilemma can be solved – I think we can circumvent it by focusing on *the processes that both inform the constitution of systems and actors*. If we can show that the same or very similar concepts are at work we come one step closer to analysing the "co-constitution" of agents and structures. [. . .]

The third goal of this article was to contribute to the "inter-paradigmatic" debate and its vagaries of the last few decades. I tried to do this by both showing the similarities between constructivist thought and some of the neo-Marxist approaches. Lately, these have made important contributions not only to the historical understanding of social institutions and politics, but have proposed a "new key" for the analysis of the social world. These approaches are less indebted to the traditional materialism than to the analysis of social relations. Here the organisation of these relations in terms of public and private, the state and society, the market and the rule of law – all of which give rise to the distinctive institutions of capitalist society, including the balance of power – let us distinguish different historical societies without reifying the market or the state. An ambitious historical research programme is thereby set up and the traditional "realist" notions of power and of the constants of human and social behaviour are critically examined. [. . .]

Whatever the answers to these questions might be and for which approach we opt, I think these approaches are not incompatible despite their distinct emphases. Thus we should be able to sustain an interesting conversation although no ultimate foundation can be appealed to in order to show what the world is "really like". Even if we think that our theories are focused questions put to "the world" or "reality" and that thereby the "things" could finally speak to us in an unadulterated form, we should remember, that we cannot get "between" the things and the words. The world will have to "speak" to us and therefore, will need a language. [. . .]

Notes

1 Jean Bodin, *The Six Bookes of a Commoweale*, facsimile of the original English translation of 1606, ed. by Kenneth Douglas McRae (Cambridge, Mass.: Harvard University Press, 1962), Bk. I, chap. 1, p. 1

2 See i.e. Bodin's reference to the king of the Tartars, who is elected but who has after that no obligations concerning the exercise of his rights as an absolute ruler. To that extent the "delegation" effectuated by the "election" is more like a "perfect gift" than a delegation proper. Bodin, *Six Books*, op. cit., Bk. I, 8.

3 See Bodin's other definition of sovereignty in Bk. I, 10: "who can deny that that person is sovereign who can make laws for his subjects, make decisions concerning peace and war, appoint the officers and magistrates, levy taxes, or free whomever he wants from them, grant pardons in capital cases."

4 See Bodin's argument against certain cannon and civil lawyers who want to diminish natural law by arguing for the primacy of positive law. Here too "property" (i.e. natural law as the "proper" domain of God) serves to make the point. Bodin, *Six Books*, op. cit., Bk I, 8.

5 See the following quote: "If the sovereign ruler is not bound by the laws of his predecessors, then it follows that he is not bound by his own laws and edicts. Although it is possible that for a person the law is prescribed by somebody else, but it is as impossible to prescribe for oneself the law as it is to give oneself a command because that is dependent on one's own will. . . . It is for this reason that we find at the end of all edicts and orders 'this is our will' wherebey it becomes clear that the laws of a sovereign ruler are solely dependent on his free will even if there are cogent and persuasive reasons for such orders". Bodin, *Six Books*, op. cit., Bk I, 8.

6 See i.e. Martin Wolfe, "Jean Bodin on Taxes: The Sovereignty-Taxes Paradox", *Political Science Quarterly*, Bd. 68 (1958): S. 268–84.

7 See Bodin, *Six Books*, op. cit., book 1, 8, S. 220.

8 See Bodin, *Six Books*, op. cit., book 1, 8. "But we can go even further and say that a ruler is bound by the compacts with his subjects, so that he cannot deviate from them on the basis of his absolute power, even if the compacts are not part of public law."

9 Morris Cohen, "Property and Sovereignty", in C.B. Macpherson, ed., *Property: Mainstream and Critical Positions* (Toronto: University of Toronto Press, 1978), chap. 10, quotation in S. 159.

10 Fredrick W. Maitland, *The Constitutional History of England* (Cambridge, England: Cambridge University Press, 1908), S. 538.

11 XVII UNGA Res. 1803 (Dec. 1962).

12 The best example is the alliance policy of England during the 7 years war which was dictated by the dynastic interests of the House of Hannover rather than by those of Great Britain. For a discussion see Julian Corbett, *England in the Seven Years War: A Study in Combined Strategy*, 2 vols. (New York: AMS Press, 1973).

13 See Stephen Krasner, "Westphalia and all that".

14 See Otto Hintze "Military Organization and the Organization of the State", in *The Historical Essays of Otto Hintze*, (ed.) and transl. by Felix Gilbert (New York: Oxford University Press, 1975), S. 178–215.

15 Charles Tilly, "Reflections on the History of European State Making" in Charles Tilly (Hrsg), *The Formation of National States in Western Europe* (Princeton: Princeton University Press 1975), S. 3–83; Charles Tilly, *Coercion, Capital and European States* (Cambridge, Mass: Basil Blackwell, 1990).

16 Rodney Bruce Hall, *National Collective Identity: Social Constructions and International Systems* (New York: Columbia University Press, 1999).

17 For an interesting discussion of the repercussions of this form of "nation-building" for domestic as well as for foreign policy see Seymour Martin Lipset, *The First New Nation* (New York: Doubleday, 1987), particularly chap. 3.

18 For a critical discussion of the liberal moral vocabulary vs. that of an ethics of "virtue" see Ronald Beiner, "The Moral Vocabulary of Liberalism" in John Chapman, William Galston, ed., *Virtue* (*Nomos* XXXIV) (New York: New York University Press, 1992), S. 145–84. For an anthology of modern approaches to a virtue ethics see Bernard Crisp, Michael Slote (eds.), *Virtue Ethics* (Oxford: Oxford University Press, 1997).

19 For a further discussion see Kurt Burch, *"Property" and the Making of the International System* (Boulder, Colo.: Lynne Rienner, 1998).

20 See Hobbes, *Leviathan*, op. cit., chap. 30.

21 See i.e. the "truths" that the sovereign has to propagate and enforce in *Leviathan*, op. cit., chap. 20.

22 For a good discussion of this type of "authorisation" theory of representation see Hannah Pitkin, *The Concept of Representation* (Berkeley: University of California Press, 1967).

23 Hobbes, *Leviathan*, op. cit., chap. 16, S. 218.

24 See Theodor Eschenburg: *Auctoritas* (Frankfurt: Suhrkamp, 1965).

25 This distinction is usually made in terms of "being an authority" and "having authority"; see e.g. Peter Blau, "Critical Remarks on Weber's Theory of Authority", *American Political Science Review*, vol. 57, June 1963: S. 305–16. See also Peter Blau, *Exchange and Power in Social Life* (New York: Wiley, 1964).

26 Karl Marx, *Grundrisse der Kritik der politischen Ökonomie* (Frankfurt: Europäische Verlagsanstalt, 1967), Karl Polanyi *The Great Transformation: The Political and Economic Origins of Our Times* (Boston: Beacon Press, 1957).

27 John Locke, The Second Treatise of Government in Peter Laslet ed., *John Locke's Two Treatises of Government* (New York: Mentor, 1965), S. 308.

28 Ibid. S. 340f.

29 For an excellent discussion of the German constitutional developments see Hans Maier, *Die ältere Staats- und Verwaltungslehre* (München: Beck, 1980).

30 See chap 4 of the Introduction by Peter Laslet in *Johns Locke's Two Treatises of Government*, op. cit.

31 See John Pocock, "Virtue, Rights, and Manners" in J.G.A. Pocock, *Virtue, Commerce and History* (Cambridge: Cambridge University Press, 1985), chap. 2, which provides an overview of the debates between Pocock, Hexter, Hill and others.

32 See also Isaac Kramnick, *Republicanism and Bourgeois Radicalism* (Ithaca, NY: Cornell University Press, 1990).

33 A good discussion of Harrington can be found in J.G.A. Pocock, *The Ancient Constitution and the Feudal Law* (Cambridge, England: Cambridge University Press, 1987), chap. 6, also a good introduction Harrington's work.

34 See the debates in England at the beginning of the 18th century and Defoe's and Addison's futile attempts to convince the English public otherwise; see G.C.A. Pocock, *The Machiavellian Moment* (Princeton: Princeton University Press, 1975), especially chaps. 13 and 14.

35 For a brief discussion of these problems see M.M. Goldsmith, "Liberty, Luxury and the Pursuit of Happiness" in Anthony Pagden, ed., *The Languages of Political Theory in Early Modern Europe* (Cambridge, England: Cambridge University Press, 1987), chap. 10.

36 Jean-Jacques Rousseau, *The Social Contract*, Bk I, chap. 8, in Lester Crocker, ed., *The Social Contract and the Discourse on Inequality* (New York: Washington Square Press, 1971) p. 22f.

37 For a fundamental discussion concerning the development of the notion of "interest" see Albert Hirschmann, *The Passions and the Interests: Political Arguments for Capitalism before its Triumph* (Princeton: Princeton University Press, 1977).

38 See Stephen Krasner, *Sovereignty: Organized Hypocrisy* (Princeton: Princeton University Press, 1999).

39 See Alex Wendt, "Anarchy is what states make of it: the social construction of power politics", *International Organization*, vol. 46 (Spring 1992): 391–425.

Part II

Writings on international law

5 Thrasymmachos revisited

On the relevance of norms and the study of law for international relations

Introduction

The place of norms in political life has always been controversial, probably because of their counter-factual validity. The possibility of violating norms has made the explanation and prediction of human action in terms of norms particularly difficult.[1] Thus the search for causes of human behaviour has been concerned mainly with the discovery of less problematic factors that could be imputed as constants in explaining particular decisions.

Such explanations, be they cast in terms of power, interest, drives, or race were thought to be more parsimonious than the complicated description of circumstances and applicable norms in a given situation. Thereby a more objective or in any case scientific explanation of human action, it was hoped, would become possible.[2] Consequently, norms have been understood solely as ideological reflections, deceptions, subterfuges or simply as an impediment to the achievement of one's goals in a "rational" way.

One of the most principled discussions in which the relevance of a normative order for man and society is defended is Plato's *Republic*. Significantly, it is also entitled a dialogue "on justice". There the debate about the relevance of norms in individual and social life takes a "theological" turn when Thrasymmachos, the sophist, maintains that the gods, as symbols and guarantors of the normative order either do not exist or do not care and are therefore irrelevant. If indeed they do care, Thrasymmachos contends, they can be bribed, thus calling into question the whole prospect of a normative order.[3]

Many students of international relations voice similar objections concerning the status of legal prescriptions in the international arena. In a realm governed by great insecurity, marginally rather than widely shared values, and great competitiveness, a modified version of the three "Thrasymmachian objections" appears relevant. Thus modern sophists argue plausibly that: 1) international law does not exist, i.e., any norm which might exist in the international arena is not legal; 2) if legal norms exist they are ineffective, and; 3) even if legal norms exist and are relevant to decisions they are constantly abused in the interest of the powerful. For these reasons the idea of an impartial regulatory system is fanciful indeed.

These assertions speak to three different aspects of the legal *problématique* in any society. The first and most radical objection, but also perhaps the easiest to refute, is based on a particular definition of law. A conceptual clarification can quickly show the inadequacies of a preconceived idea of law derived exclusively from a particular subset of legal prescriptions.[4] For example, using criminal law as the model means to mistake a part of law for law in its entirety. This shows two things. First, the question of the existence or non-existence of international law cannot be answered by nominal definitions as e.g. in Austin's theory: law is the command of the sovereign; since there is no sovereign in international relations therefore there is no law. As a corollary, it is only against the background of a broader definition of law that the question of the status of international law can be discussed intelligently.

The second aspect of the legal *problématique* deals with the influence of norms upon decision-making and, in particular, the constraining force of prescriptions. But again to focus exclusively on the constraining aspect of prescriptions – as opposed to a fuller account which includes the justificatory, enabling and communicative aspects of norms – leads to serious distortions concerning the efficacy of law in social life.

The final objection focuses on the jurisprudential issue of the link between a set of legal prescriptions and the requirements of a formal or substantive conception of justice. This in turn not only includes the specification of such criteria as fairness, impartiality or equity, but entails a critical appraisal of the actual strategies by which a more principled and just order can emerge from the interactions between states.

Those familiar with the legal literature will recognize that these three theses can serve as convenient categories in classifying a variety of scholarly efforts. The first question deals mainly with the problem of Austinian positivism and its reformulation by legal theorists such as H.L.A. Hart.[5] The third issue is most explicitly treated by writers who share a world order perspective.[6] The second issue, the influence of norms on policy-makers, has not received sufficient attention. In this context it is important to note that the work on regimes is characterized by an egregious lack of familiarity with legal theory.[7]

It is through the prism of this second objection that the other two sophistic theses, and their problematic character will be examined. This will not only help develop a broader understanding of the functions and limitations of law in general, but will highlight the distinctive features of the international legal order. Furthermore, a more appropriate appraisal of the weaknesses of international law becomes possible. This appraisal avoids mistaking the "cops and robbers" model of law for an adequate formulation of the role of norms in social life.

Such an approach is indebted to linguistic conceptual analysis and jurisprudence rather than to the positivist understanding of science. It is useful in clarifying some of the epistemological problems of the present "regime" discussion in international relations and it has important repercussions for the building of international relations theory.

The next section begins with an argument about the "ineffectiveness" of international legal prescriptions. In this context the conceptualisation of rules and norms as constraints is shown to be faulty and to lead to a mistaken view of the role of norms in social life. After determining the function of norms, the following section will examine the question of their legal character. The final section is devoted to a short summary and some concluding considerations concerning the status of theory-building in international relations.

The efficacy of international legal prescriptions

Law can be defined "as a set of prescriptions (rules and principles) that impartial judges apply to a case at hand in order to render an authoritative decision".[8] This conception of law avoids the excesses of Austinian positivism (command of a sovereign) and is specific enough to serve as a useful point of departure. Unless appropriately modified, however, this preliminary definition, which focuses upon important differences between political and legal decision-making as sub-categories of "authoritative" decisions, is problematic at best. The problem is brought out by reflecting briefly on the meaning of the term "rule of law". A government of laws does not refer to the government of judges, but, as Morton Kaplan and Nicholas de B. Katzenbach have aptly put it, it refers to:

> ... the larger formal process through which the members of the society pursue and realize values in an orderly way. It scarcely requires argument that law viewed as a body of authoritative rules pervades all the institutions of modern democratic government and is no monopoly of judges . . . .[9]

Three points are worth pondering in this context. There is the implicit argument that law is best understood as a special type of rules guiding conduct, rather than as a set of commands. Secondly, there is the distinction between the narrow conception of law as applied by impartial third parties and the wider context in which rules are used, invoked and utilized. The third point concerns the importance of legal rules for the performance of duties. Law, therefore, is not simply a "constraint", but it also functions to orchestrate and thereby facilitate, societal interaction.[10] These two functions emphasize the performative and pragmatic dimensions of law, and as such are usually neglected in the normal definition of the functions of law.[11]

From this preliminary analysis it becomes obvious that the conception of law as a coercive order needs revision.[12] The efficacy of law cannot be assessed simply in terms of the compliance or non-compliance with prohibitions. Such a procedure would be inaccurate, because it mistakes laws for commands, and because complying with prescriptions is an intensely dynamic process as opposed to passively following rules.

Mistaking legal prescriptions for commands has a long and distinguished ancestry shared by such unlikely companions as positivists, voluntarist philosophers and theologians.[13] But even in the last case, when the obligatory character of prescriptions is derived from an absolute sovereign – God – the language distinguishes between a command and a commandment. While commands are always situation-specific, commandments (which show rule-like characteristics) are always thought to be applicable to broad classes of events.[14] Rules, as Hart points out, are standing orders.[15] This is elucidated when rules are stated in the "if-then" form.[16] Rules are also valid *erga omnes* (applicable to all) and are different from commands. After all, the famous gunman asking for your wallet is not claiming to have established a norm also applicable to him or herself.[17] This surely is not part of the language game of asking for "your money or your life". Even when rules empower someone to issue commands in specific situations, the command and the rule are clearly distinguishable.[18] [. . .]

Two corollaries follow from this. First, it appears not only that one cannot equate rules with commands, but that a variety of different rule types exist, each of which exhibits characteristic differences in the incentives for compliance. Although prohibitions are adequately represented as constraints, rules that empower or enable are not. Thus while enforcement according to the "cops and robbers" model of criminal law may increase compliance with a certain type of prescription, and thus the effectiveness of a certain part of the legal order, it is clearly irrelevant to the compliance patterns of enabling rules. A serious effort in ascertaining the effectiveness of legal prescriptions in general would entail: first, the differentiation of several types of rules; second, an analysis of the social situation to which these rules correspond, and third, an empirical account of actual compliance patterns. It should be obvious that such an enterprise is at odds with the facile arguments about the ineffectiveness of the legal order mentioned above in the second sophistic objection. Actors, in the domestic as well as the international order, are not simply constrained by rules. Rules enable them to act, to pursue goals, to communicate, to share meanings, to criticise claims and justify actions. Indeed, the blue-print image of a society in which legal norms program individual action has been justly criticised by sociologists.[19] The inappropriateness of viewing laws merely as a system of sanctions or constraints has also been noted in the jurisprudential literature.[20]

These theoretical considerations conform with an unprejudiced assessment of the empirical evidence. While it is true that the international legal order is not very successful in preventing international violence, the relevance of norms in international life is manifest in the thousands of transactions that take place every day. It is precisely because policy-making machinery has become bureaucratised that it increasingly needs standard operating procedures by which to function, these conditions can be best met by the application and invocation of norms.[21]

The fact that legal prescriptions are not particularly effective in preventing violence in the international, as well as in the domestic context is not new. In both arenas the legal order is continuously violated. What distinguishes the failure of international law from that of the domestic legal order is less the frequency of violations than the catastrophic consequences these failures have for international relations. While the daily death toll from violent crimes in American cities alone might amount to 30 victims, it does not have the same saliency as a guerrilla attack or military expedition which claims ten or twenty lives and which is quickly adduced as proof of the failure of international law.

In addition, the scope of war distinguishes it from private acts of unauthorised violence. The destruction wrought, and the possibility of escalation, clearly sets international violations apart from even the worst failures of the domestic legal order, with the exception of internal strife and civil war. The issue, therefore, is not the weakness of the international prohibitions against violence but rather more effective prevention of violence. This in turn presents an array of new puzzles. Would a world in which no legal prescriptions exist against the resort to force be better off? Arguments could be made that this might lead to a less cynical attitude concerning violations. There might also be trade-offs between an increased observance of the rules of warfare *(jus in bello)* and the free resort to violence *(jus ad bellum)* as defined by the UN regime. As Louis Henkin has shown, however, the argument is not persuasive, conceptually or historically.[22]

Would it be more effective to rely on other mechanisms to the exclusion of legal considerations? Sometimes a *Realpolitik* policy depending on competing national interests and the balance of power is mentioned in this context. The balance of power model, however, can only be an effective and rational policy within a framework of conventions with normative status. Even the most hardened realists confess that the application of force is a very costly way to achieve one's objectives in international relations and that sensible powers have therefore followed a policy of "prestige".[23] Prestige itself, however, is an ambiguous concept. It might simply mean establishing a "bad reputation" similar to gangsters attempting to keep challenges to their position to a minimum. But even in that case prestige is tied to some type of rule-governed expectations about the likelihood, scope and domain of retaliatory action. The more explicit this framework becomes the more prestige becomes mediated by the normative order.[24] This means in turn that power and influence are derived from the role as a protector of certain rules and core values of the game as exemplified in the notion of a Great Power or of hegemonic leadership.[25] Whether it is useful to endow these "rules of the game" with the dignity of some type of legal prescriptive force as some scholars seem to suggest, is a difficult question.[26] Nevertheless, it shows that the alleged antinomy between "power", "balancing" and "rule following" is a mistaken one.

The role of such hegemonic aspirations is perhaps best exemplified in Thucydides' record of the Periclean Funeral Oration.[27] All those who read or interpret this book as an example of the inevitability of hegemonic wars, caused by the law of uneven growth, miss an important part of the Thucydidean intention.[28] The shifts in key governing concepts of the political discourse that occurred during the war brought about the destruction of a common normative framework.[29] The ethos of the protagonists decays and finally destroys even the set of conventions which distinguished Hellenic from barbaric society. Both cities become oppressors of their allies and lose power and prestige as the war is finally decided by an outside power, Persia.

Another possible substitute for norms is deterrence.[30] But as Alexander George and Richard Smoke have shown, the numerous failures of deterrence demonstrate its limited effectiveness.[31] Not only is such a system dependent on common sense to function, but substantive norms also provide templates in case the normal interaction has broken down.

These remarks do not necessarily prove the importance of legal prescriptions, but they do show that realist and capability analyses, deriving everything from "structural givens", are seriously misleading.[32] Realist and capability analyses share a certain naiveté about the complexities of human life, a shortcoming often attributed to legal scholars. Only legalism of the worst kind could assume that through the proliferation of prescriptions and the criminalisation of international law, the problem of war could be eliminated. However, it is an equally naive conception that the only reality of international politics is power as gauged by national capabilities.

While the preceding paragraphs illustrate how difficult it is to maintain that norms are non-existent in the international arena, there still remains the question of whether these norms can really be called "legal". The attribution of a legal character to norms requires more than simply demonstrating that norms exist in the international arena and that norms indeed mould decisions. Thus, Austinian jurisprudence did not deny the existence of norms but maintained that they are merely norms of comity or morality.

While it may be difficult to draw a clear line between legal prescriptions and moral principles – some moral precepts such as "promises have to be kept" are inherent to legal systems – a demarcation criterion between legal prescriptions and other norms serves as an important device in further clarifying the functions of law. The next section will consider this problem and then approach the last objection mentioned above, i.e. the "partial" character of norms.

The character of international legal prescriptions

Having shown the rule-guided character of human action in the domestic as well as the international arena, the problem remains to distinguish legal rules from other rules guiding interactions. There seem to be two ways to approach the character of a rule. The rule can be traced back to its origin or it can be distinguished according to its influence on an actor's decision. While fundamentalist mullahs and positivists prefer the formal tests – law is what originates from God or a basic norm – the pressure test of legal obligation is usually preferred by sociologists and psychologists. Psychologists distinguish legal norms by the severity with which they pressure the individuals to act in accordance with the rule in question.

Both approaches create severe difficulties for the determination of the legal character of norms in the international arena. Although some norms can conveniently be traced back to a source, such as those created by a treaty, the establishment of a pedigree of a norm then depends upon the logical closure of the legal system. But this leads to problems when two norms, both traceable to a valid source, lead to contradictory implications or when one party argues that "x" is a legal norm while the other party questions its legal pedigree. In such cases a rule is formulated at a meta-level, which decides the circumstances under which one norm is to be given preference over another. Or an authoritative decision is made of what the "law is", a task performed by adjudication. Since adjudicative procedures in either contentious cases or in the "advisory opinion" variety are rarely utilised in international relations, much of what is claimed to be legally relevant is never authoritatively decided. This is obviously one reason why the international legal system can be called "primitive." Nevertheless, it would not be very useful to call all the activities in which legal norms are invoked "nonlegal" simply because of the lack of authoritative decision. After all, states usually *do* make distinctions between their rights, and their desires and preferences, even if the latter are backed by persuasive reasons. Furthermore, such a perspective makes too much of the *ratio decidendi* (the reason for the decisions) of a judge and is clearly inapplicable to international law where *stare decisis* (to stand by that which was decided) is not established.[33]

Another attempt to define a criterion of demarcation focuses on the type of psychological pressure generated by legal norms as opposed to rules of comity. On the one hand, legal norms are said to be characterized by a certain gravity and seriousness; on the other hand, it is maintained that legal rules are not as compelling as moral prescriptions. Thus it is not clear which type or degree of "seriousness of pressure" qualifies a rule as legal. In addition, the most severe psychological pressures in the international arena might not be generated by legal norms but by unilateral policy commitments. But such commitments do not qualify as moral imperatives or as legal obligations. Besides, no legal order can make the private feelings of an actor the ultimate test of legal obligations quite aside from the fact that "feelings" of pressure are probably a mistaken metaphor in the case of corporate actors.[34]

If the psychological pressure model is seriously deficient, then the guidance provided by rules must be conceptualized differently. The concept should not emphasise the psychological impact, but the explicitness and the contextual variation allowed in decision-making. Legal rules "provide relatively firm guidance not only with respect to ends but to the means adopted".[35] This distinguishes legal rules from morals. Moral precepts are practically context-free and do not provide for specific ranges of application. This accounts for the open-ended nature of the moral discourse. The specificity of legal norms, on the other hand, is perhaps clearest in the rules of evidence in a legal order. The search for "truth" in a legal proceeding is subordinate to provisos specifying what counts as a "proof" and what facts are inadmissible.

Such a definition of law focuses no longer on certain institutions such as courts, or on the states or beliefs of the actors, but rather on the reasoning process (deliberation) of an actor in making decisions. The legal nature of norms can now be determined in a "system free" way. Neither logical closure nor particular institutions of a legal order are prerequisites for its existence. A legal order exists if actors accept certain rules as obligatory by making principled use of them in defining choices, by making demands as well as proposals for the settlement of disputes in terms of these rules, and by justifying action through their invocation.

In this way a legal order can be conceived of as a particular system of communicative action.[36] It informs the participants about the nature of the game by determining the type of actors who can make claims; it sets the range of permissible goals the actors can pursue, specifies the steps necessary to insure the validity of their acts and assigns priority and weight to different claims.[37] The legal order represents one of the primary means of organising social life because it makes more specific the shared general notions in practical matters which allow for interdependent decision-making. Finally, the legal order deals with the problems that arise due to scarcity and the non-identical preferences of a multiplicity of actors. These last remarks deserve further exploration and will be helpful in clarifying the concept of a "primitive" order.

The term "shared meaning" is conventionally used to designate culture, which is a comprehensive system of symbols used to explain all or particular aspects of reality. This includes practices, mythical lores and conceptual schemes. Although law as a cultural scheme has its roots in myth and magic, it emancipated itself early from the mythical origins. Ultimate meanings are increasingly relegated to theology or philosophy. The validity of legal prescriptions becomes a matter of argumentation, through quoting relevant norms as an explanation for the espoused position. This means that law undergoes thereby not only a process of rationalisation, but that law is increasingly oriented towards the practical aspects of life.[38]

But even within this realm of practical reason law becomes a much more restricted form of discourse. This becomes evident when comparing the moral and legal discourse. While from a moral point of view all norms have to satisfy the generalisation criterion to be valid, the legal discourse allows for self-interested and thereby non-universal claims if they are rights.[39] Furthermore, rights as particularly insistent claims cannot simply be defeated by showing that the pursuit of some ultimate value, even if agreed upon, is impeded.[40]

Unlike moral precepts, the legal system has a tendency to develop procedures of internal validation by which norms can be created, altered or abolished. In this context it is important to remember that specific legislative institutions are historically rather late phenomena within legal orders and that most of the development of law takes place through judicial activity (interpretation, precedents). In addition, scholars try to introduce some consistency into often contradictory practices. Long before legal orders attain their full reality status in practice they existed as ideas which gave meaning and coherence to otherwise only vaguely related activities.[41]

These considerations lead to a more appropriate assessment of the international legal order as a primitive one. As previously mentioned, primitive does not refer to the lack of differentiation between mythical and legal concepts. International law is a secular construct and thus is distinguishable from morality, religion or mythical elaborations that endow the interaction of states with some ultimate meaning. This meaning is defined in either a philosophy of history or in a mechanical interpretation such as the balance of power.[42] After all, it was no accident that the legal conceptualisation of international relations attained importance when the "right way of life" as an organising principle of political life had to be abandoned. The wars of religion demonstrated that neither the old orthodoxies nor the new forces espousing a different way of life could organise the body politic. On the contrary, each day of continued warfare led to new savageries without resolving any of the ultimate issues; the creation of a legal order appeared to be the only possibility to provide a normative framework necessary for social coexistence. An intellectual construct created by scholars ranging from Grotius to Vattel proved useful, and the idea of a "legal order" attained an increasingly concrete status.

An important problem with the primitive law analogy is that it suggests that the international legal order is largely a customary order. One of the peculiarities of the international legal order is, however, that it presupposes the distinction between a public and a private legal sphere, a division usually undeveloped or absent in primitive customary systems. This has important repercussions for the role of public officials as "agencies" of the international legal order (the famous *dedoublement fonctionelle* of Scelle).[43] Thus, unlike a primitive order where law is the set of customary norms everybody follows, international law is applied to problems by a special class of public officials. In this sense international law exhibits some features of a developed legal system. International law also possesses features of a customary order characterised by horizontal patterns of authority.[44] Finally, there is the rather unique feature of the prescriptions of transnational law.[45] These regulate the conduct of private associations, such as multinational corporations by creating a special regime.

Having stated to what extent the term primitive is equivocal and problematic when applied to the international legal order, it is now easier to show in what sense the term primitive can be used justifiably. The international legal system is most obviously primitive in that it does not automatically subject its members to the compulsory settlement of disputes by legal means. This weakness is not specific to international law, because the settlement of disputes through court proceedings is always difficult once organised groups are involved and once issues cannot be separated from the wider social context. The lack of institutionalisation of the world political process limits the more effective utilisation of the legal process.[46] Although international law provides for a rudimentary informal organisation of social life among independent actors, there are no effective formal organisations that can translate interest and issues into policy. Collective goods on the international level are thus not provided or achieved sub-optimally through hegemonic leadership and, infrequently, through some type of voluntary contributions. The world political process remains, in spite of all communications, sporadic, and is often characterised by bargaining and coercive moves rather than by persuasion and by appeals to common standards, shared values and accepted solutions. Thus not only can the legal process not be separated from the political process, but the impartiality of legal reasoning is crucially impaired by the lack of authoritative decisions concerning the applicability and scope of legal norms.

International adjudicative institutions are more often than not quite limited in their ability to determine what the law is. This is either due to general jurisdictional limitations incorporated into the statute that brings such a "court" into existence, or to the further limitations under which the parties to a dispute agree to ask for a judicial decision.[47] Thus, quite apart from the hoary institutional problem of how authoritative decisions of international tribunals can be enforced, the problem of determining the applicable legal principle is often impaired by the narrow limits to the jurisdictional domain of such tribunals.[48] This has two corollaries: first, if the relevant legal rule or principle cannot be authoritively established, many issues remain unclear. An unknown rule can neither be followed nor violated. In this way one of the major advantages of a legal settlement is diminished: i.e. that future quarrels can be avoided by taking the authoritatively established rule into account. The second corollary is that substitutes have to be found so that such impasses do not become totally disabling characteristics of the legal order. In this context advisory opinions, decisions by national institutions and scholarly expositions have to be mentioned.

In an arena that does not accept the principle of *stare decisis*, opinions defining the scope of legal principles are of decisive importance. Their weight, however, will largely depend upon their persuasive power rather than their institutional authority. Only in this sense does the importance of advisory opinions by the International Court of Justice become understandable. This also explains why legal scholars' writings are considered a "subsidiary source" of international law.[49]

National institutions often fail in establishing "the law" because of their partisan nature. The observer is then confronted with practices varying from state to state. The most obvious example of the partisan nature of decision-making is evident in the regulations of administrative agencies, whose rulings are bound by national policy. But even the independent courts have considerable difficulty acting in a detached fashion. They might have to defer to the executive agencies because of constitutional considerations or are bound by national legislative interpretations or precedents. Thus while a decision of a national court settles a particular dispute which has international legal ramifications, and while its decision might be authoritative as a precedent within a given domestic legal system, it will often fail to be considered an authoritative decision on the international law level.[50]

The lack of international credibility of domestic decisions has important implications for an assessment of international law as an instrument that impartially protects the interests of all claimants. It is clear that those parties which have the most developed domestic organisational structures as well as the most far reaching interests can adjudicate the largest number of disputes. Although no modern nation is currently in the same privileged position as England was with respect to maritime trade, differentials of development and power still matter. To that extent the third sophist objection mentioned above is not always beside the point. An even-handed assessment must admit, however, that national courts occasionally deviate from established national policies and try to come to terms with the changing structure of international society, thereby providing important new crystallisation points for the development of international law.

Finally, the lack of effective channels for an authoritative determination of what the law is and how it can be modified, changed or rescinded, sheds new light on the problem of compliance and legal change. Non-compliance is usually conceived of in terms of transgressions in which an actor works for advantages in the hope of not being discovered. Even in the domestic arena, however, there are cases of non-compliance in defence of a valued position and with the explicit purpose of changing an objectionable rule. Although the latter strategy might open the door for all types of extra-legal considerations and thus weaken the strength and autonomy of the legal order, significant distinctions exist between these two cases. Cynical acts of rascality, therefore, are treated differently than actions of civil disobedience. Nothing in the nature of the international legal order allows the neglect of such crucial differences. Precisely because the means of peaceful change in the international arena are few, and by and large ineffective, the violation of a legal norm is often not a pure act of lawlessness but rather part and parcel of a larger bargaining game for change. It would be a legalism of the worst kind to reduce the problem of compliance to the technical problem of ensuring norm conformity at the least cost through the elaboration of repressive techniques, while leaving the issue of justifying actions in terms of broader principles, demands for justice and pleas for peaceful change to history and philosophy.

The status of law in international relations theory

At this point it is useful to summarise some of the major arguments. Taking the sophistic objections as a point of departure, the argument about the non-existence and ineffectiveness of an international legal order was shown to be flawed for two reasons. First, social interactions are in need of norms, because only then can the problem of coordination and interference be regulated. Second, it became clear that the conceptualisation of rules and norms as constraints is erroneous since norms are also enabling and empowering instruments. The phenomenal growth of international and of transnational law is a response to the increasing interdependence of international life.

This in turn made the characterisation of law in general and international law in particular as a "system of sanctioning prescriptions" inappropriate. A more fundamental clarification of the concept of law was required. This essay developed a concept of law that focuses less on the organisational features of law enforcement or the systemic character of the norms, but rather of the *contexts* in which norms are used and on the particular style of *reasoning* by which they provide decision-making guidance. In this sense norms in the international arena are not to be simple rules of comity or morals, but to exhibit legal character.

These theoretical considerations provided the necessary criteria to judge the "primitiveness" of the international legal order. Primitiveness was seen to be a rather equivocal characterisation of a legal order which showed some interesting complicating features that make it a type of system *sui generis*. A discussion of the weaknesses of international law followed. Aside from the lack of enforcement, several problems that usually are not treated adequately were emphasised. One point concerned the weakness of any legal order that deals with organised groups rather than individuals, in particular, with the issue of group violence. In this case the limits of law as a means of conflict resolution could clearly be perceived, in both the international and domestic arena. This led to a more principled discussion of the role of adjudicative procedures and their function in international life. In accordance with the main thrust of the literature, this article stated that the primary contribution of such proceedings is to develop international law as an authoritative statement of what the law is rather than the settlement of a particular dispute. The frequent lack of authoritative determinations was then diagnosed as one of the major weaknesses. This weakness cannot easily be overcome by national institutions, administrative or judicial, because their determinations are not usually disinterested choices. The role of scholars as a more objective forum was emphasised in this context.

The third section ended with some short remarks concerning the problem of compliance with existing norms and the unresolved problem of peaceful change. The problematic nature of change via non-compliance with an objectionable norm was pointed out.

What remains to be sketched are the implications of a legal approach emphasising a particular style of deliberative reasoning for theory building in international politics. Since the newest rage in theorizing about international relations is a concern with "regimes", such a clarification appears useful, especially because none of the insights from international law or jurisprudence have been taken into account in the pertinent literature.[51] The subject of custom seems highly relevant to the regime discussion, but one cannot help thinking that busy social scientists are about to rediscover the wheel. Worse still, there are justifiable suspicions that the wheel will not be discovered unless fundamental changes are made in the research program.

Since norms and rules do not directly determine the outcome of decisions, what role do they play as underlying factors? While one could argue that norms influence events in a probabilistic fashion, this does not solve the dilemma. The concept of probability is problematic, for dealing with the problem of the counter-factual validity of norms. Finally, what serves and is accepted as an explanation in a given situation cannot be derived from the logical structure of the explanation but rather from interests guiding the inquiry and from contextual factors. Explaining often means elaborating, putting events in context, or perhaps only justifying the action in terms of vaguely articulated but shared standards.[52]

If this is correct – and all indications seem to corroborate the evidence – then the chances for a grand theory of international relations are small if not non-existent. A grand theory of international relations is missing exactly for the same reasons that there is no grand theory of life. True, there are models for regularities which might in certain circumstances develop the firmness of law-like forces, but this type of explanation remains tied to rigorous abstractions as the *homo oeconomicus* so amply demonstrates. The problem is not so much that these models are unreliable, but that they create blind spots (i.e., everything that does not fit these models is declared irrelevant). It is, however, simply not true that nothing sensible can be said and that nothing worth knowing exists outside the standard positivist framework.

Since the present article is indebted more to jurisprudence and conceptual analysis than the "grand theory" tradition of international relations, perhaps it illustrates a type of analysis which, through conceptual clarifications, can lead to deeper and deeper levels of reflection. It is a discourse rather than a theory. Such an approach is definitely useful when the role of law in social life is investigated. Since norms are not "causes" for behaviour but are part of the deliberation necessary to make a choice, a contextual and interpretative frame of reference had to be chosen in order to "understand" human action. Only in this way can a particular type of question sensibly be asked without being ruled out by the framework. Thus what is at issue in explaining an action is often not the cause, but whether the decision could have been made differently, whether a choice was possible, whether responsibility was incurred and can be assessed, and whether good reasons can be provided for acting in this and not in another fashion. Since such assessments include normative terms a descriptivist framework is insufficient, as shown by G.E. Moore's argument concerning the "naturalistic fallacy".[53]

International relations specialists would do well to remember the limitations of the positivist approaches and to reflect critically upon them. [. . .] The problem is not simply that Thrasymmachos can be shown to be mostly wrong, but he must be persuaded to better his ways.

Notes

1 Carl Hempel, *Aspects of Scientific Explanation* (New York: Free Press, 1965), chap. 4.
2 The argument that a "political", i.e., structural explanation of international relations is required is made in Kenneth Waltz, *Theory of International Politics* (Reading, Mass.: Addison Wesley Co., 1979).
3 Plato, *Republic*, Book II, 365d–366b. For an interpretation of the sophistic argument and Plato's response see Eric Voegelin, *Order and History*, vol. 3, *Plato and Aristotle* (Baton Rouge: University of Louisiana Press, 1957), chap. 3.
4 For a more extensive treatment of differing concepts of law and its implications for international law, see Friedrich Kratochwil, "Is International Law Proper Law?" *Archives for Philosophy of Law and Social Philosophy* 69, no. 1 (1983), 13–46.
5 H.L.A. Hart, *The Concept of Law* (Oxford: Clarendon, 1961).
6 For a short description of the world order approach, see Saul H. Mendlovitz, (ed.) *On the Creation of a Just World Order* (New York: The Free Press, 1975).
7 Stephen Krasner, (ed.), *International Organization* 36, no. 2 (Spring 1982).
8 Morton Kaplan and Nicholas de B. Katzenbach. *The Political Foundations of International Law* (New York: Wiley, 1961), 4.
9 Kaplan and Katzenbach, 4.
10 For a discussion of the function of law as a means of communication, see William Coplin, "International Law and Assumptions about the State System", *World Politics* 17, no. 1 (1965) 615–35.
11 J.L. Austin, *How to Do Things with Words* (Cambridge: Harvard University Press, 1962).
12 On the argument that law is a coercive order, see Hans Kelsen, *Principles of International Law*, 2nd ed. (New York: Holt, Rinehart and Winston, 1966).
13 For a good conceptual distinction, see Thomas Mayberry, "Laws, Moral Laws and God's Commands", *The Journal of Value Inquiry* 4, no. 4 (Winter 1970), 287–92.
14 Alf Ross, *Directives and Norms* (London: Routledge, Kegan and Paul, 1968).
15 Hart, chaps. 2, 3.
16 Gidon Gottlieb, *The Logic of Choice* (London: Allen and Unwin, 1968).
17 For a discussion of the "gun man example" see Hart, chap. 2.
18 For a further discussion of the situation-specific form of commands in contrast to the standing order character of rules see Ross, *Directives and Norms*, 99.
19 Judith Blake and Kingsley Davis, "Norms, Values and Sanctions". *Modern Sociology*, Robert Harris, (ed.), (Chicago: Rand MacNally, 1964).
20 David Miers and William Twining, *How to Do Things With Rules* (London: Weidenfeld and Nicolson, 1976).
21 Louis Henkin, *How Nations Behave*, 2nd ed. (New York: Columbia University Press, 1980).
22 On the controversy between Thomas Franck and Louis Henkin see Thomas Franck, "Who Killed Article 2.4?" *American Journal of International Law*, 64 (1970), 809–37; Louis Henkin, "The Reports of the Death of Article 2.4 are Greatly Exaggerated", *American Journal of International Law*, 65 (1971), 545–48.
23 Robert Gilpin, *War and Change in World Politics* (Cambridge: Cambridge University Press, 1981).
24 Friedrich Kratochwil, "On the Notion of Interest in International Relations", *International Organization* 36, no. 1 (1982), 1–30.

25 On the importance of a common understanding of legitimacy see Henry Kissinger, *A World Restored* (New York: Gosset and Dunlop, 1964); on the notion of a "Great Power" see Martin Wright, *Systems of States*, Hedley Bull and Carsten Holbraad, (eds.) (Leicester: Leicester University Press, 1977).

26 Richard Falk, "The Interplay of Westphalia and Charter Conceptions of the International Legal Order", *The Future of the International Legal Order*, Cyril Black and Richard Falk, (eds.), 4 vols. (Princeton: Princeton University Press, 1969), vol. 1, chap. 2.

27 Thucydides, *The Peloponnesian War*, Book II, 34–36.

28 In this context, I object strongly to Gilpin's "Leninist" interpretation of politics. See Gilpin, *War and Change*.

29 Thucydides, *Peloponnesian War*, Book III, 82–95.

30 See Robert Jervis for critical remarks about "security regimes" in which the role of norms is considered secondary to the utility calculations of each player. Robert Jervis, "Security Regimes", *International Regimes*, Krasner, ed., 357–78.

31 Alexander George and Richard Smoke, *Deterrence in American Foreign Policy* (New York: Columbia University Press, 1974).

32 See Klaus Knorr, *The Power of Nations* (New York: Basic Books, 1975): David Baldwin, "Money and Power", *Journal of Politics* 33 (1971), 578–614; see Joseph Nogee, "Polarity: An Ambiguous Concept". *Orbis* 18 (Winter 1978), 1193–1224.

33 See Miers and Twining, 159.

34 For a discussion of the problem of political and legal obligation see Richard Flathman, *Political Obligation* (London: Croom Helm, 1972).

35 Gidon Gottlieb, "The Nature of International Law: Towards a Second Concept of Law", *The Future of the International Legal Order*, Cyril Black and Richard Falk, (eds.), vol. 4 (Princeton: Princeton University Press, 1972), chap. 9, 370.

36 See Jürgen Habermas, *Theorie des Kommunikativen Handelns*, 2 vols. (Frankfurt: Suhrkamp, 1981).

37 The informal organization of social life is thus dependent upon the workings of norms that make an intersubjective understanding possible. On the emergence of such norms out of iterative bargaining situations see Edna Ullmann-Margalit, *The Emergence of Norms* (Oxford: Clarendon Press, 1977); Philip Heyman, "The Problem of Coordination: Bargaining and Rules", *Harvard Law Review* 86 (March 1973), 707–78.

38 Max Weber, *Rechtssoziologie*, Johannes Winckelmann, (ed.), (Neuwied: Luchterhand, 1960).

39 See Marcus Singer, *Generalization in Ethics* (New York: Knopf, 1960).

40 See Dworkin, *Taking Rights Seriously* (Cambridge: Harvard University Press, 1978).

41 See Nicholas G. Onuf, "The International Legal Order as an Idea", *American Journal of International Law* 73 (1979), 244–66.

42 On the process of differentiation and the elaboration of philosophical "Weltbilder" see Habermas, vol. 2, chap. 5. Although it is fashionable to interpret the balance of power as a logical outcome of an anarchic state it can easily be shown that the European-balance of power was a rather unique phenomenon. It seems rather questionable to assume that the idea of a "balance" could have been persuasive to anyone who did not share the mechanical metaphors that came into fashion after Descartes and attained prominence with Newton's physics, which demonstrated the heuristic power of equilibrium analysis.

43 Georges Scelle, *Droit International Public* (Paris: Doneat Montchrestien, 1948).

44 Richard Falk, "International Jurisdiction: Horizontal and Vertical Conception of Legal Order", *Tempade Law Quarterly* 32 (1959), 295–320.

45 On a clarification of the concept of "transnational law" see Wolfgang Friedmann,

　　The Changing Structure of International Law (New York: Columbia University Press, 1964).

46 For a fundamental discussion on the social and theoretical preconditions of a functioning legal process see Michael Barkun, *Law Without Sanction* (New Haven: Yale University Press, 1968), chaps. 6–8.

47 See Leo Gross, "The ICJ: Considerations of Requirements for Enhancing its Role in the International Legal Order", *The Future of the International Court of Justice*, Leo Gross, (ed.), 2 vols. (Dobbs Ferry, N.Y.: Oceana, 1976) vol. 1, 27; Daniel Partan, "Increasing the Effectiveness of the International Court", *Harvard International Law Journal* 18 (1977), 559–75.

48 Oscar Schachter, "The Enforcement of International Judicial and Arbitral Decisions", *American Journal of International Law* 54 (1960), 1–24.

49 See Art. 36 of the ICJ statute.

50 Thus decisions of national courts concerning the expropriation of foreign property are notorious for not having established clear rules in spite of a considerable amount of case law. Even worse is the situation in such gray areas as "creeping expropriations" by means of fiscal laws, health, or labour regulations.

51 See Krasner, (ed.), *International Organization* 36 (Spring 1982).

52 See Hannah Pitkin, *Wittgenstein on Justice* (Berkeley: University of California Press, 1972).

53 G.E. Moore, *Principia Ethica* (Cambridge: Cambridge University Press, 1959).

6   The limits of contract

I. Introduction

The roots of many international legal institutions in private law have been well established. The creative moment in which legal scholars attempted to understand the changing nature of authority after the demise of imperial formations and the intellectual assault on the viability of an ontologically based moral order has been recounted by legal scholars and political theorists alike.[1] But even more importantly, the *generative* force of private law institutions for the development of the international legal order can be seen in their capacity to provide "standard solutions"[2] to new problems by means of analogy. One of the most recent examples is perhaps the *sic utere tuo*[3] principle which has been put to good use in charting a new course for regulating trans-border pollution problems.

However, no analogy has attained as pivotal an importance as "contract". It "solved" the problem of how "persons of sovereign authority"[4] were to relate to each other in international politics, i.e. on the basis of consent and exchange. Thus, treaties as analogues to contracts gave rise to voluntarily created rights and obligations, while at the same time preserving the sovereigns' independence and authority. Of course, some obvious problems exist in using the private law structure as an analogue to an international law construct. Problems like custom and the ability of actors in that arena to determine and modify the public order – which private persons cannot do by their contracts – come readily to mind.

But such "first order objections" did little to challenge the pivotal importance of the contract metaphor for understanding the international game. As a matter of fact, its centrality was further reinforced when it was able to accommodate fundamental changes in the constitution of the actors themselves. By the 19th century, persons of sovereign authority, who originally held their title on the basis of "tradition" or even "divine" rights, could coexist with "agents" empowered by the "people" on the basis of an "original contract".

Finally, even the further differentiation between "state" and "society" in which the members of society reserved their rights as to the proper exercise of authority by the "agent" did not necessitate a major conceptual adjustment. Despite its revolutionary implications, "popular sovereignty" seemed to fit neatly into the existing scheme. All that was necessary was to follow the generative logic of "contract" itself and to reconceptualize the emerging differences between state and society again in contractual terms. Locke's "double contract" provides here the appropriate template. Domestic as well as international order could be understood as a series of consensual acts in accordance with the contractual paradigm.

Against these tenets I wish to argue that considerably more than consent is required in order to explain the emergence of political authority and obligation. Contrary to the belief that what matters is the exchange, I shall argue that it *does* matter what we exchange and that, therefore, the farther we move from spot exchanges in a market to more complex social arrangements, the less is explained by the institution of contract as opposed to other elements.

These objections, then, cast considerable doubt on the possibility of reducing the choice of political institutions to a contractual paradigm as exemplified by a theory of "justice". I also want to argue that these flaws in the contractual paradigm are not simply the result of the obliviousness to the initial assignment of "rights" without which the notion of consensual exchange is meaningless. It seems rather that the two institutions of the contractual paradigm, consent and property, have contradictory implications, because of the failure of the contract metaphor to specify criteria for membership in the contracting group. While such a neglect is of no importance in the case of bilateral "spot contracts" in which we assume no further social bonds or lasting effects outside the exchange, such an assumption is incoherent in the case of contracts setting up political authority and negotiating distributive schemes.

These difficulties are compounded when we move from bilateral, incomplete contracts to "implicit", incomplete contracts, which is precisely the situation of the hypothetical construct of the "original" contract in the state of nature. Contractual solutions to the problems of authority have either to assume the existence of a well-established community, or they have to rely on a *deus ex machina*, i.e. "territoriality" or a "nation", in order to delineate the "members". To that extent, both legal theory and the prevalent theories of international politics assume that the "people" are always the same whether they appear as "citizens", as members of a nation, or of an "ethnos". International relations theory speaks then simply of "units" in which the people, the state, the nation and the "ethnos" are neatly packaged, and legal theory "solves" this problem by assuming that the guarantee of "self-determination" is ensured by endowing individuals with rights of citizenship and participation. Above all, sovereignty and its contemporary manifestation of the territorial state, provide all the necessary conceptual tools.

However, such a theoretical construct is all the more unsatisfactory as international migrations, the revival of ethnic assertiveness, and changing notions of citizenship/nationality make a return to simple territoriality unfeasible. Domestically, the "democratic deficits" caused by the existence of increasing numbers of refugees and long time resident aliens has not only worried political theorists; the question of their legal status requires answers which cannot be obtained from the traditional conceptual grid or from the mere assertion of "human rights". In particular, if group membership is so important, [. . .] and if this problem remains unaddressed by contractarians and "rights" advocates, it seems that the discourse on rights and contractual thinking can provide less guidance than is usually claimed for the problem of "justice" either domestically or internationally.

While I obviously do not possess a fully-fledged alternative for the solution of these conceptual puzzles, this article has two more modest goals: one is to show the limits of two currently fashionable contractual paradigms in relation to the liberal reduction of the problem of domestic and international order to a question of "justice"; and two, to advocate a mode of analysis which utilizes the structure of well-established institutions and attempts to understand the logic of their extension to other areas of social reality. This mode of analysis is at odds with the usual attempts to create "grand theories" whether in the areas of "law" or "politics", or to "apply" some theory imported from some other discipline to social issues. The former attempts usually fail because of the difficulties in formulating sensible demarcation criteria that establish conceptually distinct spheres and which, therefore, quickly end up "subsuming" or marginalizing the other spheres or parts of social reality. The latter are in danger of degenerating into mistaken analogical thinking or of providing simple redescriptions in terms of the new framework rather than generating new insights.

Opting for a conceptual analysis of well-established institutions, I believe that these twin dangers are minimised by a more modest approach, i.e. it is heuristically more fruitful to examine institutions and their conceptual extensions because "anomalies" are less likely to be ignored or "normalised" instead of becoming new starting points for theoretical puzzles. Furthermore, such a procedure, because of its "realism", bears more promise than the grand "imported" theories which arrive as ready-made models that are then prematurely dispatched in search of their range of application.

In order to make good these claims, my argument will take the following steps. In Section II, I begin with the examination of different types of contracts. In this context I will distinguish the spot contract (simultaneous and sequential exchange), the long-term iterative contract, the incomplete contract and, in particular, the incomplete contract establishing "authority relationships". My analysis focuses on "problems" of enforcement and demonstrates that, contrary to the assumptions made by the "grand theories" of neo-classical economics and international politics (that view "self-help" as resulting from "anarchy"), self-help is pervasive in domestic as well as international affairs. Consequently, both the general equilibrium model as well as the predominant "theory" of international politics are badly in need of revision. In Section III, I address the difficulties which arise when the incomplete contract model is applied to ongoing relationships that are either non-specific as to scope and duration, or where these elements are simply "implied". For this purpose, I examine the institution of marriage as a contract and, more importantly, the invocation of the contractual paradigm for the determination of political obligation. Section IV draws out some of the conceptual puzzles which arise in this context when a solution is attempted by means of a Rawlsian "hypothetical contract". My interest here is not to provide a comprehensive evaluation of the Rawlsian "original position" and its recent modifications, but rather to assess the importance of the contract and consent metaphor for a "theory" of the political and legal order, domestically as well as internationally. I argue that consecutive extensions of the contractual paradigm can no longer successfully integrate the different pulls these additions have generated, and that therefore, the contractual paradigm becomes incoherent. To the extent that grand theories of "politics" and "law" originate in a contractual paradigm (social contract), I argue that they also quickly reach the limits of their capacity to provide insights for solutions to contemporary problems of domestic and international order.

II. Three types of contract

To view the problem of obligation as resulting from the institution of contract, (i.e. the exchange of mutual promises) is to treat consent as foundational for the assignment of responsibility. To that extent, it seems to matter little whether the promises concern tangible resources, more abstract property rights, such as "good will", or even the commitments or forbearances which we call political obligations. At the heart of the matter, there always lies the notion that nothing more than the voluntary choices of the parties is involved in creating order among them.

But there are peculiar difficulties that arise and that are often not properly reflected upon when we examine the institution of contract in general and when we move from "spot" exchanges facilitated by the "meeting of the minds" to the problem of "implicit" indefinite, multi-person incomplete contracts. Examples of the latter are the "social contracts" of Hobbes, Locke and Rousseau.

It might be useful to examine systematically these complications as they emerge in the contractarian enterprise. [. . .] Let us therefore begin with the simplest type of contract, the one in which two actors agree on spot exchange. Obviously such an analysis has to assume that the parties have something to exchange antecedent to their agreement, i.e. property rights must have been assigned. Similarly, the parties must know the rules which constitute the practice of contracting, such as e.g. the use of certain formulas like *do ut des* or signing certain forms. In addition, in order to insure the "voluntariness" of the exchange, rules must prevent the use of fraud, force and, depending on the case, impose a duty of disclosure of essential but not readily available information.[5] Finally, in case of non-performance, exogenous "enforcement" must be provided by the state. With the exception of the last point, ample analogies exist between domestic and international law. Not only do we have explicit rules for the acquisition and alienation of titles, but as Coplin[6] reminds us, the rules of international law also authoritatively define who is an actor, and they determine the formalities which must be observed if the parties wish to attach validity to their acts (Vienna Convention on Treaties).

Beyond the obvious analogies, the above account of the spot contract provides several lessons. One is that even simple spot contracts are the result of the interaction of highly complex institutional arrangements. Their unproblematic character depends less on the simplicity and "naturalness" of such arrangements – Adam Smith's allegation of the natural tendency of men to "truck and barter" notwithstanding – than on the discipline of the actors which makes such exchanges routine. This highlights the second lesson of the example, i.e. the recognition that the "obligation" resulting from a contractual undertaking cannot simply be reduced to the "consent" of the parties. They may have committed a mistake of form, might not have foreseen some contingencies which make the contract either wholly or partially voidable, or have provided for grossly disparate benefits for the parties, so that their contract lacked (in common law terms) "consideration".

Since I have dealt with these issues at great length elsewhere such cursory remarks might suffice here.[7] However, what is important here is the realisation that the institution of contract combines two related yet distinguishable ideals that suggest different bases for the obligatoriness of contractual obligations. As Michael Sandel points out:

> One is the ideal of autonomy, which sees a contract as an act of will, whose morality consists in the voluntary character of the transaction. The other is the ideal of reciprocity which sees the contract as an instrument of mutual benefit . . . contracts bind not because they are willingly incurred, but because (or in so far as) they tend to produce results that are fair.[8]

The last point becomes of particular importance when courts have to deal with unforeseen circumstances and when, therefore, there is no ascertainable "will" of the parties, or when losses or risks have to be allocated.

The third lesson is therefore, that "enforcement" problems cover a much wider field than the popular image of the public authority clubbing recalcitrant actors into submission. As a matter of fact, while exogenous claim enforcement figures prominently in our common sense view, as well as in the economics and law literature, "self-help measures" i.e. endogenous claim enforcement, are pervasive in private contracts. This is quite contrary to the conventional wisdom among international relations scholars, neo-classical economists and "pure theorists" of law who all, in one way or another, identify "self-help" with anarchy and consider the existence of either exogenous enforcement or of self-help as the main distinguishing characteristic of the domestic and the international arenas respectively. But not only is this dichotomy heuristically not very useful, as it makes the existence of order virtually a function of a particular kind of enforcement, it is also essentially misleading. If self-help is a rather pervasive phenomenon in both arenas, i.e. not limited to the exceptional circumstances of "self-defence", then self-help can neither be used as a defining property of international anarchy, nor can central enforcement institutions be exclusively credited for the existence of order or for the beneficial functioning of "markets".

Consider in this context a second type of spot contract, i.e. one which entails sequential performance. This is Hobbes' classical description of Prisoners' Dilemma situations. Aware of the dangers of being played for a sucker, the parties might not want to rely on costly *ex post* litigation but devise measures which alleviate the dangers of being exploited: they can agree on payment schedules, escrow arrangements, or resort to limited acts of retaliation such as notifying the Better Business Bureau, or ruining the delinquent party's credit.

It is probably no exaggeration to consider the credit reporting system as *the* most important disciplining force in our society in which credit cards and, in general, access to credit (given the low savings rate) have become a virtual necessity. The horror stories which appear periodically in the papers dealing with the consequences of erroneous credit reports make it clear that it is the effects of these private means of enforcement rather than the club of the state that keeps most of us in line. In cases in which neither the loss of reputation nor actual denial of access to future credit serves as a sufficient motivating force to honour one's obligation, resort to more stringent means of private enforcement is sometimes a viable option. Repossession by private agents acting as enforcers of the authoritative decisions of public authorities show an interesting symbiotic relationship of public and private elements in some areas of domestic "self-help".

Internationally, we possess similar remedies such as e.g. publicity – a measure in which Jeremy Bentham put considerable trust, despite its dubious efficacy in all but a few extreme cases of shunning and branding states as "pariahs" – unilateral counter-measures, such as the suspension of treaties, freezing of assets, the enforcement of arbitral awards through domestic institutions, and various other unfriendly acts falling into the categories of retorsion or reprisals.[9] Similar to domestic contract law, however, self-help measures have been limited since the inception of the Charter regime and the ICJ *Corfu Channel*[10] decision, to measures not involving the use of force. Self-defence and action authorized by the Security Council are the obvious exceptions.[11] The only other exception is perhaps intervention in case of the rescue of one's own nationals in instances of a credible threat to their safety and the inability of the foreign government to provide for minimum conditions of civil order.[12]

[. . .]

Further complications arise when we examine "long-term" iterated transactions. If, as is likely, not all contingencies can be exhaustively listed and dealt with, the contract will have to include catch-all concepts and quite non-specific, higher order "principles". Again the problem of endogenous enforcement arises, precisely because both the attempts to stipulate contingencies and their enforcement through the courts become costly, as Llewellyn has pointed out in his famous "What price Contract?" article.[13] Instead of a direct *quid pro quo* the parties face two interrelated problems: the commitment to keep the contractual relationship going which, in turn, frames the distributive bargaining problem at each iteration. It is clear that the parties will be able to maintain such a relationship only if they agree to dispute settlement "in a businesslike" or "amicable fashion". But beyond such an agreement in principle they must share fairly concrete common understandings as to what these principles mean in certain "typical situations". Here precedent, customary ways, salience, etc. are all important in particularising the higher order principles.

If situations cannot be typified, if they are not recurrent enough to develop settled ways of dealing with them, the contract becomes more and more a framework for continuous negotiation rather than an historic document which freezes the "meeting of the wills" of the parties at a given time. An example for this latter type of "long-term contract" in the international arena was SALT II. First, "enforcement" had to be entirely endogenous (national means of verification!) and compliance was based virtually entirely on "discovery" rather than on measures we traditionally associate with "enforcement". Second, since facts seldom speak for themselves but need interpretation particularly if "intent" is at issue (was it a "mistake" or a "deception"?), some method of arriving at a shared understanding becomes necessary. Third, since most of these situations could not readily be typified because they concerned technological innovations or unprecedented events (such as the building of the Krasnoyarsk radar stations), (re)negotiation of the terms of the contract became a characteristic of this particular arms control regime.[14] Commentators have not only correctly pointed to the essential part played by the Standing Group in Geneva[15] dealing with complaints about alleged violations, but have also suggested that a distinction existed between SALT as a treaty and SALT as a process. The last point was vividly brought home by the fact that SALT continued to provide the operative framework even after the "treaty" had expired.

Another interesting case in point is GATT which served as the basis for the post-war multilateral trading order. Its viability and actual resiliency over the years is hardly conceivable without both the various negotiating "rounds", creating new specific norms on the basis of the general principles of the initial "incomplete contract", and the crucial role of its dispute settling mechanisms.[16] While these chambers have certainly not "enforced" anything, they have created a large body of "standard solutions" for dealing with trade disputes.[17] Indeed, one can argue that over the years a certain "evolution" has taken place in which the chambers have moved increasingly from consensual (mediational) procedures to the more principled application of "norms" and standard solutions to a controversy.

Given the difficulties that arise for endogenous enforcement of incomplete contracts, in particular when the participants face a highly volatile environment, the development of customary practices is difficult; or when asymmetries of information create incentives for actors to act with guile, a radically new "contractual" solution can be tried. Consider in this context the "complex incomplete contract". Instead of iterated rounds of bargains providing for re-negotiation and dispute settlement, this type of contract is based on an exchange of promises of the parties which explicitly changes the *quality* of their relationship.

A good example of this type of contract is the wage contract. On the surface it is an exchange (labour for money), but it is also an incomplete contract that involves a "long-term" relationship with all the attendant difficulties of endogenous enforcement. After all, hiring people and paying them a salary or wage instead of relying on contracts for procuring the needed goods and services creates a "firm". This means that the employer not only acquires the labour power of the employee, but obtains the right of directing it. Labour has not only its price like any other commodity – a point crucial for Marxists – but, more importantly, for our purposes, the wage contract amounts to an exchange of money for the employer's *authority*. The parties cease to enjoy equal status precisely because the contract entails explicit inequality in decision-making power. Employees have to defer to the authoritative directives of their "boss"; they can no longer object to specific commands, or bargain over them because in the incomplete contract which exchanged "work" for a wage, broad areas of discretion were left to the employer to determine what "work" entails.

This authority though is not unlimited; it is circumscribed in a variety of ways. First, there is the limitation of "time" stipulated by the "working" hours. Second, there are substantive limits of discretion, such as those that govern the ability of an employer to ask his secretary to type a letter or even perhaps to make coffee, but they prohibit a solicitation of personal favours even if these demands fall within the time period covered by the employment contract. Third, limits are created to regulate hazardous activities, and there are health codes, injunctions against child labour, etc. Finally, there are normative definitions of what constitutes the scope of "managerial" (owner) directive power, and less formally articulated, but nevertheless important understandings of "how things are done". The latter rest on both experiential and/or technical knowledge and on customary conceptions of what can be expected from a worker. Thus, bosses have only limited opportunities to "pull rank" before their commands engender resistance, and if their directives do not make sense in terms of customary trade practices they will not be followed even if they are innovative or efficient. Indeed, the work force has to be "brought around" by persuasion and inducements.

In other words, since a principal/agent problem exists in the complex incomplete contract, the *de facto* terms of the "exchange" result largely from the sanctions, surveillance and a variety of other self-help measures which cannot be transferred to exogenous enforcement. While the employer can exchange money for work he cannot "make" the employee work, or "sue" or fire him for not giving his best. Rather, employers have to rely on surveillance (quotas), incentives (bonuses), threats (probationary period, contract renewal) and/or stipulation of work rules (particularly important in organisations operating in non-market environments, i.e. bureaucracies).

Against these measures, passive resistance, "yesing" the boss to death, reporting to "upstairs" what they want to hear, and – particularly in the case of bureaucracies – "working by the book" (slow-downs) are quite effective counter-strategies. Thus, while the reliance of hierarchy on command rather than exchange certainly creates "efficiencies" in some respects, it also often generates a perverse incentive system explained by the research on organisational pathologies.[18] These range from misreporting and non-compliance with directives to the extreme case of outright sabotage. Firms and bureaucracies have therefore found it necessary to inculcate feelings of "loyalty" into the employees, and rely on appeals to a "corporate culture".[19]

Finally, particular difficulties arise in assessing the efficiency of non-market organizations. They share with firms not only the endogenous enforcement problem of the incomplete wage contract, but have to face, in addition, problems resulting from the absence of a market "discipline". Since the output of the organisation is not directly related to the satisfaction of the consumers (who create through their "purchases" the resources (inputs) for the firm), the funding of the bureaucratic organisation depends to a large extent on its ability to mobilise resources from groups which are not their clients. Heads of agencies know that ties to congressional leaders are more important than customer satisfaction. In public interest or "third sector" organisations, resource mobilisation depends upon the ability of the leadership to tap into latent sympathies in the environment of the organisation. They have to persuade people or groups to contribute to various "causes" with virtually no control of the donors over the organisation's "product", i.e. its performance. While the "agency" problem, i.e. endogenous enforcement of the wage contract, is lessened if most employees are highly motivated individuals dedicated to the "cause", managing according to a "chain of command" template is virtually impossible in these organisations. In case of conflict over priorities and programs which operationalise and implement the organisational "goals", disagreements become immediately "political". Various leaders and factions will try to rally support, start intrigues, personalise the "fight", etc.; in short, they will attempt to outflank hierarchical decision control. If there is a solution, it will usually involve "exit" of one of the factions, a "sacrifice" of one of its leaders, or the establishment of a new consensus by often laborious negotiations.

These considerations have particular importance for the functioning of international organisations. First, a "contract" among states establishes, in the "charter", the organization's "domain", within which the organization is supposed to exercise its "powers". Second, this delineation is not only dependent upon the consensus among the sponsors but on the availability of technical knowledge which defines "functionally" the specific tasks. For example, Peter Cowhey has shown that the operation of the traditional telecommunications regime "implemented" by the International Telecommunications Union (ITU) was crucially dependent upon the accepted view of natural monopolies (which served as the underpinning in the creation of national Postal and Telecommunications authorities), and the resulting "technical problems" of linking national telecommunications networks through compatible switches. The establishment of the ITU in 1932 resulted in an organization in which engineers debated the technical rules and standards for the functioning of the existing networks and their linkage. At most they speculated about the adequacy of the allocation system for radio frequencies and orbital satellite slots. Although, technically speaking, the resulting "standards" were recommendations only and not "directives", the three expert bodies charged with these duties could largely proceed with technical and bureaucratic modes of decision-making, until well into the 1970s.

Change came from two sources: one from the increasingly eroding consensus that telecommunications indeed represented natural monopolies, a doubt powerfully reinforced by the emerging notion that "services" should be treated like "goods"; and two, from the new technologies of satellite and digital transmission that made it possible to bypass the switches linking national networks.[20] Both elements ushered in the end of the old telecommunications regime and upset the merely "technical" mission of the ITU. It became a forum for debates rather than a functional organisation in which authoritative decision-making is legitimised by "knowledge" of the relevant technology.

The last point brings to the fore the importance of consensual knowledge and the role of epistemic communities in institutionalising such a consensus in organisational structures and routines. These factors have been investigated by Ernst and Peter Haas.[21] It also shows that in an arena in which a domain consensus is either non-existent, or is fragmented by constitutional provisions, formal organisations will have to internalise the formation of such a consensus by providing for an appropriate forum. Ann-Marie Burley has shown that the organisational design of some of the functional organisations of the UN not only differs from the old international union model, but that its templates were the regulatory agencies of the New Deal.[22] These agencies had been designed to overcome the constitutionally mandated fragmentation of an issue area by combining legislative and executive functions in the new domain of the regulatory agency. The curious design of traditional IGOs which combines an assembly (for debate and consensus) with a council (giving shape to the "mission" of the organisation) and the "staff" (secretariat) charged with the support of the council and the administration (implementation) of some policies, is an attempt to satisfy these conflicting demands. But since bolting together different organisational designs is not the same as finding a truly integrative solution for decision-making, we should not be surprised that these different organisational forms often work at cross purposes.

Most obvious are the problems in the case of the multipurpose universal membership organisations such as the League and the United Nations.[23] There is first the General Assembly as an organ to debate and provide for the collective legitimisation of issues.[24] The Security Council represents, in a way, the directors setting policy to be implemented by personnel assigned to the organisation, either through earmarking troops and subjecting them to the machinery of Chapter VII, or to the more administrative personnel hired by the Secretary-General. It is not surprising that the former has never been tried and that the increase of direct managerial control by e.g. the Secretary-General of UNESCO has been cited as an instance of the "politicisation" of the organisation.[25]

However, most of the time, politicisation charges indicate a disagreement about the priorities of the United Nations. This is amply demonstrated by the challenge for developing nations to make the organisation serve their goal of development by redesigning the international economic order[26] rather than addressing only, or primarily, "peace and security" issues. In the case of more specialised agencies, "politicisation" concerned largely the issue of a vanishing domain consensus. For example, the quest for a New Information Order raised the fundamental issue whether information should be treated as a good supplied by private individuals and market mechanisms or as one which is subject to state regulation.[27] Similarly, addressing issues outside the original organisational domain was held to exceed the bounds of legitimacy. Under such circumstances, sponsors of the organisation have the option to resort to voice (including the withholding of funds) or to loyalty (holding exit at bay and activating voice) as means for establishing domain consensus, but both of these options are strengthened by the threat of a credible "exit".[28]

Another set of problems concerns the issue of coordination. Proposals for organisational reform have a long history in the UN system with the Bertrand report serving as only one of the most recent examples. However, given the complex parameters of this organisation, opportunities for actual reorganisation are here, even more so than in domestic politics, severely limited.[29] Furthermore, by arguing for "reform" of the organisational structures implementing the regime, one makes a subtle but important shift by implying the permanence of the regime which, so to speak, provides the "constitutional frame" for the organisations within it. This raises the question: can constitutional frames still be understood through the contractual metaphor, or does the rapid increase of theoretical inconsistencies critically undermine the consent argument as the basic template to understand social order? It is the task of the next section to address these issues.

III. Constitutional contracts: the problem of rule and consent

Enduring commitments based on a promise are often interpreted in contractual terms. In this context the institution of marriage and the "social contract" founding either "society" or the public authority of a "government" are the most prominent examples. In addition, at least one historically powerful tradition existed, which amalgamated the establishment of political rule on "patriarchal power" supposedly characteristic of the institution of marriage. In the following comments I do not want to follow this line of thought by tracing the role of Filmer's *Patriarcha*[30] in Locke's conception of the "double contract". Rather, I want to investigate the problem of whether issues of fundamental political rights and obligations can be based on the contractual paradigm. I begin with the marriage "contract" and then discuss "constitutional" contracts and the question of "justice" which arises in this context.

Is marriage really a contract, or are the specific features of this relationship amalgamated to the contractual paradigm only with great difficulty? At first, the voluntariness and the exchange of promises seems to fit it squarely within the contractual template. But a short reflection shows that, at least under modern conditions, neither a specific iterated exchange nor the creation of an authority relationship is implied, though exchanges will be part of the ongoing concern of the parties. True, traditional societies believed in the authority of the *pater familias* and the justified subordination of his wife and children under his authority; legitimised by the special concern for the well-being of those not able to make their own decisions (women and children). Apologists for patriarchal authority in the state also made recourse to the special bond created by the marriage in order to bolster traditional rule. But as Locke was quick to point out against Filmer, if marriage is based on a contract, then it can be dissolved, when the couple has raised and cared for their children.

The last issue is of particular importance since at least part of our understanding of the institution of marriage implies that the "contract" is not easily revocable if the parties' preferences change. Rather, what seems to be an important part of this institution is a commitment to the relationship "for better or for worse". The contract is not limited in scope to a set of specific activities or an identifiable time period. Rather it is conceived as a commitment to become a certain type of person, a "life-partner" for the other. Aside from the question of intimacy which thereby becomes possible, and which goes well beyond even unspecified contractual obligations, the other important element here is that the relationship as such presupposes the "endogenisation" of the contracting parties' preferences.

The language of contract becomes thereby strained and its relevance is limited to the disposal of assets brought to or acquired during the marriage in case the couple is unable to sustain the relationship. But here again, it is either a new "agreement" among the parties (rather than the original contract) or the fiat of the public authority that usually sets the terms, ranging from the property settlement to the custody of children.

The conceptual difficulties multiply when we conceive of constitutional order in terms of the contractual paradigm. Several of the difficulties which already entered the picture of the marriage contract create new difficulties. One is the question of the indefinite duration of the "contract". This is further aggravated by the fact that, unlike real persons, "societies" as ongoing and trans-generational concerns do not die. Second, the problem arises of duties we might have in the absence of actual exchanges, or even of some notions of what our preferences are since we do not know who *we* will be.

Third, unlike marriage, which has a clear inception, many constitutional orders cannot point to a clear instance of "contracting" among the parties particularly if obedience to "the law" is predicated upon the consent given by a former generation. Thus, consent is inferred by all types of devices from holding property to even travelling in a country, as these examples taken from Locke suggest.

But such constructions designed to impose obligations on people who through their action supposedly "consent" to the exercise of authority are unconvincing unless it can be shown that a rule existed which makes such behaviour a sign of consent and thereby "implies" a contract.

Fourth, our confidence in both the explanatory power and normative pull of such a use of contractual language is not enhanced when, instead of actual or implied contracts, "hypothetical" contracts are constructed. These analytical devices are supposed to clarify what type of rights and obligations we have as "citizens" of a well ordered society.

The last point leads us to the fifth difficulty which strains the contractual metaphor: its inability to provide for a clear delineation of members who are party to the contract. Who are the relevant others with whom I agree to contract and who might therefore acquire the right to "outvote" me next time around? Thus, while the contract is supposed to explain the emergence of a group either as a "society" or as a political organisation, it is painfully obvious that without a preliminary delineation of "membership" the idea of contract becomes incoherent in a multiparty situation. Finally, since the participants of the constitutional contract are not exchanging tangible assets or identifiable services but choosing constitutional principles of justice, the hypothetical contract soon has to be supplemented by the construction of *hypothetical actors*. Since such a construction has some very disturbing implications for individuals, as well as for the domestic and international order, it might be useful to examine these difficulties in greater detail.

Let us begin with the problem of implied consent. It arises, for instance, in a conflict of law situation, when a state seeks to assert personal jurisdiction on the basis of the behaviour of the defendant. But when a state defends its jurisdictional authority on the basis of "implied consent" by the individual as a condition for the permission to enter the country, then, as Lea Brilmayer correctly points out,

This implicit assumption amounts to a prior assumption of state territorial sovereignty. Only a state that has territorial sovereignty may condition entrance upon consent to obey the law. If the state possesses territorial sovereignty, however, reliance on defendant's consent, whether explicit or implicit is unnecessary. Consent is largely superfluous; indeed, it only serves to mask the fact that territorial sovereignty provides the real basis for the exercise of personal jurisdiction.[31]

Similarly, when the members of the General Council of the New Model Army – historically the *locus classicus* for contract arguments – gathered at Putney in 1647 and debated the questions of the legitimate powers of a government, Ireton used the foreigner's obligation to obey the English laws passed by "English land holders' as counterfactual against the radical theory of universal consent as the basis of obligation. He thereby not only pointed to the problem that contract presupposes a prior assignment of rights, but, in addition, by focusing on landed property, he also avoided the radical implication that territoriality, seen merely as a container for persons in their natural equality, defined without further qualifications membership in the group contracting for governmental powers. Against the demands of the first article of the *Agreement* which provided for equal representation of "every man that is an inhabitant", Ireton argued forcefully that only those with a "permanent fixed interest in the kingdom" should be allowed to vote. In Ireton's case this permanent fixed interest was based on "property" and not on any universalist notion of an "absolute natural right" which attaches to them *qua* persons rather than *qua* members of a civil society united by "civil right".

[. . .]

This is not the place to follow the changes that occur when "property" no longer means "fixity" of place (that ties people together by necessity), but becomes the collective name for a variety of arrangements (including even intangible assets valued solely for their "exchange" potential). The implications of the ascendancy of "wealth" over the original notion of property as "rootedness" have been well elaborated by Hannah Arendt.[32] As a matter of fact, the hold of land on our imagination seems unusually firm. "Land" not only provides people a "place in the world" which forces people to address their common problems and to engage in cooperative ventures, but it also becomes a symbol of continuity and an assurance of transgenerational connectedness. Thus, "the land" becomes one of the most powerful symbols of identification, invoked frequently in national anthems and in countless allusions contained in tales and folklore that contribute to the creation of a collective memory.

A further issue, equally troublesome to contract and consent theory, is the problem of how to bound the new power, i.e. authority, resulting from this complex incomplete *and* indefinite contract. On the surface, the sovereign resulting from the social contract is simply the enforcer of the rights and exchanges among its subjects. But even Hobbes knows that such a conceptualization evades the problem of "sovereignty" which means that, unlike private incomplete contracting, an authority is created that can decide *what its own competency is*. This obviously entails many new dimensions of authority including that of modifying the framework for "private" contracting, acting against hold-outs without their consent, or even modifying or overriding certain of their presumed rights, such as their property (by levying taxes), their choice of religion or their freedom of speech. Such a *"plenitudo potestatis"* cannot be derived from the concept of the sovereign as an "enforcer" of private rights.

Thus, while the language of contract is used, it is "functional necessity" rather than consent in any meaningful sense that informs Hobbes' analysis. He never tires of emphasising that only in this fashion can the sovereign create peace and the preconditions of commodious living, so eagerly sought by the subjects leaving the state of nature. Only by virtue of this authority, i.e. as the "fixer" of signs and meaning, can the sovereign avoid internal dissent and conflict. This exercise of power can neither be restrained nor can it be rationally opposed. "Law" is not only what the sovereign says it is, but the obligations arising from his commands are paramount (except in the limiting case in which physical self-preservation is at stake).

[. . .]

Some of these problems arise even in the international arena, i.e. in the absence of government but not "governance". Even here, law-making treaties adduce interpretative canons such as *ut res magis valeat* and "purposes" rather than simply relying on the intentions of the parties. Similarly, in the UN Charter, technically a multilateral treaty, the authority to take measures for peace-keeping has received a "constitutional" interpretation based on notions of functional necessity and "implied powers".

The notion of consent seems to quickly approach the vanishing point. Perhaps Rousseau put it most bluntly, that the social contract implies an *aliénation totale* for the person entering it.[33] [. . .] As even Locke suggests, "he that has once, by actual agreement, and any express declaration, given his consent to be of any commonweal, is perpetually and indispensably obliged to be and remain unalterably a subject to it".[34] If this is an exercise of my autonomy and consent then it is so only metaphorically. As Don Herzog perceptively pointed out:

> Consent theorists face an imposing structural dilemma, one built into the logic of their framework. They want to say that individuals consent to the government and that consent generates an obligation to obey the law. So they need a conception of consent that is descriptively plausible: they need to point at citizens and show us their consent. But that conception also needs to be normatively robust: whatever counts as consent has to generate an obligation. These two requirements pull in different directions. I can meet skeptical inquiries about whether people really do consent by watering down my notion of consent. But the skeptic will ask

whether *that* bit of consent is enough to generate an obligation. And if I've watered down the notion enough, I will be hard pressed to find a credible affirmative answer. Similarly, if I begin with a conception robust enough to do normative work, I may be hard pressed to say, that in fact people do consent. The consent theorist shares Goldilock's plight trying to find just the right fit. That fit may be unavailable.[35]

Although such a fit might indeed be unavailable, two strategies have traditionally been suggested to solve this problem. One, the insistence on "natural rights" preceding the "contract" and the establishment of "political" control in the exercise of public authority created by the contract. Both strategies can be found in Locke. Thus, while he declares on the one hand, "The supreme power cannot take from any man any part of his property without *his own consent*", on the other hand, when faced with the problems of holdouts and the need to procure "public goods" by means of taxation, he admits,

> governments cannot be supported without great charge, and "tis fit everyone who enjoys his share of protection, should pay out of his estate his portions for the maintenance of it. But still it must be with his own consent, i.e. the consent of the majority, giving it either by themselves, or their representatives chosen by them.[36]

The interesting point in the latter example is not only that Locke transforms the need of individual consent into one of a parliamentary majority, but that the idea of "representation" is thereby fundamentally changed. Different from the old conception of "making" present the majesty of the realm, the representatives now simply become controllers of policy; elections are no longer acclamations but rather increasingly decide controversies about the direction and scope of public authority. However, ultimately the power of members of parliament to oblige their constituents through a majority vote seems to derive more from the notion of their corporate capacity as representatives of the entire body politic than from consent via the delegation of consent by their constituents.

There remains therefore, the intractable difficulty of squaring the obligatory force, resulting from majority decision, with the paradigm of "consent". How can we meaningfully say that someone "consented" when he and his representatives were not only outvoted but had actively opposed the adopted policy? If in following the "self-imposed" law I am merely abiding by my resolution to follow the commands of a majority, whatever that might entail, then such obedience is hardly an exercise of autonomous choice. On the contrary, it looks much more like the simple submission to be a slave. Again, the tension between the notion that a contract is binding as a *result of a procedure* or on the basis of the result it tends to achieve re-emerges.

The only way to lessen the severity of this dilemma is to re-introduce cognitive factors into the voluntarist account and to move from the *actual consent of real persons* to an argument of hypothetical consent, i.e. that a decision would obtain assent if the actors were actually aware of the relevant considerations. This is, of course, the route taken by natural law, but can also be found in Rousseau's cryptic remark that the "general will" can never err and that under proper procedures majority rule would lead to the "discovery" of the general will (as opposed to merely the *volonté de tous*).[37]

Another, perhaps more sceptical version, is the appeal to the "ancient constitution", or the limitation of the discretion which inevitably forms part of "authority" through the explicit exemption of at least certain areas from its domain by ensconcing "right" which serve as bars to the exercise of public authority. The rights themselves are then either "self-evident" or natural. A decision of the public authority deserves our respect and justly imposes obligation not because we have either explicitly, or implicitly consented, but because *"reasonable" or rational men or women would consent* to such a decision.

While such a construction alleviates some of the problems, it leaves us in the lurch when "rights" conflict or when persons claim or allege rights that are non-evident to others. Under such circumstances, the justification has to rely increasingly on the "fairness" of the procedure by which the decision was made, rather than on the assertion of self-evident underlying factors.

One of the most elaborate and sophisticated versions of this cognitive reconstruction of the voluntarist contract paradigm is of course Rawls' contract in the "original position". But in a way there is a striking resemblance between this version of contractarianism and "legalism", i.e. the notion that obligations result from following rules and norms in a principled fashion. Not only is the question of obligation transformed into the cognitive issue of validity of norms and their "fair" application, but consent as the basis of obligation is pushed to the margin. It figures only as a validating reason for the "basic norm" which is "accepted" as in Kelsen's pure system of law, or as the ground for the duty imposing character of principles chosen behind the "veil of ignorance". Having thereby entered "Law's Empire",[38] we must not only take "rights seriously"[39] but the problem of the scope and limits of public authority is no longer a matter of bargaining, compromise or the acceptance of solutions actual people can live with. It is rather the task of "rule-handlers" who are charged with the "Herculean" task of arriving at a correct solution by being neutral as to the substantive definitions of the "salus publica" and by insisting on the primacy of "justice" as procedural fairness over any other value.

At this point it may be useful to take one step back and examine more closely the conceptual transformation that has occurred in conceiving of the "constitutional" contract in such a fashion. First, it seems clear that much of the persuasive power of this construction results from the linkage between two powerful metaphors; that of a "game" constituted by rules, and that of contract. Second, the purpose is clearly to provide a transcendental foundation for the primacy of justice as fairness, instead of relying on the problematic link between the logic internal to the system of rules and the "sociological" fact of acceptance of the *Grundnorm* or on the "normative force of facticity". Similarly, the reduction of issues of legitimacy to a question of overall utility is logically faulty because such purely instrumental reasoning is incompatible with the notion of "rights" as trumps against both public and private claims.

But if the intention of such a constitutional construct is Kantian it is considerably more ambitious than the Kantian categorical imperative serving as the transcendental criterion in our assessment of duties. While Kant's imperative can be used to evaluate certain practices after they have gained currency in a society – and how successful such an enterprise is, remains highly debatable – it cannot constitute them and, *a fortiori*, it cannot be used for setting up a society, as the social and the constitutional contract pretends to do. Kant seems quite clear that "*pure reason* which legislates a priori" is the transcendental principle – rather than contract as such, or common goals (such as happiness) – which justifies public authority.[40] Similarly, while Kant's postulate to treat others as ends rather than as means has been translated by liberal theorists to mean respect for other persons and their "rights", a more accurate reading suggests that Kant's respect is centred on the morality of "law" and thus much more on the "worthy" parts of persons in so far as they order their actions and lives in conformity with moral ends, rather than on their rights per se. To that extent the Kantian respect for persons only partly "operates as the practice of respect for rights and integrity that is admired by so many"[41] liberal theorists who have adopted him as one of "their" canonical writers. But if this is so, then the primacy of justice seems much less defensible than most "liberal" legalists suggest.

The crucial question then is whether the concept of a constitutional contract overcomes these difficulties and can provide a coherent account of duties and obligations flowing from the adoption of principles of justice. Rawls is clear about the fact that such a "contract" must be of a special kind in order to deal with the problem of "the further question" (yes it is a contract, but is it just?), or the problematic argument that it is simply an agreement to keep agreements. For this purpose, Rawls not only chooses a hypothetical contract but places the parties behind a veil of ignorance to mask their knowledge of their own capacities, risk propensities, and likely position in the society for which they are to choose the principles of justice.

Through this device, the contract is doubly hypothetical since it brings together hypothetical actors, i.e. persons who have been stripped of their individuating differences – in Rawlsian terms they are "theoretically defined"[42] in a hypothetical choice situation. The choice in the original position is to "nullify the effects of specific contingencies which put men at odds and tempt them to exploit social and natural circumstances".[43] Thus there is no bargaining, actually not even a discussion. Since each of the participants is "equally rational, and similarly situated, each is convinced by the same arguments".[44] The result is that under such circumstances the principles of justice as "fairness" are adopted "unanimously".

At this point one justifiably gets nervous. After all, why should anyone feel obliged by the results of a "contract" in which hypothetical actors chose in ignorance? What does it mean to talk in that case of "agreement"? Gone is not only Rawls' original commitment to "reasonable empiricism" on which he insisted against Kant's metaphysical presuppositions (transcendental deduction), gone also is the assumption of diversity among persons, which was the main reason for preferring a deontological scheme of rules, in particular of rights, rather than a utilitarian criterion.[45] After utilitarianism was (correctly) dismissed for "extending to society the principle of choice for one man"[46] we can only be surprised by Rawls' admission that the adoption of principles of justice is "unanimous", or even stranger still, that it is tantamount to the "choice" of *one* person, *any person*, taken at random. He writes: "Therefore we can view the choice in the original position from the standpoint of one person taken at random. If anyone after due reflection prefers a conception of justice, then they all do, and a unanimous agreement can be reached".[47]

The attractiveness of this type of hypothetical contract for legalists dealing with difficult constitutional issues is obvious. The popularity of such "contractual" thinking is not merely superficial, but has obvious implications for a "legalistic" theory of how "law" ought to work, producing clarity and finality of choices. The conjunction of "contract" with the notion of a game suggest that the "finality" of decisions in moral, legal and political affairs results from a simple appeal to some institutional rules, very much as "moves" function in a well-structured game. But, as we all know, judgments in the public and legal spheres can be opposed with good reasons and are therefore considerably more complex than even the "judgment calls" of a "neutral" referee.

This problem becomes painfully obvious when one considers Rawls' categorical denial of "desert" as a valid basis for claims to distributive justice. Since people do not even "possess" their natural assets, no "just" claims can be made on the basis of desert prior to the establishment of particular institutions. Rawls' argument is that natural endowments as well as cultural privileges are accidental and should not be considered as valid, inchoate claims antecedent to the constitutional choice of the principles of justice. In order to ensconce the radical equality of the choosers in the original position and in order to ensure the adoption of the difference principle, Rawls has to argue that a person's natural assets are not his or hers but are actually *owned* by the community.[48] This not only makes for a strange theory of "rights", it also makes "the community" a mystical entity far beyond the "organic" conceptions he so ardently opposes. In fact, the perhaps unintended but furtive introduction of substantive criteria, with neither a (logically weak) "communal" (i.e. in terms of, for example, an actual distribution of moral sentiments in a population), nor a (logically strong) "transcendental" justification makes this project based on a contract in the original position incoherent. As John Gray suggests,

> The significance of Rawls' neglect of entitlement and, in general, of historical principles of justice is that, since nowhere does he justify their absence from the list of alternative conceptions of justice he has no independent chain of reasoning which might warrant end state rather than historical principles. The point, then, is not that Rawls' construction of the original position is designed only to yield end state principles, nor yet that his list of alternative principles of justice is far from exhaustive (which Rawls readily admits), but that Rawls' reasoning becomes viciously circular, in so far as he can give no good reasons for accepting stipulations regarding the original position other than that they allow him to derive the outcome he wants.[49]

Finally, the primacy of justice advanced in contractual terms as a voluntary undertaking, is quickly transformed into a simple problem of cognition which, however, far from being "neutral" imposes a particular discipline hidden in the original position. Since the actors in the original position cannot even adopt provisional rules to be revised in the light of subsequent experience, because no matter who enters or when one enters into the original position, the same principles "are always chosen",[50] parties never need to learn. They are always assured of a "right perspective" on the issues that might arise. A nearly Hobbesian quiet settles over the entire enterprise. The institutions based on the principles of justice become the fixers of meanings. Now that everything has been rendered predictable and reduced to the "administration of justice" what is required is some proper instruction by Herculean teachers of law, and an occasional adjustment of one's vision provided by the "perspective" of the original position [. . .].

IV. The problems of "grand theorising"

This examination of the various forms of contract and the limitations of the contractual paradigm when extended to "constitutional contracts" has hopefully, even if only indirectly, strengthened my argument against "grand theories" in general, and against an overarching "legal" theory in particular. I have attempted to engage in a type of theorising that is thematically open but sharply focused. It is open in that it does not take for granted the traditional disciplinary limitations, such as those existing between law, politics or philosophy. But I have resisted advancing a new grand or integrated "theory" by keeping the investigation focused on a fairly well developed institution and examining systematically the problems that arise from the conceptual extensions of the notions of contract and consent.

This procedure allowed me to address a variety of issues whose connectedness usually eludes us because of the blinders thrown up by "disciplines".

One such issue was "self-help" in the domestic arena which is usually neg-lected by both neo-classical economics – as many of the beneficial effects of the general equilibrium model only hold if "exogenous" claim enforcement can be "assumed" – and by political science, precisely because the discipline of international politics is characterised by anarchy and self-help in stark contrast to the domestic arena.

But the disciplining force of the established "fields" goes still further. Even the traditional definition of international law as "a body of rules binding upon states' becomes an accomplice in this distortion of understanding social reality. It attempts to separate a "set of rules", in terms of a "system", outside the context of shaping interactions. By this very distinction, such an attempt enters into a symbiotic relationship with similar efforts to cleanse inter-national politics of most of its normative elements and founding its auton-omy on "power", the distribution of capabilities, or whatever. The connec-tion of "great debates", – such as the one between "utopians" and "realists"[51] in the interwar and post WWII era – and the establishment of disciplinary boundaries becomes visible. Although proponents of such disciplinary boundaries differed, of course, on many significant points, both shared a peculiar understanding of "politics" and "law" that valorised the disciplinary boundaries.

Utopians, as long as they were good legalists – and were not exclusively comprised of social activists, fundamentalists, or Marxists – argued that unless all politics is transformed into the paradigm of "just" action no stabil-isation of expectations, crucial for the establishment and maintenance of social order, is possible. For international politics the agenda seemed clear: if not world government, at least "war" had to be outlawed. Furthermore, the uncompromising character of justice made it impossible to subject the role of unprincipled adjustments that are part of social life but depend on bargain-ing or even coercion, to critical appraisal. There was either justice or chaos.

The flip side of this argument was of course, that "an entirely extravagant image of politics, as essentially a species of war, has to be maintained. Only thus can the sanctity of rule-following as a social policy be kept from com-promising associations".[52] This was then grist to the mill of "realists" who defined politics in terms of the limiting situation of "emergency" and of the fundamental distinction between friend and foe (Carl Schmitt),[53] as the *libido dominandi* (Reinhold Niebuhr),[54] or the idea that force is the first and fore-most "ratio" in the international arena (Waltz).[55] Thus the autonomy of the political sphere is based on the foundationalist assumption of politics as potential physical violence.

This is after all why today's realists claim that the brutal killings we see in Bosnia/Herzegovina dampen not only our optimism concerning the advent of a new world order, but "prove" the correctness of neo-realist theory.[56] Thus "anarchy", with its concomitant security dilemma, remains the master key that unlocks the "Sesame" of international politics.[57] But contrary to (neo)realism's assertions, there is no singular logic of "anarchy" nor does self-help mean the resort to force. Even internationally, the "structural" conflicts between Germany and France, and between France and England have been transformed. What we witness today is rather a security community in which resort to force becomes unimaginable.[58] Furthermore, groups that are suddenly faced with the issue of securing their own way of life after secession or central government collapse, have not *inevitably* interpreted their situation as a security dilemma. Why are some of the more benign outcomes so facilely ignored? Sweden and Norway parted amicably in 1905, and their relations probably have been better since. The Czech and Slovak republics were able to work out a "velvet divorce", even Quebec and Canada, as well as Catalonia, the Basque region and Spain could compromise. Although their relations are certainly full of tension, it is equally certain that they are not appropriately characterised by the "anarchical" logic of a security dilemma.

Underlying such misinterpretations is, of course, the nearly metaphysical assumption that such anomalies are only temporary respites from the inexorable logic that forces "units" to become alike. But contrary to formulations which consider the "nation-state" to be the rule, this organisational form has always been the exception. Historical experience shows that the theoretical equivalence of nation and state has always been contestable, that it has been *actively* contested, and that, at present, the logics of sovereignty and "nationalism" are heading in different directions. This is a phenomenon that ought to be investigated by an adequate "theory" of international politics, but the "evolutionary" logic of the international system entitles our present scholars in the "discipline" to pay only the scantiest attention to "real" politics. As in the world of true love, reality increasingly proves nothing.

Meanwhile legalists are busy at work promoting human rights by drafting new documents and advocating the establishment of new judicial institutions for their "enforcement". As is fitting for "liberals", here, as anywhere else, "more" is better than "less" and, therefore all that is required is to transform anything desirable either by a conceptual extension or by a new draft convention into a "right". From there it is then easy to construe not only a licence but a duty whose determination is entrusted to legal experts, without much attention to the social realities or even the intervening conceptual problems.

Thus, extravagant claims are made for "the people's" right to "democratic" participation,[59] and third parties' interventions for violations of human rights are justified by a simple "liberation of Paris principle": if the "people" throw flowers intervention by outsiders is okay, if they throw bottles or anything else, it is illegal.[60] Unfortunately, such parodies of analysis are not uncommon, resulting directly from a particular mode of approaching issues. The legalist's work is done as soon as he has, in true Kelsenian fashion, established something as a "right" or a "delict", or asserted that "human dignity" is impaired by the violation of guaranteed human rights. But since, even domestically, the status of justice as the supreme virtue is contested, "law's empire" is often felt to be little more than legal imperialism, often ensconcing policies of dubious value. It is therefore not surprising that different cultures, in which the concepts of law, courts, the insistence on rights and adversarial procedures, resonate much less than in the Western tradition, are hard to convince that behind the universalist claims of human rights is only the imperialism of law, and not imperialism pure and simple.

In contra-distinction to the ideal that there are "solutions" in accordance with legal justice, the dilemmas of politics fail to be silenced. Examples come readily to mind: the (Haitian) refugee problem, Somalia and the Bosnian crisis. In the latter case our tolerance for cognitive dissonance is severely tested when we see that under the auspices of the same organisation, one set of lawyers is busy preparing the documents for prosecuting as war criminals the very same persons with whom another set of jurisconsults attempts to mediate the dispute. Apparently the problem of establishing the conditions of social coexistence among groups, caught in the throes of a violent struggle, is somewhat more complicated than serving "justice" by enlarging "law's empire", or even of enforcing some of its basic injunctions.

Against these "grand" theories [. . .] I have advanced more modest claims based on the careful analysis of the logic of institutions. Grand theories, whether legal or political, are usually not very helpful precisely because as "grand" theories they tend to "normalise" discordant facts instead of making them occasions for further analytical development.

Nowhere does this become clearer than in the case of the thorny issue of a right to "self-determination". The normalization of international relations theory consists in leaving the connection between nation and state unexplored and by representing problems of ethnicity and nationalism as appendices to the well known "anarchy" problematic. Legalism on the other hand, even if it takes "rights seriously" misrepresents these problems as "human rights" issues.

Consider in this context the assertion of the Universal Declaration of Human Rights which provides: "everyone has the right to take part in the government of his country directly through freely chosen representatives".[61] Here the question of self-determination is clearly viewed not only in individualistic terms but as part and parcel of a consent theory to governmental authority. But even if we agree that the right to self-determination might indeed be an individual right, it does not follow that it has much to do with participation in government. Only if we assume a complete identity between two sets of distinctive memberships, i.e. the nation and the citizen, does this inference follow. Here, the lack of an articulated theory of community and the criteria of membership, (despite their logical necessity for any contract theory), becomes visible.

One need not be an adherent of the communitarian critique of contractarianism in order to appreciate the conceptual befuddlement in this area. As Tamir aptly put it,

> . . . self-rule and national self-determination are two distinct concepts. They differ in their individualistic and communal aspects, represent two

distinct human goods and derive their value from two separate human interests. The individualistic aspect of both of these rights celebrates personal autonomy and the right of individuals. Whereas in the right to self-rule this aspect points to the right of individuals to govern their lives without being subject to external dictates, in the case of self-determination, it concerns the way in which individuals define their personal and national identity.[62]

Thus, many "minorities" striving for self-determination are understandably hard to convince that their struggle is "really" only about voting and civil rights in a community they want to leave without forgoing the claim to some territory (as do refugees). [. . .]

[. . .]

Using the terminology of civil rights in order to protect minorities, the Charter suggests not only that "in a world where individual rights are fully protected, minority groups will not only disappear with time" but also that the nationality problem will "cease to pose a threat to world stability".[63] But is the quest for self-determination really only about territorial claims that can be amalgamated by the traditional logic of "sovereignty"? In short, is the generative logic really one in which "the state" again masters the "nation", or is the present preoccupation with "ethnicity" pointing to the importance of identity which has quite different, but probably equally deep, implications for politics and law as contract and consent? One can reasonably suspect that this is the case, but it is less clear what this would entail for our institutions and concepts of political order and citizenship. This is obviously a problem going far beyond the scope of the present paper and will have to be taken up at another time.

Notes

1 For a comprehensive treatment of the origins of many international legal institutions in private law see Sir H. Lauterpacht, *Private Law Sources and Analogies of International Law* (1927). For a more historical account of the intellectual ancestry of international law see H. Bull, B. Kingsbury and A. Roberts (eds.), *Hugo Grotius and International Relations* (1990). See also C.F. Murphy, *The Search for World Order: A Study of Thought and Action* (1984).
2 For the importance of "standard solutions" for the development of international law see Nicholas Onuf, "Legal Theory", in N. Onuf (ed.), *Global Law-making and Law-making in the Global Community* (1982) 1–82.
3 See, e.g., *Lake Lanoux Case* (Arbitration between France and Spain; 1866 – ILR 101, 1957) and *Trail Smelter Case* (*U.S. v. Canada* – 3 U.N.Rep.Int.Arb.Awards 1911; 1941).
4 This is Hobbes' term in *Leviathan*, Penguin Classics, London (1968) chap. 13.
5 For a discussion of these problems see, for example, the works of P. Atiyah, *The Rise and Fall of Freedom of Contract* (1979); G. Gilmore, *The Death of Contract* (1974); C. Fried, *Contract as Promise* (1981); M. Horowitz, *The Transformation of American Law* (1977) especially chap. 6.
6 Coplin, "International Law and Assumption about the State System", 17 *World Politics* (1965).

7 See my *Rules, Norms, and Decisions* (1989) chap. 4.
8 M. Sandel, *Liberalism and the Limits of Justice* (1982) 106 and 107.
9 For a good discussion of unilateral countermeasures in international law see E. Zoller, *Peacetime Unilateral Remedies* (1984).
10 *United Kingdom v. Albania* (1949) ICJ 4. (a.k.a. *Corfu Channel Case*). See also *Nicaragua v. U.S.* (1985) ICJ 169.
11 For a general discussion see O. Schachter, *International Law in Theory and Practice* (1985) especially chap 7: "The Prohibition of Force". Additionally, see A. Verdross and B. Simma, *Universelles Völkerrecht: Theorie und Praxis* 3rd ed., (1984) especially chap. 12: "Die Erlaubte Selbsthilfe". See also Waldock, "The Regulation of the Use of Force by Individual States", 81 *RdC* (1952-II) 451–517.
12 For a discussion of rescue mission vs. a broader right of "humanitarian intervention" see the discussion of Schachter, "Self-help in International Law: US Action in the Iranian Hostages Crisis", 37 *Journal of International Affairs* (1984) 231–46; Donnelly, "Human Rights, Humanitarian Intervention and American Foreign Policy: Law, Morality and Politics", 37 *Journal of International Affairs* (1984) 311–28; and my "Sovereignty as Dominium: Is there a Right to Humanitarian Intervention", in G. Lyons (ed.), *After Westphalia* (1994 forthcoming).
13 Llewellyn, "What Price Contract: An Essay in Perspective", 40 *Yale Law Journal* (1931) 704–51.
14 For a further exploration of the relation between contracting and regimes see my "Contract and Regimes: Do Issue-specifity and Variations of Formality Matter?", in V. Rittberger (ed.), *Regime Theory and International Relations* (1993) Chapter 4.
15 On the Standing Consultative Commission, see S. Talbott, *Deadly Gambits* (1985) 228–32, 319–21. See also S. Talbott, *Endgame: The Inside Story of Salt II* (1979).
16 For a good discussion of the results of the Tokyo Round of Gatt and its various conventions see J. Grieco, *Cooperation Among Nations: Europe, America, and Non-tariff Barriers to Trade* (1990).
17 See J.H. Jackson, *Restructuring the GATT System* (1990) Part II.
18 The locus classicus for this argument is O. Williamson, *Markets and Hierarchies* (1975).
19 For an excellent discussion of this point see Kreps, "Corporate Culture and Economic Theory", in J. Alt, K. Shepsle (eds), *Rational Perspectives on Positive Political Economy* (1990) 90–143.
20 See Cowhey, "The International Communications Regime: The Political Roots of Regimes for High Technology", 44 *International Organization* (1990) 169–99.
21 See, e.g., E. Haas, "Is there a Hole in the Whole?", 29 *International Organization* (1975) 827–76; and E. Haas, "Why Collaborate?: Issue Linkage and International Regimes", 32 *World Politics* (1980) 357–405; and P.M. Haas, "Do Regimes Matter? Epistemic Communities and Mediterranean Pollution Control", 43 *International Organization* (1989) 377–404.
22 Burley, "Regulating the World: Multilateralism, International Law and the Projection of the New Deal Regulatory State", in J.G. Ruggie (ed.), *Multilateralism Matters: The Theory and Praxis of an Institutional Form* (1993) chap. 4.
23 The history of the underlying ideas for the universal organisation is well-elaborated in David Kennedy, "The Move to Institutions", 8 *Cardozo Law Review* (1987) 841–988.
24 On the importance of collective legitimisation by the UN see Claude, "Collective Legitimization as a Function of the UN", 20 *International Organization* (1966) 267–79.
25 See M. Imber, *The USA, ILO, UNESCO and IAEA: Politicization and Withdrawal in the Specialized Agencies* (1989).
26 See Bhagwati, "Rethinking Global Negotiations", and Ruggie, "Another Round – Another Requiem? Prospects for the Global Negotiations", both in J. Bhagwati

and J.G. Ruggie (eds.), *Power, Passion and Purpose: Prospects for North-South Negotiations* (1984).

27 For a comprehensive discussion of these problems see Drake, Nikolaides, "Ideas, Interests and Institutionalization: Trade in Services and the Uruguay Round", 44 *International Organization* (1992) 37–100.

28 For the fundamental discussion of these strategies see A. Hirschman, *Exit, Voice and Loyalty* (1970).

29 For a survey of the issues dealing with the political rhetoric and reality of reforming the United Nations, see Taylor, "The United Nations System Under Stress: Financial Pressures and their Consequences", 17 *Review of International Studies* (1991) 365–82.

30 R. Filmer, *Patriarcha*, in J. Locke, *Two Treatises of Government*, ed. by T. Cook (1947).

31 Brilmayer, "Consent, Contract, and Territory", 74 *Minnesota Law Review*, No.1 (1989) 1–35; quote at 6.

32 H. Arendt, *The Human Condition* (1958) especially chap. II, sec. 8.

33 J.J. Rousseau, *The Social Contract*, ed. by L. Crocker (1967) Book I, chaps. 8 and 9.

34 J. Locke, *Two Treatises on Government*, ed. by P. Laslett (1970) 365.

35 D. Herzog, *Happy Slaves: A Critique of Consent Theory* (1989) 185.

36 J. Locke, *supra* note 35, at 378, 380.

37 J.J. Rousseau, *supra* note 34, Chapters 3 and 4.

38 R. Dworkin, *The Law's Empire* (1986).

39 See R. Dworkin, *Taking Rights Seriously* (1978).

40 See, e.g., his essay, "On the Common Saying: This May be True in Theory but it Does Not Apply in Practice", in H. Reiss (ed.), *Kant's Political Writings* (1970) 61–92, particularly 73 s.

41 B. Honig, *Political Theory and the Displacement of Politics* (1993) 18.

42 J. Rawls, *A Theory of Justice* (1971) 147.

43 Ibid., at 136.

44 Ibid.

45 Ibid., at 3–4.

46 Ibid., at 28.

47 Ibid., at 139.

48 For a further discussion of some of the implications of this type of "egalitarianism", i.e. *asset egalitarianism*, see Arrow, "Some Ordinalist-Utilitarian Notes on Rawl's Theory of Justice", 70 *Journal of Philosophy* (1973) 245–62. For a trenchant critique of the type of "end state theories of justice" to which such asset egalitarianism gives rise, see R. Nozick, *Anarchy, State, and Utopia* (1974) 155ff.

49 Gray, "Social Contract, Community and Ideology", in J. Gray, *Liberalism: Essays in Political Philosophy* (1991) chap. 3, quote at 32.

50 Rawls, *supra* note 43, at 139.

51 See the reflection on this great debate in E.H. Carr, *The Twenty Years Crisis, 1919–1939* (1964).

52 J. Shklar, *Legalism: Laws, Morals and Political Trials* (1986) 122.

53 C. Schmitt, *Der Begriff des Politischen* (1979) chap. 2.

54 See, e.g., R. Niebuhr, *The Children of Light and the Children of Darkness* (1944) chap. 1.

55 K. Waltz, *Theory of International Politics* (1979) especially 113. For an argument that it is this substantive understanding of politics rather than the "logic" of a generative structure, see my "Errors Have Their Advantages", 38 *International Organization* (1984) 305–20. For recent arguments that "anarchy" is not determinative of outcomes, see A. Wendt, "Anarchy is What States Make of it", 46 *International Organization* (1987) 391–425; and B. Buzan, C. Jones, and R. Little, *The Logic of Anarchy* (1993).

56 Such claims are made by J. Mearsheimer and B. Posen in their recent essays on "hypernationalism". See Mearsheimer, "Back to the Future: Instability in Europe after the Cold War", 15 *International Security* (1990) 5–56, and Posen, "Nationalism, the Mass Army and Military Power", 18 *International Security*, No. 2 (1993).

57 See, i.e., the articles by Mearsheimer and Posen, ibid.

58 See K. Deutsch *et al., Political Community and the North Altlantic Area* (1957), reprinted in *International Political Communities: An Anthology* (1966) 1–92.

59 Fox, "The Right to Political Participation in International Law", Paper presented at the Annual Meeting of the American Political Science Association, Washington, D.C. Sept. 1993.

60 Michael J. Levitin, "The Law of Force and the Force of Law: Grenada, the Falklands, and Humanitarian Intervention", 27 *Harv. Int'l L.J.* (1988) 621–57, at 654.

61 *Universal Declaration of Human Rights*, G.A.Res. 217, 1948.

62 Y. Tamir, *Liberal Nationalism* (1993) 70.

63 As quoted in Tamir, *supra* note 63, at 76.

7 Has the "rule of law" become a "rule of lawyers"?

An inquiry into the use and abuse of an ancient *topos* in contemporary debates

I. Introduction

The argument that a free society should be governed by laws rather than men is one of the oldest political *topoi* – one that has proven its resilience over the centuries. It was used in ancient Greece (in terms of the *nomos basileus* argument),[1] later became part of the republican tradition in Rome, played a decisive role in modernity (as exemplified by Rousseau), powerfully shaped the constitutional struggles in England[2] and the founding of the US,[3] and has survived to make an appearance in discourses on the global order. Here the UN and its subsidiary organisations such as the World Bank[4] mention the rule of law in connection with their efforts at establishing viable democracies, effective and legitimate international regimes, and universal respect for human rights.

To that extent this notion seems to have travelled well, despite the vastly changing political and social terrain that it has traversed. Thus its "success story" could be amalgamated with the discourse of modernity and its idea of "progress" and enlightenment. Such a reading of the historical record, however, which charts the course from the claims made by the free and equal members of a specific political association – the English gentry which "remembers"[5] the traditional rights of an Englishman, exemplified by the Magna Carta and the *habeas corpus* – sits uneasily with the contemporary emphasis on *universal rights* accruing to individuals as part of their status as individuals and moral agents. It is my purpose in this chapter briefly to sketch out these changes in use of the *topos*, but also to analyse the implications of such a change from a key concept of the political discourse to a virtually exclusively legal conception.

The initial bewilderment caused by this brief historical reflection has some methodological implications. It casts doubt on the viability of our usual means of clarifying the meaning of concepts, that is of ascertaining to which events, objects or actions this term "refers". However, given the vastly differing circumstances and projects in which this argument has played a role – ranging from the efforts to preserve the integrity of the political association, to claims to legitimate resistance against state power, to the universalist aspirations enshrined in the human rights discourse – we might be hard pressed to identify a clear set of identifiable phenomena or even problems to which the rule of law consistently "refers". One of the likely reactions to this conundrum could therefore be to consider this formula merely to be an "ideological" tool, employed to legitimise particular goals, or as a simple "aspiration" or general principle. Like the moral command "do good and avoid evil", it might not be entirely meaningless but offers little help in solving real-life questions. However, the conclusion that it can be discarded because of its imprecision or a value-taintedness that subverts attempts to provide an "objective" analysis of its referent object[6] is far from established. What we also readily see is that the invocation of the rule of law serves as a trump card in discursive strategies to legitimise and de-legitimise particular policies and institutional arrangements.

To that extent the concept is part and parcel of our heritage and of our way of tackling certain practical issues by making claims and counter-claims. Thus, in spite of its lack of a stable reference, the term plays a decisive role in the realm of *praxis* where we try to work out our legal and political problems. Its meaning therefore consists in its *use* and in the connections it establishes to other concepts within a semantic field, and in the way in which certain actions and practices are thereby authorised or prohibited. Thus any analysis of this *problematique* must always be historical as well as analytical and must be alert to its "ideological" dimension. Because it addresses practical issues, the rule of law is bound to deal with political projects,[7] and these, in turn, always transcend the world as observed from an (allegedly) "objective" point of view.

In short, political projects can never show the social world as it "really" is, even though the move to "naturalise" it and treat it like the material world is a frequently used gambit of skilled debaters and social "scientists" alike.[8] The value of such "projects" does not consist in their descriptive accuracy, but rather in their productive power. Consequently, their appraisal cannot be reduced to some deictic procedure, or "operationalisation", but has to be "tested" through criticisms, both internally and externally. Here the criteria of consistency, but even more so of practicability in the light of historical experience, and comparisons with alternatives, provide the appropriate yardsticks.

In this chapter I want to examine the "arrival" of the rule of law argument within the discourse of global order. Of course, no fully-fledged account of the historical twists and turns of its development can be attempted here. Nevertheless, a few references to some important historical shifts are in order. As already argued, the shift from the political project of safeguarding the liberties of the members of a *particular society* to one of *universal human rights* entails a significant change in meaning. Thus in contrast with the traditional use of the rule of law argument that had as its regulative ideal the notion of the free citizen, the present use emphasises a notion of "victim" who must be protected through – among other things – the "punishment" of the perpetrators of traditional or newly defined "crimes".

While such a trend is well in tune with arguments about new threats and the crisis of the state, it is also powerfully reinforced by the discourse of modernity. After all, within this discourse "progress" is assessed by eliminating all the particularities of politics. But it is precisely these particular social and political facts that made the law among "persons of sovereign equality" possible, stemming from their contractual undertakings, from custom, as well as from the analogies borrowed from Roman private law.[9] Nowadays, however, universal humanity has attained pride of place and the capacity to punish, always a crucial element in the constitution of a political association, has to be "transferred" to the "universal level". The boundaries between constitutional law and international law thereby become increasingly permeable. Similarly, while most if not all goals in the old rule of law were entrusted to politics, they are now conceptualised as individual "rights". There is a subjective right to a "clean environment",[10] to "development"[11] or even to "democracy". Often these new postulates are voiced with little concern as to who the actual duty-bearers of all these new rights are and how these goals requiring collective action can be implemented.[12] Given the still-segmented character of "world society" and scant evidence that we have been transformed from Humean beings of "little generosity" into ones who accept and feel at home in a system of "cosmopolitan" justice, such a conception of the rule of law does indeed require a leap of faith.[13]

But not only these openly avowed goals but also the "silences" deserve some mention. There is, for example, little discussion in current international discourses about the property rights of the initial assignment of titles, which always presupposes a political decision. Virtually all discussions centre on the "protection" of these rights, which are then "justified" by some highly questionable economistic ideas about "incentives", and by the liberal tendency to mystify power by assigning property to the "private" sphere. The result is a curious mix of statism projected on a global scale, and of professionalism,[14] which on the basis of expertise is prepared to take over the functional tasks of "governance" previously entrusted to states and their "governments".

From these initial remarks, the remainder of the present chapter will be structured as follows. In the next section I examine some of the inherent tensions in the conception of the rule of law that provide – so to speak – the "enabling" conditions for its "ideological" use. In Section III, I analyse the implications of applying this method to problems of "governance" in the international arena. It is my contention that, following Foucault, this shift from government and from bilateral and multilateral co-operation of governments to one of governance implies a significant shift in the *loci* and sources of power. This new form of "governmentality" implies not only new forms of surveillance but also of capillary control of all social sectors as well as an atrophied notion of politics.[15] The chapter concludes (in Section IV) with a brief summary of the arguments.

II. The complex language game of the "rule of law"

The above analysis suggests not only that the rule of law is not a thing-like entity brought under a concept, but also that it is a concept that bridges within its penumbra a variety of political and value concerns. The first and most obvious concern is that of combating arbitrariness, as the opposition between law and "men" indicates. This speaks to two dangers simultaneously. One concerns a problem intrinsic to "rule" namely the distinction between the governing and the governed. It addresses the potentially coercive character of any regime that tries to overcome collective action problems. Given this structure of inequality, as indicated by the existence of a "subject" on the one hand and the ruler, magistrate or sovereign on the other, the rule of law also addresses the potential for the abuse of power flowing from such inequality. Here the traditional remedy lies in "generality" or "even-handedness": the imperative that the potentially coercive power of rule is applied to all, and proportionally in similar situations, reduces the risk of idiosyncratic uses of power. The distinction between the arbitrary exercise of power and law's "generality" has been one of the constants in the debate, as has been the issue of the "discretion"[16] of those entrusted with official power.

Here another difficulty comes to the fore. Since general rules do not decide concrete cases, additional safeguards have to be introduced. Two further dilemmas arise. One concerns the nature of "exceptions", the other the power of naming things. Both point beyond law to the general understandings limiting the bounds of sense and thus of interpretation. Carl Schmitt most notably addressed the first kind of "decision dilemma" by focusing on the "exception".[17] For him, unfathomable extra-legal grounds are part of the sovereign's prerogatives which have to be beyond appeal. But his argument, drawing its force from the emergency situation, is too spectacular and at the same time too particular. It fails, therefore, to provide proper guidance for understanding the general *problématique* of legal discretion and interpretation.

It is too spectacular in that it forgets that emergencies and exceptions are "special situations" only because we (perhaps mistakenly) believe that all bets are off when the situation under consideration seems to be no longer one of routines and procedures of law and of politics *as usual*. But this argument implies that the relevance of the exception for explaining the "normal" might be severely limited. I also do not believe that the old adage that the "exception" confirms the rule is fitting, or even helpful, even though it correctly identifies the parasitic character of exceptional reasoning upon "normal" decisional rules. What is at stake in the "exception" is that obviously the "speech act" of a public authority signals that different strategies are required that might justify "special measures" and deviations from precedents. But this does not imply that indeed all bets are off and that we have to accept a blind form of decisionism. Similarly, the Copenhagen school of security has pointed out that "security" does not refer to existing "objective" conditions, but that by naming specific circumstances they are thereby "made" into threats. When successful, such a speech act justifies special measures that go beyond politics as usual.[18] But this power of "naming" usually sets off a series of debates and challenges rather than ending up in the eerie silence that comes with universal compliance.

Thus it seems such an argument, made differently by both Schmitt and the Copenhagen school, suffers from a Hobbesian myopia. Of course, in the Hobbesian universe such determinations are unequivocally binding and not subject to further scrutiny – a limitation that is justified by the belief that otherwise a return to the state of nature is unavoidable. But it is precisely because we know that such a consequence is neither inevitable nor even likely in most cases, that the contestation of such determinations is part and parcel of the political game, notwithstanding attempts of decision-makers to "stand" on this prerogative. Even in well-ordered societies such speech acts at best establish a (more or less) powerful "presumption". As President Nixon found out, claiming supreme national security interests for covering up a partisan and illegal action (Watergate) cannot resolve this question either legally or politically. Similarly, while the argument of the Copenhagen school without doubt correctly characterises security issues by pointing to their genesis in a speech act, it misses the point by not emphasising the merely *prima facie* character of such characterisations and the subsequent intense contestation. Governments differ in their capacity and willingness to limit these contestations, but even dictatorial regimes basing their claims on Hobbesian premises of the non-reviewable nature of such determinations are subject to popular reactions which they ignore only at their peril.

The second reason why Schmitt's "theory" is defective is that by focusing on the spectacular it misinterprets the decision-making process in "normal" cases. Here too the ultimate determination does not follow strictly either from the rules or from the facts, but rather involves a decision based on a particular judgement that is not simply "entailed" by either of them. To that extent *all* decisions involve some form of "leap" that is not simply reducible to the "mechanisms" of rule application or fact recognition. Thus what distinguishes an emergency situation from one of routine decision is neither their contestability nor the need to reach a closure, but the scope and seriousness of the decision in the former case. "Routine" decisions are simply characterised by their "isolation" from the ongoing concerns of a society and from general social interaction – having one's day in court precisely means that no "others" are or should become involved, since the case is removed from the public agenda and entrusted to the "appropriate" institution for resolution. However, no such isolation is possible when the community as a whole is challenged (as in the case of national security) or when a "case", even if entrusted to a "court", becomes emblematic for some generally perceived social ill. In that case new ways of dealing with it might be required and attempts to limit its relevance by claiming that the case represents only a particular controversy could be of no avail.

While the most important concern of the rule of law *topos* is the substitution of human caprice or frailty by the objective force of law, in practice such a gambit is unavailable,[19] at least in this categorical fashion. Historically this difficulty has led to the laying of emphasis either on the actual social conditions that inform law, or on "formalism" whereby the issue of the "authorship" of law or its "source" moves the question one step further back. The first strategy, that is the retreat to some substantive customary standards limiting the discretion of judges by traditional understandings specific to a particular society, is observable when, for example, arguments are made to resurrect the "ancient freedoms" of Englishmen. The second becomes apparent when "discretion" is limited to largely procedural notions, such as *lex posterior*, the hierarchy of norms (statutes versus laws versus constitutional provisions), *lex specialis* and so on. This sooner or later results in a notion of law as a system of norms or in a "pure theory" which abstracts from all contingencies and limits the contact between "reality" and law to one point, that is the *Grundnorm*. The latter is both part of law and beyond law and thus provides the hinge between the "ought" and the "is".[20]

Of course it is only possible to internalise all reasons for the normative force of law and make it appear that this question is simply a question of "validity" if we accept that "legality" addresses all issues of legitimacy at the same time. But even if we fail to take into account the fact that judges always have to support their decisions with substantive reasons – aside from showing that they are applying "the law" – usually via "principles" that allow for such support to be drawn from morals, philosophy or particular customs, the construction of the *Grundnorm* or the "rule of recognition" as the keystone of the legal edifice draws attention to the fact that a formal understanding of legality requires a broader legitimisation. Ultimately, in modernity when both God and "nature" (in the sense of an intelligible order of being) have been marginalised, there remains only the "sovereign people" and its law-creating declarations as a foundation.

It is not necessary, and indeed there is no space here, to trace these developments to their roots in theology, as Rousseau's remarks about the need of a civil religion clearly indicated, a problem which has been taken up by Schmitt,[21] Voegelin[22] and, more recently, Agamben.[23] What is important here is rather the recognition that it is only through the introduction of "the people" as a source that both the formalism of law and its legitimacy can be maintained. Rather than assessing the substantive justice done in a single case – Weber's *kadi justice* orienting itself solely to a notion of "output legitimacy" – modern "rational" law relies largely on "input legitimacy". As Weber reminds us, the legitimacy of "rational" legal order relies on a procedural notion, namely the process of norm creation. In this sense, law and politics are not only intrinsically linked through the concept of the "state", where legislation is produced, but the state itself derives its legitimacy "from" the people – or even understands itself as an expression of a particular people (nation state).[24] Consequently, legitimisation deficits will appear in all instances of institutionalised inter-state co-operation that go beyond the

classical alliance patterns or *ad hoc* limited purpose arrangements. No further argument is necessary to conclude that international regimes as well as
the regulatory activities of international organisations, be they the UN or
even more so the EU, thereby become suspect. Indeed, it is no accident that
discussions over the ultra vires character of a given Security Council (SC)
decision are paralleled by discussions centred on the general democratic def-
icit of the EU.

The responses to this dilemma range from denial to efforts at addressing
these deficits through determined measures at constitutionalisation. While
for regimes the argument is often made that their "beneficial" character and
their enabling rather than merely constraining character creates some form of
output legitimacy,[25] denser forms of institutionalised co-operation in areas of
"high politics" require additional legitimisation. Here, some form of judicial
review of SC actions, (although it seems highly unlikely that the International
Court of Justice (ICJ) would be interested in taking over this role), as well as
making the SC a more representative body, has been suggested as a remedy.
In the case of the EU, a more serious effort of creating a "constitution" has
recently been undertaken, despite at best lukewarm interest on the part of the
European public(s).[26]

Both attempts attest, however, to the difficulty of creating such legitimising
structures in the absence of a concrete, historical *demos* which is ready and
willing to understand itself as the author of its legislative acts. While there is
of course no dearth of speculation about a "cosmopolitan democracy" or
about a "world (civil) society", the question still remains as to whether such
characterisations are appropriate. What has to be established is whether these
new social formations – whatever their characterisation might be – can act as
a substitute for the historical "peoples" which are mentioned in the UN
Charter as the "authors" of the United Nations.

III. The uses of the rule of law argument in (inter)national political discourses

The casual observer of contemporary debates in international law and politics is confronted with several discourses emphasising different elements of
contemporary political and legal issues. Thus the cumulative effect of the end
of the Cold War and the phenomenal increase in transnational transactions
made a realist understanding of international relations based on the traditional anarchy *problématique*[27] simply incoherent. A whole new vocabulary,
rather than some minor adjustments, was required. This task was accom-
plished in two interdependent moves. The first entailed a shift from a formal
model of law to a plurality of norms governing actual interactions. The
second move involved the substitution of the anthropocentric concept of the
sovereign's "will" by a more "functional" notion of problem-solving in an
"issue area". Both changes were, of course, features of the "regimes" that
provided a new research programme for international relations and inter-

national law. Within this context, attention increasingly was directed to new organisational forms, such as "networks", where public and private stakeholders and experts cooperate. Due to their "thick" institutionalisation, these arrangements were a far cry from the one-shot contracting that even realists had accepted in the area of high politics when alliances were forged. The new forms of cooperation also differed from patterns in the area of "low politics", where co-ordination problems had to be resolved, and were also quite different from the "move to institutions"[28] characteristic of the post-World War I and World War II era. At that time the new type of regulatory agencies familiar from the New Deal were transferred to the international level. It became part of the "multilateral" realisation of "embedded liberalism"[29] that reconfigured domestic and international institutions.

The success of regimes, of course, came at a price; namely the splitting of law into functionally differentiated areas or islands of co-operation, whether "trade", "the environment", "human rights" or even "security". Each "issue area" seemed to be independent and managed by a different group of experts, thus raising issues of "fragmentation" and of "legitimacy". Consequently, the solution to both problems seemed to lie in a further constitutionalisation of international law.[30] Here the Charter was mentioned, as well as the World Trade Organization (WTO), because of its "dispute settlement" mechanisms. But as the controversy over the potential ultra vires character of some SC actions had shown, in the absence of some effective means for adjudication – an arrogation of power for which the ICJ, in contrast to the US Supreme Court in *Marbury v Madison*, was clearly not prepared – there were clear limits to the constitutionalisation argument.[31] Thus, aside from the difficult issues of the "representative" character of the UN and of the SC in particular, neither state practice nor even the "development" of UN law provided auspicious prospects for making the Charter the basis for a future global rule of law. The case for the WTO was even weaker, even if one tried to construe a comprehensive but rather imaginary "right to free trade" as the basis for the rule of law.[32]

Aside from these "practical" objections there was the equally significant theoretical question of whether or not such a step was sensible at all, given the constitutional experience with state-building. The capacity to address problems of interference through hierarchy and clearly delineated competences (separation of powers) has become under modern circumstances itself more of a problem than a solution. After all, as students of decision-making have pointed out, modern decisional processes, even within states, resemble much more complex bargaining games – akin to multi-level governance and techniques of "muddling through" – than the clearly defined constitutional procedures of law-making, law application or execution.[33]

Thus, to some, constitutionalisation seems rather a throwback to distant times in which the illusion of a comprehensive steering of political and social processes through law seemed to provide a map for orienting oneself within social reality. But the functional differentiation of autonomous and interpenetrating systems no longer fits such a model. An alternative conceptualisation becomes necessary, which is sometimes likened to a legal Bukowina[34] characterised by multiple free-standing, even overlapping regimes without any overarching order. This might be a more adequate description, and might also allow us more successfully to locate the levers of influence for our political projects. Here adherents of Luhmann[35] find themselves strangely affiliated with some critical legal studies proponents who, like David Kennedy, have advocated a shift from structural givens to "policies" and their potential for realising a "progressive" agenda.[36]

It is, however, hard to understand why "policies" should be easier to handle than rules or principles. After all, policies also come with exceptions and have different implications depending on the context. Thus puzzles reappear in a different disguise, as a choice between "policies" and as the question of *who shall decide* in the face of deep-seated disagreements. The focus on policies, on output legitimacy and perhaps even on the "coherence" of a particular norm or policy with other elements of the legal order – as suggested by Franck[37] – cannot avoid sooner or later asking the *cui bono* question, suggesting an answer "in whose name" a particular law is made or applied. To raise this question is not to engage in some debunking of law, so familiar from Thrasymmachian realists and Marxists alike. It is rather to point out that part of the rule of law argument has been that even beneficial outcomes might be subversive of public order if they are the result of the benevolence of an otherwise unrestrained despot or procedure. Only in this way can we avoid the biases that come with the unreflective use of expertise, when fundamental choices between values are resolved through some "naturalising" move. In that case we usually argue that we "really" have no choice but must defer to the trade expert, the environmental scientist or even the peacemaking "professional" who pushes "best practices" because this is just "the way the ball bounces", how "transaction costs" can be lowered and actors "in equilibrium" are made to "comply".

Large-scale co-operation between governmental networks *à la* Slaughter,[38] or even among public and private actors, is certainly an important corrective to the "anarchy" argument promulgated by political realists. By their sustained efforts, these new forms of organisation might even have attained some "intrinsic" value – often referred to in popular economistic parlance as "consumption good". Nevertheless, they hide important forms of power that accrue to a hegemon or a modern form of empire. Traditionally such commanding power – sometimes only idiosyncratically exercised, sometimes hidden by *law*'s empire – was originally dependent on the acquisition and physical domination of territory with a view to laying down the law (*jurisdictio*). Given the dramatic costs of such an expansion and of exercising those rights, traditional empires were, not surprisingly, often little more than associations of relatively independent political units enjoying considerable autonomy.[39] Imperial programmes were usually part of a particular "theology" authorising the particular rule. Modern forms of the imperial project work both on the "macro level" – via an intellectual hegemony (the way in which the bounds of sense are drawn and "problems" and solutions are identified) – and on the micro level – via specific disciplining and surveillance regimes.

Nevertheless, some significant differences exist that need to be mentioned. The old conception of law was largely based on deterrence and required an *ex post* authoritative finding of a transgression before its concomitant punishment could be meted out. The imposition of a sanction served as a "warning" to others and thus also allowed for prospective ordering. The new disciplinary modes, on the other hand, rely on near omnipresent surveillance through monitoring, (self-)reporting, transparency requirements, periodic evaluations and benchmarking exercises, of both public and private institutions. These methods of "governmentality", as Foucault has called it, have considerably changed the ways in which compliance with one's commands can be sought and power can be mystified. Above all, no territorial expansion or physical control is necessary, as in old forms of imperialism.[40] It also does not seem to be of particular importance whether this new form of governmentality is administered by a single centre or is "contracted out" to some other agency which acts on behalf of the centre and its "mission".

Thus it is hardly surprising that trade lawyers today are in favour of uniform and transparent systems of administrative law. For the implementation of liberalisation and anti-dumping commitments, foreign investors desire fair and transparent enforcement of commercial contracts. Human rights advocates favour changes in constitutional arrangements in order to safeguard civil and political rights. All these attempts – covered by the neutrally sounding term of "best practices" – lead to standardisation and increases in the capacity of control of the "standard setters" without involving them directly in the political or administrative system of another "jurisdiction". On the other hand, it should also not come as a surprise that the "subjects" of these disciplining moves might not particularly care whether the orders originate in the imperial centre or in one of the multilateral organisations that have become the harbingers of "democracy" or "responsibility" for "failed" states. This predicament creates considerable difficulties in implementing the "rule of law", a problem known in the literature as the "will to reform dilemma".[41] Furthermore, the strategies, even if they are – against all odds – successful, might be counter-productive and defeat some of the central objectives of equity and the traditional "rule of law". As will become clear from the discussion below, these two problems are strangely interdependent.

The admission of "implementation" difficulties considerably weakens the universalist appeal upon which modern "rule of law" exports are built. After having cleansed law of all particularities and historical contingencies and having appealed to "rational" criteria whose allure consists in being applicable at any time, anywhere and in respect of anybody, the admission that such programmes can be successful only if the recipients are persuaded to "co-operate" considerably undermines the claim to universality and "innateness".

Knowing the "locals" and their peculiar ways of thinking seems suddenly more important than getting the universal principles right (after all, the latter were supposed to do the work more or less on their own, since they possess the "force of the better argument"). Furthermore, the shift from a concern with law and its integrity to one of "incentives" is telling and suggests that the rule of law involves more than the reform of a country's legal system and its administration of justice. It is above all a "disciplinary" practice aimed at "constituting subjects willing to accept the values of Western liberal democratic values".[42]

While the "others" might have reasons to be suspicious of the particular political project, there is an even greater difficulty in that the "imposition" of such a regime defeats one of the central values of the rule of law, namely autonomy. As Martti Koskenniemi has pointed out:

> The worry about new global law reflects concerns about the absence of structures of political representation, contestation and accountability, of a public sphere institutionally linked to global power . . . Whatever the managerial mindset has to say about the difficulties of effective governance today fails to address the sense that these difficulties are undermining freedom, in the sense of leading one's life only under the authority of one's own (good) will.[43]

Just as an individual cannot be forced to be moral, so too a community cannot be forced to respect the rule of law on its own. It might be cajoled into adopting in part or in whole regulations which have been made by others, but such a move usually lacks the "authorship" and the concomitant obligatory force to bind citizens. This was, after all, Kant's "free will" argument establishing the autonomy and freedom of the agent and, by analogy, the right of every people to give themselves a "civil constitution of the kind that sees fit without the interference from other powers".[44] Thus while Kant has little to say about the law's function in the international arena – one is indeed struck by his dismissal of such eminent international lawyers as Pufendorf, Grotius and Vattel, who are belittled as *"leidige Troester"* ("pathetic comforters")[45] – central to his conception of law is his notion of authorship of a self-determining will. It is therefore the "moral politician" rather than the expert or "political moralist" who is charged with the arduous task of guiding the project of the league (*foedus pacificum*) so that over time it becomes a genuine "security community" in which the resort to force becomes unthinkable and the submission of disputes to mandatory settlement is routine.

These arguments have several implications for our rule of law argument. First, while Kant does not explicitly utilise the vocabulary of "citizenship", casting his *Rechtslehre* in more universalistic terms, the emphasis on the "authorship" of law clearly links him to the original rule of law arguments made by common lawyers and dissenters in the seventeenth century. They had deployed the more particularistic vocabulary of "ancient freedoms" and of "consent" to law-making and taxation in order to stem the tide of absolutism and establish the supremacy of Parliament against the King's prerogatives. But in doing so they also had to contest the conception of individual rights as simple grants by the sovereign to his subjects. Second, Kant more than anybody else defends the rule of law project as a *political project* and not as one of technical expertise, or of some (right-Hegelian) notion that what exists is also reasonable and therefore legitimate, arguments about "reality" notwithstanding.

In other words, Kant directly inveighs against the normative force of facticity, while at the same time arguing that the particular political solution can consist neither in the mere "application" of universal principles nor in the historical singularity of a "lucky" coincidence (as later exemplified by the "Whig interpretation" of history). Instead, what is required is a judgement that is singular but which, as in aesthetics, goes far beyond idiosyncratic grounds of indicating personal likes and dislikes.[46] In short, what is involved here is a *validity claim* that is subject to critical reflection and evaluation in the light of shared standards. Kant's "solution" therefore seems to be as far removed from the decisionism of Hobbes (or Schmitt) as it is from the unreflected satisfaction with decisions that somehow "worked out" – a viewpoint characteristic of the attitudes of *status quo* powers. Yet it is also far removed from the universalist fantasies of "infinite justice" promised by some imperial project.

In a way, the contrast with present conceptions of the rule of law could not be more striking. Rather than laying emphasis on citizens as the "authors" of law we notice that the dominant figures in the contemporary project have become the "victim" and the "perpetrator". The former is to be "helped" by the proper "professionals", whilst the latter has to be prosecuted and punished, again by a specialised cadre of "experts". By a strange twist the rule of law has changed from an empowering instrument of citizens taking their fate into their own hands to a construct that gives the individual pride of place as a pre-political being endowed with subjective rights. But such a shift places man's social and political existence at the mercy of those who are ministering to "humanity" at large.

Since the "protection" of the individual is now the *spiritus rector* of the legal enterprise, the notions of "crime", prosecution and coercion become equally important. This is, of course, a *novum* for international law, whose classical "countermeasures" – including acts of force (aside perhaps from war) – were only designed to bring the wayward state back into the fold.[47] Thus retaliation and reprisals were measures of self-help intended to make the opponent desist from illegal acts rather than to serve as a punishment for the transgressions committed. The closeness of the new notion with its emphasis on criminality to an imperial conception of "law and order" (Vergil's *Tu regere imperio, memento Romane: parcere subjectis et debellare superbos*[48]) is not accidental. However, given the enormity of the task of providing equal and universal justice, it is hardly surprising that the aspirations of the rule of law have to be sacrificed on the altar of contingent "reality". The result is an ever-widening gap between aspiration and practice. Most problems in the international arena are still dealt with by "oversight", as Rwanda, Darfur or the Congo demonstrate, and one need not be a "realist" to see that particular interests and saliency rather than universal aspirations or a notion of duty do most of the explaining.

But even in the latter cases – which are admittedly few and far between – there are some conceptual issues worth pondering. Justice cannot be achieved through the even-handed and general application of existing rules by independent judges who are nevertheless subject to the constraints of a particular constitution. Instead, it is supposed to work in the newly opened up space of international "universality" and through some form of "exemplary justice" that is visited upon individuals, be they state agents or "private" persons. Here two further questions arise: one concerns the specificity of criminal acts, and the other the issue of how deterrence connects with the prospective ordering of law. It is precisely because many international crimes, such as genocide or the use of force, are not part of normal "individual" cost-benefit calculations but are distinctly "political" considerations that one might seriously doubt the efficacy of deterrence. This scepticism is enhanced by the fact that enforcement is selective and thus arbitrary.

It does not lack a certain irony that "deterrence", which has gone out of fashion among most penologists, has suddenly found some fervent adherents among international lawyers, a group not known for their familiarity with criminology. My suspicion is therefore that the persuasive force of the recent efforts at criminalisation in international law has less to do with its expected effectiveness or prospective ordering function – indeed the recent record of highly selective enforcement makes a mockery of that hope – but with the ideology of progress. Part of that ideology is the near-messianic hope in a transformative change that is supposed to result from the challenge to the state's monopoly on legitimate force. True, the right to punish was always a jealously guarded right of states or communities. But whether sporadic verdicts handed down by tribunals which stand "above" the state determining what the law is can also instil new loyalties by speaking in the name of "human dignity", of "collective humanity", or at least the "international community", seems rather doubtful.

The inability to name the "source" which can hold individuals "responsible" is telling. Is the relevant group the community of states, the "domestic" order, which has incorporated certain universal principles, the "peoples" of the world, or "humanity" at large? These are no idle word games. It seems that having purged law of all historical peculiarities and contingencies, the identifiable thrust of the argument requires a narrative explanation of the end of the state, or even of "history". In this sense, "humanity" itself and not only "mankind" in its contingent diversity becomes the all-encompassing point of reference. Both the "peoples" and the (concrete) people of a given order have vanished. What remains is "human dignity" as the ultimate source from which all law emanates and to which it refers back.[49] But since "humanity" cannot act, the question of *quis judicabit* thus becomes all the more important.

We sometimes catch a glimpse of the complexities that arise in these contexts. Thus in the *Tadic* case[50] before the International Criminal Tribunal for the former Yugoslavia (ICTY – a tribunal created by the SC), faced with a challenge to its legality, the trial chamber rejected the motion by disclaiming competence to pronounce on the legality of the court's establishment. The Appeals Chamber, on the other hand, argued that as a "self-contained system" it did indeed possess such competence, as otherwise it would be at the mercy of the SC. Such dependence, in turn, would undermine its judicial character. But such a justification clearly goes beyond the authorising instrument. In other words, in order to advance the rule of law, something more is required than the establishment of a tribunal entrusted with the responsibility of judging according to universalist standards.[51]

Similarly, considerable uneasiness can be detected in Carla del Ponte's opening statement at the trial of the former Kosovar Prime Minister Ramush Haradinaj. He was praised by the US State Department, the UN, the French Foreign Ministry and other "representatives", while being delivered up for trial at The Hague for the murder of 40 of his countrymen. "It is a prosecution," Del Ponte said, "that some did not want to see brought, and that few supported by their cooperation at both the international and local level."[52] What she significantly omitted was that the culprits were not simply other Kosovars who stayed loyal to their leader, but also UN diplomats who had hoped to broker an agreement for which they needed Haradinaj's co-operation. Consequently – and clearly violating the rules for the detention of persons charged with war crimes – Hardinaj was released and allowed to return to Kosovo after entering a not guilty plea.

These instances not only demonstrate the "intrusion" of politics but also the fact that the administration of justice and the effectiveness of the rule of law depend on the institutionalisation of a political process contained in a constitution to which "the law" has to defer. It is in this way that "the people" come to see themselves as authors of their own choices, and in this way a constitution can then claim "loyalty" and respect for the limiting and enabling conditions of such an order. What the rhetoric of universalism simply leaves out is that the duties which flow from loyalty are quite different from those resulting from contracts or universal norms. Loyalty is owed to those people and institutions which define us as particular historical subjects – which establish who we "are". One might be obliged to strangers, due to the promises one has made or due to the general principles underlying their status as persons which thus deserve recognition. But one can only be "loyal" to friends and "others" who are or have become part of "us". Loyalty connects us to particular groups and invokes specific historical experiences. It cannot be tailor-made as a free-standing "de-contextualised" structure that is imposed upon a group. The "law" must be the repository for their particular experiences and meaning, even if the "text" produced satisfies the criteria of justice and makes reference to universal human values. Consequently, Hirschman considers "loyalty" as one of the fundamental social mechanisms that cannot be reduced either to "exit" or to "voice".[53]

The usual tendency to explain our political obligations in terms of the "justice" of the regime to which we are subject misses precisely the point that we, as Frenchmen, for example, have special obligations to abide by French law and not by the law of Australia or Switzerland, even if the latter are also "just regimes". These "special obligations" therefore do not result from the benefits we receive in the pursuit of our goals, nor from the general maxim that laws are necessary to avoid conflict and regulate interference, nor even from universal values which are part of our projects. Rather, the obligations derive from the realisation of who we are as historical beings. As such we can never start from scratch, as the imagery of a market or even a "game" suggests, both of which we might enter or exit *ad libitum*. Rather, here we become aware that we are always part of a "drama" in which what happens today has a long past that casts its shadows and which sets the stage for our actions and their success and failure.

Strangely enough, liberal theory recognises the power of the "shadow of the future" ("discounted" at different rates). It seems, however, entirely blind to the role of the past, except when viewed as a "constraint" on our ability to maximise our choices. But what remains outside its view is the influence of those forces which call our attention to *who we are* and what our particular predicament is. These realisations must come before any game we enter and any maximising strategy we might choose. Benedict Anderson's curious question of why there is in virtually all states a memorial to the unknown soldier, but none to the unknown Marxist[54] (or the "fallen liberal", or "disappointed progressive") is perhaps no longer so puzzling if we understand the dynamics in the construction of "meaning" and law's role in it. It is therefore no accident that the original use of the rule of law argument was couched in terms of the specific "ancient freedoms" once allegedly enjoyed by all free Englishmen, or as an argument about the constitution of a specific public thing (*res publica*) that locates each individual within a specific context and signals to a "people" that they are thereby enabled (and not only constrained) to work out their individual and collective destinies.

The issue here is not to rehash the mistaken idea of a "primordial" existence of a people which "gives" itself a constitution, or to argue that since this "theory" is clearly problematic, any other "multitude" can be created through contract. The point is rather to understand that law is not only a co-ordination device, regulating the interactions among "rational" self-interested actors, but also a vehicle for the generation of meaning and that this constitutive function is deeply embedded in our historical experiences and our political imagination. To that extent it is true that "the people" is not a pre-political fact but rather a strategy of sense-making in which "fictions" are established and put beyond question. Hence Kant's dictum that people should not inquire into their origin "with any practical aim in view",[55] as otherwise their dogmatic force lending legitimacy to a system of laws would be undermined. It also should be borne in mind that the "social fact" of "a people" defining itself through a specific "founding" is largely "mythical", even if it is related to a concrete historical incidence.

Admittedly, such a conception of law which emphasises its role as a repository of meaning rather than as a simple instrument for avoiding collisions between "rational" actors is difficult to grasp for a tradition that considers only individuals and their wishes to be "real". In this way, their (political) projects and their recollections remain simply a matter of idiosyncratic "tastes" (*de gustibus non est disputandum*). However, such a perspective leads to a variety of conceptual and practical political impasses that are worth pondering as they create significant difficulties for both "theory" and practice.

Consider in this context the historically contingent fact that none of the existing social arrangements can be justified in terms of universalist criteria since the historical world shows their utter contingency, and neither is the construction of common political projects in terms of individual rights able to provide a coherent account of what is happening. Both problems deserve therefore a brief discussion. On the first issue, Habermas remarks:

> Since the voluntariness of the decision to engage in law giving praxis is a fiction of the contractualist tradition, in the real world who gains power to define the boundaries of a political community is settled by historical chance and the actual course of events – normally the arbitrary outcomes of war and civil war.[56]

This, of course, is a far cry from any justification in terms of universal principles of humanity. But things are not looking up for the "liberal" programme when due to the requirements of methodological individualism all mediating institutions are construed as an aggregation of "subjective rights".

This leads me to the second problem mentioned above: the reframing of collective political projects in individualist terms. Democracy then suddenly becomes an individual "right to democracy", the environment is similarly protected by the subjective "right to a clean environment" and "development" is somehow wished into existence by the postulation of a "right to development".[57] It needs only a moment's reflection to realise that the construal of these "rights" is the result of considerable conceptual befuddlement. The last "right" can at least arguably be understood as a manifesto claim – as addressing a recognised grievance. In the absence of a clearly defined class of correlative duty-bearers, a flaw in the existing order is identified that awaits further specific initiatives in order to address this problem.

The other two rights are simply based on faulty reasoning. To put it bluntly, the "right" to democracy is not a human right accruing to agents as part of their natural liberty. It is at best a status assignment bestowed upon a person as member of a particular society. Thus "democracy" is not a subject-ive right inherent in, or explicating the notion of, personhood or agency. It is rather a principle of organising for political purposes and failure to see the difference involves a category mistake of the first order.[58] Similar difficulties arise if the protection of the commons is "derived" from the subjective right to a clean environment. Again, while the assignment of exclusive property rights might alleviate certain pressures that otherwise result to tragedy of the commons, this is a far cry from the notion that a part of nature should be set aside, so as to remain "unspoilt" or become subject to severe limitations on use. A more appropriate conceptualisation would therefore be one of com-mon ownership that explicitly prohibits individual appropriation and the exercise of individual rights. However, such a conception requires something like a notion of "corporate" rights that cannot be reduced to the individual rights of persons forming the corporation. In consequence, such a construc-tion has to be contrary to the notion of a universal human right.

The practical political consequences of such muddled thinking are no less deleterious. Given the impoverishment of the international legal ontology which recognises an overarching goal, such as human dignity (but little else), everything becomes dissolved in a process where strategic claims and coun-terclaims are advanced. The only "relevant" question then becomes whether one is "on the side" of universal values. The underlying imperial aspirations of such a mode of thinking are not difficult to fathom. It comes as no surprise that a special role is then claimed on the basis of the *mission civilisatrice*, the white man's burden, or American exceptionalism.

In this context both the New Haven school of international law around Myres McDougal[59] and the more cynical analysis supplied by some of the lawyers of the present US administration provide some striking examples. In McDougal's case the dissolution of law into a process of "appraisal" of political claims and counterclaims was at least not intended to impair the possibility of rendering a judgement of legitimacy, but simply that the criteria were no longer those of legal formalism but rather of "policy analysis". His argument was that policies can be evaluated depending on their capacity to further (or impair) "human dignity". Not surprisingly, the appraisal usually concluded with an approval of US policies as they were allegedly conceived and executed in the pursuit of "human dignity".

Compared to this fig-leaf conception of law the writings of some inter-national lawyers presently advising the US government in its war on terror seem more cynical. For them, the "theory of public goods", particularly in the area of security,[60] explains why the US has to act unilaterally. It also shows why any conception of legality or of the binding force of norms has no place in their "theory". For them, nations comply with laws to minimise transaction costs and out of fear or retaliation and reputational loss.[61] It is not quite clear why reputation should matter in such a world where there is a market with clear prices or at least a transparent system of "incentives" that determines once and for all "how the ball bounces". Furthermore, why should reputation matter – even under conditions of "market imperfections" – if one possesses all the wherewithal necessary to pursue one's goals? To that extent, any "reputation" will be a function of the "big stick" one carries rather than of "speaking softly", because the latter is in any case most likely to be dismissed as "cheap talk".

At this point the astonished and disbelieving reader is directed to the international relations literature which is alleged to provide a more "sophisticated analysis" (*sic*) of international law and the reasons for compliance.[62] This comes, of course, as a shock to all of us who have worked in the mines of social science over the years. Obviously we must have failed to notice the brilliance of some of the allegedly high-carat diamonds that are now being paraded in front of us, which must have hitherto been hidden in the familiar chaff. But could it be that all that the "hired guns" of the present administration have encountered is some pieces of broken glass, the pathetic remnants of some past food-fights in the abode of the "fraternity" of international relations specialists? Lawyers are unlikely to know or to be able to judge the rather arcane debates in political science, given the disciplinary boundaries, unless, of course, they are confirmationist ideologues who simply "assume" that something which supports their view has been established as "truth" somewhere else.[63] Thus the "arguments" advanced by Yoo,[64] Goldsmith *et al* turn out to be little more than a cheap debating trick. We all know that "over there" the grass is always greener, the girls are always more beautiful and so on . . .

The tragedy, however, is not only that we end up with some problematic "theory". The tragedy consists rather in providing incredibly bad policy advice. Inquiring only into the ends and "testing" them in terms of their universalisability or "progressive" nature, while dismissing all mediating structures and considerations of particularity, leads not only to imperial aspirations, but ultimately to *hubris*. It is precisely because the exclusive focus on instrumental "rationality" prevents us from distinguishing between irrational wish-fulfilment and legitimate modes of pursuing one's goals that such a tunnel vision of law makes us forget that law is a structure of meaning. It is not only about issues of regulating strategic interaction, but also equally about the legitimacy of the *means employed* and also about *"who we are"*.[65] It is in this way that the notion of the rule of law attains its importance. If the messianic mission of spreading democracy abroad is possible only by subverting both legal and political processes at home – by threatening the constitutional separation of powers and civil liberties, not to speak for the moment of the victims created abroad – such a "mission" does not amount to a "tragic" bargain but rather to a pathetic delusional goal.[66]

As we all know, one of the fastest ways to nowhere is to get caught in misplaced dichotomies; for example, arguing that given the challenges of terrorism and existential threats we will either have to "adjust" (that is, practically abolish the traditional safeguards of the rule of law) or face disaster. Another equally problematic argument is that any change or infringement of a given regime can only eliminate the rule of law. But, as we have seen, both positions are untenable because they subvert the very notion of a "balance" that is an intrinsic part of this *topos*. In other words, the problem of the rule of law is thus neither one of efficiency nor one of simply protecting the law's purity. It entails attending to the task of preserving the integrity of law, which can only be safeguarded if the institutional arrangements are capable of dealing reasonably well with the *twin dangers* of anarchy and unrestrained power. It necessarily becomes part and parcel of a larger "security" theory that transcends the purely military dimension. As Daniel Deudney has shown, this awareness figures in a "republican"[67] security theory that addresses four dangers simultaneously:

> As its most elemental level, republican security theory holds that insecurity results from the extremes of both anarchy and hierarchy, both of which can manifest themselves internally and externally, thus producing four situations of gross insecurity: the internal anarchy of civil war (stasis), the external anarchy of total or annihilative war, the internal full hierarchy of tyranny, despotism, and totalitarianism, and the full external hierarchy of imperial rule.[68]

While it was formerly the common lawyers who rediscovered and used the rule of law argument to impose limits on the political projects of a centralising and more "universal" (statist) political order, the new use of the rule of law *topos* as part of a messianic "universalist" project of human rights suggests that this concept has not travelled well over the years. But then again this is not unusual and there are good reasons to be sceptical of attempts to press such concepts into the service of new projects, even if this is done by "experts" in the field. We know that war is too serious a matter to be left to the military, and the rule of law might be too important to be left to the lawyers. Its function is certainly neither to bring about the "end of history" nor to provide a strategy for the propagation of some technical expertise to "underdeveloped" societies. Rather, its purpose is to make us aware of the need for critical appraisal of our political projects in the light of our condition as finite "historical" beings. This seems to me the core meaning of this concept. Only in this way can we avoid the rule of law becoming the nightmare of messianic politics or an equally frightening prospect of a rule of lawyers who function as "experts" by emasculating politics.

IV. Conclusion

This chapter has analysed the rule of law, not by attempting to "define" it according to the usual taxonomic criteria and then see how the various policies and practice instantiate this concept. Rather, it began from a Wittgensteinian notion that the meaning of a concept – particularly in the social world, which is not natural but entirely constructed by shared meanings – is not its reference but its "use". Consequently, the inquiry had to be historical and analytical at the same time, seeking to sketch instances and contexts in which the rule of law argument was used. It also examined the historical links to other concepts and practices which were thereby authorised or prohibited. This allowed us to see its trajectory throughout various epochs and also served as a useful reminder that the narrative in which the rule of law argument is usually embedded is one of "progress" and increasing enlightenment.

While we cannot judge the narratives by comparing them directly with the historical world telling us how things "really were" – an illusion Leopold von Ranke still had at the birth of modern historiography but which any critical reflection on historiography clearly shows to be mistaken[69] – analysing the changes and seeing what "work" the arguments did in different periods is a useful first step. It insures against the dangers of a totalising perspective, certain hidden teleologies or the well-known tendency to project our present meanings back onto the historical record. The realisation that the *topos* was for long periods part of the *political discourse* rather than jurisprudence, or a theory of law, provides a useful corrective, particularly when a concept is taken from the "limited" context of domestic politics and projected onto the global sphere.

As we have seen, such shifts result in a de-emphasis of the importance of the state, sovereignty and most of the traditional "sources" of law. Instead, a new form of "naturalism" has emerged whereby it is no longer particular individuals but rather "humanity", or even more abstractly, "human dignity" which becomes the exclusive legitimising source. It foregrounds different problems, such as those of the "victim" who has to be rescued, suggesting different strategies for implementing the rule of law, such as the punishment of criminal perpetrators. Thus, not only is any form of legal "formalism" devalued as we shift from government to governance, but even the status of the "person" is increasingly less that of an agent and more that of one who is in need of help by "others". Significantly, these "others" are not necessarily those who have particular duties derived from the social and political arrangements in which they and the victim participate, since the authorisation for action does not flow directly from "membership" of a specific historical society but from a pre- (or a-) political notion of human existence.

Both *foci* lead to an entirely new *problematique* which the rule of law *topos* has to address. It has to raise the question of authorisation that potentially engenders imperial pretensions on the one hand and cynicism on the other hand. The latter consequence results from the widening gap between universalist aspirations and the inevitable unevenness and controversial nature of enforcement "above" the state. The other big issue concerns the interface between constitutional law and international law. In contrast to the contemporary debate that sees in the further strengthening of the "commander in chief" powers of the US President the only solution to the problems of new security challenges, British experiences of Empire pointed exactly in the opposite direction. This resulted in the ascendance of Parliament (after the Glorious Revolution) or at least in a strengthening of the rule of law in terms of civil liberties (as in the nineteenth century). The reason for these two different outcomes seems to lie in a conception of law that, as of late, has been successfully emptied of all traces of any concrete society and that stresses solely the instrumental functions of law. Not even a constitution is any longer treated as a text in which the historical experiences of "a people" are inscribed, whereby they can understand themselves as the "authors" of their laws. Instead, almost any arrangement seems to be sufficient as long as it is competently drafted and makes reference to "universal" values. The result is a rather strange debate on the "constitutionalisation" of international law, which is supposed to ban the dangers of "fragmentation" but in which nearly any halfway "effective" regime will do. Thus "professionals" working in the field of the WTO have suggested that this organisation might serve as a constitutional framework due to its effective dispute-settlement mechanism and due to the individual "right to free trade" which, in one way or another, also nicely entails and links in with the "right to democracy" and other human rights.[70] Here the world has, for all intents and purposes, become a "shop", and "persons" are not only ahistorical and prepolitical entities but little more than "consumers".[71]

Against this instrumentalisation of law a notion of law as a system of meanings has been emphasised. It transcends the notions of "facilitating" strategic interactions or arguments of utility. It is in this context that the *topos* of the rule of law has played a particularly important role. It would be a misunderstanding to treat it as a shorthand for best legal practices, ready prepared for export, or to dismiss it as an outmoded concept of constitutional politics in an era of globalisation and universal human rights.

Notes

1 See i.e. Aristotle, *Politics* 1287a at 15–23: "It follows that it is preferable that law should rule rather than any single one of the citizens. And following this same line of reasoning ... these persons should be appointed as guardians of the law as its servants ... Therefore he who asks law to rule is asking God and intelligence and no others to rule; while he who asks for the rule of a human being is importing a wild beast ... for desire is like a wild beast and anger perverts rulers and the very best of men."
2 See i.e. the Petition of Rights of 1628.
3 See *Marbury v Madison*, 5 US (1 Cranch) 137 at 163: "The government of the United States has been emphatically termed a government of laws, and not of men."
4 World Bank, *Governance and Development* (Washington, DC: World Bank, 1992).
5 See i.e. the arguments made by Sir Edward Coke and his followers in the early Stuart parliaments, who used Bracton and Littleton as their authorities. For a general discussion of the English tradition see Q. Skinner, "States and the freedoms

of citizens" in Q. Skinner and B. Stråth (eds.), *States and Citizens* (Cambridge: Cambridge University Press, 2003), chap 1.

6 For a further discussion of the misconception of a purely referential function of political language see W. Connolly, *The Terms of Political Discourse*, 2nd edn (Princeton, NJ: Princeton University Press, 1983); see also J. Davis, *Terms of Inquiry* (Baltimore, MD: Johns Hopkins University Press, 2005).

7 "Old" realists like Carr have known that and so, in spite of Carr's denunciation of the legalist approach to international politics, which he criticises as utopian, he is well aware that all politics possesses such a "utopian" element since it is concerned not simply with the description of an existing world but with its construction: E.H. Carr, *The Twenty Years Crisis 1919–1939* (New York: Harper and Row, 1964).

8 On this point see my "Constructivism: what it is (not) and why it matters" in M. Keating and D. della Porta (eds.), *Approaches and Methodologies in the Social Sciences: A Pluralist Perspective* (Cambridge: Cambridge University Press, 2008).

9 H. Lauterpacht, *Private Law Sources and Analogies of International Law* (Hamden, CT: Archon, 1970).

10 See i.e. C. Tomuschat, *Human Rights: Between Idealism and Realism* (Oxford: Oxford University Press, 2003) p 49*ff.*

11 R.L. Barsh, "The Right to Development as a Human Right: Results of the Global Consultation" (1991) 13 *Human Rights Quarterly* 322–38.

12 See the criticism by O. O'Neil in "Transnational justice" in D. Held (ed), *Political Theory Today* (Cambridge: Polity, 1991) chap 11.

13 For a further discussion see my argument in "Global Governance and the Emergence of World Society" in N. Karagannis and P. Wagner (eds.), *Varieties of World-Making: Beyond Globalization* (Liverpool: Liverpool University Press, 2007) chap 14.

14 On the international "professionals" and the underlying ideology see D. Kennedy, "The Politics of Invisible College: International Governance and the Politics of Expertise" (2001) 5 *European Human Rights Law Review* 463–97.

15 On Foucault's notion of "governmentality" see G. Burchell, C. Gordon and P. Miller (eds.), *The Foucault Effect: Studies in Governmentality* (Chicago: University of Chicago Press, 1991).

16 Here the debate started by Dworkin and his mythical judge "Hercules" come to mind. See R. Dworkin, *Taking Rights Seriously* (Cambridge, MA: Harvard University Press, 1978).

17 C. Schmitt, *The Concept of the Political* (Chicago: University of Chicago Press, 1996).

18 See i.e. B. Buzan, O. Weaver, M. Kelstrup and P. Lemaitre, *Identity, Migration and the new Security Agenda in Europe* (London: Pinter, 1993).

19 See I. Kant, *Critique of Pure Reason* (1781) 132–4.

20 See H. Kelsen, *Principles of International Law*, (ed.) Robert Tucker (New York: Holt, 1966).

21 C. Schmitt, *Political Theology: Four Chapters on the Concept of Sovereignty* (Chicago, IL: University of Chicago Press, 2005).

22 E. Voegelin, "The Political Religions" in M Hennigsen (ed.), *The Collected Works of Eric Voegelin, Vol 5: Modernity Without Restraint* (Columbia, MO: University of Missouri Press, 2000).

23 G. Agamben, *Homo Sacer: Sovereignty and the Bare Life*, trs. D. Heller-Roazen (Stanford, CA: Stanford University Press, 1998).

24 See Y. Tamir, *Liberal Nationalism* (Princeton, NJ: Princeton University Press, 1993).

25 See my discussion in "On Legitimacy", (2006) 20 *International Relations* 302–8.

26 See Neil Walker's contribution to the present volume (chap 6).

27 For an exposition of the anarchy problematic see R. Ashley, "The Poverty of Neorealism" (1984) 38 *International Organization* 225–86.

28 See D. Kennedy, "The Move to Institutions" (1987) 8 *Cardozo Law Review* 881–988.

29 For a further discussion see my "The Genealogy of Multilateralism: Reflections on an Organizational Form and its Crisis" in E. Newman, R. Thakur and J. Tirman (eds.), *Multilateralism under Challenge* (Tokyo: UN University Press, 2006) chap 8.

30 See i.e. B. Fassbender, "The United Nations Charter as Constitution of the International Community" (1998) 36 *Columbia Journal of Transnational Law* 529–620.

31 See i.e. the argument by J. Alvarez, "Constitutional Interpretation in International Organizations" in J.M. Coicaud and V. Heiskanen, *The Legitimacy of International Organizations* (Tokyo: UN University Press, 2001) chap 4.

32 E.U. Petersmann, "Time for a United Nations 'Global Compact' for integrating Human Rights into the Law of Worldwide Organizations: Lessons from European Integration" (2002) 13 *European Journal of International Law* 621–50.

33 See i.e. A. Benz, F. Scharpf and R. Zintl, *Horizontale Politikverflechtung* (Frankfurt: Campus, 1992); F. Scharpf (ed.), *Games in Hierarchies and Networks* (Boulder, CO: Westview, 1993).

34 See G. Teubner, "Global Bukowina: Legal Pluralism in the World Society" in G. Teubner, *Global Law without a State* (Aldershot, USA: Dartmouth, 1997).

35 See i.e. A. Fischer-Lescano and G. Teubner, "Regime Collisions: The Vain Search for Legal Unity in the Fragmentation of Global Law" (2003) 25 *Michigan Journal of International Law* 999–1042.

36 See D. Kennedy, *The Dark Sides of Virtue* (Princeton, NJ: Princeton University Press, 2004) pt 1.

37 See T. Franck, *Fairness in International Law and Institutions* (Oxford: Oxford University Press, 1995).

38 A.-M. Slaughter, *A New World Order* (Princeton, NJ: Princeton University Press, 2004).

39 Take, for example, the Persian Empire and the original Roman arrangements of the *foedus aequum* and the *foedus iniqum* for exercising control.

40 This is a point well made by M. Hardt and A. Negri, *Empire* (Cambridge, MA: Harvard University Press, 2000).

41 See i.e. T. Carothers, *Promoting the Rule of Law Abroad: In Search of Knowledge* (Washington, DC: Carnegie Endowment for International Peace, 2006).

42 J. Beard, "The Confessional Framework of Law Development: How to Offer Salvation to Willing Legal Subjects" (2005) 75 *Nordic Journal of International Law* 409–49 at 411.

43 M. Koskenniemi, "Constitutionalism as Mindset: Reflection on Kantian Themes about International Law and Globalization" (2007) 8 *Theoretical Inquiries in Law* 9–36 at 26.

44 I. Kant, *Der Streit der Fakultaeten* A144*ff*, in W. Weischedel (ed.), *Immanuel Kant: Schriften zur Anthropologie, Geschichtsphilosophie, Politik und Paedagogik* (Frankfurt: Suhrkamp, 1977) at 358.

45 I. Kant, *Zum ewigen Frieden* (1796), BA 33, 34.

46 See I. Kant, *Critique of Judgement*, trs. W. Pluhar (Indianapolis, IN: Hackett Publishing Co, 1987).

47 See E. Zoller, *Peacetime Unilateral Remedies* (Dobbs Ferry, NY: Transactional Publishers, 1984).

48 "You remember to guide the peoples with power, Roman, to impose the way of peace, to spare the conquered and to battle down the proud" (*Aeneid*, Book 6, lines 852–3).

49 See also A.-M. Slaughter, *A New World Order* (Princeton, NJ: Princeton University Press, 2004) p 267; see also A.-M. Slaughter and W. Burke White, "An International Constitutional Moment" (1990) 43 *Harvard International Law Journal* 866–76.

50 (Judgment) ICTY 94–1 (26 January 2000).

51 See the discussion by V. Popowski, "Legality and Legitimacy of International Criminal Tribunals" in R. Falk and R. Thakur (eds.), *Legality and Legitimacy in the International Order* (Tokyo: UN University Press, forthcoming).

52 See the article in the *Chicago Tribune*, 1 May 2007, "US praises indicted former Kosovo PM" at www.balcanpeace.org/index.php?index=article&articleid=14323 of 26/07/2007.

53 A. Hirschman, *Exit, Voice, Loyalty* (Cambridge, MA: Harvard University Press, 1970).

54 B. Anderson, *Imagined Communities: Reflections on the Origin and Spread of Nationalism* (London: Verso, 1980) p 10.

55 I. Kant, *Metaphysics of Morals*, trs. M. Gregor (Cambridge: Cambridge University Press, 1996) p 462.

56 J. Habermas, "The European Nation State: On the Past and Future of Citizenship" in C. Cronin and P. De Greiff (eds), *Inclusion of the Other: Studies in Political Theory* (Cambridge, MA: MIT Press, 1998) p 115.

57 B.R. Lawrence, "The Right to Development as a Human Right: Results of the Global Consultation" (1991) 13 *Human Rights Quarterly* 322–38.

58 See J. Cohen, "Whose Sovereignty: Empire vs. International Law" (2004) 18 *Ethics and International Affairs* 1–24.

59 Out of the numerous publications of McDougal and his disciples see a concise outline of their project in M. McDougal, "Some Basic Concepts about International Law: A Policy Oriented Framework" in R. Falk and S.H. Mendlovitz (eds.), *The Strategy of World Order, vol 2* (New York: World Law Fund, 1966).

60 For a justification of the unilateral use of force due to the nature of security as a public good see J. Yoo, "Using Force" (2004) 71 *University of Chicago Law Review* 729–98 at 784–7.

61 J. Goldsmith and E.A. Posner, *The Limits of International Law* (Princeton, NJ: Princeton University Press, 2005) p 90.

62 Ibid, p 15.

63 On the danger of engaging in confirmatory research see K. Popper, *The Logic of Scientific Discovery* (New York: Harper and Row, 1970).

64 See i.e. J. Yoo, *The Powers of War and Peace: The Constitution and Foreign Affairs after 9/11* (Chicago, IL: University of Chicago Press, 2005).

65 This point is persuasively argued by Ulrich Haltern in "Internationales Verfassungsrecht? Anmerkungen zu einer kopernikanischen Wende?" (2003) 128 *Archiv des oeffentlichen Rechts* 511–57.

66 As a useful corrective to Yoo's argument that the new circumstances require "imperial" solutions, see the discussions in nineteenth-century England which came to the conclusion that only a strengthening of the position of Parliament could prevent an abuse of power and the subversion of the rule of law: see i.e. R.W. Kostal, *A Jurisprudence of Power: Victorian Empire and the Rule of Law* (New York: Oxford University Press, 2005).

67 For a discussion of the tradition of "republican" thought which focuses on the "separation" of powers and disabling as much as it does of its enabling functions see J.G.A. Pocock, *The Machiavellian Moment: Florentine Political Theory and the Atlantic Republican Tradition* (Princeton, NJ: Princeton University Press, 1975); Q. Skinner, *Liberty before Liberalism* (Cambridge: Cambridge University Press 1998); N. Onuf, *The Republican Legacy in International Thought* (Cambridge: Cambridge University Press, 1998); M. Viroli, *Republicanism* (New York: Hill and

Wand, 1999); J. Appelby, *Liberalism and Republicanism in the Historical Imagination* (Cambridge, MA: Harvard University Press, 1992). See also P. Onuf and N. Onuf, *Federal Union, Modern World: The Law of Nations in an Age of Revolutions 1776–1814* (Madison, WI: Madison House, 1993).

68 D. Deudney, *Bounding Power: Republican Security Theory from the Polis to the Global Village* (Princeton, NJ: Princeton University Press, 2007) p 46.

69 In this context see my "History, Action, Identity" (2006) 12 *European Journal of International Relations* 5–29.

70 See EU Petersmann, "Time for a United Nations 'Global Compact' for integrating Human Rights into the Law of Worldwide Organizations: Lessons from European Integration" (2002) 13 *European Journal of International Law* 621–50.

71 See the criticism by P. Alston, "Resisting the Merger and Acquisition of Human Rights by Trade Law" (2002) 13 *European Journal of International Law* 815–44; see also R. Howse, "Whose Rights, What Humanity, Comment on Petersmann", and Petersmann's rejoinder: E.U. Petersmann, "Taking Human Dignity, Poverty and Empowerment of Individuals More Seriously: Rejoinder to Alston" (2002) 13 *European Journal of International Law* 645–51.

Part III
Writings on epistemology

8   Constructing a new orthodoxy?

Wendt's "social theory of international politics" and the constructivist challenge

Assessing "progress" in the scientific study of international politics faces several difficulties. There is initially the issue of the objects of study and how the subject matter shall be delineated. Subsequently, there is the issue of the criteria by which we can produce warranted knowledge. One position argues that true knowledge can only be gained by following a particular method. Popular since Descartes, this stance is nowadays best represented by the unity of science position whereby anything claiming to have scientific status has to follow a specified method. An alternative contention proposes that, first of all, "knowledge" should not simply be identified with one mode of knowing, particularly since even within science there exist many different warrants that cannot be reduced to one criterion.

[. . .]

These difficulties are further exacerbated when the objects of our theoretical inquiries are not the "things" in the world, but when they are, as in the social sciences, characterised by recursivity. Social objects are not simply describable in terms of purely observational categories or measurement procedures. Rather their descriptions must make reference to the shared representations underlying the actions of actors that allow us to identify, for instance, the marks on a piece of paper as a "signature". Different from an "autograph", a signature might bind those having attached it to a document. If we could do with simple descriptions, then there could be no difference between some marks on a paper, an autograph, or a signature, since observationally all descriptions entail more or less the same movements and marks.

Most recently, these controversies have been revived in IR by the constructivist critique of logical positivism. But a similar challenge has been mounted by the rational choice approach which has become a major contender for bestowing the coveted warrant of "science" to a piece of research. Constructivists can be found not only in the cultural sciences. Indeed, some of its most prominent exponents have been biologists (Humberto Maturana, Francisco Varela) who, in turn, influenced an entirely new system theory in sociology (Niklas Luhmann).[1] Nonetheless, there is more than an elective affinity between constructivists and those who have focused on "meaning" in the past. Many constructivists have been influenced by ordinary language philosophy and speech act theory, even if such an orientation is not a necessary precondition for research in the constructivist mode.

Given these elective affinities it is, therefore, rather surprising that the recent *magnum opus* of a leading constructivist attempts to provide a new solution to the old dilemmas through some radical compromises.[2] Alexander Wendt claims not only to be a scientific realist, i.e., he puts ontology first and method second, but he also espouses some form of the unity of science position despite his acknowledgement of the ontological differences between natural and social objects. While I think Wendt's attempt is not as successful as claimed, there is no doubt in my mind that this is a work of outstanding scholarship. [. . .]

It is, therefore, quite instructive to take on Wendt on this principled level and see why and how his attempt of steering a middle course between the major existing schools of thought runs into heavy weather despite his tranquil exposition of the explosive issues involved. In a way, I am more worried that instead of remaining a provocative and fruitful new departure, true to its constructivist premises, the "reasonable middle ground" that emerges from Wendt's engagement with unreconstituted Waltzian realists, with the somewhat disoriented political scientists of the mainstream, and with rational choice believers, might actually succeed in becoming the new orthodoxy. Precisely because I think that Wendt has done a yeoman's job in sensitising us to the complexities in building better social theories, it is important to call into question some of his conclusions, and reopen some controversies which have been papered over.

We all profess to like debate and controversy, relying in due course on John Stuart Mill and Karl Popper, who extolled the necessity and virtue of debates for the growth of knowledge.[3] But as even the example of the latter shows, we do not always practice what we preach.[4] Despite our alleged love for debates, we seem to like the quiet of certitude even more and prefer the monologue of instruction rather than the arduous give-and-take of serious engagements with those who disturb our self-assuredness. After all, mathematicians do not argue, they demonstrate!

The conception of science as a set of "true", a-temporal, and universal statements clashes with the notion of science as a praxis, in which all insights are preliminary and debates about the meaning of "tests" and the allocation of the burdens of proof, rather than demonstration, are the important elements. We feel understandably uneasy with the jurisdictional metaphor, considering "truth" as the result of certain procedures, and abandoning the foundational idea that "truth" is a property of the "world".

In this context, I shall argue that because Wendt's *Social Theory* is based on a particular version of "scientific realism", it relies on some problematic foundationalist notions (although he protests this several times). I suggest that the "representational" dimension of such foundational theories is convincing only on the basis of rather unreflected conventional wisdom and experience. Here, metaphors become exceedingly important, but also misleading. We feel that there has to be some foundation on which the edifice of science is erected. Only then are we able to square the preliminary character of our knowledge with the representational theory of truth by simply depicting it as "coming closer to" the line which once and for all determines facticity. Below, I shall argue that these spatial metaphors are misleading and that some other ways of thinking about "progress" in science might be more helpful. I suggest that the image of a crossword puzzle or of playing Scrabble provides a better analogy to science as a practice than the idea of erecting a house on some "rock bottom" (materialist, of course, given the current fashion!). On the basis of this argument, I then explore the notion of science as an argument in which coherence and various strategies of shifting the burden of proof are taken as criteria for leading to both legitimate and final determinations, even though both criteria can seldom be satisfied together.[5]

The argument proceeds as follows: I provide an overview of Wendt's *Social Theory*, followed by some criticisms that are largely internal to Wendt's argument and concern clarifications or the repair of inconsistencies. In the subsequent section, I address the question of what can be learned from Wendt's truly impressive attempt as well as from its shortcomings: where might we look for further enlightenment when no secure foundations in the "observables" or in some *a priori* method can be discovered? While I obviously cannot provide some firm resting place which ends all debates by pointing to "God's" view of the world – precisely because such a view "from nowhere",[6] is not available to us – I address the allegation of "relativism" that such a negation entails [. . .].

Wendt's social theory

For Wendt, the problem of a theory of IR entails substantive "first order" questions, but also "second order" problems of social theory. To that extent, Wendt is well aware of the interdependence of the two issues above. Indeed, Wendt claims that IR theory would not only greatly benefit from systematically raising such second order issues, but also that such a mode of inquiry would result in a considerably deeper social picture of the international arena. In using Kenneth Waltz's structural theory as a foil, Wendt argues that there is not one single logic of anarchy but rather several, depending on the nature of the actors who populate the international system, i.e., whether they approach the Hobbesian, Lockean, or Kantian ideal-types. Instead of the usual threefold division of theories in IR texts, Wendt's trichotomy is not introduced *ad hoc* by looking around what is available, but instead is carefully derived from some theoretical concepts, i.e., from roles by which states represent themselves and each other.[7]

This time around Wendt has resisted deducing his argument of "anarchy is what the states make of it" from a hypothetical situation of a "first encounter" between some space aliens and humans in favour of a more historical example emphasizing the role of shared ideas.[8]

The role of ideas

Wendt's present innovation consists in the explicit inclusion of a common system of meanings (culture) and a more stringent derivation of interests from both conceptions of the self and the identification with others. Such moves allow him to dismiss some traditional red herrings, such as the dichotomy of explanation by "material interests" as opposed to "ideas". Insofar as power and interest are constituted by ideas, Wendt renders ineffective the tactic of neoliberals, rational choicers, and realists alike of treating power and interests, even institutions, "as idea-free base-lines against which the role of ideas is judged".[9] He maintains

> what makes a theory materialist is that it accounts for the effects of power, interests, or institutions by reference to brute material forces – things which exist and have certain causal powers independent of ideas, like human nature, physical environment, and, perhaps, technological artefacts. The constitutive debate between materialists and idealists is not about the relative contribution of ideas versus power and interest to social life. The debate is about the relative contribution of brute material forces to power and interest explanations. Materialists cannot claim power and interest as their variables; it all depends on how the latter are constituted.[10]

This argument disposes quickly of the sterile debate about the "role of ideas" that has been limping along in IR circles. It also clearly puts Wendt, in terms of the predominant taxonomy, in the "idealist" camp. Wendt is careful not to be identified with a "radical" form of idealism that claims it is only ideas that count ("turtles all the way down"), but embraces some "rump materialism".[11] Although this commitment is allegedly "rooted in scientific realism's naturalistic approach to society", Wendt has to admit that this "rump" does not do much of the explaining,[12] thus explicitly alerting us to the dangers of conflating the "objective" with the "material".[13] In this context, "emergence" or "supervenience" – taken up later in the book – play a crucial role. Wendt's warnings could not be clearer:

> When Neorealists offer multipolarity as an explanation for war, inquire into the discursive conditions that constitute the poles as enemies rather than friends. When Liberals offer economic interdependence as an explanation for peace, inquire into the discursive conditions that constitute states with identities that care about free trade and economic growth. When Marxists offer capitalism as an explanation for state forms, inquire into the discursive conditions that constitute capitalist relations of production . . . Enmity, interdependence, and capitalism are to a large extent cultural forms and to that extent materialist explanations that presuppose those forms will be vulnerable to . . . idealist critique.[14]

In short, as in the case of language – which is only possible when individuals are capable of making some noises for which moving one's tongue is causal – there is not much that can be learned from such a study of causality. If we are interested in communication, we had better get involved in the deciphering of the structure of language and of the meanings that are connected with certain utterances. As a matter of fact, not much remains of "rump materialism" (making some noises) when we realise that we can communicate even without such "noises", as reading and writing demonstrates. Although we might need some material marks on a paper, these preconditions are again different from the formerly mentioned causes. This argument, in turn, suggests that neither of them can be the necessary or sufficient cause and, therefore the true "fundament" for communication.

The last issue raises two further important problems for social theory. First, whether all explanations have to be causal in nature, as the unity of science position seems to suggest. Second, how are we to conceptualise the common understandings that are part of the idealist explanation. Given the commitment to methodological individualism, it seems that this common knowledge among actors has to be the aggregate of the ideas individuals have. To that extent, any hope for an holistic social theory that also wants to be based on some notion of scientific realism seems to be illusionary.

In an analysis of great subtlety and persuasiveness, Wendt's answer to the first question is *not* that causal accounts are privileged because they represent the true "scientific" form. Yet, he does not endorse the notion that non-causal accounts are the proper way of analysing social phenomena either, as adherents of the autonomy of the cultural sciences claim. Instead, he shows that in both the natural and the social sciences, at least two different types of questions and of explanations are used: there are "causal" statements that answer "why" questions. And there are "what" and "how possible" questions that are inquiries into the constitution of things. The latter takes a different form than explaining the occurrence of an event by its efficient (antecedent) causes. In causal accounts both cause and effect have to be independent of each other while in the case of a constitutive relationship no such independence is implied.

The request in constitutive explanations is rather for explicating the structures that constitute the phenomenon in the first place (e.g., "what is sovereignty", not what "causes" it). Wendt shows that some of the most important explanations in the natural sciences, such as the kinetic theory of heat, or the double helix model of DNA, fall into the constitutive category. Since both questions are logically irreducible to each other (despite some conceptual links), and since both are occasioned by different interests that cut across the nature/culture divide, neither can be automatically privileged.

Such a view also quickly disposes of the problem that any explanation has to satisfy the subsumption model familiar from Carl Hempel and Popper. For them the conjunction of the initial conditions of universal laws leads to a singular hypothetical statement (prediction) that is derived via a logical inference. Because of the logical equivalence of prediction and explanation in this model, singular statements could be used to falsify the universality of "laws" by means of the *modus tollens*.[15] Wendt acknowledges the problematic nature of this position popularised by logical positivism. He sides with those who accept "theories" in which explanations do not exhibit the logical equivalence of prediction and explanation (the theory of evolution is the best example). Furthermore, he points out in true "scientific realist" fashion that the identification of a *causal mechanism*, rather than the logical subsumption, does the explaining in any case.[16]

Taking the democratic peace argument as a foil, Wendt suggests

> subsumption under a law is not really explanation at all, in the sense of answering *why* something occurred, but simply a way of saying that it is an instance of a regularity. In what sense have we explained peace between the US and Canada by subsuming it under the generalization that "democracies do not fight each other"? When, what we really want to know is why democracies do not fight each other, to answer that question in terms of still higher order laws merely pushes the question one step back. The general problem here is failing to distinguish the grounds for expecting an event to occur (being an instance of regularity) with explaining why it occurs. Causation is a relation in nature, not in logic.[17]

Clearly, this outlined position is very critical of the traditional unity of science position, endorsed by most "mainstream" approaches to IR. But most "theoretical" debates in the field are seldom aware of the complexity of these problems. Political scientists happily take parts and pieces from Popper and Hempel, fit some Thomas Kuhn with it, enhance it by some elements of Imre Lakatos, add perhaps a little Milton Friedman, (the "as if" character of basic assumptions is here truly a favourite) while holding on to the idea of testing against reality which is entirely incompatible with any of these elements. To his credit, instead of proceeding in this fashion, Wendt provides a controversial, but independently articulated alternative that is sensitive to these differences.

Equally controversial to many will be Wendt's answer to the second question above: how to conceptualise the beliefs that give meaning to our actions and allow us to engage in cooperative ventures, limit conflicts, justify claims, and make demands on each other. Most members of our cohort decisively opt for the individualist notion that such "common knowledge" has to be explained by aggregating the individually held beliefs. But this procedure poses the further problem of how these beliefs "got in there", i.e., the heads of the actors and why these beliefs happen to coincide.

Furthermore, issues of selection and of socialisation make, in turn, a discussion of social structure and of the interdependence of agency and structure necessary. Thus, Wendt's exchange with Waltz is more than a rhetorical ploy. The aspiration to provide some final answer ("theory is" . . ., "a system is" . . .) is common to both theories.[18] Wendt claims that his theory is clearly the wider one; his approach is systemic, cognitive, and interactionist, instead of structural, materialist, and static. Wendt's approach also allows for a more comprehensive analysis of change instead of reducing IR to the alternatives of hierarchy versus anarchy, or to positional changes within the system. Such an alternative necessitates fundamental changes in the analytical instruments, in the selection of criteria of reductionism, and in the evaluation of interaction as an important theoretical concern. I can focus here only on a few of the themes which seem to me the most important and innovative.

Individualism versus holism

Let me start with the debate on individualism and holism in social science. It is here that Wendt provides some interesting evidence that "culture" is indeed something different than the individualist notion of common knowledge in game theory. [. . .] Thus, his discussion is ultimately devoted to the demonstration of the importance of social structures which are systemic but cultural rather than materialist. These structures link micro-level and macro-level through both constitutive and causal effects that can be observed in actual interactions. Wendt distinguishes in this context between (minimal) social situations, in which interaction takes place without mediation by common knowledge, and those where common knowledge shapes such interactions.

The term "social action" is used by Wendt in the traditional sense in that an action is viewed from the actor's perspective and possesses a strategic dimension, i.e., the interacting "other" is taken into account. Thus, to take Wendt's example, when the Aztecs and Spaniards in 1519 encountered each other, they both possessed some knowledge of how to treat the other, which informed their actions. The Aztecs probably "mistook" the Spaniards as gods whose arrival had been prophesised, while the Spaniards dealt with them as "savages". As in the "original encounter" it would have been surprising if such a meeting could have evolved without degeneration. While the interaction between these two parties was "social", it was neither informed by "common knowledge" nor by shared meanings (culture). Only the latter provides the taken-for-granted knowledge of, for instance, modern international politics that frame interactions in the state system. Thus, what a "state" is has to be "known", and actors have to understand the implications of "sovereignty" for their practices. Indeed,

> compared to the situation facing Cortez and Montezuma, this represents a substantial accretion of culture at the systemic level, without an understanding of which neither statesmen nor neorealists would be able to explain why modern states and state systems behave as they do.[19]

These puzzles suggest that collective representations are something different from the common knowledge of game theory. Wendt argues that the relationship between the collective structures of meaning and individual beliefs is one of "supervenience and multiple realizability".[20] To that extent "culture", as the shorthand for collective representations cannot exist or have effects apart from the beliefs of individual actors, but is not reducible to them. As in the case of language, it exists only insofar as it is used by individual speakers but cannot be conceptualised as the "private" possession of each speaker. Drawing on Emile Durkheim, Philip Pettit, and Margaret Gilbert, Wendt argues:

> Structures of collective knowledge depend on actors believing something that induces them to engage in practices that reproduce those structures; to suggest otherwise would be to reify culture, to separate it from knowledgeable practices through which it is produced and reproduced. On the other hand the effects of collective knowledge are not reducible to individual's beliefs . . . Indeed, as Margaret Gilbert points out, we can ascribe beliefs to a group that are not held personally by any of its members, as long as members accept the legitimacy of the group's decision and the obligation to act in accordance with its results.[21]

The latter point is of particular importance as it explains Wendt's often criticised state centrism.[22] It is not that Wendt does not "see" other actors populating the international arena, or that he wants to deny their influence. Instead he is interested in the reproduction of the state system and, therefore, states and their constitution have to be at the centre of his attention. If one wants to criticise Wendt here, one has to do this via his conception of politics as it is "protection" that defines the state's "essence". Thus, it is not a neutral conception of politics as, for instance, the formal definition of making collective choices, or of representation, or as an even more substantive notion such as the Aristotelian good life. Wendt's definition comes rather close to the Hobbesian (and perhaps impoverished) notion of politics, which holds that no other social relations are possible unless they are "compatible with the 'forces' and especially the 'relations of destruction'".[23]

Without organisation and social cooperation, however, the "forces of destruction" cannot even be conceptualised, since war is, after all a social phenomenon that presupposes groups and politics. Consequently, it cannot serve as the foundation of all politics even if force plays an extremely important role. Thus, "the war of all against all" which supposedly lies at the "bottom" of the social contract is an impossible construction, both historically (as Hobbes was well aware)[24] and logically. It is surprising to see how easily Wendt falls into the Hobbesian trap.[25] This understanding of politics unites him with the (neo)realists but it does not make much sense if one espouses a constructivist approach. Let me be clear about this: the reason is not that constructivists believe in the inherent goodness of man or have peace as a political project, as opposed to realism's preoccupation with security and defence. The reason is rather that there are no simple givens for constructivists, such as "structures" or "forces" that are not again results of particular actions and "constructions" that require further explanations.

Similarly, Wendt's attribution of intentions, desires, and beliefs to "states" might seem like strange anthropomorphism, but it is not much stranger than the everyday acceptance of corporate personality. In that case too, we make important distinctions between shareholder rights and the rights of the corporate entity itself, and we assert their irreducibility.[26] We may not be convinced by Wendt's neo-Weberian emphasis on centralisation of the coercive means as the state's essence. [. . .] Yet, Wendt is certainly correct by following Weber:

> individual actions have to be oriented toward the corporate idea does not mean that everyone in the group must have this idea in their heads [*sic*] . . . What matters is that individuals accept the obligation to act jointly on behalf of collective beliefs, whether or not they subscribe to them personally.[27]

A new systemic theory?

All this sets the stage for Wendt's new systemic theory and his take on the agent/structure debate. Wendt cannot subscribe to a systemic theory recognising only capabilities and systematically neglecting interactions. As he suggests:

> The debate is not between *systemic* theories that focus on structure and *reductionist* theories that focus on agents, but between *different theories of system structure* and how structures relate to agents.[28]

He therefore not only abandons Waltz's unhelpful conceptual grid, but takes issue with the entire account of structures reproducing themselves across times. Without going into Wendt's detailed (but rather meekly voiced) criticism of Waltz, it is important to note that he clearly opts for an explanation of "sameness" in terms of *cognitive structures*.

Furthermore, he argues *contra* Waltz that social structures not only affect the "behaviour" but the actors' very identities. In short, social structures have not only behavioural effects, but also "property effects". Furthermore, these effects cannot be reduced to simple causally efficient influences. The latter presuppose independence between the entities concerned, but "property effects" obviate such independence. To that extent, any "theory" based on radical individualism cuts itself off from analysing this constitutive influence of ideas as they affect properties. It also automatically reduces the agent/ structure problem to one of co-determination or interaction, rather than one of mutual constitution and *conceptual dependence*.

Wendt wishes to steer clear of the Scylla of postulating some mysterious "group mind", and the Charybdis position of pure methodological individualism, in which any idea can only be a "subjective" representation. Thus, Wendt introduces George Mead's distinction between "I" and "Me", and between *individuality per se* and the *terms of individuality*. The latter term (Me, or the "terms of individuality") refers to those properties of an agent's constitution that are intrinsically dependent upon culture. The "I", or the "individuality per se", designates an agent's sense of the "self" as a distinct locus of thought, choice and activity.[29]

Wendt then distinguishes between four types of identity, a move that is somewhat problematic, since he tries to graft his ideas to the scheme of Jim Fearon. The first, the personal or corporate identity, seems to correspond to the "I" in the above discussion, the second involves a "type identity" which seems based sometimes on nothing more than classificatory rules, such as age. Third, "role identities", which "are not based on intrinsic properties and as such exist only in relation to others".[30] And finally, the "collective identity" in which the boundary between self and other is blurred through identification, i.e., the self is categorised as "other". Collective identification is never total, as otherwise the extinction of the "self" would result and there are apparently powerful psychological mechanisms at work that prevent total identifications. Nevertheless, to view, for example, an attack on a "friend" as an attack on oneself is one of the basic facts of international life on which even the famous "inherent" right to "collective *self-defence*" [sic] is founded.[31]

With these conceptual instruments in place, Wendt can attack the core of neo-realism's main tenet: the "logic" of anarchy. He argues that three distinct macro level structures develop out of the permissive environment of anarchy, depending on how "others" are conceptualised. These structures could be called in accordance with their most prominent theorists: a Hobbesian, Lockean, or Kantian system of anarchy. Wendt's interesting next step is then to free the notion of "culture" from too close an identification with the internalisation of norms, a mistake commonly made. Thus, the Hobbesian world is believed to be one in which norms are followed because they are "guaranteed" by a credible enforcer. If norms are better internalised, as is traditionally maintained, they give rise to a Lockean system. Here "rivalry" and "cost-calculations" channel conflicts. Finally Wendt suggests the Kantian perspective represents the deepest level of internalisation; no longer are force or price calculations determinative, but the legitimacy of the norms represent the dominant motive.

This conceptualisation, however, leads to the conflation of two distinct problems: that of the existence of norms and their internalisation on one hand, and that of "political order" or the possibility of inducing large-scale cooperation on the other. For Wendt, the existence of a stable Hobbesian culture in certain periods seems to indicate that certain norms and expectations have been thoroughly internalised without opening a path towards greater cooperation. Such a "stickiness" depends also on a process and the "lock-in" of certain assumptions about the relationship of self and other. If more and more members of a system represent each other as enemies, there comes a point at which these representations define "reality":

> At this point actors start to think of enmity as a property of the system rather than just of individual actors and so feel compelled to represent all Others as enemies simply because they are part of the system. In this way, the particular Other becomes Mead's "generalized Other", a structure of collective beliefs and expectations that persists through time even as individual actors come and go and into the logic of which actors are socialized.[32]

Consequently, Wendt holds that change at the macro level requires above all a redefinition of the posture of the self to the other, in particular with respect to force as a strategy of pursuing one's goals.[33] Thus, violence among "rivals" is self-limiting as total wars are prevented by the accepted right of the "other" to exist. To the extent that the right to life and liberty are non-controversial, conflicts are largely limited to "property" issues. Finally, in a Kantian world the threat of force has receded and the presumption of non-violence dispute-settlement in such a "security community" is the dominant maxim.

This thesis leads to two surprising results: first, the logics of anarchy are not dependent upon how deeply a culture is internalised:

> Hobbesian logics can be generated by deeply shared ideas and Kantian logics by only weakly shared ones. Each logic is multiply realisable: the same effect can be reached through different causes.[34]

Second,

> Realist pessimism notwithstanding, it is easier to escape a Hobbesian world, whose culture matters relatively little, and harder to create a Kantian one based on deeply shared beliefs. It is Realists who should think that cultural change is easy, not constructivists, because the more deeply shared ideas are – the more they matter.[35]

With this Wendt has provided some strong arguments for the ideational notion of social structures, and for the thesis that these structures are instantiated by the roles and representations of self and other. Wendt clearly considers the Lockean version of international politics as the most apt description since the Westphalian settlement. He also interprets the subsequent low death rate of states as a persuasive proof that *cultural*, not natural, selection, advanced by imitation and learning, provides the best analogy for the exploration of systemic change. Cultural selection occurs through changes in the mechanism of "reflected appraisal" rather than through (re)distribution of capabilities. Since he has argued that fundamentally different systems emerge depending upon whether the actors conceive of each other as enemies, competitors, or friends, his last chapter is devoted to the investigation of how the actors "learn to see themselves as a reflection of how they are appraised by significant Others".[36] The self still has to take, reject, or modify the identity which the others have "cast" for it, but his interactionism leads Wendt to identify the representational practices of others – rather than the actual choice of an identity by the actor – as the important puzzle. Wendt realises, of course, that in determining the options powerful states will have significantly more influence than weaker ones. Nevertheless, he is (strangely) uninterested in both problems, i.e., in how powerful states influence the menu of available choices and in the "final choice".

Since "we are – or become – what we do", Wendt reverts to a general discussion of "collective identity formation" and to the master variables that govern that process (interdependence, common fate, homogeneity, and self-restraint). The first three are termed "efficient causes", the last a "permissive cause". Under conditions of interdependence the incentives for co-operation – in the sense of making for extended identifications – are checked by fears of exploitation. The situation of "common fate" depends on the perception that the survival or welfare "depends on what happens to the group".[37] While this might seem like a strong identification, Wendt argues that common fate perceptions (usually provided by an "external threat") have not prevented states from not cooperating because of the fear of exploitation.[38] One might ask then what purchase "identifications" have.

The last of the efficient causes is "homogeneity", or likeness. Categorising others as being similar to oneself does not necessarily lead to "identification". But Wendt claims that homogeneity reduces conflict that otherwise could arise out of differences in corporate and type identity. In short, recognising that someone is like us is an inducement to treating him alike.[39] Finally, self-restraint, i.e., knowledge that the other is unlikely to resort to force, engenders "trust". In choosing the assurance the citizens of the Bahamas have concerning a US invasion, Wendt elaborates:

> When Bahamian foreign policy makers wake up each morning, they *know* that the United States is not going to conquer them, not because they think the US will be deterred by superior power, not because they think that on that day the US will calculate that violating the norms of sovereignty is not in its self-interest, but because they know that the US will restrain *itself*. Like all knowledge this belief is not 100 percent certain, but it is reliable enough that we would think it irrational for the Bahamanians to act on any other basis.[40]

There is certainly something to this stress on "routines" and "discipline" in social life. But whether or not this example can carry the weight placed upon it depends on the assessment of the theory as a whole. It is to this problem that I want to turn in the next section.

Clarifications, criticisms, and disagreements

A work of such scope and complexity is likely to engender a series of questions that arise from ambiguities in the argument, or out of mistakes in logic or fact. One prime candidate for theoretical elaboration or correction is Wendt's assertion concerning the respective advantages of rationalist and constructivist models. Wendt argues (correctly) that the former are useful for analysing decisions in which interests and identity are stable, while the latter are more appropriate for longer term-change. There is a certain plausibility to this argument, but the juxtaposed "lesson" does not follow, that is, that "rationalism is for today and tomorrow and constructivism for the *longue durée*".[41]

First of all, anyone familiar with Fernand Braudel's work will realise that the *longue durée* is the domain for structural explanations precisely because identities and interests do not matter because they "wash out" over long periods. Someone who changes the priorities has to show why his version of the *longue durée* should be accepted. Second, the reader who has just worked through a rather demanding text of some 300-plus pages which emphasises process over structure, and actors and their ideas over material factors, and who also remembers the unravelling of the former Soviet Bloc within a few years, might question Wendt's judgement. Since rationalist models – through their simplifying assumptions concerning interests and identities – can be shown to be a special case of constructivist models, their relationship is not one that can be described in terms of their fitness for short versus long-term types of analysis. Rather the problem consists in deciding whether by the introduction of simplifying assumptions, problems of interest-formation, roles, and identities can be neglected in a concrete case.

Further, such an assessment will have to go beyond traditional risk-analysis since, by definition, new identities and interests change the type of actor and, thus, also the "known" universe on which the frequency distributions and probabilities relied. What makes such events as the French Revolution or even the Cuban Missile crisis so frightening is that the "roles" used as yardsticks for assessing actions are no longer valid. This brief discussion alone suggests that the conceptualisation of long versus short run is seriously misleading and does not do justice to the problems involved.

Similarly, Wendt's "proof" that despite significant differences between natural kinds and social kinds, the same methods are applicable to each is less than convincing, particularly since it is based on a simple *non sequitur*. After explicitly acknowledging the reflexivity of social life, i.e., that actors can come to understand themselves as the authors of their structures and thus transcend the subject/object distinction, Wendt admits that social scientific theories alone have the potential to become part of the "world". Consequently, "such transformations violate the causal theory of reference, since reality is being caused by theory rather than vice versa".[42] After one further sentence, Wendt presents his conclusion: "In sum, the ontology of social life is consistent with scientific realism".[43] This conclusion, however, does not follow; having postulated the primacy of ontology, having furthermore acknowledged the important difference between natural and social kinds, the surprising conclusion is that none of all this matters!

Now let us examine the Bahamian example more closely. Despite its intuitive appeal it seems that too much is claimed. After all, given the absence of a concrete conflict of interest, even hardened realists would not claim that an attack has to follow necessarily from structural givens.[44] The "indifference" that arises out of isolation is for Rousseau the nostrum that minimises violence in the state of nature, even if the actors' motivation is no longer that of the *amour de soi* but of the *amour propre*. Wendt is certainly right in holding that many decisions (or rather non-decisions) do not result from explicit cost/ benefit analyses. But in order to show the "mechanisms" at work here, one needs something like "hidden faces of power" or the "disciplinary" understandings of Michel Foucault, in which the limits of sense are not neutral descriptions of the things, but are recognised as being part of a disciplinary program according to which actors fashion themselves. Similarly, Pierre Bourdieu's concept of "habitus" might be illuminating.

[. . .]

Wendt (re)discovers scientific realism

I have already mentioned in passing that Wendt's interactionist perspective seems to neglect the "final choice" of why and how an actor takes the role he or she is cast in. In the discussion above, the factors internal to the actor remained obscure as role and expectations were emphasised. Now I want to add a more principled criticism of the neglect of language's role in social life. This omission has various implications ranging from simple anomalies and blind spots to methodological commitments strangely at odds with constructivism.

Obviously, the last remark flags something more than mere criticism which might even fall into the category of deep-seated and irresolvable disagreements. Let me be clear that this criticism is not part of some contest who is the "better" or "truer" constructivist, in which self designations and quotes from others ("he or she also says x and he or she is a constructivist") are persuasive. Important theoretical and metatheoretical problems are at stake. The issue is not whether somebody says or believes she or he is a constructivist, but whether or not such a (self)-identification makes sense in view of some of the tenets defining constructivism.

In this context Wendt's commitment to, and version of, "scientific realism" can be questioned on two counts. First, whether his rendition of this perspective is indeed appropriate and second, whether his version of "realism" is compatible with constructivism as a metatheoretical orientation. Given the rather different emphases among scientific realists concerning methodological and ontological issues, one can indeed doubt whether "realism" is a well-defined philosophy that can serve as a foundation and carry the weight Wendt places upon it.[45] Moreover, the virtually complete neglect of the *social* component of scientific realism, most notably in the work of Roy Bashkar, on which Wendt often relies, is especially surprising. [. . .]

This brings us back to the dilemma of the apparent incompatibility of two standards for knowledge – truth and consensus – and the strategies by which we mediate these tensions. The most obvious strategy is the attempt of making consensus dependent upon truth, based on the hope that either logic or reality, if properly questioned, will adjudicate. But most problems cannot be solved that way because they belong to the category of "undecidable" questions. Thus, neither the logical tool of the "excluded middle" (bivalence principle), nor the test against reality are applicable. The second strategy is to assert that truth is a function of consensus in a scientific community sharing criteria of what represents "good science". Results are considered "true" as they emerge from particular procedures and practices. Truth is then not only contingent on some theoretical framework and some taken-for-granted or background knowledge (measurement), but is also derived from argumentative procedures. The arguments among the practitioners centre on the importance or meaning of tests, on the justifications for calling something an anomaly (rather than a refutation), an error (rather than a "discovery"), and so forth. In other words, reaching the final decision is based on some legitimate procedure that allocates burdens of proof.

Interestingly, such a perspective dethrones science as a paradigm of knowledge since it undermines foundational claims of the scientific method to show things as they really are. Instead, the choice between finality and legitimacy of a decision arises. Given the fact that these two criteria often point in different directions, it is more appropriate to use the analogy of a court and its formal procedures to "establish" the truth, rather than making the notion of truth a function of representing reality. The fact that scientists have even asked for such a "court", and that many scientific associations and enterprises increasingly use quasi-judicial procedures,[46] suggests a deep-seated change in both the practice of science and in the public's acceptance of scientific statements as self-justifying instruments of "truth".[47] Wendt's attempt to found not only *a* social theory, but *the* (generic) "social theory" seems, therefore, somehow old-fashioned, hardly compatible with his own constructivist perspective, and curiously out of sync with some of the most important developments in "science".

Since much depends on the assessment of "scientific realism", its further examination is in order. The first thing to notice is that despite Wendt's claim, the term scientific realism applies to people with rather disparate epistemological orientations; it seems rather difficult to fathom what Bashkar's "realism" has in common with David Lewis' realism. In the title of one of his books, Lewis challenges the normal conception of "reality" by arguing for the "plurality of worlds",[48] and Rom Harre suggests that there is a *variety* of realisms.[49] Thus, there is considerably more debate and controversy among these philosophers of science than the rather unified position Wendt invokes when grounding his social theory in this school. But be this as it may, scientific realists according to Wendt share certain commitments, such as the following:

1   the world is independent of the mind and language of individual observers;
2   mature scientific theories typically refer to this world;
3   even when it is not directly observable.

I am not sure whether this rather general characterisation is apt for Wendt's purposes. That there are "unobservables" in every theory is hardly controversial, strict empiricists excepted. Such a view is shared by pragmatists, postmodernists (whatever that means), constructivists, and logical positivists alike. Instead, the controversies centre on the meaning of the two other statements. Here again, hardly anyone – even among the most ardent constructivists or pragmatists – doubts that the "world" exists "independent" from our minds. The question is rather whether we can recognise it in a pure and direct fashion, i.e., without any "description", or whether what we recognise is always already organised and formed by certain categorical and theoretical elements. Thus, Kant's "thing in itself" is "there", but it is unrecognisable and as such uninteresting until and unless it is brought under some description. Consequently, there remain two problems that need further clarification: first, whether this "naming" is indeed a function of the congruence of our concepts and the "things", as this provides the yardstick for "truth"; or second, whether "truth" is a matter of the conditions governing the justifiability of *assertions* rather than a matter of the "world".

Most "realists" not only believe in natural kinds and some essence that "correctly" names the things in the world, but they also must hold some form of "iconic" theory of truth. As the latter has come increasingly under attack, Wendt explicitly states that his "theory" does not imply such a foundational stance (since theories are always tested against other theories and not against "the world").[50] However, I cannot see how such an argument can be squared with his emphasis on "essences" and natural kinds. Even more astonishing is Wendt's argument "that 'truth', does not do any interesting work" in the realist philosophy of science. While pragmatists, who rely on usefulness rather than truth, can espouse such a position, this stance is incoherent for a scientific realist.[51] As Wendt himself argues elsewhere, "science is successful because it gradually brings our theoretical understanding into conformity with the deep structure of the world out there".[52]

Thus, the suspicion mounts that several incompatible things are being bolted together. There is first of all the problem that too much is made out of the "miracle" theory of science which allegedly justifies scientific realism. While the success of science is no problem, the inference that it is due to its "correct" apprehension of reality is a difficulty. After all, a theory can be successful without necessarily referring to something real. Thus, contrary to the conception of a Popperian "Third World", where all these true entities are housed, one might wonder where all these entities like atoms, phlogistons, even elements like fire – about which even Kant was still writing a dissertation – have gone.

Furthermore, how do we know that we have got nearer to the truth instead of only substituting one theoretical concept with some other? The new concept allows us to ask interesting questions but they might lead us again down a blind alley, while a former allegedly refuted truth might suddenly provide some new starting point. As the history of science has shown these are not imaginary examples.[53] Instead, they correct the view that "science" can be described as a simple process of monological demonstration in which, by conjectures and refutations, a self-correcting process of progress commences. Although Wendt does not base his account on Popper and his followers, he still shares much of their "plot" and "rational reconstruction" of the history of science. Without wishing to enter the discussion about Popper's intellectual development, it is important to realise that he increasingly moved away from his original monological understanding of science by stressing the importance of exchanges among scientists. This adjustment was important since it united Popper's philosophy of science with his political theory.

As Popper suggested: "Rational discussion is central to the open society and to science. In both, the purpose of rational discussion is to criticise and refute".[54] This argument shows the constitutive character of debate and criticism for scientific knowledge and thus dethrones "demonstration" and purely logical criteria from their position as guarantors of truth. As Popper proposes, unanimity – the goal of logical demonstration – is not "fruitful" and might actually be the death of science. This idea is most explicit in his last book, *The Myth of the Framework*.[55] There Popper not only tried to show that there is virtue in disagreements, and that fruitful communication among scientists is not dependent upon a shared framework, a late answer to Kuhn's notion of incommensurable paradigms. Rather scientific inquiry is based on the respect of certain *ethical* principles that govern arguments and the allocation of burdens of proof in the debates.

Regardless of whether one is persuaded by Popper's strategy, it certainly was one of the most discussed epistemological issues during the past two decades. Even realists like Bashkar have emphasised the importance of this "social" component of knowledge. This component is not some part of a sociology of knowledge that can be neglected in a rational reconstruction of science.[56] It is rather intrinsic to "science" as a practice, even if it does not fit some problematic rational reconstruction of scientific progress. The virtual omission of this entire dimension of scientific activity and of two decades of epistemological debate by Wendt, his implicit embrace of the "monological" ideal buttressed by the bivalence principle of logic (either the world is so, or not so), is all the more surprising as this neglect centrally touches upon important issues of theory-building. As the scientific realist Rom Harre has pointed out, realism has to answer to the criticisms made during the last few decades,[57] and can be reconstructed only in a more modest form that is close to scientific practice and avoids previous fatal errors.[58]

[. . .]

Given this perspective, Wendt's *Theory* looks curiously old-fashioned. Although he repeatedly emphasises that science is not logic and that real "causal mechanisms" rather than logical implications have to be investigated, he misses entirely the larger point addressed by Popper and Harre.

One can only guess why Wendt, who is certainly familiar with this literature, has chosen to pass over this problem. One reason could be that the audience he tries to persuade to embrace his position as the new middleground is deeply committed to the notion that logical closure and deductive rigor are the characteristics of good science. After a prolonged period of mindless empiricism, the recent insistence of some stringency in the argumentation seems like an important corrective. Unfortunately, the stridency with which this new ideal is advocated and the questionable nature of the claims involved suggest that it is not "science", but success in terms of power within the "profession" that is the motive for such a dogmatic attitude.

[. . .]

The failed marriage: scientific realism meets constructivism

There remains the question of whether and to what extent "realism" and constructivism are compatible. This involves not only the status of ideas as opposed to natural forces – a problem that I think Wendt solves quite nicely – but also the problem of the status of "social kinds" and of "essences", as adumbrated above. Even if we do not consider "essences" to consist in a single feature or property that differentiates an object from all others, there is the assumption that objects have to fall under one description which is fitting or correct, as opposed to (all?) others.[59] Thus, Wendt somewhat ironically contrasts his essentialist account with those of some postmodernists, who suggest that even observable entities such as "dogs and cats do not exist independent of discourse".[60] Elaborating on a "dog" Wendt argues that: "Human descriptions and/or social relationships to other natural kinds have nothing to do with what makes dogs dogs".[61] This seems clear enough and well in tune with our common-sense understandings. However, a moment's reflection shows that the matter is a bit more complicated.

The first thing we notice is that defining man's essence in terms of some biological properties commits a category-mistake of the first order. The fact of a certain genetic endowment clearly locates humanity within the "animal kingdom" and shows us that some of the human capacities, such as speech, or reflexivity, are related to biological features such as a movable tongue or a well-developed cortex. But these facts do not entitle us to assume that such an essentialist description is particularly helpful for answering our questions concerning humankind's social life and for investigating the symbolic structures upon which social orders are based. Thus, humanity's essence is not a question about some unique feature only, but is crucially related to the questions we are interested in asking. Focusing on some unique feature might not be helpful at all. For instance, it is certainly true that "man" is the only featherless biped, but this characterisation is neither very useful for biology nor for the analysis of social order. To that extent, it is correct that we have to be interested in the "generative" aspect of "essential" characterisations rather than on some unique feature. Nevertheless, essentialism must hold that there is one and only one "true" description of a thing.

This leads us to a second difficulty with Wendt's argument. His insistence that the existence of things is not only independent of our descriptions, but that our descriptions of the things are independent from particular frames of reference. That the second argument does not follow from the first should be clear, especially to constructivists. Contrary to Wendt, and without necessarily embracing the postmodern position, the problem constructivism raises in a big way *is not* the one of *existence* but of recognising *what* the existing thing is. In other words, we cannot talk about "things in themselves", but need descriptions; these descriptions are not neutral and somehow objective but embrace all types of social practices and interests that then make the things into what they are called or referred to. Thus, while "dog" might be a name for an animal, it is not a description which is appropriate under all circumstances. Part of what defines a "dog" for us is not only its zoological characteristics, but a socially significant property such as "tameness", which brings a dog under the description of "pet". When we encounter an animal that lacks this property we are entirely justified in calling it something different, such as "dingo", even if its genetic code is the same as that of a dog!

Similarly, it is difficult to say what a fork or a broom "is" unless we understand the uses and the roles of these instruments in our practices. Why do we perceive a "broom" in the corner, and not some elongated piece of wood with some bristles on top, held together by a wire, and how do we decide which of these properties or materials is its "essence"? Similarly, would a "fork" be a fork if we did not use it for holding food but rather think it is an instrument for gouging one another's eyes, as some knights in the play by Thomas Becket apparently thought when this newfangled instrument was introduced? The object itself certainly cannot tell us!

In short, what is at issue is not the existence of the "thing in itself" but its recognition as "something" which can only be established by bringing it under a description. Thus, a table *is* different depending on whether I bring it under the description of a physicist, a chemist, or avail myself of the common-sense language in referring to it. It is, therefore, pretty useless to argue in the abstract (i.e., without specifying the interests and purposes) which of these descriptions is the "true" one, as it should be clear that "truth" is not a function of the "things", or of the "world", but of assertions that are made within certain frames and descriptions. Short of taking a position of extreme reductionism, i.e., that all descriptions and frames can be reduced without loss to one description – the favourite game of "materialists" who want to hit "rock bottom" somewhere, as well as of Platonists who claim for themselves God's view of the world – the talk about "essences" seems pretty sterile. Wendt himself is right when he resists this turn in his discussion of "rump materialism".[62] But his argument makes it then all the more unintelligible, why he hangs on to some of its red herrings. Whatever merits different versions of essentialism have, be they material or ideational, it is certainly no accident that the growth of science occurred only after we had given up on the idea that the world could either speak for itself, or that it can be comprehended from a Platonic perspective.

Similarly, if social systems are not simply "there" but arise as the result of construction, then one of the interesting questions is that of the boundaries of such systems: how they are drawn and how they mediate between the environment and the system. Thus, Luhmann's systems theory has fruitfully taken an analytical stance that analyses the operations by which a system draws its boundaries and reproduces itself, instead of focusing on the elements of the system.[63] Even if one does not share Luhmann's decentred approach, the problem of boundaries and their maintenance is an important issue that can not be aborted by some ontological fiat.[64] Thus, it is more than disappointing that such questions are practically ruled out by Wendt's insistence on the ontological priority of the state.[65] He also cuts himself off from the analysis of the shifting boundaries of the political, as exemplified by the debates in political economy.[66] He thereby excludes the possibility of engaging with crucial issues of inclusion and exclusion that animate the discussion of citizenship and the state's capacity to act, and from the analysis of secular changes by which systems and actors get reconstituted, as Rodney Hall has so nicely shown.[67] To deal with such interesting and important questions by definitional exercises or apodictic statements (e.g., a system is . . ., the state is ontologically prior to the system, etc.) is to dismiss them and to needlessly impair the heuristic power of a systemic theory of international politics, particularly when the dismissal is based on a mistaken analogy.[68]

Finally, there seem to be different conceptions of "system" at work in Wendt's book. On the one hand, there is the residual Waltzian notion of a system as a sum of states positioned vis-à-vis each other. In other words, Wendt retains a conception of system (even if enriched by interaction) that comes close to a natural system. In chapter four, though, the concept shifts, as the system is now understood as a combination of material factors, ideas, and interests (*vide* the discussion of "rump materialism"). Finally, in chapter six we arrive at the virtual conflation of "system" with culture. But as Jens Steffek has asked, can one define a social structure simply by "culture"? Usually, when we talk about structures we do distinguish them from the more encompassing notion of "culture" (that might house or be compatible with several structures).[69]

Moralité, or what can be learned from it

If we cannot rely on a firm foundation, then we seem to question the existence of "truth", along with "science" as a method of arriving at it. This raises the problem of relativism and often engenders the charge of nihilism. While a more critical perusal of my argument indicates the unjustifiability of such an inference (as only a dogmatic epistemology and conception of science is called into question) there is clearly some uneasiness in dispensing with notions of secure foundations. Admitting that forgoing such foundational claims might be painful, the more interesting question is what can be done given our predicament.

As I tried to show there are various attempts to "fox" these issues, such as recognising the force of the sceptics' criticisms while holding on to the notion of a truth which we approach, but never reach. Similarly, we might claim to dispense with foundationalism while keeping the "realist" vocabulary and conceptual framework intact. All these gambits are problematic responses to the crisis. As a first step it may be useful to offer some middle position, counteracting both the fears of hopelessness (nihilism) and of arrogance that comes from the alleged possession of "truth". As a second step, however, it is necessary to critically reflect on such a middle position and perhaps embark on a different strategy, especially when it becomes clear that the "middle" course has no particular virtues but many of the disadvantages of the positions it tries to mediate.

I believe that turning away from foundational notions, such as the bivalence or the rationality principles, and interpreting the question of decidability as one of a fair procedure provides a more honest approach. Here, some ethical principles rather than demonstration and deduction are critical. Basically, this amounts to the recognition that finality and legitimacy of a judgement coincide only in logic. These criteria point to different directions not only in practical matters, but also in science. The problem of fairly allocating the burdens of proof is therefore not as simple as Lakatos suggested, who distinguished between naïve and sophisticated falsificationism and progressive and degenerative problem shifts.[70] Nevertheless, ethical reflections provide scientists in such situations with some standards. As Paul Diesing, when summarising the debate about "research programs", points out:

> there is no rule that says that scientists ought to abandon a degenerating research program and shift to a progressive one. Two or three rival programs may develop side by side for a long time, each striving to produce the novel facts that mark it as progressive and their fortunes might fluctuate several times. The only rule Lakatos suggests that each program should keep an honest score.[71]

In this context, Wendt's rather apodictic statement that scientific study depends on "publicly available evidence and some possibility of falsification", is trivial.[72] It does not address issues of judgement, of the criteria that govern the weighing of the evidence, or of the discharge of one's responsibility for either sticking to one's (possibly refuted) theory or of abandoning it. The core controversy is usually *not* about evidence at all, as Jervis correctly points out, but rather about assigning strategic burdens of proof.[73] It is the "default position" that usually invites controversies of a quite different and serious kind than problems of evidence or of the formal adequacy of some model or theory.[74] The emphasis on ethics points precisely to these difficulties. It brings to the fore the silent presuppositions, invites us to critically reflect upon them, and establishes the importance of practical reason and judgement (not only of deduction and theoretical reason). These considerations also provide the strongest possible rationale for pluralism, not as the "second best", but as the most promising strategy for advancing our knowledge.

Nevertheless, ultimately the loss of foundations is unsettling precisely because foundations promise (however falsely) some security. In this way, we keep our bearing and are assured that our questions will somehow come to a rest. One way of dealing with the loss of the "metaphysical comfort" is to inquire into the reasons why we felt such comfort in the first place, why certain metaphors such as that of a chain, of a circle, or of a fundament provided such persuasive power, despite the realisation that the hopes built upon them will be disappointed.

Consider in this context the notion of coming nearer to truth while never quite arriving there. Here, the idea of successive polygons used for determining the content of a circle gives some plausibility to this stance. The problem is, however, that in the case of the circle we do have the perimeter given, while the entire problem of scientific knowledge is that there is no way in which we can know its limits. Progress in the latter case consists in being able to ask questions which were not even thinkable before, even while there is no perimeter from which we could determine whether we have come closer to truth. In this respect, the notion of knowledge as a procedure analogous to exhausting the interior of the circle does no longer make much sense.

Furthermore, the metaphor of the circle seems to be a double-edged sword. When we focus on the perimeter instead of the interior, the fear rises that we might get caught in a circle that turns "vicious". Consequently, recursivity becomes suspect and the generative capacity of the circle metaphor has to give way to that of a chain, or that of a foundation. Both the chain metaphor and the "ground" metaphor suggest an absolute "beginning" or (end) as Aristotle shrewdly observes.[75] Both rely on rudimentary spatial experiences for their suggestive power. The "ground metaphor" implies that our knowledge is structured like a building, in which the upper echelons receive support from lower ones. To that extent, the image of "justified belief" (or warranted knowledge) resembles the figure of a pyramid below:

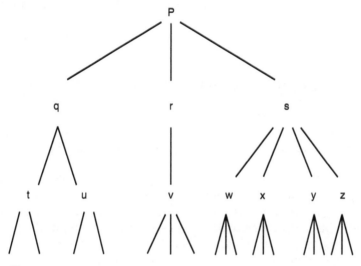

Figure 1[76]

At some point, we have to assume some basic beliefs that are not justified by further beliefs but some immediate perceptions. Unfortunately, this problem led to the downfall of strict empiricism. Besides, without changing the architectural metaphor, we realise that not all beliefs need independent support. As the image of an "arch" suggests, it is the "mutual support" of the parts that can carry great weight. While this example shows that independence of beliefs is too demanding a criterion, it is the "solid ground" or rock bottom, as experienced by gravity, that gives this metaphor its generative power.

When with the change in the view of the world as a disc, such notions as "above" and "below" lost their naïve ontological status, the answer to the new insecurities and conceptual puzzlements was the construal of an absolute point of view. In this "view from nowhere", space became a system of co-ordinates within which everything could be located.

The metaphor of the "chain", on the other hand, supports our naïve version of scientific progress as a sequence of discoveries of cause and effect that is somewhere anchored in reality. This image is also well in accordance with some textbook version of the "path" of science. But as the physicist John Ziman pointed out, this metaphor is seriously misleading as an account of scientific progress:

> This point is of the greatest importance, since it explains so much of the strange sense of unreality that scientists feel when they read books on the philosophy of science. It is abundantly obvious that the overall structure of scientific knowledge is of many, many dimensions . . . The initial path to a new discovery may be apparently one-dimensional with no more

reliable authority than a simple causal chain. But the strategy of research is to seek alternative routes, from other starting-points, to the same spot until the discovery has been incorporated unequivocally into the scientific map.[77]

The interesting point of these observations is not only that a new metaphor is proposed, but also the realisation that by choosing the metaphor of a "map" rather than that of a circle, or that of a pyramid, the fears engendered by the previous metaphor vanish. In addition, former fears are actually turned into strengths, mutual support is no longer seen as vicious, but *as proof of superiority*!

But even the map might not be the most fruitful metaphor. After all, it presupposes a "land", pre-given and virtually unchanging, that has to be discovered and mapped. It is, therefore, still beholden to the notion of representation. But if in at least some part of science the aim is not the discovery of something "pre-existing" as, for example, some experiments in high-energy physics suggest, but an endeavour in which "the process to be observed has never occurred before in the history of the Universe: God himself is waiting to see what will happen!",[78] then notions of representational accuracy quickly lose their usefulness. Similarly, when we accept the thought that we cannot get in between the "things" and our description of them, but that in true constructivist fashion, their "ontology" depends on the purposes and practices embedded in our concepts, then we no longer need to hold on to the "thing in itself" as an anchor. We are finally free to address the question of how to go about our inquiries.

Perhaps the metaphor of a game of Scrabble provides a better image. We begin with a concept that makes certain combinations possible. In criss-crossing we can "go on", and our additions are justified by the mutual support with other words and concepts. Sometimes, we cannot proceed as our attempts of continuing get stymied. Then we begin somewhere else, and might, by circuitous routes, reach again some known terrain. Potentially there are innumerable moves, and no two games are identical since moves at different times will have different consequences. On the other hand, no move of them is free in the sense that "anything goes". But none could have been predicted by the "view from nowhere". Without making too much of this metaphor, because like all metaphors it eventually breaks down, I think it captures our predicament in generating knowledge and of the constructivist challenge.[79] To that extent, no new middle-ground, no new orthodoxy is needed.

Notes

1 See Humberto R. Maturana and Fransisco J. Varela, *The Tree of Knowledge: The Biological Roots of Human Understanding* (London: Shambhala Publishers, 1992) and Niklas Luhmann, *Soziale Systeme* (Frankfurt: Suhrkamp, 1984), and *Die Gesellschaft der Gesellschaft*, 2 vols. (Frankfurt: Suhrkamp, 1998).

2 Alexander Wendt, *Social Theory of International Politics* (Cambridge: Cambridge University Press, 1999).
3 See John Stuart Mill, *On Liberty*, ed. David Spitz (New York: Norton, 1975); Karl Popper, *The Myth of the Framework*, (ed.) Mark A. Nottumo (London: Routledge, 1994).
4 Popper did not mince words when he and his opponents disagreed and he did seldom "learn" from his enemies who had refuted some of his tenets. See the useful discussion of Paul Diesing, *How Social Science Works* (Pittsburgh: University of Pittsburgh Press, 1991), chap. 2.
5 I am partially influenced here by Laurence BonJour, *The Structure of Empirical Knowledge* (Cambridge, MA: Harvard University Press, 1985).
6 See Thomas Nagel, *The View from Nowhere* (Oxford: Oxford University Press, 1986).
7 Wendt, *Social Theory*, chap. 4.
8 For Wendt's construal of a first encounter with extraterrestrials, see his "Anarchy is What States Make of it: The Social Construction of Power Politics", *International Organization* 46, no. 2 (1992): 391–425; for a principled critique of this position, see Maja Zehfuss, "Sprachlosigkeit schränkt ein", *Zeitschrift für Internationale Beziehungen* 5 (1998): 103–37.
9 Wendt, *Social Theory*, 94.
10 Ibid., 94.
11 Ibid., chap. 3.
12 Ibid., 136.
13 Ibid., 95.
14 Ibid., 135.
15 If p, then not q, q therefore not p; whereby p represents the alleged universal law and q the singular hypothetical statement.
16 For an argument for social mechanisms instead of covering laws, see Jon Elster, *Nuts and Bolts for the Social Sciences* (Cambridge: Cambridge University Press, 1989). For a more recent discussion, see the anthology assembled by Peter Hedström and Richard Swedberg, (eds.), *Social Mechanisms* (Cambridge: Cambridge University Press, 1998).
17 Wendt, *Social Theory*, 81.
18 Kenneth Waltz, *Theory of International Politics* (New York: Addison Wesley, 1979).
19 Wendt, *Social Theory*, 158.
20 Ibid., 162.
21 Ibid.
22 Ibid., chap. 5.
23 Ibid., 8, 198.
24 Hobbes explains that "It may preadventure be thought, there was never such a time, nor condition of was as this ... (*bellum omnium contra omnes*) ... But though there had never been any time, wherein particular men werre in a condition of warre one against another ..." See his *Leviathan*, (ed.) Crawford B. Macpherson (Harmondswoth: Penguin, 1968), 187.
25 For a further elaboration of this point, see Friedrich Kratochwil, *Rules, Norms, and Decisions* (Cambridge: Cambridge University Press, 1989), chap. 4.
26 See, for example, the discussion of the *Barcelona Traction Case* of 1970 *(Belgium v. Spain)*. *Reports of the International Court of Justice* (The Hague, 1975).
27 Wendt, *Social Theory*, 219.
28 Ibid., 12, emphasis in original.
29 Ibid., 182.
30 Ibid., 227.
31 See United Nations Charter, Article 51.

32 Wendt, *Social Theory*, 264.
33 Ibid., 258.
34 Ibid., 254.
35 Ibid., 255.
36 Ibid., 341.
37 Ibid., 349.
38 Ibid., 353.
39 Ibid., 354.
40 Ibid., 360.
41 Ibid., 367.
42 Ibid., 76.
43 Ibid.
44 See Hobbes's explicit argument, "For warre consisteth not in Battell only, or the act of fighting; but in a tract of time wherein the Will to contend by Battell is sufficiently known" in his *Leviathan*, 185.
45 See here also Martin Hollis and Steve Smith's warnings in their "Beware of Gurus: Structure and Action in International Relations", *Review of International Studies* 17, no. 4 (1991): 393–410.
46 On the federal advisory apparatus, see Joel Primack and Frank von Hippel, *Advice and Dissent: Scientists in the Political Arena* (New York: Basic Books, 1974). For an interesting discussion of the general problems involved, see Albert Matheny and Bruce Williams, "Scientific Disputes and Advisory Procedures in Policy Making: An Evaluation of the Science Court", *Law and Policy Quarterly* 3 (1981): 341–64.
47 See, for example, Arthur Kantorowitz, "Controlling Technology Democratically", *American Scientist* 63 (1975): 505–9; see also the attempts to establish a "court" for good scientific practice: US Department of Commerce, *Proceedings of the Colloquium on the Science Court* (Washington, DC: Commerce Technical Advisory Board, 1977), which reports on the results of a conference in which the Commerce Department, the National Science Foundation, and the American Association for the Advancement of Science participated with the purpose of vetting the proposals for a science court.
48 David Lewis, *On the Plurality of Worlds* (Oxford: Basil Blackwell, 1987).
49 See Rom Harre's excellent introduction to various schools of thought and the issues involved in his *Varieties of Realism: A Rationale for the Natural Sciences* (Oxford: Basil Blackwell, 1986).
50 Ibid., 58.
51 See, for example, the various essays in Richard Rorty, *Objectivity, Relativism, and Truth* (Cambridge: Cambridge University Press, 1991).
52 Wendt, *Social Theory*, 65.
53 See, for example, the studies by Popper's own disciple, Joseph Agassi, *Science in Flux*, Boston Studies in the Philosophy of Science, no. 28 (Dordrecht: Reidel, 1975).
54 As quoted in ibid., 34.
55 See Popper, *The Myth of the Framework*.
56 See, for example, Roy Bashkar's argument, "To see science as a social activity, and as structured and discriminating in its thought, constitutes a significant step in our understanding of science" in his *A Realist Theory of Science* (Leeds: Leeds Books, 1975), 9. Similarly: "What the orthodox tradition omits from its account of science is the nature of scientific activity as work; or when, as in transcendental idealism, it does recognise it, it considers it only as intellectual and not as practical labour. Accordingly, it cannot see knowledge, or at least the achievement of a closure as a transient social product." See *The Possibility of Naturalism: A Philosophical Critique of the Contemporary Human Sciences* (Brighton: Harvester Press, 1979), 19.

57 "Many realists have based their defences of scientific realism on the doctrine (one might almost say, the dogma) of bivalence, the principle that most theoretical statements of a scientific discourse are true or false by virtue of the way the world is ... Other realists have persisted with the idea that the essence of scientific discourses and material practices, such as experimentation, is some abstract logical framework. Sceptics had little difficulty in demonstrating that no real scientific research program could come anywhere near realising the bivalence principle in practice, nor have they had much trouble in showing that real scientific thinking could make little use of logical schemata if its cognitive and material practices were made explicit. It looks as if the work of a scientific community can be rational only at the cost of being impossible, while, on the other hand, the extreme sceptical reaction offers nothing but a caricature of what we know the scientific achievement to have been." Harre, *Varieties of Realism*, 3.

58 Ibid., 5.

59 See, for example, the attempt to proceed with such a definition of "essence" in Andrew Sayer, "Essentialism, Social Constructionism and Beyond", *Sociological Review* 45, no. 3 (1997): 453–87.

60 Wendt, *Social Theory*, 49.

61 Ibid., 73.

62 Ibid., chap. 3.

63 See Luhmann, *Die Gesellschaft der Gesellschaft*.

64 For an interesting treatment of boundaries and their role in social systems and international politics, see Matthias Albert, David Jacobson, and Yosef Lapid, (eds.), *Identities, Borders, Orders: New Directions in International Relations Theory* (Minneapolis: University of Minnesota Press, 2001).

65 See, for example, the claims to this effect in *Social Theory*, 198, 240.

66 See, for instance, Philip Cerny, "Globalization and Collective Action", *International Organization* 49, no. 4 (1995): 595–626 and Richard Stubbs and Geoffrey Underhill, (eds.), *Political Economy and the Changing Global Order* (New York: St. Martin's Press, 1994).

67 Rodney Bruce Hall, *National Collective Identity and International Systems* (New York: Columbia University Press, 1999).

68 See Wendt's claim "states are ontologically prior to the state system. The state is presocial to other states in the same way that the human body is presocial" in *Social Theory*, 198. First, the question is not whether one or the other state is "prior" but what the relationship between systems and states is. Second, there is the question whether the state, which is not a natural kind, can be likened to a "body" and thus whether the priority claim makes any sense, and third, whether such a biological priority tells us anything interesting about the specific social character of man (aside from his extreme dependence in infancy and thus the need for particular care in early developmental phases).

69 Jens Steffek, communication to the author, 8 February 2000.

70 See Imre Lakatos, "Falsification and the Methodology of Scientific Research Programmes", in *Criticism and the Growth of Knowledge*, (eds.), Imre Lakatos and Alan Musgrave (Cambridge: Cambridge University Press, 1970), 91–196.

71 See Diesing, *How Social Science Works*, 46.

72 Wendt, *Social Theory*, 373.

73 As Robert Jervis suggests, "we should not adopt the Whiggish stance that the fate of a research program is predominantly determined by the extent to which it produces propositions that anticipate and fit with empirical facts. Programs – and even more, their first cousins paradigms – are notoriously difficult to confirm or disconfirm. Not only do they shape what counts as a fact at all, but there are so many steps between the assumptions and outlooks on the one hand and empirical findings on the other that neither in social nor natural science can the evidence ever

be unambiguous." See "Realism in the Study of World Politics", *International Organization* 52, no. 4 (1998): 975.

74 For an interesting treatment of this problem in law and science, see Richard Gaskins, *Burdens of Proof in Modern Discourse* (New Haven, CT: Yale University Press, 1992).

75 Aristotle, *Nicomachean Ethics* 1095b31; actually after Aristotle has discussed his famous chain of goals and has arrived at the notion of a supreme good for which everything else is being done he then distinguishes the procedure as to inquiring into the nature of this good either by proceeding from the facts to the good or from the good to the facts, like runners "run either from the judges stand to the far end or in the reverse direction".

76 For a further discussion of the problems of such a "foundationalist" account, see Susan Haack, *Evidence and Inquiry: Towards Reconstruction in Epistemology* (Oxford: Blackwell, 1993), 24.

77 John Ziman, *Reliable Knowledge: An Exploration of the Grounds for Belief in Science* (Cambridge: Cambridge University Press, 1991), 84.

78 Ibid., 62.

79 For a similar view of constructivism as a metatheoretical commitment see Stefano Guzzini, "A Reconstruction of Constructivism in International Relations", *European Journal of International Relations*, 6, no 2 (2000), 147–82.

9   History, action and identity

Revisiting the "second" great debate
and assessing its importance for
social theory

Introduction

Assessing progress in theory-building in International Relations involves
two issues. First, what are the criteria for appraising theory development
and, second, what are the factors driving this development? Is it mainly the
changing political *problématique*, or the debates within the discipline, or
the organisation of the field as an academic discipline that explains theory
development?

Each of these factors seems to provide a plausible account that can mar-
shal some empirical support. According to the hypothesis of policy-driven
development it was no accident that the study of IR emancipated itself in the
inter-war and post-World War II period when revolutionary changes brought
the European state system to a close and ushered in a global system of
unprecedented heterogeneity. Presently we can see again that a changed political agenda and new policy problems, such as terrorism, make it appear that
most of what we know about deterrence and security are rather quaint
reminders of a time gone by, rather than part of a cumulative disciplinary
knowledge. Furthermore, depending on how we count the various debates in
the field, at least since the "third" debate, we have to admit that the discussion
has been driven more by epistemological and methodological issues than by
politics (Lapid, 1989). Finally, more recently, students of the disciplinary
development have pointed to the importance of national and social settings
for the development of the field (Joergensen, 2000; Friedrichs, 2004).

One trend showing itself in different disguises is the turn to history either
by focusing on the practical problems determining the IR agenda, or by
examining directly the history of the field and tracing over the years the
"bounds" of sense within the academic discourse. To that extent the endless
debates about "science" and method, about "rigour" and "parsimony" have
been replaced by a critical examination of traditions in the field and by a
more pragmatic approach in choosing one's methodology. Some of these
points were of course already voiced in the Second Grand debate where Bull
pleaded for a "classical approach" instead of being enthralled by "theory".
This trend is also powerfully reinforced in "science studies", by the turn away

from treating epistemology and its attempt of formulating trans-historical, universal and field independent criteria for knowledge, to a focus on science as a communal practice for knowledge generation.

Without wanting to enter a full-fledged discussion of the second debate – precisely because I believe that some of Bull's (1966) central points need a much more careful restatement – I shall use Bull's arguments as a foil in order to demonstrate the importance of historical reflection for an adequate understanding of politics. The appropriate knowledge in this case is then not simply that of a science or even an applied science, but the combination of a strong diagnostic element (knowing "what") with the "knowing how" (rather than knowing only "why").

I want to argue, therefore, that these substantive reasons will by necessity point us to history. However, the engagement with the historical will obviously be quite different from encountering or distilling some "lessons" from history, or from testing our theories by historical "facts". As to the first, given that under conditions of rapid change, the past can no longer provide us with exemplars, which we can apply to the case at hand. Thus the function of a historical reflection can neither be the collection of "lessons" (on the change in our historical understanding of the past see the fundamental discussion by Koselleck, 1985) of history, nor consist in the knowledge of what "really" happened. Rather, I claim that it is through historical reflection that we become aware of the "dialectic of choice" in which from the present the past is recollected and joined with the future by means of a political "project". To that extent the model of "rational action" is expanded, as it is no longer limited to the present preferences whose genesis remains, however, exogenous. [. . .] Instead, the agents' valuations are now systematically tied to individual and collective identities, as well as to future "projects" (utopias) which, in turn, are not restricted to probabilities by which one assesses the occurrence of events.

Precisely because we know that things could have been different, the more we deepen our understanding of the past, we begin to sense the opportunities forgone and thereby become aware of our own potential as agents. Of course, this does not mean that everything is now possible only because most constraining "structures" are now "deconstructed" in this reflective process. On the contrary, historical awareness clearly indicates that not everything is possible, as disagreements are rife, collective action problems abound, dilemmas are real and institutions are sticky. Historical reflection does not provide us with a warrant to engage in fantasies of omnipotence solely because the "necessities" to be confronted turn out to be mostly man-made. Such a reflection is, nevertheless, the precondition for a proper appreciation of action and agency.

These might seem rather heady claims and in order to make good on them I want to take the following argumentative steps. In the next section I want to review briefly Bull's arguments to show the problems of using history as a tool in theory-building. In particular, I shall concern myself with the problems of measurement, judgement and the alleged role of generalizations or laws in the social sciences. To illustrate the problematic "use" of history, I draw on two further debates in the discipline, namely the democratic peace argument and the place of macro-sociology in the field. While in both cases history is largely used as a storehouse for data which allegedly allow us to test theories, some of the recent discussions concerning historical facts have brought to the fore the problem of their "emplotment", i.e. the realization that historical "facts" are always part of a story. To that extent history is not simply "there" (like a collection of facts or things), but is a product of "recollection", i.e. memory, the subject of part three. This argument about memory then sets the stage, in the fourth section, for a discussion of the role of individual and collective memory in a theory of action. A brief summary characterising the type of knowledge applicable to practical problems concludes the article.

The need for historical reflection vs. reducing history to a storehouse of "data"

I begin with Bull's critique of the obsession with measurement in the social sciences which in his view misdiagnoses the problems of conceptualisation and the way in which warranted knowledge is created. Here the role of judgement and the question of the historical nature of the social world become the relevant issues. Both points have important implications for theory-building and for the *kind of* theory we need in order to address questions of *praxis*. But despite the fact that Bull's argument seems essentially right, some of its steps were badly stated and ought to be clarified. For example, it is hardly convincing to argue against the search for universal laws and then say that the "models" of IR "could just as well have been expressed as an empirical 'generalisation'" – quite aside from the fact that laws and generalisations work rather differently (Bull, 1966: 370). Similarly, to maintain that "rigor and precision" to which the scientific approach aspires can be achieved "wholly within the classical approach" (see his point six in Bull, 1966: 375) seems rather off. After all, this argument contradicts two other major points of his – that the subject matter of politics might require different standards from those provided by logical calculi, and that by choosing an erroneous methodological ideal one is likely to end up in an empty formalism and with an impoverished research agenda (points 1 and 7).

Furthermore, Bull claims that if the proponents of the scientific approach have led us to insights, it was because they had left the narrow confines of their own methodological criteria. Again, to the extent that the failure to match one's own standard is a common failing among researchers of all colours, Bull's plea for a classical approach requires then a more principled argument. It would have to go beyond merely indicting the "fetishistic"(!) character of measurement and argue, instead, that the *notion of field-independent scientific criteria* – endorsed by the unity of science position –

is in itself not a useful "regulative idea". Moreover, a more principled restatement of Bull's concerns about the failure of theory to appreciate the challenge posed by problems of *praxis* has to be extended in order to question the belief in the "objectivity" of the "scientific approach", *as propagated in mainstream social science*, since it relies on several metaphysical assumptions. This requires further explanation.

The most important of these assumptions is the idea that "social kinds" do not differ in any significant way from "natural kinds".[1] But if we take seriously Weber's (1974) claim that in the social sciences it is not simple observable elements (natural kinds) but *values* that determine the operations of our concepts, Bull's argument about the need for judgement attains a special weight. What counts as an instance of, for example, war or democracy, is neither answerable by a closer look at the phenomena, nor is it solved by strict operationalisation and inter-coder reliability. Equally problematic is a second assumption, i.e. that only trans-historically valid generalisations provide insights and warranted knowledge. As Paul Diesing once correctly pointed out, generalisations, about US voting behaviour, for example, can be valid even though they apply only between 1948 and 1972 and only to Americans. "Truth does not have to be timeless. Logical empiricists have a derogatory name for such changing truths: relativism, *but such truths are real, while the absolute fully axiomised truth is imaginary*" (Diesing, 1992: 91 emphasis added).

A third metaphysical assumption concerning "objectivity" becomes visible here. It is beholden to a rather suspect Platonic ontology that something truly "is" only when it does not change. The whole Western tradition has always distinguished "true being" from different forms of being. The former is eternal while the latter is the realm of growth and decay. On the basis of modern physics we might, however, rather think about "things" and "objects" not as fixed entities, but as temporary stabilisations of various processes. In that case a totally different ontology emerges, as time and change are not identified with decay or lack of truth. Instead, change is the normal, i.e. true, condition. Thus, in the case of "social kinds", getting the context for these "stabilisations" right, both conceptually and historically – a problem that cannot be answered by building, for example, rigorous models, as Bull correctly suggests – is then more important than focusing on two or three unchanging variables.

Given these difficulties that seem to open the floodgates of "relativism", several gambits are available to the adherents of "universality", all of which depend, however, on the elimination of history as a proper concern. One is the idea that historical laws, explaining transitions from one epoch or period to another, can capture even transformative changes. The other involves the opposite assumption, i.e. the existence of some trans-historical structures that work themselves out, irrespective of the changes "on the surface".

However, a moment's reflection shows the problematic nature of both gambits (quite aside from the incompatibility of the claims). The first relies on a philosophy of history (for a scathing criticism of this idea see Popper, 1961), in which the philosopher plays now the role of God who looks upon the "developments" from an absolute point beyond time. For him everything is contemporaneous and history can only be conceptualised as some type of unfolding, be it of the Hegelian spirit, or of Marx's productive forces, or democracy as in the "end of history" (Fukuyama, 1992). It was one of the merits of Popper's analysis to have debunked the myth of such historical laws. Even if three or four events are causally related, there is no way to construct out of this chain an historical law.

The other gambit, as we have seen, is to radically de-emphasise problems of change by focusing on the existence of allegedly trans-historical systemic structures (for a much more heuristically fruitful notion of a system allowing for great historical variation see Buzan and Little, 2000). In this fashion even transformative change, such as the one we encountered in the demise of the Soviet Empire, becomes a mere "data point" that is hardly of significance (for a useful collection of essays on this point see Lebow and Risse-Kappen, 1995). Having defined the "system" in such a way that nothing but the emergence of an empire would count as a transformative change, the actual investigation into the changing patterns of politics can then safely be sequestered to "confirmatory" research. However, as the discussion about "unipolarity" vs. "hierarchy" suggests, such a research programme is seriously flawed. Obviously the two systems differ in whether or not the principle of legitimacy has changed, rather than in a change in the distribution of capabilities. While the preponderant state in a unipolar system might have as much influence as an imperial centre, part of the rules defining the international game differ significantly. In an empire the centre can give orders, in a unipolar system such orders are illegitimate and will, in all likelihood, engender resistance.

To the extent that the foregoing points are valid, the development of an objectivist conceptualisation of a social system without any recourse to the ideas and values the actors themselves hold seems futile indeed. Precisely because social reality is not simply "out there" but is made by the actors, the concepts we use are part of a vocabulary that is deeply imbricated with our political projects. Nowhere does this become clearer than in the "empirical" evidence presented in support of the theory of democratic peace. Behind the efforts of operationalisation, measurement and coding lie not only language but a political project that informs our conceptual apparatus. Drawing the lines will depend more on judgement in the light of our values than on operationalisation and the development of "over-all" scores. Attributing a case to a type requires, therefore, (contestable) *judgements* rather than abstraction and the type of inferences familiar from statistics and quantitative methods.

For example, what are we to do with "illiberal democracies" (see the discussion by Collier and Levitsky, 1997), that is, political systems that might provide for contested elections and changes in government, but not for an effective civil rights regime? But if such additions stand for relevant dimensions, could the development of an "over-all score" not perhaps deal with these problems? Unfortunately, the idea of an over-all score does not really solve the problem, as the following discussion shows. In operationalising the democratic peace argument, for instance, a polity-score could be calculated by substracting an "autocracy" index from that of a "democracy index", which then yields a number that supposedly tells us how democratic a country is. But, as David Spiro (Spiro, 1994: 56) has pointed out, by using this data set and the operationalisation suggested by Maoz and Russett for autocracy and democracy France is then not "democratic" after 1981, but El Salvador is, and Belgium was not a democracy until 1956! (Maoz and Russett, 1993). Here obviously some implicitly or explicitly held values concerning the importance and weight of the several dimensions of democracy play a role, a problem that cannot be reduced to one of increasing coding reliability, or to one of looking harder at the facts.

Similarly, the comparison between the measures constructed by the Finnish social scientist Tatu Vanhanen (1990) for democracy (operationalising the concept along the lines of Dahl's definition) and that of Doyle (Doyle, 1983, 1986) shows, that on the "Finnish" score the US ranks consistently low, far behind West European political systems. [. . .] In Doyle's treatment, on the other hand, the US scores always highest historically as well as at present. It does so despite the fact that historically the franchise was limited, slavery was part of the picture and party competition virtually non-existent in large parts of the country, not to speak of apparently widespread alienation, indicated by the low voter turnout. Thus in the American scientific discourse the liberal norms are usually those that correspond with the *ongoing political project* of the US and it is this yardstick that is then applied to other countries.

[. . .]

The upshot of this discussion is that data banks are not simple storage places for our unadulterated facts, but they are part of our political understandings and projects. *It is through historical reflection and not through generalisation* that the genesis of such data becomes visible, that the role of judgement is uncovered, and that the criteria for counting a phenomenon as an instantiation of a certain concept become explicit. [. . .]

Similar controversies emerge from the renewed interest in macro-historical studies in sociology (see the controversy between Mann, Goldthorpe, Mouzelis and Hart, 1994) and political science (Lustick, 1996). While the discussion among the sociologists created more heat than light, Ian Lustick correctly identified the central point of this controversy – expressed in the language of normal social science it concerns a "selection bias". Thus in examining the "empirical" basis of such macro-historical works as Barrington Moore's *The Social Origins of Dictatorship and Democracy* (1966) or Theda Skocpol's study on *States and Social Revolutions* (1979), Lustick points out that both authors had used, as their factual basis, histories by authors who implicitly or explicitly shared their own theoretical biases. Moore – in order to make good on his claim that the English Civil War was actually a bourgeois revolution – had for example to show that the bourgeoisie emerged as an important social force by the second quarter of the 17th century. His proof was provided by the historian Tawney's somewhat problematic class analysis that had amalgamated not only the burghers and the gentry into one revolutionary movement, but that also had postulated the emergence of an entrepreneurial "proto-capitalist class". These facts were, however, forcefully debunked by Hexter (1961) and other historians studying the same era. In other words, Moore relied on Tawney and Campbell for the facts, without any critical appreciation that these facts were the result of interpretations and of theoretical dispositions similar to his own, and thus could not provide a neutral set of data by which the theoretical propositions could be established.

Somewhat counter-intuitively we have to conclude that the primary problem for macro-historical work is, therefore, not the difficulty of getting enough information about the past. As Lustick suggests, "The more daunting question is how to choose sources or data without permitting correspondence between the categories and implicit theoretical postulates used in the chosen sources to ensure positive answers to the questions being asked about the data" (Lustick, 1996: 608). Of course, historians have long been familiar with this difficulty. In a seminal article the eminent historian Carl Becker (see the discussion of Becker in Barnes, 1927) tried a long time ago to explode the notion of hard "historical facts" that are directly accessible to us. For example, the historical fact that Caesar crossed the Rubicon existed not as a simple description of the physical acts involved in crossing a river, but only in virtue of its relations to other facts and its *emplotment in a narrative*, putting these things in perspective. [. . .]

I have used the two examples above to suggest that the recursivity problem arises particularly clearly in the social sciences, because the actors' understanding influences the world. Therefore, the causal arrows run from our (or the agent's) understanding *to* the world and not *from* "the world" to our understanding or theory. This point explodes the notion that all true explanations have to be cast in terms of efficient causes, and that objectively given things are mirrored by our concepts, as the scientific approach suggested. I also argue that this leads us straight back to Bull, who suggested an exposure to history in order to deal with the substantive issues arising in the world of *praxis*.

The above discussion concerning the employment of historical facts and the nature of historical data has also tried to drive home the point that although history is past and seems therefore objective, fixed, and thus presumably provides a secure source of knowledge, actual historical reflection shows that matters are quite different – history is malleable because it is always *remembered* and part of a story, which, in turn, is usually confronted not only by counter-arguments concerning this or that "fact" but also by different narratives "contesting" the conventional or hegemonic version of things passed. This is often forgotten even by authors who engage in research and adduce historical data in support of their theories. Often such historically enriched research represents little more than a "confirmatory" engagement with history, precisely because only supporting evidence is presented and the crucially important element of the criticism of "sources" often remains underdeveloped.

As recent debates show, dyed in the wool realists are wont to find the workings of anarchy everywhere (Fischer, 1992; for a criticism of the abuse of history in general by neo-realists see Schroeder, 1994; a critique of Fischer's treatment of medieval sources can be found in Hall and Kratochwil, 1993). [. . .] Finally, what is often forgotten is that "history" always remembered from *a certain situation in the present*, for which things past now have relevance. Thus "recollecting" the past means putting it in a frame which bestows importance on the actions and events by connecting the past through the present with our personal and political projects. In this reflection we establish our identity as agents and societies and understand ourselves as the "same" despite all the changes. In this sense "history" is the encounter with the "self" rather than simply a storehouse of data, or an agglomeration of examples or presumptive lessons.

Memory, identity and action

Below I explore the link between historical reflection, agency and notions of the individual and collective self. For if we can show how agency depends on historical reflection, this evidence will cast further doubt on the coherence of an absolute, objective scientific vantage point for problems of praxis, as Bull suggested. In order to build my case I want to approach the problem by relying on Nietzsche's reflections on historicity, before coming back to Bull's "classical" approach.

It was Nietzsche (1954) who probably most strongly emphasised the role of historical reflection in the construction of the self. He reserved special criticism for viewing the past as fixed – a misconception of history that he labelled "antiquarian". In addition, by seeing history as a product of memory, Nietzsche not only realized that every recollection also presupposes the "ability to forget" (Nietzsche, 1954: 281) and that any "history" exists in the tension between recalling and forgetting, he also highlighted the fact that the past is deeply involved in constructing the individual as an agent. In order to be able to act, agents have to first recover their history.

Furthermore, history, defined as a "re-collection" of all those things *worth remembering*, provides in itself the antidote (Nietzsche, 1954: 281) to the poison of an assumed necessity, of the logic of systems, of the "blind forces of the real" (Nietzsche, 1954: 265) and the hopelessness that comes from the invention of a tradition which makes out of us only "epigones" of a glorious but unreachable past. We can see now from this vantage point why new beginnings stand in such a close relationship to the past, as exemplified by the various "renaissances", from ancient Sumer[2] to Egypt,[3] to the Italian

Renaissance, or even to the French or the Russian Revolution.[4] A new link to the past was intrinsic to the new beginnings that were sought.

Another important thing we notice in Nietzsche – irrespective of whether or not we agree with his philosophy of life – is that, seen from this perspective, the process of individuation is not simply a biological process but is mediated by communication with others and by the sharing of certain collective memories with the group. As all societies are "imagined communities", to use Anderson's felicitous phrase (Anderson, 1991), the individual memory is built up by participation in communicative processes. Two processes are important in this context. One concerns the shared rules and practices we need for both daily interactions and the inevitable conflicts that arise. The other concerns the common recollections that help us understand *who* we are.

The *first* kind of processes (dealing with conflicts and interactions) has usually been treated as a problem of order and justice. Norms governing this process allow us to interact even in the face of disappointments, as the most important function of norms is their capacity for "prospective ordering" as well as their counterfactual validity. Contrary to the realist explanations of social order – that is, the supposed need for an enforcer who metes out *ex post* punishment – enforcement can always only be a residual strategy, as no society could exist if it had to rely solely on the command of the sovereign and his sanctions. Here Hobbes's point was much subtler as his analysis is based on the generative force of expectations.

The *second* type of process involves, however, the diachronic link of connecting the past through the present to the future via our individual and common projects. Who we are is significantly shaped by where we think we come from. This process has therefore to do with identities and collective memories that allow us to function as a person and a group and that make "society" an ongoing and trans-generational concern of all members.

Furthermore, these two ways of connecting the individual and the group are much more intrinsically linked than they appear at first. After all, what has to be done and what we are obliged to do is often directly the result of *particular recollections* that powerfully shape us precisely because *they are not universalizable* or can claim general applicability. For example, obedience is due to the traditional ruler, because he is the legitimate son of the previous ruler and, thus, only a flaw in the genealogy would exculpate the nobles and vassals if they failed to obey. Similarly, historical events may have particular meaning and obligatory force for a society. "Remember the Maine", "remember the Boyne" (the battle of 1690 between Protestants and Catholics in Ulster), "remember St Vitus' day" (1389, battle of Kosovo), "remember Auschwitz", "never again must Masada fall", etc. – all those exhortations refer to recollections of particular relevance to a given group, but they are at the same time powerful sources of obligations.

Obviously the dead are of particular importance in this context. Traditional society has dealt with this specific obligation in terms of *piety* (i.e. what is due to one's ancestors)[5] (Virgil, 1990) and *fama* (kudos), where others may participate although they might have no particular personal link to the deceased. How *political* this cult of the dead had become after the move from a tribal society to the classical polis can nicely be gathered from Pericles' famous Eulogy for the dead (Thucydides, 1972, Bk II, paras 34–46). At first, somewhat strangely for us, we notice that it is the *city* and not the fallen that is the object of the encomium. But Pericles followed here only the very spirit of the Athenian legislation that had made honouring the dead a *public* rather than a family or clan obligation (Loriaux, 1986). While the family was allowed to keep the fallen for some days, both burial and public display were now the task of the city, thereby powerfully reinforcing the notion that loyalty was owed to the community at large, rather than to the clan or tribe.

These examples make several points. *One* is the malleability of the past as it is created by memory through a recording[6] (and forgetting) of the events one considers (un-)important. As the individual re-writes continuously his/her biography in which events and decisions take on different meanings – even relegating some of them to oblivion – so collective memories, recorded or not, show similar plasticity. Of course, with the invention of writing, those memories which have been discarded remain somewhere and can be "re-collected" again and become sometimes in the future again part of the collective remembrance.

The best example for this phenomenon is the Masada incident that played virtually no role in Jewish collective life during the nearly 2,000 years of the Diaspora. As originally recorded by Josephus Flavius (1970) it was a story highly critical of the various groups of zealots who had revolted against the Romans. They had succeeded in seizing the fortress near the Dead Sea and finally committed collective suicide after the Romans had breached the walls. Josephus blamed the zealots[7] for ending the last vestiges of Jewish political life since the Romans laid waste the land and dispersed the entire Jewish population thereafter. But with the experience of the Holocaust, with Zionism becoming a political force, and with the creation of a beleaguered state in the 1940s, Masada took on an entirely new meaning. What was now remembered was the uncompromising sacrifice for independence and a particular way of life rather than the political failure of the former state. Something that had been forgotten was "re-collected" – even though from quite a different angle, as suggested by the political situation of the period – and became part of the new collective memory.

The *second* point is that individual and collective memories differ in some important respects but not those usually considered. Usually we assume that the individual as the "unencumbered" self, rooted in the notion of pure reflexivity, is the proper beginning for theoretical reflection. Indeed, Descartes took this as the *fundamentum inconcussum*. Society and all other collective notions are later additions as they are based on experience and aggregation. However, we always start out as "encumbered selves", as members of a concrete society, in a specific time and with particular obligations. It is only through a long process of differentiation that we acquire the abstract form of the individual or the modern person and with it, the "view from nowhere". This Archimedean point characterizes not only our apprehension of the world – since it is constitutive of scientific objectivity – it is also supposed to provide the criteria for assessing our moral commitments. The categorical imperative establishing the criteria of moral autonomy is then the last step in this process in which generalisability becomes the most important requirement. Now all obligations resulting from a shared way of life, such as special duties to our family, children and fellow-countrymen, have to be justified as the ethos itself no longer suffices.[8] [. . .]

It was not only Hegel and the later communitarians who objected to such a construal of ethical reflection. Even Locke (and later Hume) – by no means enemies of moral or scientific enlightenment – recognised that this conceptual move might not be as progressive or unproblematic as it at first appears. Different from the pure Cartesian *cogito*, Locke sees that the actual person is the result of acting, recollecting and forgetting. Consciousness, the timeless certainty of self-reflexivity, cannot provide that foundation, as it is subject to the same processes of emergence and decay as all other human sense impressions. Thus neither the "clear and distinct ideas", nor the ego emerging from radical doubt, can sustain the weight placed upon them in construing identity and agency.

> The memory in some men 'tis true, is very tenacious, even to a miracle; but yet there seems to be a constant decay of all our ideas, even those which are struck deepest, and in minds most retentive . . . Thus the ideas . . . of our youth, often die before us: and our minds represent to us those tombs, to which we are approaching; where though the brass and marble remain, yet inscriptions are effaced by time.
>
> (Locke, 1975: 151f.)

Despite the tenaciousness of memory, the identity of a person does not exist in the material substratum, even though we are dealing with the "embodied self". Rather it is a unity imposed on the events and actions, which lets us understand ourselves as the same person, despite all the obvious changes and all the various roles we play in our lives. Locke uses here the metaphor of the "owner" of one's own actions in order to drive home this fact. He contrasts it sharply with the "unity of substance" such as the body, as a materialist interpretation would suggest.

> That with which the consciousness of this present thinking can join it self, makes the same person, and is one self with it, and nothings else; and so attributes to it self, and owns all the actions of that thing, as its own, as far as that consciousness reaches and no farther . . .
>
> This may show us wherein personal identity consists, not in the identity of substance, but as I have said, in the identity of consciousness.
>
> (Locke, 1975: 341ff.)

Even if we are not entirely convinced by this "proof", one thing has become clear – identity is richly textured by all types of conceptual links to notions of responsibility and agency, all of which cannot be reduced to "pointing" to some incontrovertible fact (for the social character of individual memories see Halbwachs, 1992). Instead what counts as a "self" joins subjective elements and imputations of outside observers, with those self-definitions of the individual in question. Nevertheless, the difference between personal (or individual) identity and collective identity is that the former has normally – and here pragmatic criteria are of obvious importance as the quote above suggests – as a reference the "embodied self", while the latter is purely a social construct.

From these follows as a *third* point – that it is easier to "forget" one's collective identity than the personal one since in the former case life can go on and need not result in the same pathological problems that are frequently associated with the loss of a personal identity. However, as the above considerations also showed, we ought to be careful in thinking that the former is real while the other is a simple figment of the imagination. Collective memories are real and not simple aggregates of individual memories. [. . .]

Fourth, it seems also to follow that the present infatuation with simultaneous "multiple identities" is a problematic notion. It confuses the notion of "role" with that of identity, and it commits the fallacy that if something is not fixed, it has to be arbitrary and therefore changeable at will. If someone experiences his or her personal past merely as a sequence of events, s/he will experience life as largely meaningless, s/he will not be able to learn, but is likely to get stuck in (destructive) routines. For avoiding such a fate s/he will have to "work through" the past – to use the Freudian vocabulary – in order to become again an autonomous actor in its full meaning. Usually such an alienation from one's own past and such a decentred stance is the result of a trauma, which therapy tries to overcome by constructing an alternative historical narrative. True, the individual might decide to change part of his or her identity by leaving home, converting to a new creed or getting "naturalised" somewhere else. But these are usually exacting processes, more akin to learning a new language than to becoming for example a member of a club, or making a choice between apples or oranges.

Fifth, since emotions play such a crucial role in remembering and forgetting (*vide* the trauma mentioned above), special rites and ceremonies are powerful means for mobilising them and for enabling us to "re-collect". These rites play a particularly important part in cultures that are not dependent on writing for the preservation of memory (see in this context the discussion of the *tepe* ritual among the Osages in Assmann, 2000: 23ff.). The *hieros gamos*, the yearly ritual of the marriage between heaven and earth, existing in many societies, provides the best example. The periodic "reliving" of the original creation by re-enacting the cosmological myths is for non-literate societies of utmost importance for the maintenance of order.

In societies in which memory is largely transmitted by texts, coherence is no longer created solely by actual presence and the re-living through rites but mainly by the canonisation of certain texts. This results not only in "closure" of what belongs to the tradition and what is apocryphal, but also in the "purification" of the texts themselves, expunging from them what seems foreign or accidental. However, even in cultures whose memory has been transformed by writing, memorial days – when rites and ceremonies call attention to the "commonality" of the public in an emotionally significant way – are not simply supplanted, but remain part and parcel of the cultural heritage.

The implication of the above discussion is that those who forget their history are not only condemned to repeat their mistakes as Santayana pointed out. The problem is even more serious since those who cannot recall the past from the ever-changing problems of the present and connect it meaningfully to a future are impaired in their agency and therefore prone to misunderstand the issues and choices that have to be made. While history cannot be the "teacher" of all things practical, the critical reflection on our historicity is an indispensable precondition for grasping our predicament as agents.

Conclusion

This article began with a critical question of how to evaluate progress in theory building. Instead of postulating *a priori* epistemological criteria I began the discussion with an "historical" turn, approaching the problem via a history of the field. I did this for two reasons. One, reconstructing the past of a field is an important corrective to aprioristic notions of science and epistemology, as Thomas Kuhn (1970) and many historians of science have shown. Two, given that the subject matter of politics is "praxis", the question of what type of knowledge is appropriate for it is prejudged if one assumes that it had to be "scientific" and that the criteria can be formulated in a field-independent fashion, as the epistemological monism of the unity of science (logical positivism) suggests.

I tried to show the difficulties of that position by first emphasising the practical aspects of all knowledge production that does not fit the "theoretical" mould. Here disciplinary histories are particularly important. Second, through this historical approach I was able to highlight the eminently practical nature of knowledge production. In a third step, using Bull as my foil, I tried to show that a certain type of theory-building, which attempts to "test" theories with multi-variable historical data, fundamentally misunderstands the nature of historical data, for these data consist not in brute facts but are always employed and thus part of larger structures of meaning. "History" is not simply "there" but is largely a product of memory. What is considered worth remembering is, therefore, constituted by our value-attachments and interests, as Weber already remarked.

Furthermore, if history is produced by memory, as I argued, then it is always viewed from a particular *vantage point of the present*. It is this present problem that informs the selection of what is considered worth remembering. To that extent historical reflection is not some collection of interesting facts one could do without, but is intrinsic to our notions of agency and identity. By approaching history not in terms of the fixity of the past, but through the modality of remembering, individuals and collectivities can transcend the confinements imposed by seemingly autonomously operating systems, and find new ways of mastering their destiny.

If agency depends on the appropriation of the historical world rather than on the development of an absolute vantage point, then Bull's classical approach provides an important corrective to the absolutist claims of science. It points to the variability of the social world that results from its artificial nature (there are no natural kinds,[9] and from the importance of the practical interest guiding our inquiry. Both factors interact with each other and have important implications for orienting actual research and for the criteria by which we try to assess the results. One emphasises the "situated-ness" of political problems, the other the specific duties practical political problems impose upon actors. Both problems deserve some cursory treatment hinting at the special characteristic of the "knowledge" appropriate for *praxis*.

The first problem raises the question of what is a "case" and how we should treat it for analytical purposes. Here two different types of "case" treatment are discernible. One is the *population/analytical* approach, the other the *historical case* study. There is no doubt that the traditional epistemological canon favours the population/analytic approach over the single case, as only the former allegedly can provide knowledge warrants according to the generalisability criterion and the canons of statistical inference. Consequently, if there are not enough cases around the researchers are encouraged to increase their observations. [. . .]

The single (historical) case study, on the other hand, focuses right from the beginning on the issue of delimiting the case by providing a narrative "plot" and examining its coherence and "followability" critically. Here getting the context right and making judgement calls as to the important dimensions that develop throughout the observation is the actual puzzle. The attributes of the case take their meaning then largely from the "case context", *and not from the values of the variables* themselves, as Ragin has pointed out (Ragin, 2000: ch. 3). Fuzzy boundaries are assumed for any "historical individual" (case), so not all variables can be identified *ex ante* and the issue is the explanation of "case transformation" rather than the reduction or transformation of the problem to an issue of different mixes of attributes. As Andrew Abbot suggests:

> The case/narrative approach to explanation thus differs from the popula-
> tion/analytical one in important ways. It ignores variables (in its language
> "type of events") when they aren't narratively important . . . Rather than
> assuming universal or constant relevance, it explains only "what needs to

be explained" and lets the rest slide along in background. This selective attention goes along with an emphasis on contingency. Things happen because of constellation of factors, not because of a few fundamental effects acting independently. And the roving focus of the case/narrative approach has another distinctive advantage over the population/analytic approach. It need make no assumption that all causes lie on the same analytical level (as in standard sociological models). Tiny events (assassinations) can have a big effect.

(Abbott, 1992: 68)

Thus judgement and quick recognition (reasoning by analogy rather than through logical inference or subsumption), both of which depend substantively on experience rather than deductive rigour and formal elegance, are required and provide help for orientation. To that extent the knowledge appropriate for such an environment is exposure to many cases, the actual training of recognition for conjunctures rather than abstraction and formalisation.

As to the issue of the responsibility imposed on practical knowledge, consider the following problems. First, since we know that often we "make" the situation rather than act within its known constraints, the argumentative side of political interaction can seldom be discounted (Risse, 2000), even if strategic and argumentative steps are in actual negotiations and bargaining hardly separable (Schimmelfennig, 2001). Second, since we know that we act not only in an environment of risk (we do know what we do not know) but at times of the truly "unknown" (we do not know what we are ignorant of), precautionary measures rather than maximising principles suggest themselves as maxims for action. Doing no harm, not foreclosing options, rather than instrumental reasoning is then necessary. Third, when we take *practical interest* seriously then – like doctors, lawyers, teachers and decision-makers – we have to learn quickly, that our tasks are powerfully shaped by our *responsibility for the single patient, client, pupil or the particular community*. This task cannot be achieved by retreating to a timeless world in which we have the luxury of being concerned only with what is generally true for mankind in its universality.

Finally, because we know that even in the absence of a catastrophe such as nuclear war, there is a possibility that such an event *could* happen, we also have an obligation to worry about non-events and have to think up cases and scenarios that engage both in counterfactual analysis and in process tracing of single cases. A satisfactory explanation will then no longer be one that plots a case as a "data point" in some multi-variate analysis, but that accounts for the "stream of behaviour" through time. It is by this procedure that we discover contextual features that deeply influence outcomes and modify supposedly causal relationships between the identified variables. Thus, George's examination of actual deterrence failures corrected in significant ways the explanations derived from highly abstract but rigorous models of deterrence and contributed thereby also to the development of far less pro-vocative policy stances (George and Smoke, 1974).

[. . .]

It is this notion of responsibility and the importance of time and of change in human affairs that give Bull's arguments their particular seriousness and urgency. His point is not that theories often mystify their origins in a political project by pretending to deal with the social world as it "is". Such arguments have been made by Gramsci (1971) and Cox (1981), and both have asked for the development of a "critical" rather than a simple problem-solving theory. The former contains as an intrinsic element an "archaeology", that is, the recounting of how this social world and its actors were made. Bull's point though is, I think, even more principled. Even for a "problem-solving" the-ory, we need to understand the peculiar problems of *praxis* and that entails an awareness of our predicament as historical beings.

Notes

1 This is the assumption behind the assertion in the leading graduate school primer that "research designed to help us understand social reality can only succeed if it follows the logic of scientific inference" (King *et al.*, 1994: 229).

2 As Jan Assman notes, the Dynasty of Sargon (ended 2154 BC) attained during the first millennium BC paradigmatic status and the Mesopotamians of that time became a "digging society", obsessed with preserving and finding the remnants of this dynasty which by then had all but disappeared (Assmann, 2000: 42f.).

3 See for instance the attempts of the founders of the 12th Dynasty to "revive" the Old Kingdom and to accord to the Pharao Snofru of the 4th Dynasty a certain "canonical" importance (Assmann, 1990: ch. 2).

4 See the revival of the cult of the Roman Republic and of virtue, particularly among the most radical exponents of the French Revolution.

5 Thus piety meant first loyalty to one's own "house", parents and the gods protect-ing the family and its abode. This is why Aeneas was called "pious" as he took his old father and his son and wife and in order to settle somewhere else when every-thing else was lost at Troy (Virgil 1990: *Aeneid*, BK II).

6 That here emotions play a particular role in "selecting" and making important the things one "records" is shown by the etymology of the word. Not simply the storage of data is involved but something is entrusted to the "heart" (cor!) for keeping.

7 Echoing almost the mood of Thucydides' description of the revolution in Corcyra, Josephus writes of the various groups that often used "religious" motives to justify their terrorist attacks "so corrupt was the public and private life of the whole nation, so determined were they to outdo each other in impiety towards God and injustices to their neighbours, those in power ill-using the masses and the masses striving to overthrow those in power. One group was bent on domination, the other on violence and on robbing the rich" (Josephus, 1970: 394f).

8 Perhaps this is also one of the reasons why analytical ethics has become so barren or when it actually contributes to solving our practical problems it has to rely on "interpretation" and that means on "forms of life" rather than from the calculi of pure models. For a criticism of formalism in ethics see Kratochwil (1998).

9 While it might be problematic to speak about a "classical" approach one could nevertheless argue that Aristotle's argument about the artificiality of the human world might be the "core" example of this approach that can then be extended

to other similar cases. In distinguishing the "political" element as a subclass of "gregariousness" and relating this difference to the notion of "speech", i.e. the ability to use concepts (as opposed to "voice" that serves only as a signalling device), Aristotle shows the importance of "concepts" for the creation of social order. Finally, by demonstrating that these concepts are not simple descriptions of observed "patterns of behaviour" but are a result of agreement on values he clearly shows that concepts do their work not via the "representation" or accurate description of an external reality but are "productive" of the social world, by always being part of a "project". Thus even if we no longer share Aristotle's commitment to "purpose" in nature his remarks remain valid (Aristotle, *Politics*, 1253 a 7–18).

References

Abbott, Andrew (1992) "What do Cases Do? Some notes on Activity in Sociological Analysis", in Charles C. Ragin and Howard S. Becker (eds.) *What is a Case? Exploring the Foundations of Social Inquiry*, pp. 53–83. Cambridge: Cambridge University Press.

Anderson, Benedict (1991) *Imagined Communities* (rev. edn). London: Verso.

Aristotle (1972) *Politics*, trans. T.A. Sinclair. London: Penguin.

Assmann, Jan (1990) *Maat: Gerechtigkeit und Unsterblichkeit im alten Aegypten*. Munich: Beck.

Assmann, Jan (2000) *Religion und kulturelles Gedächtnis*. Munich: Beck.

Barnes, Elmer (1927) *A History of Historical Writing*. Norman, OK: University of Oklahoma Press.

Bull, Hedley (1966) "International Relations Theory: The Case for a Classical Approach", *World Politics* 18(April): 361–77.

Buzan, Barry and Richard Little (2000) *International Systems in World History*. Oxford: Oxford University Press.

Collier, Davis and Steven Levitsky (1997) "Democracy with Adjectives: Conceptual Innovation in Comparative Research", *World Politics* 49(April): 430–51.

Cox, Robert (1981) "Social Forces, States and World Order: Beyond International Relations Theory", *Millennium* 10(Summer): 125–55.

Diesing, Paul (1992) *How Does Social Science Work?* Pittsburgh, PA: Pittsburgh University Press.

Doyle, Michael (1983) "Kant, Liberal Legacies and Foreign Affairs", *Philosophy and Public Affairs* 12(3): 205–35.

Doyle, Michael (1986) "Liberalism and World Politics", *American Political Science Review* 80(4):1151–69.

Fischer, Markus (1992) "Feudal Europe 800–1300: Communal Discourses and Conflictual Practices", *International Organisation* 46(Spring): 426–66.

Friedrichs, Joerg (2004) *European Approaches to International Relations Theory: A House with Many Mansions*. London: Routledge.

Fukuyama, Francis (1992) *The End of History and the Last Man*. New York: Free Press.

George, Alexander and Richard Smoke (1974) *Deterrence in American Foreign Policy*. New York: Columbia University Press.

Goldthorpe, John (1994) "The Uses of History on Sociology – A Reply", *British Journal of Sociology* 45(1): 55–77.

Gramsci, Antonio (1971) *Selections from the Prison Notebooks*, ed. and trans. Q. Hoarc and G. Nowel Smith. London: Lawrence and Wishart.

Halbwachs, Maurice (1992) *On Collective Memory*, (ed.) Lewis Coser. Chicago, IL: University of Chicago Press.

Hall, Rodney and Friedrich Kratochwil (1993) "Medieval Tales: Neo-Realist 'Science' and the Abuse of History", *International Organisation* 47(Summer): 479–91.

Hart, Nicky (1994) "John Goldthorpe and the Relics of Sociology", *British Journal of Sociology* 45(1), 31–6.

Hexter, J.H. (1961) *Reappraisals in History*. Chicago, IL: University of Chicago Press.

Joergensen, Knud Erik (2000) "Continental IR Theory: The Best Kept Secret", *European Journal of International Relations* 6(1): 9–42.

Josephus [Flavius] (1970) *The Jewish War*, trans. G.A. Williamson. New York: Dorset Press.

King, Gary, Robert Keohane and Sidney Verba (1994) *Designing Social Inquiry: Scientific Inference in Qualitative Research*. Princeton, NJ: Princeton University Press.

Koselleck, Reinhart (1985) "*Historia, magistra vitae*: The Dissolution of the Topos into the Perspective of a Modernized Historical Process", in Reinhart Koselleck, *Futures Past: On the Semantics of Historical Time*, trans. Keith Tribe, pp. 21–38. Cambridge, MA: MIT Press.

Kratochwil, Friedrich (1998) "Vergeßt Kant: Reflexionen zur Debatte über Ethik und internationale Politik", in Christine Chwaszcza and Wolfgang Kersting (eds.) *Politische Philosophie der Internationalen Beziehungen* (pp. 96–152). Frankfurt: Suhrkamp.

Kuhn, Thomas (1970) *The Structure of Scientific Revolutions*. Chicago, IL: University of Chicago Press.

Lapid, Yosef (1989) "The Third Debate", *International Studies Quarterly* 33: 235–54.

Lebow, Richard Ned and Thomas Risse-Kappen (eds.) (1995) *International Relations Theory and the End of the Cold War*. New York: Columbia University Press.

Locke, John (1975) *An Essay Concerning Human Understanding*, ed. Peter Nidditch. Oxford: Clarendon Press.

Loriaux, Nicole (1986) *The Invention of Athens: The Funeral Oration in the Classical City*. Cambridge, MA.: Harvard University Press.

Lustick, Ian (1996) "History, Historiography and Political Science: Multiple Historical Records and the Problem of Selection Bias", *American Political Science Review* 90(3): 605–18.

Mann, Michael (1994) "In Praise of Macro Sociology: A Reply to Goldthorpe", *British Journal of Sociology* 45(1): 37–54.

Maoz, Zeev and Bruce Russett (1993) "Normative and Structural Causes of Democratic Peace", *American Political Science Review* 87(3): 624–38.

Moore, Barrington (1966) *Social Origins of Dictatorship and Democracy: Lord and Peasant in the Making of the Modern World*. Boston, MA: Beacon Press.

Mouzelis, Nicos (1994) "In Defence of Grand Historical Sociology", *British Journal of Sociology* 45(1): 31–36.

Nietzsche, Friedrich (1954) "Unzeitgemaesse Betrachtungen, Zweites Hauptstueck: 'Vom Nutzen und Nachteil der Historie' ", in Friedrich Nietzsche, *Werke*, 3 vols, (ed.) Karl Schlechta, vol. 1, pp. 135–438. Munich: Hanser.

Popper, Karl (1961) *The Poverty of Historicism*. New York: Harper.

Ragin, Charles (2000) *Fuzzy Set Social Science*. Chicago, IL: University of Chicago Press.

Risse, Thomas (2000) "Let's Argue: Communicative Action in World Politics", *International Organization* 54 (Winter): 1–39.

Schimmelfennig, Frank (2001) "Liberal Norms, Rhetorical Action and the Enlargement of the EU", *International Organization* 55(Winter): 47–80.

Schroeder, Paul (1994) "Historical Reality vs Neo-Realist Theory", *International Security* 19(Summer): 108–48.

Skocpol, Theda (1979) *States and Social Revolutions.* Cambridge: Cambridge University Press.

Spiro, David (1994) "The Insignificance of the Democratic Peace", *International Security* 19(Fall): 50–86.

Thucydides (1972) *The Peloponnesian War*, trans. Rex Warner. London: Penguin.

Vanhanen, Tatu (1990) *The Process of Democratization: A Comparative Study of 147 States.* New York: Crane Russak.

Virgil (1990) *The Aeneid*, trans. Mortimer Adler. Chicago, IL: Encyclopaedia Britannica.

Weber, Max (1974) *Gesammelte Aufsätze zur Wissenschaftslehre*, (eds.) von Johannes Winckelmann. Tübingen: Mohr.

10 Ten points to ponder about pragmatism

Some critical reflections on knowledge generation in the social sciences

Readers of the contemporary literature in international relations (IR) increasingly find calls for a pragmatic reorientation in theorising the field. Some scholars, for instance, advocate a more pragmatic version of constructivism and a greater concern with the relevance of academic knowledge to our political life (Bernstein *et al.* 2000). Others interpret the increasingly scholastic debates as a "flight from reality" (Shapiro 2005) and call for a more decisive "pragmatic turn" (Bohman 2002; Owen 2002). It is no accident that the former argument is made predominantly by students of foreign policy and diplomacy. They traditionally have been ill at ease with the project of a general "theory" of international politics, particularly after the dissolution of the bipolarity that gave some *prima facie* legitimacy to "systemic" approaches.[1] [. . .]

The more principled calls for a pragmatic approach, however, come from some IR specialists who have participated in previous "great debates". Here the present anthology, as well as the recent contributions by P.J. Katzenstein and R. Sil (forthcoming), or my Tartu lecture (Kratochwil 2007) resulting in a symposium, could be mentioned. These calls usually not only entail a move away from some of the foundationalist criteria of classical positivist science – be it those of empiricism, logical positivism or scientific realism – but they also invite us to give up on the universal suspicion of critical theory, or the endless deconstructions of some postmodern attempts of "theory construction". Instead, the actual problem that such a pragmatic turn identifies is the mistaken attempt of reducing issues of *praxis*, and of the knowledge appropriate for it, to "philosophical" or even metaphysical questions. Here the postulated primacy of ontology over epistemology (or *vice versa*), of "rump materialism" over "idealism" debates, come to mind (Wendt 1999).

[. . .]

Classical pragmatists such as William James (James 1909; see also Dewey 1917) had little patience with this type of "metaphysical disputes", which are obviously interminable. Pragmatists notoriously argued for an active engagement with actual problems and strategies through creative experimentation, accepting the always incomplete nature of our knowledge. In fact, pragmatism is fundamentally misunderstood if it is treated as "second best" try at "theorising", just as when we are "satisfied" with less than perfect solutions because they somehow work. Instead, the emphasis is on pluralism and analytical and methodological eclecticism, which underlie a pragmatic orientation are elements intrinsic to the generation of knowledge. As the rest of this chapter shows, this pragmatic orientation holds promise because of its heuristic potential. This is considerable when we analyse actions and practices that pose problems quite different from the traditional criteria specified for good "theories". "Completeness" and "timeliness", rather than "rigour" or atemporal "validity", come to mind here. [. . .] Furthermore, if our perspectives on the social world always involve us as actors, who make and at the same time observe social reality, there is no single Archimedian point (the view from nowhere) from which everything can be viewed and appears "as it is".

To that extent, the *argument for a pluralism* of methods and approaches follows from the fact that all knowledge is always part of a certain perspective, and that direct tests against "reality" are not available. Consequently, the orthodox notion that scientific "progress" consists in coming nearer and nearer to the truth shows its ideological character. For one, it is on all fours with the empirical evidence of how the scientific enterprise developed. Thus the notion of a simple accumulation not only was debunked by Kuhn and the general criticisms developed by the history of science (Kuhn 1970) but, more importantly, involves us in a logically untenable contradiction. Without knowing "reality" independently of our specific theoretical inquiries, we can never know whether we are "nearer" to the "truth" (rather than being simply "somewhere else"). Otherwise we would need to argue that we can determine that we are nearer to the "goal", even if we have no goal line against which we can make that assessment.[2] This recognition puts a premium on "dialogue" among practitioners utilising competing theories rather than on the idea of "demonstration" that speaks for itself.

Analytical and methodological eclecticism recommends itself precisely because, in practical contexts, we cannot wait until we know "the truth", whatever it might be. To that extent, insisting on methodological purity seems a problematic regulative idea. Instead, what we need is a self-conscious "trespassing", *à la* Hirschman, of various research traditions, and a flexible utilisation of their contribution to the problem at hand (Hirschman 1981). Trusting "paradigms" might hinder rather than help with diagnosing the problem. Similarly, a blind reliance on methods in the sense "one size fits all" is unlikely to deliver the desired "data" (King *et al.* 1994). What is needed is a careful combination of methods and approaches that understands and respects the strengths and limitations of different research traditions and methods, and that combines and adapts (through "translation" and other techniques) the different parts, while being fully attentive to their moorings in different descriptions of the world.

While we are usually aware that this is the way to proceed, disciplinary limitations powerfully counteract these insights. For the strict disciplinarian, everything becomes a problem of "inference" (as if problems of conceptualisation did not exist). Similarly, elegance and rigour very often stand in competition with informational value, so that relying on them exclusively is hardly promising (Walt 1999). Finally, policies are prescribed as if, for example, economic data spoke for themselves, and as if measures such as large-scale dismissals of the workforce might not be interpreted differently in Tokyo and New York. We know, however, that in the former arena it might cause panic, while in the latter stock prices might rise as the observed "restructuring" promises higher returns.[3]

In this chapter I want to defend pragmatism understood as an approach to knowledge generation. Pragmatism relies on pluralism and analytical eclecticism, and crucially takes its departure from *acting* rather than from reason itself. Against the "disciplinary" injunctions familiar from Descartes and the "epistemological project" underlying the standard arguments of positivism, I shall argue, firstly, that the emergence of a "pragmatic turn" in the social sciences is not accidental. There is indeed a logical progression from the criticisms by the history of science, exemplified by Kuhn and others who first undermined the epistemological project, to the new "sociology of knowledge" that emphasises the communal aspects of scientific practices. This line continues in the reconfiguration of epistemology in science studies and the praxiological concerns that characterise Foucault's and Bourdieu's work. Secondly, I argue further that it might be illuminating to link these research enterprises with the more philosophically oriented concerns of everyday language, conventions and institutions – *à la* Searle and Rorty – and reconnect them with a philosophical tradition that explicitly addresses the problem of producing "useful" knowledge, such as the classical pragmatism of Peirce and Dewey. This strategy promises to help us in identifying criteria for assessing our theoretical efforts, now that the old notions of universality, necessity, methodological rigour and near-automatic self-correction through "testing" have been fatally undermined.

Thirdly, beyond placing IR and the analysis of politics in a wider context – quite different from the largely phantasmagoric understanding of a physics and a science that never was (Toulmin 2001) – I show that attempts of developing a "theoretical" understanding of practice distort and hide important dimensions of action by either amalgamating practical knowledge to "theory" or to *techné* (know-how or "applied" knowledge). To the extent that pragmatism starts with *action*, instead of some preconceived ontology or epistemology, it becomes a distinct and promising orientation for the analysis of practices and actions.

With these considerations in mind, the chapter proceeds as follows. In Section two, I briefly outline the reasons why the epistemological project has failed and why recent work in the philosophy of science has stressed the "social" character of knowledge production. Here "science as a practice" has largely supplanted the notion that science could be understood as a mono-logic process of self-correction or of simple though "rigorous" demonstration. Section three outlines the "case" for a pragmatic approach in terms of ten points that address problems of knowledge generation in general, and of the social world more specifically. Rather than summarising the arguments, distilling, so to speak, my anti-epistemological message at the danger of involving myself in a performative contradiction, in the conclusion I leave the reader with these reflections and encourage him or her to begin with actual research.

From epistemology to the study of science as a practice

In what follows, I claim that the shift in focus from "demonstration" to science as practice provides strong *prima facie* reasons to choose pragmatic rather than traditional epistemological criteria in social analysis.

Irrespective of its various forms, the epistemological project includes an argument that all warranted knowledge has to satisfy certain field-independent criteria that are specified by philosophy (a "theory of know-ledge"). The real issue of how our concepts and the world relate to each other, and on which non-idiosyncratic grounds we are justified to hold on to our beliefs about the world, is "answered" by two metaphors. The first is that of an inconvertible ground, be it the nature of things, certain intuitions (Des-cartes' "clear and distinct ideas") or methods and inferences; the second is that of a "mirror" that shows what is the case.

There is no need to rehearse the arguments demonstrating that these under-lying beliefs and metaphors could not sustain the weight placed upon them. A "method" *à la* Descartes could not make good on its claims, as it depended ultimately on the guarantee of God that concepts and things in the outer world match. On the other hand, the empiricist belief in direct observation forgot that "facts" which become "data" are – as the term suggests – "made". They are based on the judgements of the observer using cultural criteria, even if they appear to be based on direct perception, as is the case with colours.[4]

Besides, there had always been a sneaking suspicion that the epistemo-logical ideal of certainty and rigour did not quite fit the social world, an objection voiced first by humanists such as Vico, and later rehearsed in the continuing controversies about *erklären* and *verstehen* (Weber 1991; for a more recent treatment see Hollis 1994). In short, both the constitutive nature of our concepts, and the value interest in which they are embedded, raise peculiar issues of meaning and contestation that are quite different from those of description. As Vico (1947) suggested, we "understand" the social world because we have "made it", a point raised again by Searle concerning both the crucial role played by ascriptions of meaning (*x* counts for *y*) in the social world and the distinction between institutional "facts" from "brute" or natural facts (Searle 1995). Similarly, since values are constitutive for our "interests", the concepts we use always portray an action from a certain point of view; this involves appraisals and prevents us from accepting allegedly "neutral" descriptions that would be meaningless. Thus, when we say that someone "abandoned" another person and hence communicate a (contestable) appraisal, we want to call attention to certain important moral implications of an act. Attempting to eliminate the value-tinge in the description and insisting that everything has to be cast in neutral, "objective", observational language – such as "he opened the door and went through it" – would indeed make the statement "pointless", even if it is (trivially) "true" (for a powerful statement of this point, see Connolly 1983).

The most devastating attack on the epistemological project, however, came from the history of science itself. It not only corrected the naive view of knowledge generation as mere accumulation of data, but it also cast increasing doubt on the viability of various field-independent "demarcation criteria". This was, for the most part, derived from the old Humean argument that only sentences with empirical content were "meaningful", while value statements had to be taken either as statements about individual preferences or as meaningless, since *de gustibus non est disputandum*. As the later discussion in the Vienna circle showed, this distinction was utterly unhelpful (Popper 1965: ch. 2). It did not solve the problem of induction, and failed to acknowledge that not all meaningful theoretical sentences must correspond with natural facts.

Karl Popper's ingenious solution of making "refutability" the logical criterion and interpreting empirical "tests" as a special mode of deduction (rather than as a way of increasing supporting evidence) seemed to respond to this epistemological quandary for a while. An "historical reconstruction" of science as a progressive development thus seemed possible, as did the specification of a pragmatic criterion for conducting research.

Yet again, studies in the history of science undermined both hopes. The different stages in Popper's own intellectual development are, in fact, rather telling. He started out with a version of conjectures and refutations that was based on the notion of a more or less self-correcting demonstration. Confronted with the findings that scientists did not use the refutation criterion in their research, he emphasised then the role of the *scientific community* on which the task of "refutation" devolved. Since the individual scientist might not be ready to bite the bullet and admit that she or he might have been wrong, colleagues had to keep him or her honest. Finally, towards the end of his life, Popper began to rely less and less on the stock of knowledge or on the scientists' shared theoretical understandings – simply devalued as the "myth of the framework" – and emphasised instead the processes of communication and of "translation" among different schools of thought within a scientific community (Popper 1994). He still argued that these processes follow the pattern of "conjecture and refutation", but the model was clearly no longer that of logic or of scientific *demonstration*, but one that he derived from his *social* theory – from his advocacy of an "open society" (Popper 1966). Thus a near total reversal of the ideal of knowledge had occurred. While formerly everything was measured in terms of the epistemological ideal derived from logic and physics, "knowledge" was now the result of deliberation and of certain procedural notions for assessing competing knowledge claims. Politics and law, rather than physics, now provided the template.

Thus the history of science has gradually moved away from the epistemological ideal to focus increasingly on the actual practices of various scientific communities engaged in knowledge production, particularly on how they handle problems of scientific disagreement.[5] This reorientation implied a move away from field-independent criteria and from the demonstrative ideal to one in which "arguments" and the "weight" of evidence had to be appraised. This, in turn, not only generated a bourgeoning field of "science studies" and their "social" epistemologies (see Fuller 1991), but also suggested more generally that the traditional understandings of knowledge production based on the model of "theory" were in need of revision.

If the history of science therefore provides strong reasons for a pragmatic turn, as the discussion above illustrates, what remains to be shown is how this turn relates to the historical, linguistic and constructivist turns that preceded it. To start with, from the above it should be clear that, in the social world, we are not dealing with natural kinds that exist and are awaiting, so to speak, prepackaged, their placement in the appropriate box. The objects we investigate are rather *conceptual creations* and they are intrinsically linked to the language through which the social world is constituted. Here "constructivists", particularly those influenced by Wittgenstein and language philosophy, easily link up with "pragmatists" such as Rorty, who emphasises the productive and pragmatic role of "vocabularies" rather than conceiving of language as a "mirror of nature" (Rorty 1979).

Furthermore, precisely because social facts are not natural, but have to be reproduced through the actions of agents, any attempt to treat them like "brute" facts becomes doubly problematic. For one, even "natural" facts are not simply "there"; they are interpretations based on our theories. Secondly, different from the observation of natural facts, in which perceptions address a "thing" through a conceptually mediated form, social reality is entirely "artificial" in the sense that it is dependent on the beliefs and practices of the actors themselves. This reproductive process, directed by norms, always engenders change either interstitially, when change is small-scale or adaptive – or more dramatically, when it becomes "transformative" – for instance when it produces a new system configuration, as after the advent of nationalism (Lapid and Kratochwil 1995) or after the demise of the Soviet Union (Koslowski and Kratochwil 1994). Consequently, any examination of the social world *has to become in a way "historical"* even if some "structuralist" theories attempt to minimise this dimension. [. . .]

Therefore a pragmatic approach to social science and IR seems both necessary and promising. On the one hand, it is substantiated by the failure of the epistemological project that has long dominated the field. On the other, it offers a different positive heuristics that challenges IR's traditional disciplinary boundaries and methodological assumptions. Interest in pragmatism therefore does not seem to be just a passing fad – even if such an interpretation cannot entirely be discounted, given the incentives of academia to find, just like advertising agencies, "new and improved" versions of familiar products.

The pragmatic turn and its implications

It might be useful at this stage to clarify a bit further the variety of uses of the terms "practice" and "pragmatic", since this will give us also some clues as to the discussion of the ten points for pragmatism in the third section of this chapter, and their interrelationships. In what follows, I briefly address the "practice turn" argument and the issue of pragmatism. Then I examine more closely questions of "practice", as these shed some light on the confusion that exists in the use of the former two terms.

Even the most casual perusal of the "practice turn" in social analysis reveals an astonishingly wide variety of quite different types of effort that are subsumed under this label (Reckwitz 2002). Ethnomethodological studies examining the practices of strategic behaviour in the enactment of everyday life *à la* Goffman (1966) are put next to studies of the reverse adaptation of man-machine routines á la Latour (1987; Latour and Woolgar 1979), or of the "praxeological" and disciplinary inquiries of Foucault (1977). Analyses based on rule-following by Wittgenstein and his adherents (Schatzki 1996) are lumped together with examinations of "virtuosity", transcending all rule-bound behaviour, as exemplified in Bourdieu's account of a Kabyle chieftain (Bourdieu 1977). Thus deliberate action and "tacit knowledge" *à la* Turner (1994), or the near-automatic reflexes caused by a specific acquired "habitus" (Bourdieu 2000), are being investigated.

When we turn from the varied landscape of the "practice turn" to *pragmatism*, we see that our focus becomes somewhat narrower. Yet one would be hard pressed to establish a clear-cut definition of a school of thought comprising "classical pragmatists" such as Peirce and Dewey; neopragmatist thinkers such as Rorty, strongly influenced by language philosophy; and again Toulmin (1986, 2001) or Habermas (1984) whose "universal pragmatics" displays some American influence but represents a distinct orientation. One would also have to include some thinkers who have contributed to the revival of "practical philosophy", even if the latter would not characterise themselves as "pragmatists".[6] In any case, in one way or another, as a philosophical orientation pragmatism seems to have some identifiable features that allow for the lumping together of otherwise quite distinct approaches.

What the thinkers mentioned above are all concerned with is the clarification of action and agency and the nature of the knowledge appropriate for it. Their approach to knowledge takes its departure from *acting* rather than reason itself – or "being", or speculation. Their mode of knowing is based on reflection, deliberation and the awareness of its historical embeddedness, rather than on the construction of ahistorical universal laws, "ideal languages" or efficient causality.

The notion of practice, on the other hand, seems wider than that of "pragmatics". While the latter focuses specifically on action and on the features that differentiate actions from events and acting from "happenings", the term practice is used in several rather distinctive ways. Firstly, it stresses the elements of a disciplinary instruction that we get something right finally after having tried it repeatedly. For example, I have to practise playing the violin if I want finally to "perform" the Beethoven concerto without much effort or conscious control and nearly effortlessly master the difficult octaves. In this sense, both Foucault's (1977, 1985) studies about self-fashioning and disciplinary control, and Bourdieu's (1977, 2000) and Flyvjerg's (2001) focus on virtuous performances fit this use, as do the arguments about common intentions, and the specific forms of continuously monitored but half-consciously carried-out cooperation, as in the case of dancing or playing a duet, analysed by Bratman (1987).

Secondly, we also use the term for activities that imply some form of knowledge and "craft". Exercising this knowledge or craft entails discretion and perhaps some form of skill. These are sometimes bound by certain special responsibilities, but their exercise does not seem to be specifiable by rules or a decision algorithm. In this sense, we speak of practising law or medicine, or maintain that the statesman's activities are part of statecraft. Obviously, the old distinction between theoretical knowledge and prudence plays a significant role here. On the other hand, it would be odd to say that someone "practised engineering", even though he or she has an office like a medical doctor, or is a "professional" in the sense of having to go through studies and certifications before being allowed to set up shop. Similarly, simple as well as complicated activities, such as fishing or building a car, are not "practised". Thus these two examples show us that we make distinctions between instrumental actions, productive activities and practical activities. To that extent, the old Aristotelian distinction between *techné, poesis* and *praxis* still seems relevant (Höffe 1971).

Thirdly, we speak of a practice and practices when we want to characterise certain assemblies of interrelated actions, like Bratman's collective intentions, but we do it from the observer's rather than the actor's perspective. To that extent, ceremonies, rituals and institutions (often defined as "settled practices") fall within this category. Searle has elaborated on the peculiarities of institutional practices, and particularly on two aspects that have analytical import. On the one hand is the recognition that their *fiat* character depends on a status ascription mediated by language – "I hereby appoint you ... X", or "this token of paper shall count as ... money, a diploma, etc." On the other hand, understanding their functioning and explaining an act in terms of institutional actions inevitably involves a type of recursive move. Thus an explanation of money, for instance, cannot do without invoking the concept of money. While such recursivity seems to violate the criteria of logical purity, the "circle" involved here is far from vicious. In other words, it is not the kind of logical paradox in which "Epimenides the Cretan says that all Cretans are liars", thereby involving himself in a performative contradiction. Rather, the circle here is more like a hermeneutic one, where we understand, for example, the meaning of a sentence from the "text", which is in turn made up of its sentences.

Faced with such heterogeneity in the meaning and use of "practice", the impulse would be to look for some "working" definition, listing certain "essential" properties, and to use this template for organizing the materials and separating the sheep from the goats. Yet such a strategy might come at a heavy price. This is, after all, a rather familiar problem in social analysis, the traditional remedy for which has been to insist on unequivocal "definitions". A short reflection shows, however, that conceptual moves are less promising than they first appear. Take the attempts to "define" power once and for all. As the various stages of the power debate have shown, no such easy procedure is available, because the social world is not one of "natural kinds". For example, power turned out to be better understood as a cluster-concept, linking various "forms" without it being clear that all of them have a common core. Sometimes it can be "possessed", at other times it is more diffuse (as in the case of intellectual hegemonies or structural power), sometimes it has certain observable effects (as in Weber's or Dahl's definition), and in other cases it can be "seen" only on the basis of a counterfactual thought experiment (as in the case of the power of anticipated reaction). None of these variations, however, disqualifies any of these manifestations from being properly called an instance of power, and eliminating any of them might entail significant heuristic costs.

The lesson seems clear. Even at the danger of "fuzzy boundaries", when we deal with "practice" (just as with the "pragmatic turn"), we would be well advised to rely on the *use* of the term rather than on its *reference* (pointing to some property of the object under study), in order to draw the bounds of sense and understand the meaning of the concept. My argument for the fruitful character of a pragmatic approach in IR, therefore, does not depend on a comprehensive mapping of the varieties of research in this area, nor on an arbitrary appropriation or exegesis of any specific and self-absorbed theoretical orientation. For this reason, in what follows, I will *not* provide a rigidly specified definition, *nor* will I refer exclusively to some prepackaged theoretical approach. Instead, I will sketch out the reasons for which a pragmatic orientation in social analysis seems to hold particular promise. These reasons pertain both to the more general area of knowledge appropriate for *praxis* and to the more specific types of investigation in the field. The following ten points are – without a claim to completeness – intended to engender some critical reflection on both areas.

Firstly, a pragmatic approach does not begin with objects or "things" (ontology), or with reason and method (epistemology), but with "acting" (*prattein*), thereby preventing some false starts. Since, as historical beings placed in a specific situations, we do not have the luxury of deferring decisions until we have found the "truth", we have to act and must do so always under time pressures and in the face of incomplete information. Precisely because the social world is characterised by strategic interactions, what a situation "is", is hardly ever clear *ex ante*, because it is being "produced" by the actors and their interactions, and the multiple possibilities are rife with incentives for (dis)information. This puts a premium on quick diagnostic and cognitive shortcuts informing actors about the relevant features of the situation, and on leaving an alternative open ("plan B") in case of unexpected difficulties. Instead of relying on certainty and universal validity gained through abstraction and controlled experiments, we know that completeness and attentiveness to detail, rather than to generality, matter. To that extent, likening practical choices to simple "discoveries" of an already independently existing "reality" which discloses itself to an "observer" – or relying on optimal strategies – is somewhat heroic.

These points have been made vividly by "realists" such as Clausewitz in his controversy with von Bülow, in which he criticised the latter's obsession with a strategic "science" (Paret *et al.* 1986). While Clausewitz has become an icon for realists, only a few of them (usually dubbed "old" realists) have taken seriously his warnings against the misplaced belief in the reliability and usefulness of a "scientific" study of strategy. Instead, most of them, especially "neorealists" of various stripes, have embraced the "theory"-building based on the epistemological project as the *via regia* to the creation of knowledge. A pragmatist orientation would most certainly not endorse such a position.

Secondly, since acting in the social world often involves acting "for" someone, special responsibilities arise that aggravate both the incompleteness of knowledge as well as its generality problem. Since we owe special care to those entrusted to us, for example, as teachers, doctors or lawyers, we cannot just rely on what is generally true, but have to pay special attention to the particular case. Aside from avoiding the foreclosure of options, we *cannot refuse* to act on the basis of incomplete information or insufficient knowledge, and the necessary diagnostic will involve typification and comparison, reasoning by analogy rather than generalization or deduction. Leaving out the particularities of a case, be it a legal or medical one, in a mistaken effort to become "scientific" would be a fatal flaw. Moreover, there still remains the crucial element of "timing" – of knowing when to act. Students of crises have always pointed out the importance of this factor but, in attempts at building a general "theory" of international politics analogously to the natural sciences, such elements are neglected on the basis of the "continuity of nature" and the "large number" assumptions. Besides, "timing" seems to be quite recalcitrant to analytical treatment.

Thirdly, the cure for anxiety induced by Cartesian radical doubt does not consist in the discovery of a "foundation" guaranteeing absolute certainty. This is a phantasmagorical undertaking engendered by a fantastic starting point, since nobody begins with universal doubt! (Peirce 1868). Rather, the remedy for this anxiety consists in the recognition of the unproductive nature of universal doubt on the one hand, and of the fetishisation of "rigour" on the other. Letting go of unrealisable plans and notions that lead us to delusional projects, and acquiring instead the ability to "go on" despite uncertainties and the unknown, is probably the most valuable lesson to learn. Beginning somewhere, and reflecting critically on the limitations of the starting point and the perspective it opened, is likely to lead to a more fruitful research agenda than starting with some preconceived notions of the nature of things, or of "science", and then testing the presumably different (but usually quite similar) theories (such as liberalism and realism). After all, "progress" in the sciences occurred only after practitioners had finally given up on the idea that in order to say something about the phenomena of the world (*ta onta*), one had to grasp first "being" itself (*to ontos on*).

Fourthly, by giving up on the idea that warranted knowledge is generated either through logical demonstration or through the representation of the world "out there", a pragmatic starting point not only takes seriously the always preliminary character of knowledge, it also promises that we will learn to follow a course of action that represents a good bet.[7] Thus it accounts for changes in knowledge in a more coherent fashion. If the world were "out there", ready-made, only to be discovered, scientific knowledge would have to be a simple accumulation of more and more true facts, leading us virtually automatically closer and closer to "the Truth". Yet, if we have learned anything from the studies of various disciplines, it is the fact that progress consists in being able to formulate new questions that *could not even be asked previously*. Thus whatever we think of Kuhn's argument about "paradigms", we have to recognise that in times of revolutionary change the bounds of sense are being redrawn, and thus the newly generated knowledge is not simply a larger sector of the encircled area (Kratochwil 2000).

Fifthly, pragmatism recognises that science is social practice, which is determined by rules and in which scientists not only are constitutive for the definitions of problems (rather than simply lifting the veil from nature), but also debate seemingly "undecidable" questions and weigh the evidence, instead of relying on the bivalence principle of logic as an automatic truth-finder (Ziman 1991; Kratochwil 2007a). To that extent, the critical element of the epistemological project is retained, but the "court", which Kant believed to be reason itself, now consists of the practitioners themselves. Instead of applying free-standing epistemological standards, each science provides its own court, judging the appropriateness of its methods and practices. Staying with the metaphor of a court, we also have to correct an implausible Kantian interpretation of law – that it has to yield determinate and unique decisions. We know from jurisprudence and case law that cases can be decided quite differently without justifying the inference that this proves the arbitrariness of law. Determinacy need not coincide with uniqueness, either in logic (multiple equilibria), science (equifinality) or law – Ronald Dworkin (1978) notwithstanding!

Sixthly, despite the fact that it is no longer a function of bivalent truth conditions, nor anchored either in the things themselves (as in classical ontology) or in reason itself, "truth" has not been abolished or supplanted by an "anything goes" attitude. Rather, it has become a procedural notion of rule-following according to community practices, as nobody can simply make the rules as she or he goes along. These rules do not "determine" outcomes, as the classical logic of deductions or truth conditions suggest, but they do constrain and enable us in our activities.

Furthermore, since rule-following does not simply result in producing multiple copies of a fixed template, rules provide orientation in new situations, allowing us to "go on", making for both consistency and change. Validity no longer assumes historical universality, and change is no longer conceived of as temporal reversibility, as in differential equations, where time can be added and multiplied, compared with infinity, and run towards the past or the future. Thus "History" is able to enter the picture, and it matters because, differently from the old ontology, change can now be conceived of as a "path-dependent" development, as a (cognitive) evolution or even as radical historicity, instead of contingency or decay impairing true knowledge. Consequently, time-bound rather than universal generalisations figure prominently in social analysis, and as Diesing, a philosopher of science, reminds us, this is no embarrassment. Being critical of the logical positivists' search for "laws" does not mean that only single cases exist and that no general statements are possible. It does mean, however, that in research:

> there are other goals as well and that generality is a matter of degree. Generalizations about US voting behaviour can be valid though they apply only between 1948–72 and only to Americans. Truth does not have to be timeless. Logical empiricists have a derogatory name for such changing truths (relativism); but such truths are real, while the absolute, fully axiomatized truth is imaginary.
>
> (Diesing 1991: 91)

Seventhly, the above points show their importance when applied not only to the practices of knowledge generation, but also to the larger problem of the reproduction of the social world. Luhmann (1983) suggested how rule-following solves the problem of the "double contingency" of choices that allows interacting parties to relate their actions meaningfully to each other. "Learning" from past experience on the basis of a "tit for tat" strategy represents one possibility for solving what, since Parsons, has been called the "Hobbesian problem of order". This solution, however, is highly unstable, and thus it cannot account for institutionalised behaviour. The alternative to learning is *to forgo* "learning". Actors must abstract from their own experiences by trusting in a "system of expectations" which is held to be counterfactually valid. "Institutionalisation" occurs in this way, especially when dispute-settling instances emerge that are based on *shared expectations about the system of expectations*. Thus people must form expectations about what types of arguments and reasons are upheld by "courts" in case of a conflict (Luhmann 1983).

Eighthly, a pragmatic approach, although sensitive to the social conditions of cognition, is not simply another version of the old "sociology of knowledge", let alone of utilitarianism by accepting "what works" or what seems reasonable to most people. It differs from the old sociology of knowledge that hinged on the *cui bono* question of knowledge (Mannheim 1936), since no argument about a link between social stratification and knowledge is implied, not to mention the further-reaching Marxist claims of false consciousness. A pragmatist approach, however, is compatible with such approaches as Bourdieu's (1977) or more constructivist accounts of knowledge production, such as Fuller's (1991) social epistemology, because it highlights the interdependence of semantics and social structures.

Ninthly, as the brief discussion of "science studies" above has shown, it is problematic to limit the problem of knowledge production to "demonstrations" (even if loosely understood in terms of the arguments within the scientific community), thus neglecting the factors that are conducive to (or inhibitive of) innovation in the definition of problems. To start with, antecedent to any demonstration, there has to be the step of "invention", as the classical tradition already suggested. Secondly, although it might well be true that "invention" does not follow the same "logic" as "testing" or demonstrating, this does not mean these considerations are irrelevant or can be left outside the reflection on how knowledge is generated. To attribute originality solely to a residual category of a rather naively conceived individual "psychology of discovery", as logical positivists do, will simply not do. After all, "ideas" are not representations and properties of the individual mind, but do their work because they *are shared*; innovation is crucially influenced by the formal and informal channels of communication within a (scientific) community.

While the logical form of refutability in principle is, for logical positivists, a necessary element of their "theoretical" enterprise, it does not address issues of creativity and innovation, which are a crucial part of the search for knowledge. Corroborating what we already suspected is interesting only if such inquiries also lead to novel discoveries, since nobody is served by "true" but trivial results. Quite clearly, the traditional epistemological focus is much too narrow to account for and direct innovative research, while pragmatic approaches have notoriously emphasised the creativity of action (Rochberg-Halton 1986).

Tenthly, the above discussion should have demonstrated that a pragmatic approach to knowledge generation is not some form of "instrumentalism" *à la* Friedman (1968), at basement prices, or that it endorses old wives" tales if they generated "useful predictions", even though for rather unexplainable reasons. Thus, buying several lottery tickets on the advice of an acquaintance to rid oneself of debts and subsequently hitting the jackpot hardly qualifies as a pragmatically generated solution to a problem, neither does it make the acquaintance a financial advisor. Although "usefulness" is a pragmatic standard, not every employment of it satisfies the exacting criteria of knowledge production. As suggested throughout this chapter, a coherent pragmatic approach emphasises the intersubjective and critical nature of knowledge generation based on rules, and it cannot be reduced to the *de facto* existing (or fabricated) consensus of a concrete group of scientists or to the utility of results, the presuppositions of which are obscure because they remained unexamined.

Conclusions

No long summary of argument is necessary here. Simply, a pragmatic turn firstly shows itself to be consistent with the trajectory of a number of debates in the epistemology of social sciences; secondly, it ties in with and feeds into the linguistic, constructivist and "historical" turns that preceded it; and thirdly, it is promising for the ten reasons listed above. While these insights might be useful correctives, they do not by themselves generate viable research projects. This gain might have been the false promise of the epistemological project and its claim that simply following the path of a "method" will inevitably lead to secure knowledge. Disabusing us of this idea might be useful itself as it redirects our efforts at formulating and conceptualising problems that are antecedent to any "operationalisation" of our crucial terms (Sartori 1970), or of any "tests" concerning which "theory" allegedly explains best a phenomenon under investigation.

As anyone familiar with an IR dissertation can testify, we often encounter claims that there are three theories explaining the dissertation topic. Unfortunately, this "theory-generated" research is not only often "scholastic" in nature, but also frequently woefully inadequate in its conceptual development. This is precisely because one's fascination with numbers or deductive rigour renders one prey to the misconception that "precision" can be ascertained by how well a concept "covers" the "reality out there".

A pragmatic approach reminds us that "truth" and meaning are, however, not problems of simple reference, but problems of relation with other concepts in a semantic field, and of linking the problem under investigation to actions and practices which are the stuff of "politics". Moreover, it draws attention to the historical nature of the social world, a problem that is frequently misunderstood when "history" is treated as a warehouse of "data" for the "testing" of atemporal "theories". As the historian Paul Schroeder has shown in his criticism of neorealism and its "historical" relevance, the "cases" and the "empirical" support they allegedly provide for a structural "theory" of IR are largely phantasmagorical exercises in confirmatory research that make for bad histories and – one might add – for even worse social "science" (Schroeder 1994). But when everything is said and done, in research as in life, in the beginning there is the deed or the action (Onuf

1989), not some universal doubt or the vain search for incontrovertible foundations.

Notes

1 For instance, the work of Henry Nau (2002), who tried to explain US foreign policy as the result of an interactive process between balance of power and balance of identity (US exceptionalism), comes to mind.
2 Incidentally, the argument that scientific progress "has" to be conceived of as approximation (otherwise it would be an absolute miracle) – an argument popular with some scientific realists – has the same logical structure as the argument that from the perfect designs we encounter in nature – we have to conclude that there has to be a (perfect) designer. Both are, of course, logically faulty, as Kant has shown in his chapter on antinomies (Kant 1787: A420ff./B48ff.).
3 I owe this thought to Oliver Kessler. As Stiglitz noted, measures that are usually the standard means to stem the tide of capital flight might induce capital flight and worsen the situation if, during a crisis, they are interpreted as a holding effort, especially if they had been imposed by a "supervising" financial agency (Hall 2003).
4 On the colour concepts and their cultural variations, see the discussion of cognitive research in Davis (2005).
5 The arguments that dominated this discussion since the 1980s are exemplified by Knorr-Cetina (1981) and Bourdieu (1977).
6 Here Schwemmer (1980) and the German Erlangen school of practical philosophy come to mind.
7 Points four to eight draw on Kratochwil (2007).

References

Bernstein, S. *et al.* (2000) "God Gave Physics the Easy Problems: Adapting Social Science to an Unpredictable World", *European Journal of International Relations,* 6: 43–76.

Bohman, J. (2002) "How to Make a Social Science Practical: Critical Theory, Pragmatism and Multiperspectival Theory", *Millennium: Journal of International Studies,* 31: 499–524.

Bourdieu, P. (1977) *Outline of a Theory of Practice,* Cambridge: Cambridge University Press.

Bourdieu, P. (2000) *Pascalian Meditations,* Cambridge: Polity Press.

Bratman, M. (1987) *Intention, Plans and Practical Reason,* Cambridge, MA: Harvard University Press.

Connolly, W.E. (1983) *The Terms of Political Discourse,* 2nd edn, Princeton, NJ: Princeton University Press.

Davis, J.W. (2005) *Terms of Inquiry: On the Theory and Practice of Political Science,* Baltimore: Johns Hopkins University Press.

Dewey, J. (1917) "The Need for a Recovery of Philosophy", in J. Dewey *et al.* (eds.) *Creative Intelligence: Essays in the Pragmatic Attitude,* New York: Henry Holt.

Diesing, P. (1991) *How Does Social Science Work? Reflections on Practice,* Pittsburgh: University of Pittsburgh Press.

Dworkin, R.M. (1978) *Taking Rights Seriously,* Cambridge, MA: Harvard University Press.

Flyvbjerg, B. (2001) *Making Social Science Matter: Why Social Inquiry Fails and How It Can Succeed Again*, Cambridge: Cambridge University Press.

Foucault, M. (1977) *Discipline and Punish: The Birth of the Prison*, New York: Random House.

Foucault, M. (1985) *The Uses of Pleasure*, Vol. 2 of *The History of Sexuality*, Harmondsworth: Penguin.

Friedman, M. (1968) "The Methodology of Positive Economics", in M. Brodbeck (ed.) *Readings in the Philosophy of the Social Sciences*, New York: Macmillan.

Fuller, S. (1991) *Social Epistemology*, Bloomington: Indiana University Press.

Goffman, E. (1966) *Behavior in Public Places: Notes on the Social Organization of Gatherings*, New York: Free Press of Glencoe.

Habermas, J. (1984) *The Theory of Communicative Action*, 2 vols, Boston, MA: Beacon Press.

Hall, R.B. (2003) "The Discursive Demolition of the Asian Development Model", *International Studies Quarterly*, 47: 71–99.

Hirschman, A.O. (1981) *Essays in Trespassing: Economics to Politics and Beyond*, Cambridge: Cambridge University Press.

Höffe, O. (1971) *Praktische Philosophie: Das Modell des Aristoteles*, München: Pustet.

Hollis, M. (1994) *The Philosophy of Social Science*, Cambridge: Cambridge University Press.

James, W. (1909) *Pluralistic Universe*, Cambridge, MA: Harvard University Press.

Kant, I. (1787) *Critique of Pure Reason*, Cambridge: Cambridge University Press 1998.

Katzenstein, P.J. and Sil, R. (forthcoming) Beyond Paradigms: Analytic Eclecticism in the Study of World Politics, Palgrave Macmillan.

King, G., Keohane, R.O. and Verba, S. (1994) *Designing Social Inquiry: Scientific Inference in Qualitative Research*, Princeton, NJ: Princeton University Press.

Knorr-Cetina, K. (1981) *The Manufacture of Knowledge: An Essay on the Constructivist and Contextual Nature of Science*, Oxford: Pergamon Press.

Koslowski, R. and Kratochwil, F. (1994) "Understanding Change in International Politics: The Soviet Empire's Demise and the International System", *International Organization*, 48: 215–47.

Kratochwil, F. (2000) "Constructing a New Orthodoxy? Wendt's 'Social Theory of International Politics' and the Constructivist Challenge", *Millennium: Journal of International Studies*, 29: 73–101.

Kratochwil, F. (2007) "Of False Promises and Good Bets: A Plea for a Pragmatic Approach to Theory Building (the Tartu Lecture)", *Journal of International Relations and Development*, 10: 1–15.

Kuhn, T.S. (1970) *The Structure of Scientific Revolutions*, 2nd edn, Chicago: University of Chicago Press.

Lapid, Y. and Kratochwil, F. (eds.) (1995) *Nationalism, Citizenship and Identity*, Boulder, CO: Lynne Rienner.

Latour, B. (1987) *Science in Action: How to Follow Scientists and Engineers through Society*, Cambridge, MA: Harvard University Press.

Latour, B. and Woolgar, S. (1979) *Laboratory Life: The Social Construction of Scientific Facts*, London: Sage.

Luhmann, N. (1983) *Rechtssoziologie*, Opladen: Westdeutscher Verlag.

Mannheim, K. (1936) *Ideology and Utopia: An Introduction to the Sociology of Knowledge*, New York: Harvest.

Nau, H.R. (2002) *At Home Abroad: Identity and Power in American Foreign Policy*, Ithaca, NY: Cornell University Press.

Onuf, N.G. (1989) *World of Our Making: Rule and Rules in International Relations*, Columbia: University of South Carolina Press.

Owen, D. (2002) "Re-orienting International Relations: On Pragmatism, Pluralism and Practical Reasoning", *Millennium: Journal of International Studies*, 31: 653–73.

Paret, P., Craig, G.A. and Gilbert, F. (eds.) (1986) *Makers of Modern Strategy: From Machiavelli to the Nuclear Age*, Princeton, NJ: Princeton University Press.

Peirce, C.S. (1868) "Some Consequences of Four Incapacities", in L. Menand (ed.) *Pragmatism: A Reader*, New York: Vintage Books 1997.

Popper, K.R. (1965) *Conjectures and Refutations: The Growth of Scientific Knowledge*, New York: Harper and Row.

Popper, K.R. (1966) *The Open Society and its Enemies*, Princeton, NJ: Princeton University Press.

Popper, K.R. (1994) *The Myth of the Framework: In Defence of Science and Rationality*, M.A. Notturno (ed.), New York: Routledge.

Reckwitz, A. (2002) "Toward a Theory of Social Practices: A Development in Culturalist Theorizing", *European Journal of Social Theory*, 5: 243–63.

Rochberg-Halton, E. (1986) *Meaning and Modernity: Social Theory in the Pragmatic Attitude*, Chicago: Chicago University Press.

Rorty, R. (1979) *Philosophy and the Mirror of Nature*, Princeton, NJ: Princeton University Press.

Sartori, G. (1970) "Concept Misformation in Comparative Politics", *American Political Science Review*, 64: 1033–53.

Schatzki, T.R. (1996) *Social Practices: A Wittgensteinian Approach to Human Activity and the Social*, Cambridge: Cambridge University Press.

Schroeder, P. (1994) "Historical Reality vs. Neo-Realist Theory", *International Security*, 19: 108–48.

Schwemmer, O. (1980) *Philosophie der Praxis: Versuch zur Grundlegung einer Lehre vom moralischen Argumentieren in Verbindung mit einer Interpretation der Praktischen Philosophie Kants*, Frankfurt am Main: Suhrkamp.

Searle, J. (1995) *The Construction of Social Reality*, New York: Free Press.

Toulmin, S.E. (1986) *Place of Reason in Ethics*, Chicago: University of Chicago Press.

Toulmin, S.E. (2001) *Return to Reason*, Cambridge, MA: Harvard University Press.

Vico, G. (1947) *De Nostri Temporis Studiorum Ratione*, Godesberg: Kupper.

Walt, S.M. (1999) "Rigor or Rigor Mortis? Rational Choice and Security Studies", *International Security*, 23: 5–48.

Weber, M. (1991) *Schriften zur Wissenschaftslehre*, Stuttgart: Reclam.

Wendt, A. (1999) *Social Theory of International Politics*, Cambridge: Cambridge University Press.

Ziman, J.M. (1991) *Reliable Knowledge: An Exploration of the Grounds for Belief in Science*, Cambridge: Canto.

Part IV

Drawing boundaries

The inter/external and the private/public nexus

11 Of systems, boundaries, and territoriality

An inquiry into the formation of the state system

I. Introduction

Changes in the function of boundaries throughout history help to illuminate differences in the nature and patterns of interactions of different domestic and international systems. Such a clarification has become important for the analysis of international relations at a time when the world system appears to be characterised by two conflicting trends. On the one hand, we observe the virtually universal recognition of territorial sovereignty as the organising principle of international politics. On the other hand, because of the growth of transnational relations and interdependencies, there is a tendency toward erosion of the exclusivity associated with the traditional notion of territoriality. This disjunction between the organising principles and social reality creates dilemmas for conflict management. An investigation of these tensions and of the varying patterns in which they manifest themselves in different international systems is therefore of historical as well as analytical interest.

In this article, I intend to lay the groundwork for such an historical and comparative analysis of international systems. An examination of shifts in the functions of boundaries is particularly helpful for a better understanding of the origins and evolution of the present territorial state system. Without intending to bring back the old controversy of whether such changes can be taken as indicators of either the demise or the revival of the territorial state,[1] I maintain that territoriality, like property, is not a simple concept, but comprises a variety of social arrangements that have to be examined in greater detail. For that purpose, I first investigate the function of boundaries in nonterritorial and territorial social organizations and give reasons for the transition from one form of organising societies to the other. Second, within the class of territorial orders, I distinguish between empires and territoriality in a state system. Finally, I will examine changes in the relationships and exchanges between international systems and their environment by contrasting the function of boundaries in territorially based orders with those based on functional regimes.

[. . .]

Section II deals with territorial and nonterritorial social organisations and the function of boundaries in each. Within the territorial category, those systems that are based on the mutual recognition of rights and acknowledged common practices are distinguished from "imperial" orders. The importance of these conceptual distinctions is shown by two brief case studies. The first examines Mongol society, which allows us to trace the changes in the function of boundaries when societies move from a nomadic (nonterritorial) to a sedentary (territorial) form of social organisation. The second case study is a comparative examination of imperial boundaries, exemplified by the relations of the Chinese, Roman, and British Empires with outsiders who were never accorded equal status. By contrasting the patterns of interaction in imperial orders and in the state system, we can show that the function of boundaries is significantly different.

In Section III, the conceptual distinctions developed thus far are used to discuss techniques of conflict management in the state system. Two strategies are examined in particular. One is the movement of the *location* of the boundary; the other concerns the manipulation of the *function* of boundaries through untying the bundle of rights conventionally associated with full territorial sovereignty. The first strategy or technique was characteristic of territorial adjustments during the classical balance-of-power period; the untying of sovereign rights through imposed neutralisation, the creation of suzerainties, buffer states, spheres of influence or preponderance, and so forth, was used primarily by European powers in order to manage competition in the colonial world.

In Section IV, I investigate the creation of spheres of special responsibility in the contemporary system. I argue that the impossibility of reviving spheres of influence under modern conditions was one of the contributing causes of the Cold War, and that the failure to agree on the meaning of spheres of abstention led to the demise of détente. In addition, I discuss transborder resource arrangements and functional regimes and their implications for a theory of international relations.

Finally, in Section V, I draw some preliminary conclusions as to the power and parsimony needed in a systems approach to international relations.

II. Territoriality and the social formation of states

In contemporary social science, groups are often classified either as communities based on kinship or as communities built upon the recognition of mutual rights subject to a common law within a given territory. This distinction between tribal and territorial communities may be empirically and conceptually difficult to make, however.[2] After all, even nomads do not wander aimlessly.

> The primitive nomad who depends for survival on what he can find . . . must know the territory in which he roams: locales of water holes, where certain plants grow, the habits of game, etc. . . . . Thus, each nomadic band

establishes rights over the territory within which it migrates although its members may visit bands of other territories.[3]

In such nomadic communities, the right to move prevails over the right to camp, and "ownership means in effect the title to a cycle of migration".[4] Lattimore studied the implications of these forms of allocating territorial use-rights among the Mongols.[5] He followed the change of territorial use from common, tribally owned land administered by a prince to the establishment of fixed private ownership through the introduction of the monastic rule of Lamaism. The social consequences were startling. The original Mongol tribes were never static because disputes over the right of movement led to the splitting and coalescence of small clan-like groups. This allowed an exceptional leader like Genghis Khan to gather into his tribe those who, in search of protection, had fled from their abusive or ineffective overlords. Fundamental changes in the balance of power could be effected through such a gathering of followers by a leader.

The allocation of fixed property, on the other hand, prevented the process of agglomeration and led to the parcelling and repartitioning of tribal territory. The emphasis on fixed property first introduced by Lamaist monasteries led to further important internal as well as external changes. The former tribal customs emphasized mobility and forbade the digging of wells and intensive agriculture in order to adjust the Mongol way of life to the steppe rather than to the marginal areas that could have sustained a mixed form of economy. Exclusive property titles, however, led to the ascendancy of wealth over mobility and drew the Mongols closer to China through trade. This development brought them under the influence of the Manchus, whose vassals virtually all of them became – especially when the Chinese intervened successfully in church affairs and divided northern from western Mongols.

Most Western travellers in the 19th century commented on the peaceful character of the once warlike Mongol people; Chinese official writings and Western observers attributed this development to the teachings of Lamaism. Matters were more complicated, however: some of the bloodiest wars between northern and western Mongols had been conveniently neglected in these accounts.[6] Lamaism had not only divided the Mongols and broken their ability to invade the Chinese Empire, but the settlements following the introduction of fixed property had also abolished the mobility that had been one of the strategic assets for raiding the border. The development of territoriality in the new sense made a more fixed relationship with China necessary. Unable to unite and maintain an independent basis of power, the Mongols became suzerains of the Manchu emperors. Similar arrangements could be found all along the Chinese frontier; only the clash with Russia necessitated a more precise definition of the relationship between the suzerains and Russia. [. . .]

The treaty of Peking (1860) between Russia and Imperial China was an important step in this direction. It fixed the boundary as "following the mountains, great rivers and the present lines of Chinese permanent pickets". This delimitation still left a substantial part of the Sinkiang region on the Chinese side, but the Imperial government did not decide to include Sinkiang formally in the Chinese Empire until 1884.[7] Even after that date, it was still treated as an "outer region" inhabited by "barbarians" over which largely indirect control was exercised. According to Wheeler, Sinkiang remained substantially independent of governmental control by Peking until the 1940s.[8] The governors appear to have determined all pertinent internal and external policies. Thus, although the Western state system imposed a particular mode of territorial rule upon China's relationships with its clients and the rest of the world, the old social formation of China prevented the new international boundary from serving its function. Local leaders and Russian and Chinese clients made the attribution of the area to either state problematic in spite of its internationally settled boundaries. By the end of World War I, the region was ruled by various warlords who – as the case of Sheng Shih-tsai shows – were more sympathetic to the Soviets than to the National Chinese government under Chiang Kai-shek.[9] The region was firmly in Chinese hands only after the Chinese Revolution. Still, the first treaties signed between the new China and Moscow protected Soviet interests in the area by setting up joint oil- and mineral-exploiting companies in Sinkiang; the Soviets had a majority vote.[10] Stalin had used the same arrangement quite effectively in Eastern Europe in order to cement his political influence over Soviet client states. The arrangement with China continued until 1955.

The case of the Mongols has significant implications for our inquiry. If boundaries are important because of their role in mediating exchanges, a closer look at the *types of relationships* mediated by boundaries will prove instructive. At the most general level, boundaries are points of contact as well as of separation between a social system and an environment. As Luhmann remarks:

> They reduce the points with the environment, thus allowing the internal conditioning of various relations with the environment. Only where boundaries do exist, relations between system and environment can increase their complexity, their differentiation and their controlled mutability. Boundaries are permeable to causality; they only make sure that each causal process involves the entire system.[11]

The natural boundary of a mountain crest or a watershed that separates societies is natural only because such areas are usually sparsely populated and bereft of natural resources. [. . .]

It is important though to distinguish between two types of exchanges: system-environment, and system-other systems.

> As long as the contacts with the people on the other side were rare, it was possible to manage relations with a relatively low level of understanding.

The others were "barbarians", primitive, etc., which could be classified as part of the wild "environment" because not much came of them . . . Long-range contacts were essentially reserved to higher strata and traders and supplied the system with "strange" objects and were thus only strengthening the awareness of a deep difference between system and environment.[12]

When contacts increase and political and economic interdependencies are recognized, a differentiation arises between inter-system and system-environment relations. Exchanges between systems (states) are increasingly regulated by normative structures, even in cases of interstate violence. Thus, a "negative community" – one not united by a common purpose or a vision of the good life, but only by common practices and the mutual recognition of rights – comes into existence.[13] Boundaries become lines (although their exact demarcation must wait until better means of geodesy develop) instead of remaining zonal frontiers. The importance of centre-periphery relations becomes visible and the task of boundary maintenance presents itself.

In the European context, we see these patterns in the development of the state system and in the emergence of the classical conception of boundaries that define exclusive zones of jurisdiction. The Treaty of the Pyrenees, which set up a joint commission for deciding where the exact boundary line between Spain and France would be drawn, inaugurated the first official boundary in the modern sense (1659).[14] Although similar attempts to determine boundaries were recorded earlier (e.g., Philip le Bel's attempt in 1312 to determine the boundaries of Flanders),[15] the largely personalistic political organisation of the time made such attempts at delineation a different matter. Under feudal rule, loyalty was owed, depending on circumstances, to various overlords simultaneously. Thus, although the limits of the realm were quite well known, there was a tendency to obfuscate the boundaries of the kingdom. Nobles made war on their own and had pretensions on domains in other realms; interventions and counter-interventions were the order of the day, preventing the kingdoms from acting like unitary states.[16]

In the case of the German Empire before the Thirty Years War, the lack of clear demarcation of a public realm for decision-making purposes was paralleled by the confused status of the imperial powers with respect to "external affairs". According to C. V. Wedgwood, a population of about "twenty-one million depended for its government on more than two thousand separate authorities", and although free tenants and knights might form federations, there were still "over three hundred potentially conflicting authorities in Germany".[17]

[. . .]

The different meanings of boundaries in such a political system thus become clear. The King of Bohemia, although a legitimate elector, was not entitled to participate in the meetings of the Electors' circle since his kingdom lay outside the confines of the Empire. The Elector of Brandenburg was a member of the Empire as a prince of Brandenburg – but, as ruler of Prussia since 1618, a vassal of the King of Poland. Similarly, the Duke of Lorraine, which was nominally within the Empire, also owed fealty to the King of France. Thus, even though the Hapsburg family had secured the imperial crown for generations through the control of votes within the Electors' circle, the Emperor's power was virtually non-existent except within his own possessions. The approval of the Electors' circle had to be sought for imperial initiatives such as the convening of the Diet and for any new tax, alliance, or declaration of war. The Emperor was left without any right to independent action even in serious emergencies.

> Fiscal and military organization was as little in imperial control as legislation. For these purposes the Empire had been divided into ten circles, each with its local Diet and elected president. Should a circle be attacked, the president could appeal to the two neighboring circles to assist him, and if the three together were still unable to defend themselves, a further two might be called in. If this did not ease the situation, the five circles might then ask the Elector of Mainz to call the leading members of the Diet to Frankfort, a form of meeting without imperial consent which was called a *Deputationstag*. If this meeting agreed that the attacked district needed further help, they in turn appealed to the Emperor for a general Diet. By this amazing procedure it was possible for one-half of the Empire to be fully engaged in civil or external war before anyone was bound so much as to inform the Emperor.[18]

Only exclusive sovereignty made defence and internal administration the primary and increasingly exclusive task of the central authorities. This development illustrates the complexity of the concept of sovereignty. It denotes internal hierarchy as well as external equality. The similarities and differences between boundaries in a state system and those developing in the frontier zones of empires are striking; they show the usefulness of separating centre-periphery relations from those of inter-system interactions and system-environment exchanges. Although the Great Wall of China and the Roman *limes* appear to be examples of linear boundaries, they are not boundaries in the modern sense. Owen Lattimore points out that

> . . . the concept of a man-made Great Wall . . . was more a product of the kind of state created within China than of the kind of pressure against China from the steppe. Naturally enough, it is the military aspect of the Great Wall that has commanded most attention, and this has distorted its historical significance.[19]

Considering the immense military strength of Ch'in at the end of the period of the warring states, the border changes of the Great Wall were not very extensive when compared to the territories of the former feudal kingdoms that Ch'in had united, nor was there any imminent menace by northern barbarians. Most of the military threats came from the still unconquered south. The destruction of feudalism resulted from Ch'in's deliberate policy of exterminating the nobility and of converting feudal serfs into peasants who owed rent to their overlord and taxes to the state. The nobles could no longer use serfs as soldiers and were only entitled to rent; the peasants could now be approached directly by the state for taxes and conscripted labour without the intercession of the feudal lord. With these changes, the defence of the boundaries became the task of the central authorities. Imperial boundaries did not operate to demarcate areas of exclusive jurisdiction on the basis of shared practices and mutual recognition of rights, but to keep the environment safe through the establishment of clients and the control of trade.

Similarly, the Roman Empire conceived the *limes* not as a boundary, but as a temporary stopping place where the potentially unlimited expansion of the *Pax Romana* had come to a halt.[20] The political and administrative domain often extended beyond the wall[21] or stayed inside it at a considerable distance. Boundaries – i.e., legally relevant distinctions – existed only in private legal relations, where they governed property rights. The *ager publicus*, or public domain, had no boundaries; it ended somewhere, but this end was not specifiable by means of a legally relevant line. (The expression used was *fines esse*.) The boundary was therefore essentially a floating zone within which tributary tribes as well as Roman legions with local barbarian recruits were used to keep the peace.[22] Other barbarian tribes were to be slowly acculturated and integrated, or subjugated and suppressed. Caesar's political plan, expressed in his *Commentaries*[23] as well as in Plutarch,[24] not only represents his personal political thinking but the policy consensus in Rome – at least until Commodus: to conquer the world up to the "earth-surrounding ocean." After Commodus, these plans came to naught and Rome developed client relationships with the northern Germanic tribes until internal decay and the crushing defence burdens brought the imperial organisation to its knees.

A closer investigation of such client relationships as well as the similarities and differences in managing inter-societal affairs in the state system is now appropriate.

III. Boundaries and the management of the international system

The distinction between frontiers and boundaries, as well as the examination of how boundaries function under conditions of various social formations, is particularly helpful for understanding some issues of conflict management in international relations. Basically, two classes of techniques were available: management of the *types* of exchanges mediated by boundaries, and manipulation of the *location* of the boundaries. The latter was characteristic of the European balance-of-power system that attempted to "preserve the equilibrium in Europe"[25] through territorial gains and divisions such as the division of Poland and the territorial adjustments at the Congress of Vienna.[26] The former was employed most consistently around the edges of the various European empires that subjugated the colonial world. Institutions such as buffers, protectorates, spheres of interest (or influence), suzerainties, and neutral zones were commonly used to impose European rule on more or less recalcitrant "locals" and to manage potential conflicts with other expanding European powers;[27] as in Europe, the institutions of servitude and imposed neutralisation (rather than division of territory) also played a role.

With the abolition of the colonial frontiers, many of the lines formerly marking off spheres of interest became permanent boundaries of successor states; some of the present boundary disputes result from such spheric agreements. The dispute between Ethiopia and Somalia, and the Indian-Chinese boundary problem concerning the meaning and understandings underlying the McMahon line in Tibet (dividing Tibet into two spheres but acknowledging the "suzerainty" of China), are cases in point.[28] Nevertheless, some parallels or spheric boundaries, such as the 49th parallel in North America, are still in existence and serve as functioning boundaries at present.

Why have some meridians, designed primarily as markers indicating agreements in principle for uncharted territory, become boundaries without engendering conflict, and why have others not? One or more of the following conditions seem to have helped in mitigating potential disputes. First, most of the spheric boundaries still in existence are in deserts or polar regions. The maintenance of such lines can be explained in terms of the costs of demarcation in an uncharted and hostile environment. Second, straight lines persisted when a colonial power gained possession of adjacent territory that was once marked off as lying in some other power's sphere of influence. Former spheric demarcations therefore became internal administrative boundaries and only later, through state succession, international boundaries. The Egypt-Sudan, Tanganyika-Kenya, and Botswana-South West Africa borders are cases in point. The acceptance of the 49th parallel as the boundary between Canada and the United States has a different explanation. Jefferson advocated this line in 1818 on the basis of a putative agreement between the Hudson's Bay Company and French Canada. This proposal was acceptable to England precisely because the British had wanted that boundary since 1697, but it had never won the acceptance of the French.

Most of the time, however, former demarcation lines marking off the spheres of European power rivalry have been the cause of complicated arrangements. For instance, the treaty that established the Anglo-German sphere of influence in Africa in 1890 specifically provided for future adjustments in accordance with local requirements.[29] Consequently, the boundaries that emerged between Malawi and Tanzania, Uganda and Rwanda, and Kenya and Tanzania show alterations (or are still in dispute).

The other method – the imposition of a special regime on a zone on the frontier – has given rise to patterns of interaction that are quite different from those between the sovereign territorial regimes of Europe. For example, in the 19th century the Balkans represented a "frontier zone" in which Austrian, Russian, and British influence met, and which could not be effectively dealt with by the nominal power, the Ottoman Empire. At that time, Turkey was not considered a European state; it only came to be regarded as a "civilised" nation, accepting the common practices and mutually recognised rights of the European state system, after the Crimean War. The Treaty of Adrianople (1829) gave the Tsar, as protector of the Christians, a right of intervention in certain Ottoman possessions, a circumstance that led to the Crimean War. Later on, the Bosnian crisis of 1908 was the result of the incorporation of the nominally Turkish provinces of Bosnia and Herzegovina into the Austrian Empire, although Austria had "administered" these provinces since 1878.

On the lowest level of formalisation is the "sphere of interest", which is either backed by formal or informal agreements among competitor states alone (when "the locals do not matter"), or by additional arrangements with the local authorities. As to a sphere of influence, according to Lord Curzon, "no exterior power but one may reassert itself in the territory so described".[30] Spheres of influence have therefore also been called "semi-suzerainties". Other arrangements, such as the institution of a protectorate, or (full) suzerainty, or condominia, were also developed. The tripartite condominium between Germany, Britain, and the United States over Samoa, and the Anglo-French arrangements in Sudan and the New Hebrides, are examples of such joint administrations. The term "sphere of influence" appears to have entered the vocabulary of European diplomacy only in the late 19th century. It is somewhat ironic that this term originally was used by Russia to declare its *disinterest* in controlling Afghanistan. Count Gorchakov is reported to have assured Lord Clarendon in 1869 that "Afghanistan lay completely outside the sphere within which Russia might be called upon to exercise her influence".[31]

The application of this device to Africa during the Berlin Conference of 1884–1885 resulted in a relatively uncomplicated division of Africa among the colonial powers; they thus acquired vast territories without having to perfect their title through effective occupation and administration of the vast hinterlands to their colonial enclaves.[32] Since these areas were technically *terra nullius* (i.e., they belonged to nobody), considerable conflict could have developed from the inchoate titles in the absence of a multilateral agreement.[33]

A slightly different problem arose when the European powers faced a local state that, on one hand, could not effectively resist foreign penetration but, on the other, could not be wholly absorbed within one exclusive sphere of influence. For such purposes, "spheres of preponderance" were designed; they nominally preserved the integrity of the country, but allocated influence on an exclusive basis for certain areas or zones. An example of such an arrangement is the Anglo-Russian Convention of 1907 concerning Persia. Originally this idea had been floated by Salisbury precisely in order to preserve the integrity of Persia; the practical implication, however, was the division of a nominally independent state into exclusive spheres of influence. Keal describes Persian affairs after the 1907 convention:

> Although both signatories had affirmed their intention to maintain the independence and integrity of Persia and to allow equal facilities for trade to all nations, that was not what happened in practice. The two powers sent a joint note to the Persian government, declaring that they would refuse to sanction loans from other powers if these loans involved granting concessions to any other power or their subjects contrary to Russian or British political and strategic interest. Persia protested, both about this and the Anglo-Russian Agreement, whereupon Petrograd and London reacted by warning other powers against taking up Persia's cause.[34]

Surveying the range of various frontier arrangements in 1945, Duncan Hall found the following rather surprising (but not exhaustive) set of mandates, international regimes, trusteeships, and so forth:

> reading from south to north, . . .: the mandates (now trusteeships) of Ruanda Burundi and Tanganyika; the Uganda Protectorate; rivalries and spheres of influence over Abyssinia; Eritrea, in turn Turkish, Egyptian, Italian, and now a projected international trusteeship; rivalries of Britain and France over Egypt and the valley of the Nile culminating in the Fashoda incident; the condominium of the Sudan; the former condominiums and protectorate over Egypt; the neutralized and demilitarized Suez Canal, with its international regime; the mandates over Transjordan, Palestine, and Syria; the projected international trusteeship regime for Jerusalem; the checkered history of Alexandretta, in turn Turkish territory, League mandate, international regime, and again Turkish territory. As we shall see, the line of phenomena of the international frontier continues historically through Anatolia, along the Straits, through the Balkans, and thence on to the Baltic and even to the Arctic.[35]

Finally, there were neutral zones and buffer states, which allowed the local inhabitants considerable autonomy. Neutral zones stopped functioning when local refugees or even brigands used the lack of a strong internal or external authority for their own purposes. The neutral zone between the British and German territories of the Gold Coast and Togo had to be abolished in 1899 for that reason. All such areas without political authority were set aside in modern times when the exclusivity of territorial rule became more and more important. Thus, the neutral zone between Saudi Arabia and Kuwait was divided up equally between these states in 1965.[36]

A good example of a buffer state is Afghanistan, which was created to separate British and Russian influence more effectively. Having failed in 1879 to impose a protectorate upon the resisting tribes, the British, with Russian consent, persuaded the Emir of Afghanistan to accept sovereignty over Vakhan, thereby creating the curious extension of Afghan territory toward China. To a large extent, the treaty of 1907 ended the rivalries of these European powers in that area. In a similar vein, Siam was successful in defending its autonomy against direct interventions by becoming a "neutral" in the British-French contest over Indochina.

As in Europe, neutralization was contingent upon the agreement of the Great Powers as well as upon the difficulty or costliness of extending the imperial boundaries.[37] This was the case when the territory in question was effectively administered by some sort of government that could prevent easy penetration. Otherwise, various client arrangements had to be developed in order to prevent the excluded states from invading, or – in cases where the border people were poorly organised – to prevent internal pressure from colonists, traders, military careerists, and others from involving the imperial state in further expansion at great cost. The social formation of the imperial state is therefore as important as that of the outer "barbarians" or tribes. We find historical examples for such imperial expansion due to the activities of traders and entrepreneurs in the machinations of Rhodes and Luederitz, who extended British and German influence in Africa by forcing their governments to protect their private acquisitions. The debate concerning the causes of imperialism and the arguments that "empire does not pay" are familiar. The acquisition of Texas in the American frontier setting also shows the extension of influence originally brought about by private initiative.

The dynamics created by this clash of internal and external factors can be seen in Britain's policy in India. In the case of the British Northwest Frontier, London vacillated between a "closed-border" policy and a "forward" policy. The closed-border policy involved strict patrols of the border by the British, negotiations limited to representatives of transborder societies, and British insistence on the right of supervising and controlling transborder affairs. This policy was usually accompanied by an otherwise non-interventionist stance toward tribal affairs, and punctuated by occasional punitive expeditions when the security of British India was threatened. The forward policy, on the other hand, as exemplified by the Sandeman system of consultation and more active intervention in tribal affairs, offered arbitration and subsidies in order to keep the peace while not discouraging contacts between the subjects and the outsiders.[38]

IV. Unspoken rules, networks, and regimes

After a survey of a variety of forms by which states have tried to modify the exclusionary nature of territorial sovereignty and thereby to manage their relations, the present world system appears to be considerably simpler. The emancipation of the colonial world not only abolished most of these arrangements – except when former spheres evolved into actual boundaries – but sovereign equality and the assertion of absolute territorial rights gained new salience. Especially in the third world, sovereignty has been invoked in order to modify domestic legal arrangements and international obligations resulting from state succession. Thus, the affirmation of "Permanent Sovereignty over Natural Resources",[39] which justifies nationalisation without the conventional compensation,[40] is another way of reasserting *independence*; this often means that the domestic economy has to be isolated from foreign penetration through emphasis on "borders of separation." Attempts to establish codes of conduct, for multinational corporations for instance, must thus be understood as a means to master the problem of loss of control that is concomitant to increasing *interdependence*. As Krasner has pointed out, the New International Economic Order is less a distributive bargaining for larger shares of wealth than a struggle for control.[41] This struggle is primarily, or at least ostensibly, designed to ensure the sovereign independence of the developing countries within their own territorial confines; at the same time, it is an effort to control influences that originate beyond territorial borders and that have an impact on national life.

Nevertheless, a variety of contradictory tendencies can be found in present international life. The *first* is the universal recognition of territorial sovereignty as the differentiating principle in the international arena. But there is also a *second*, conflicting trend: the erosion of boundaries through the increasing interdependencies of modern economic life. Thus, while political systems are boundary-maintaining systems, markets – although dependent for their creation upon political power and economic networks – are not.[42] It is precisely this difference that led to Wallerstein's argument concerning the success of European capitalism: the penetration of the entire world became possible only after the European powers had given up on the creation of a world empire and contented themselves with economic networks.[43]

This expansion, however, did not eliminate differentiation of centre and periphery, which sometimes made it necessary to extend direct political control into the penetrated areas. The establishment of colonial rule became necessary when the original informal agreements between the local rulers and their European counterparts broke down.[44] Thus, far from proving the automatic and unproblematic nature of economic expansion, the history of European imperialism, especially in its rush into Africa, proves the importance of political underpinnings for the functioning of unbounded economic exchanges.

A *third* identifiable trait is the result of the power differentials among nations and the tensions between bounded political systems and unbounded exchanges such as economic, ideological, or informational transactions. The issues of dependency, propaganda, and transborder data flows come to mind. Thus, problems necessitating careful conflict management have not disappeared while many of the old techniques of modifying the functions of boundaries for such purposes are no longer available. In short, although the system is based on sovereign territoriality, new conceptions modifying this exclusive regime have evolved that make the management of the international system possible without violating authoritative prescriptions.

Three types of new management devices have evolved: they are usually subsumed under the term "rules of the game".[45] These devices are: *spheres of responsibility, spheres of abstention*, and *functional regimes*. Of these, only functional regimes are clearly legal in character in that they usually rely, among other things, on treaties (bilateral or multilateral) and thereby create explicit rights and obligations. Spheres of responsibility mix legal rights with the unilateral arrogation of competence – which, if respected at all, gives rise only to a norm with the character of an "unspoken rule". Spheres of abstention are the least formal arrangements. They are susceptible to breakdowns as demonstrated by the short-lived détente between the United States and the Soviet Union in the seventies.

Spheres of responsibility

Spheres of responsibility may be defined either functionally or territorially. The functional definition shaped the role of the Great Powers (a role that came into existence after the Congress of Vienna). It designated powers with system-wide interests – those that were to have a say in matters pertaining to the management of the system.

In the classic conception of politics, management questions primarily involved the issue of balances of power. But Metternich's attempts to stretch the meaning of security to include the internal constitution of the states (Congress of Verona), and England's reluctance to accede to such an understanding of the Concert,[46] showed that the purely functional system-wide specification of the responsibilities of a Great Power were problematic for two reasons: (1) varying conceptions of legitimate sovereignty existed among the conservative and liberal participants, and (2) the respective interests of various Great Powers showed significant geographic discontinuities.

Gradually, spheres of interest reemerged as the predominant concept, most clearly in the Balkans. As the clashes between Russia and Austria in this region demonstrated, conflict increasingly involved "internal" political groups (Pan-Slavism) or territorial division and incorporation (the Bosnian crisis of 1908). Incorporation became increasingly difficult as the system's flexibility decreased because of nationalism and a new understanding of politics as the "survival of the fittest". A rational balancing in terms of territorial adjustments thus created scores that had to be settled. Territorial adjustments no longer could fulfill the task of restoring an acceptable status quo for all.[47]

The notion of a special sphere of responsibility surfaced at the end of World War II, when the Allies discussed the structure of the postwar international order. In this connection, it is worth mentioning Roosevelt's idea of the "four policemen" charged by the general international community with "enforcing the peace" in their respective areas, and Churchill's idea of a world organisation as a framework for *regional arrangements*.[48] The inability of the great powers to come to substantive understandings concerning either their collective responsibilities or their mutually accepted preponderance in certain regions demonstrates not only that these notions were imprecise, but also that they contained conflicting elements.

The Western conceptions of the future international order never resolved the tension between the principles of universalism and the regionalist bias exhibited by Churchill and even sometimes by Roosevelt. The U.N. was based, from the beginning, on an uneasy compromise between the claim of universal competence to deal with all matters of peace and security (even with respect to non-members) – as the Security Council was entrusted with the enforcement of peace – and the claim to collective self-defence that spawned regional alliances.[49] In addition, the two main antagonists, the Soviet Union and the United States, did not have a common understanding of the legitimacy and limits of Great-Power influence in their respective spheres. For this reason, informal agreements – such as Churchill's proposal on apportioning influence in the Balkans on the basis of either exclusive or shared zones of preponderance – were doomed to fail.[50] The U.S. refused to recognise such deals, but even if they had been accepted, the Soviet conception of interest was so extensive that it came to mean the virtual exclusion of all foreign influence, or even constitutional limitations. Instead of exerting power through alliances and informal means, Stalin's mistrust of his client governments – especially when they showed interest in Western economic recovery plans – led to an absolute *Gleichschaltung* of the Soviet satellites.[51]

In this way, we can establish the similarities and differences between the management devices of the 19th century and of modern times. First, there appears to be a similarity in the change from the more universal conception of a functionally defined general responsibility for peace and security to a more solidly defined territorial sphere of influence. What is surprising is the rapidity with which this change occurred in the postwar era. Various forms of the European Concert had functioned (admittedly with different degrees of success) for several generations,[52] but the drastic shift in the postwar era took only a few years. This remarkably quick change, which was accompanied not by mutual accommodation but instead led to the exacerbation of cold-war tensions, was caused by the lack of commonly accepted practices that could guide and set limits to the exertion of influence.[53]

A second comparison between the developments in the 19th century and those of the 20th shows an inverse historical sequence. Metternich's extensive interpretation of Austria's security interest failed to win acceptance and then quickly led to a more moderate interpretation of domestic challenges to the international order; Soviet insistence on an implausibly extensive security interest initially led to hostility and the breakdown of interactions, but ultimately to a *de facto* accommodation. A measure of ideological preponderance was added to the classical notion of a sphere of influence: regimes based on ideologies that do not agree with that of the regional great power can be changed or suppressed. The similarities between the U.S. assertion of primacy in the Western hemisphere (including American interference with non-conformist regimes) and Soviet behaviour in the Eastern bloc have been noted. Moreover, both powers have developed extensive rationales or doctrines for their purposes, as Franck and Weisband have pointed out.[54]

Differences also exist. The accommodation that occurred in the late sixties and early seventies was not backed by explicit agreements, and the rules of the game that have emerged in regard to spheres of influence resemble "unspoken" rules. This last point constitutes a significant dissimilarity between the European state system and the modern international system.

In the old conception, a sphere of influence or interest was usually the result of bilateral, explicit agreements. This had two consequences: (1) the agreements created enforceable rights among the contracting parties; and (2) they imposed a regime upon the local inhabitants. Because agreements in international law cannot bind non-participating third parties (*pacta tertiis nec prosunt nec nocent*), the non-recognition of the local powers as full subjects of international law was formerly a precondition for such legal arrangements. With the acceptance of territorial sovereignty as the universal organising principle in present international relations, the legal expression of such agreements is not possible. Consequently, such understandings can have only the status of tacit or *unspoken* rules, as Keal has called them.[55]

Such rules generally emerge through unilateral calculations (which take verbal as well as non-verbal cues into account); their root lies in the coincidence of the perception of a common interest. Unilateral calculation occurs on the basis of expectations about the other's reaction to the self's action:

> *A's* expectation of *B* will include an estimation of *B's* expectations of *A*. This process of replication, it must be noted, is not an interaction between two states, but rather a process in which decision-makers in one state work out the consequences of their beliefs about the world; a world they believe to include decision-makers in other states, also working out the consequences of their beliefs. The expectations which are so formed are the expectations of one state, but they refer to other states.[56]

Although expectations that prove correct in a number of instances attain a certain stability and provide some guidance for future decision making in similar situations, compliance with these unspoken rules will be unproblematic *only* when the perception of a common interest is sufficiently strong. Obviously, this will be the case in instances in which the situation resembles a game of coordination – i.e., when the interests of the interacting parties are neither opposed nor mixed.[57] To that extent, Hume's example of two men coming to a "tacit" agreement about how to row a boat is instructive, as a common interest can be assumed.[58] If states perceive the situation as resembling a Prisoners' Dilemma, however – i.e., when mixed motives are given and the incentives to defect are larger than those to cooperate – rules and norms that attempt to shore up the cooperative solution will be endangered. This problem is further aggravated by the imprecision of the tacit rule. Since it is not based on explicit verbal agreements and thus secured by the meanings of ordinary language,[59] but only on unilateral imputations of motives for actions and other non-verbal acts, its institutionalisation is weak; no explicit discourse about the tacit rule is possible, and therefore neither scope nor applicability to certain contexts can be discussed.

Spheres of abstention

In the foregoing considerations I referred to spheres of abstention, which were either tacitly agreed upon by the superpowers or created by the United Nations through "preventive diplomacy".[60] Such arrangements broke down in the Congo when the interjection of U.N. troops was identified with the policy goals of a particular faction that possessed outside sympathies. As soon as the question arose for what purposes the U.N. troops were being used – aside from reestablishing minimal control of the situation – the idea of preventive diplomacy failed. The opposition of the Soviet Union and its refusal (together with France) to pay for the operation led to a financial crisis of the world organisation which clearly and narrowly circumscribed future activities of this kind.

The tacit understanding among the superpowers to leave most of the developing world to its own devices came to naught during the Ford administration and contributed significantly to the demise of détente. The arrangement was susceptible to subversion because of the perception of relatively large gains for limited involvements, particularly in the weak states of Africa. In addition, intervention by proxy (Cuba) appeared to enable the intervening party to disclaim responsibility.

Finally, détente itself was problematic. It was based on the recognition of the Soviet Union as an equal world power, but the United States increasingly tried to de-link the Soviet-American understandings concerning nuclear parity and arms control from the substantive consensus concerning certain regions. For example, attempts by the Soviet Union to propose a joint undertaking in the Middle East and thereby to transform détente into an entente were rebuffed by the United States through the drastic measure of a nuclear alert.[61] "Linkage" was advocated by the U.S. and opposed by the U.S.S.R. in certain areas (détente and economic help), but it was invoked by the Kremlin and negated by the White House in others (condominia).

Negative understandings are weak – aside from the extreme case of mutual assured destruction or, as Hobbes would have called it, the "fear of violent death". They are subject to defeating considerations precisely because an agreement of abstention is often too ambiguous about the limits of allowable influence. Furthermore, the perception of *mutual interest* is not shored up by "rights" that demonstrate to the participants the tangible *quid pro quo* in cases of conflict and insulate an issue from the overall patterns of social interaction.[62] A "right" implies that one is no longer dependent upon the opponent's approval and goodwill in all circumstances.

Functional regimes

The third important device for managing international relations in the modern state system is that of functional regimes. Basically, functional regimes "unbundle" the package of rights inherent in territorial sovereignty. Functionalism has therefore sometimes been advocated as an alternative organisational principle for international life. Functional regimes, it was hoped, would not only downgrade the importance of national boundaries, but could, through the expansion of transboundary cooperative networks, lead to "peace in parts."[63] In addition, some recent developments seem to indicate that the traditional package of territorial rights is being modified. Several new arrangements have emerged from the Law of the Sea draft treaty (UNCLOS III) by which competing resource uses can be accommodated without the all-or-nothing regulation of territoriality. Only in this fashion could the competing interests in security, resource management, access (navigational rights), pullution abatement, and freedom of research of the new "whole" called "oceans"[64] be guaranteed. The creation of an Exclusive Economic Zone, the new definition of the continental shelf, of international straits, of archipelagic regimes, and of provisos for resource recovery from the deep sea through the International Seabed Authority all show such features.[65] Similarly, a variety of specific resource regimes within the framework created by the Antarctic Treaty has carefully avoided the territorial issues between those countries claiming certain sectors and those not claiming any territory, and between states whose claims overlap (e.g., Argentina, Chile, and the United Kingdom).[66] One of the most remarkable successes of the Antarctic regime is its demilitarisation and denuclearisation backed by a unique inspection system.

[. . .]

Functional regimes also need continuous updating and upgrading, depending upon the emergence of new issue areas and the realisation of interaction effects of various regimes. The discovery of mineral resources in Antarctica, for example, made negotiations for such a regime a matter of urgency. Furthermore, the effect that mining will have on the other regimes (particularly the living resources and the Antarctica fauna and flora regimes) will make stringent environmental regulation necessary. Such a proliferation of regulations not only necessitates continuous negotiations and cooperation, but also the institutionalisation of procedures to settle disputes in order to manage the inevitable conflicts. The advantage of the all-or-nothing principle of territorial sovereignty in this respect is not merely its simplicity, but the implicit presumption that, in the face of newly emerging problems, the territorial unit – and only the territorial unit – has the right to regulate matters. Thus, although clear boundaries create problems by excluding others, they also simplify international life. In the political arena, they appear at present to be the precondition for the existence of national independence, constitutional rule, and responsible government by creating and reinforcing significant breaks within the stream of transactions of world society.

V. Conclusion

I have addressed the problem of the function of boundaries in territorial and non-territorial social orders for historical as well as for theoretical reasons. The historical interest is rooted in the need for a better understanding of those changes that led to the emergence of the European state system in the 17th century, after the demise of the medieval empire. The theoretical interest concerns the appraisal of the present world system. This system is characterised by conflicting trends in the universal recognition of territoriality as the organising principle in international politics and by the observable countertrend of increasing interdependencies that undermine territorial exclusivity.

In the present approach, I investigated three types of exchanges that determine the function of boundaries, By systematically examining the exchanges that take place between a unit and its environment, the exchanges among units, and the exchanges between a unit's centre and its periphery – as well as their various interaction effects – I developed a parsimonious explanation of systems characteristics in a wide variety of territorial and non-territorial social systems. The heuristic power of this approach was further evidenced by its ability to relate the characteristics of systems to modes of conflict management by means of boundaries. Two techniques were discussed: the movement of the location of a boundary, and the changing function of boundaries brought about by allowing or excluding certain types of exchanges. The first strategy was characteristic of the European balance of power and its territorial adjustments. The second was used predominantly in the colonial world, where spheres of influence or preponderance, as well as buffer states, became the standard devices for managing conflict with other European powers.

Beyond these historical examples, I discussed modern attempts of creating functional regimes and formulating tacit rules in order to manage conflicting uses of resources and political interests. I also examined the robustness, or rather the reasons for the limitations and the lack of effectiveness, of these techniques.

Some difficulty is created by attempts to place this approach in the wider context of theoretical efforts in international relations. However, it is apparent that this inquiry is more indebted to a system-of-action perspective[67] than to structural theories of international relations[68] that emphasise the unintended consequences of the actors' choices. Although structural theories explain an important aspect of interactions in an anarchical environment, they fail to suggest further avenues for research beyond the original market analogy and utility-maximising actions under constraints. It is here that the advantages of a more historically oriented approach become apparent. By focusing on the changing function of boundaries rather than on the configur-ation and number of actors or the "rationality" of their actions, the present approach provides for a richer and more detailed treatment of the historical material while preserving parsimony and explanatory power.

Notes

1 See, for example, the debate in the late sixties focusing on the probable con-sequences of various integration efforts in Europe and Latin America. For a critical appraisal, see Stanley Hoffmann, "Obstinate or Obsolete, The Fate of the Nation State and the Case of Western Europe", in Joseph Nye, ed., *International Regionalism* (Boston: Little, Brown, 1968), 177–230.
2 On kinship or "primitive" societies see, e.g., Henry Sumner Maine, *Ancient Law* (London: John Murray, 1866); Lewis Henry Morgan, *Ancient Society, or Researches in the Lines of Human Progress from Savagery through Barbarism to Civilization* (New York: Holt, 1877). For a critique of this dichotomy, see Robert Lowie, *Primitive Society* (London: Routledge & Kegan Paul, 1949).
3 T. S. Murty, *Frontiers, a Changing Concept* (New Delhi: Palit & Palit, 1978), 50.
4 See, e.g., the extensive discussion of "nomadism" in Owen Lattimore, *Inner Asian Frontiers of China* (Boston: Beacon Press, 1951), chap. 4; quote at 66.
5 Owen Lattimore, *The Mongols of Manchuria* (New York: John Day, 1934).
6 For a further discussion of Lamaism and its impact on Mongol affairs, see Lattimore (fn. 4), 86–97. For an account of the wars among the northern and western Mongols, see Gavin Hambly, ed., *Central Asia* (New York: Delacorte Press, 1969), chaps. 7, 9, 11, and esp. 17.
7 For a fascinating account of the freewheeling rule of the local warlord Yakub Beg who attempted to fend off Russian, English, and Chinese influence until he was defeated by the Chinese general Tso Tsung-tang in 1878, see Jack Chen, *The Sinkiang Story* (New York: Macmillan, 1977), chap. 6.
8 For a general discussion, see Surya Sharma, *International Boundary Disputes and International Law* (Bombay: Tripathi, 1976), 194 ff, and Geoffrey Wheeler, "Sinkiang and the Soviet Union," *The China Quarterly* (November–December 1963), 57 ff.
9 See Chen (fn. 7), chaps. 8–10, for an extensive discussion of the fluid and often shifting political situation under the rule of Sheng Shih-tsai who transferred his sympathies from the Nationalist Chinese government to Stalin, but in 1941 began to persecute Communists with Russian leanings (betting on a defeat of Stalin), only to seek a rapprochement in 1944.
10 See P. P. Karan, "The Sino-Soviet Border Dispute", *Journal of Geography*, 63 (1964), 220–42, at 221.
11 Niklas Luhmann, "Territorial Borders as System Boundaries," in Raimondo Strassoldo and Giovanni delli Zoti, eds., *Cooperation and Conflict in Border Areas* (Milan: Franco Angeli, 1982), 235–45, at 236.
12 Luhmann (fn. 11), 238.
13 I use the term "negative community" for denoting a situation in which there is an agreement on common practices and rights, but not on common purpose. For further discussion, see Terry Nardin, *Law, Morality and the Relations of States* (Princeton: Princeton University Press, 1983).
14 For the argument that the European state system depended upon a variety of conventions and institutional rules, see Maurice Keens-Soper, "The Practice of a State System", in Michael Donelan, ed., *The Reason of States* (London: George Allen & Unwin, 1978), 25–45.

15 Sharma (fn. 8), 14.
16 For further discussion of this point, see Gianfranco Poggi, *The Development of the Modern State* (Stanford, CA: Stanford University Press, 1978), and Joseph Strayer, *On the Medieval Origins of the Modern State* (Princeton: Princeton University Press, 1970).
17 C. V. Wedgwood, *The Thirty Years' War*, paperback ed. (London: Methuen, 1981), 34ff.
18 Wedgwood (fn. 18), 36.
19 Lattimore (fn. 4), 434.
20 This thesis has been put forward most eloquently by Paul de Lapradelle, *La Frontière* (Paris: Les Editions Internationales, 1928). For some important modifications of Lapradelle's thesis, see *Studien zu den Militärgrenzen Roms*, Vorträge des 6. Internationalen Limes Kongresses in Süddeutschland (Cologne-Graz: Böhlau Verlag, 1967).
21 See, e.g., the extensive discussion of Roman boundary arrangements in Franz Altheim, *Niedergang der Alten Welt*, 2 vols. (Frankfurt: Vittorio Klosterman, no date), II, chaps. 2 and 3.
22 Ibid., chap. 4.
23 Julius Caesar, *De bello gallico* (*Commentaries*), trans. by John Warrington (New York: Dutton, 1953).
24 Plutarch, *Vitae Caesarum* (New York: Heritage Press, 1941), chap. 58, sec. 6.
25 This was the formula in the preamble to the Treaty of Utrecht, which ended the War of Spanish Succession (1713).
26 See, e.g., the various compensation schemes of the Congress of Vienna, in Edward Gulick, *Europe's Classical Balance of Power* (New York: Norton, 1967), chap. 9.
27 For further discussion, see H. Duncan Hall, *Mandates, Dependencies, and Trusteeships* (Washington, DC: Carnegie Endowment for International Peace, 1948), chap. 1, "The International Frontier".
28 See J. R.V. Prescott, H. J. Collier and D. F. Prescott, *Frontiers of Asia and Southeast Asia* (Melbourne: Melbourne University Press, 1977), chap. 18.
29 Art. IV, as quoted in K. C. McEwen, *International Boundaries of East Africa* (Oxford: Clarendon Press, 1971), 178 ff. An example is the shift of the boundary from the shore to the middle of Lake Jipe on the recommendation of a boundary commission working in 1904–1906, which modified the original agreement between Germany and Britain (1893); this line has become the modern Kenya-Tanzania boundary.
30 Lord Curzon, *Frontiers* (Oxford: Clarendon Press, 1907), 42.
31 Ibid.; see also G. N. Curzon, *Russia in Central Asia in 1889 and the Anglo-Russian Question* (London: Frank Cass, 1967), 326 ff.
32 Although the principle of contiguity was virtually discounted in establishing a valid title in the *Island of Palmas* decision, Lauterpacht has shown that there is a sound core to this doctrine. For the Palmas decision, see Louis Henkin and others, eds., *International Law, Cases and Materials* (Minneapolis: West, 1980), 256–62. On contiguity, see Hersh Lauterpacht, "Sovereignty over Submarine Areas", *British Yearbook of International Law 27* (1950), 376–433.
33 This was the reason for the Latin American doctrine of *uti possidetis*, which foreclosed attempts of other countries to establish title to sparsely administered or even unknown parts of their respective territories. For further discussion, see Friedrich Kratochwil, Paul Rohrlich, and Harpreet Mahajan, *Peace and Disputed Sovereignty* (Lanham, MD: University Press of America, 1985), case studies on the Beagle Channel and Peru-Ecuador.
34 Paul Keal, *Unspoken Rules and Superpower Dominance* (London: Macmillan, 1984), 31.
35 Hall (fn. 30), 44.

36 See S. H. Amin, *International and Legal Problems in the Gulf* (London: Middle East and North African Studies Press, 1981), 124.

37 For a discussion of the problems involved, see Cyril E. Black and others, *Neutralization and World Politics* (Princeton: Princeton University Press, 1968).

38 For a discussion of British policy, see I. Coatman, "The Northwest Frontier Province and Trans-Border Country under the New Constitution", *Journal of the Royal Central Asian Society* 18 (July 1931), 335–48, and C. E. Bruce, "The Sandeman Policy as Applied to the Tribal Problems of Today", *Journal of the Royal Central Asian Society* 19 (January 1932), 45–67.

39 See, e.g., United Nations General Assembly Resolution 1803 (XVII), 1962, U.N. Doc. A/5217 (1963).

40 On this point, see Eduardo Jimenez de Aréchaga, "State Responsibility for the Nationalization of Foreign-Owned Property", *New York University Journal of International Law and Politics* 11 (Fall 1978), 179–95; reprinted in Richard Falk, Friedrich Kratochwil, and Saul Mendlovitz, eds., *International Law: A Contemporary Perspective* (Boulder, CO: Westview, 1985).

41 Stephen Krasner, "The United Nations and Political Conflict between North and South", in Toby Trister Gati, ed., *The U.S., the U.N., and the Management of Global Change* (New York: New York University Press, 1983), 210–26, at 211–14.

42 This point is made by Raimondo Strassoldo, "Boundaries in Sociological Theory: A Reassessment", in Strassoldo and Delli Zotti (fn. 11).

43 Immanuel Wallerstein, *The Modern World System: Capitalist Agriculture and the Origins of the European World Economy in the 16th Century* (New York: Academic Press, 1976).

44 This is the argument in John Gallagher and Ronald Robinson, "The Imperialism of Free Trade", *Economic History Review*, 2nd series, 6 (1953), 1–15.

45 For a more extensive discussion of the "rules of the game" in the postwar era, see Friedrich Kratochwil, *International Order and Foreign Policy* (Boulder, CO: Westview, 1978). See also Richard A. Falk, "The Interplay of Westphalia and Charter Conceptions of the International Legal Order", in Cyril E. Black and Richard A. Falk, eds., *The Future of the International Legal Order*, I (Princeton: Princeton University Press, 1969), chap. 2. Falk is one of the few "process-oriented" international lawyers who would be inclined to grant some quasi-authoritative status to "rules of the game".

46 See Henry A. Kissinger, *A World Restored* (New York: Gosset & Dunlap, 1964), chap. 15.

47 On this point, see Friedrich Kratochwil, "On the Notion of Interest in International Relations", *International Organization* 36 (Winter 1981–82), 1–30.

48 For a discussion of Roosevelt's plan for a world organization after the war, see Willard Range, *Franklin Delano Roosevelt's World Order* (Athens: University of Georgia Press, 1959). For the various incompatible conceptions emerging from the interactions before and during the San Francisco Conference, see Thomas Campbell, *Masquerade Peace* (Tallahassee: Florida State University Press, 1973).

49 This point is further elaborated in Thomas Franck, "Who Killed Article 2.4?" *American Journal of International Law* 71 (April 1977), 224–47.

50 For an extensive treatment of Churchill's proposal, see Herbert Feis, *Churchill, Roosevelt, Stalin* (Princeton: Princeton University Press, 1966), 447–51.

51 For a discussion of Stalin's policies in Eastern Europe, see Zbigniew Brzezinski, *The Soviet Bloc* (Cambridge: Harvard University Press, 1971).

52 For a discussion of the European Concert, see Richard Rosecrance, *Action and Reaction in World Politics* (Boston: Little, Brown, 1963).

53 For a further development of this theme, see Kratochwil (fn. 48), throughout.

54 Thomas Franck and Edward Weisband, *Word Politics: Verbal Strategy Among the Superpowers* (New York: Oxford University Press, 1972).

55 Keal (fn. 37), part I.

56 Ibid., 50.

57 These thoughts are more fully developed in Friedrich Kratochwil, "Rules, Norms, Values and the Limits of Rationality", *Archiv für Rechts- und Sozialphilosophie* (forthcoming).

58 David Hume, *Treatise on Human Nature, Book III, Of Morals*, in *Hume's Moral and Political Philosophy*, ed. Henry Aiken (Darien, CT: Hafner, 1970), 59 ff.

59 In this context, see Article 31 of the Vienna Convention which establishes that "a treaty shall be interpreted in good faith in accordance with the ordinary meaning to be given to the terms of the treaty in their context and in the light of its object and purpose". See also Jimenez de Aréchaga, "International Law in the Past Third of a Century", 159 *Recueil des Cours* (1978), 42–48.

60 For a good discussion of this technique, see Inis Claude, *Swords into Ploughshares*, 4th ed. (New York: Random House, 1984), chap. 14.

61 For an extensive discussion of détente and the reasons for its failure, see Coral Bell, *The Diplomacy of Detente: The Kissinger Era* (London: Martin Robertson, 1977).

62 Luhmann makes the point that rights are means by which conflicts can be limited and resolved without endangering the overall relationship. See Niklas Luhmann, *Soziologie der Aufklärung*, 2d ed. (Opladen, Germany: Westdeutscher Verlag, 1975) II, 29–33.

63 See Joseph Nye, *Peace in Parts: Integration and Conflict in Regional Organization* (Boston: Little, Brown, 1971).

64 A discussion of the emergence of new "wholes" on the basis of new knowledge is in Ernst Haas, "Is there a Hole in the Whole?" *International Organization* 29 (Summer 1975), 327–77.

65 For a text of the UNCLOS III Draft Convention, see *International Legal Materials*, XXI (November 1982), 1261–354.

66 An extensive discussion of the Antarctic regime can be found in F. M. Auburn, *Antarctic Law and Politics* (London: C. Hurst & Co., 1982).

67 Talcott Parsons, *The Structure of Social Action* (New York: Free Press, 1968); see also Niklas Luhmann, *Soziale Systeme* (Frankfurt: Suhrkamp, 1984).

68 See, e.g., Kenneth Waltz, *Theory of International Politics* (Reading, MA: Addison-Wesley, 1979).

12 The politics of place and origin

An enquiry into the changing boundaries of representation, citizenship and legitimacy

Introduction

There seems to be a growing disparity between the practices which comprise international relations, and the conceptual apparatus with which we attempt to analyse these practices. This divergence is most obvious in the case of sudden fundamental change, as in the case of the disappearance of the Soviet Union, or the (re)emergence of the problematique of nationalism. Such cases provide crucial evidence which contravenes the adequacy of our conceptual apparatus and the theories based on it. Nevertheless, denials are more common than serious reconceptualisation. Since Yosef Lapid and I have dealt with this phenomenon, exemplified by the neo-realist treatment of nationalism in a separate paper (Lapid and Kratochwil, 1996), I do not want to rehearse those arguments any further here.

Equally surprising, though, is the fact that the treatment of long-term secular changes seems to have little impact on the conceptual lenses with which we analyse the ongoing practices of international politics. There is, for example, a growing literature on the inadequacy of our traditional understanding of the state as a unit, based on the impact of growing interdependence, the communications revolution and the globalisation of production, all of which undermines the capacity of states to make autonomous choices. But if autonomy represented a significant part of our understanding of sovereignty, then the basic building block on which our understanding of international politics was based becomes increasingly problematic. The "internationalisation of the state", i.e. international regimes, on the one hand enables states to pursue their interests, but also restricts the domain of their autonomy. Similarly, the conjunction of international migration and human rights, or the development of a global civil society, all suggest that new conceptual tools have to be forged in order to understand politics at the end of the century. David Held has discussed this phenomenon in terms of the several *disjunctures* that political theorists, international relations scholars and students of the state alike encounter.

> The "disjunctures" . . . reveal a set of forces which combine to restrict the

freedom of action of governments and states by blurring the boundaries of domestic politics, transforming the conditions of political decision making, changing the institutional and organizational context of national politics, altering the legal framework and administrative practices of governments, and obscuring the lines of responsibility and accountability of national states themselves. These processes alone warrant the statement that the operation of states in an even more complex international system both limits their autonomy and impinges increasingly upon their sovereignty. Any conception of sovereignty which interprets it as an illimitable and indivisible form of public power is undermined. Sovereignty itself has to be conceived today as already divided among a number of agencies – national, regional and international – and limited by the very nature of this plurality.

(Held, 1991, p. 222)

The upshot of the above argument is that an analysis that examines the concepts singly and in term of simple dichotomies – the favourite pastime of empiricists that either something is, or is not, the case – is seriously misleading, since it neglects to enquire into the changing meaning of related concepts within an entire semantic field.

It is the task of this paper to examine the changing relations among the concepts of sovereignty, citizenship and legitimacy. I argue that by investigating these three fundamental concepts and their relations we gain crucial insights into the changing meaning of politics at the century's end. Such an enquiry seems mandated not by purely academic interest, but by the increasing divergence between the *demos*, on the one hand, and the "subjects" who, according to democratic theory, are understood to be the "citizens" who legitimate decisions by their "consent". Liberal theory in particular has focused on the issue of "consent" as a validator of decisions, given inevitable hold-out problems and the emergence of strategic behaviour among the participants in a political setting. It is doubtful whether such a construction can carry the weight that is placed upon it. The relevance of such an enquiry is further enhanced by a second problem. At present, massive international migrations are calling into question the very notion of a national community of fate that was fundamental to the modern sovereign democratic state.

While I am certainly not able to solve the practical problems that arise in this context of deciding who belongs to the "us", I still hope to clarify some of the issues. In particular, I think that the dynamics of politics emerge from a definition of the group, from an attempt to locate this group in a place, and from the establishment of representative groups which are entitled to make public choices. To that extent membership (citizenship), sovereignty and legitimacy cover this *problematique*.

In elaborating on these issues, my argument takes the following steps. In the next section I begin with the last problem mentioned, i.e. legitimacy, and try to show that "consent" as the legitimising source of political authority fails and necessitates a theory of representation. Unfortunately, and contrary to the liberal claim that "the people" are the ones represented, it can be shown that the language game of representation comprises considerably more complex issues, quite aside from begging the question of who "the people" that can advance claims to representation are. In Section 3, I analyse two conceptions of "the people", one more influenced by classical republican and participatory images, and one more by cultural and historical myths of a common descent. I also want to show how the state, defining itself both as a membership organisation and as a territorial/jurisdictional sphere, has always served as a mediating organ by ascribing the status of "citizenship". This ascription was either skewed towards the "political" or towards the "cultural", but could never be decided according to a "pure" model of political participation or of origin. These considerations in turn open conceptual space for the discussion of the dimensions and problems of citizenship in the fourth section. A brief summary in Section 5 concludes the paper.

The problem of consent

One of the fundamental tenets of liberal theory is that the exercise of public authority has to be based on the consent of the governed. This principle has two corollaries: (i) that the actions of the public authority are legitimate only insofar as they can be construed as the result of the consent of the subjected; and (ii) that there should be a congruence between "the people" and the jurisdiction of the public authority. It is the latter problem that leads in the case of large-scale migrations to a certain legitimation crisis of modern states, although historically the existence of large segments of "foreigners" (*metoikoi*) was not unusual. Not only is the symmetry between the governing and the governed disturbed by the existence of such "aliens", but the legitimacy of governmental acts *vis-à-vis* foreigners somehow has to be inferred from a specific act, such as entering a country or transacting business there.

Although this has been the standard account since Locke made the argument that even travelling on the highways of a foreign country implies "consent" (as does the owning of property), such an argument is open to a variety of objections. First, if one is to infer consent from some silent or non-explicit act, then such an inference seems valid only if there was an antecedent rule that such and such an act meant precisely the uptake of an obligation. In the absence of an institutional rule to that effect, it is hard to fathom how one could infer normative consequences from merely factual observations. This leads to a *second* difficulty: if this rule is construed as the crossing of the boundary by a "foreign" individual against whom the state asserts jurisdiction, it is the state's assertion of jurisdiction which does most of the explaining and the person's "consent" hardly does any work. As Lea Brilmayer aptly put it,

The implicit assumption amounts to a prior assumption of state territorial sovereignty. Only a state that has territorial sovereignty may condition entrance upon consent to obey the law. If the state possesses territorial sovereignty, however, reliance on defendant's consent, whether explicit or implicit is unnecessary. Consent is largely superfluous; indeed it only serves to mask the fact that territorial sovereignty provides the real basis for the exercise of personal jurisdiction.

(Brilmayer, 1989, p. 6)

Here, a *third* problem emerges that makes the individualistic consent metaphor problematic, unless it is buttressed by some notion of representation. Brilmayer's remark that only states can do certain things, reminds us that acts of sovereignty are *sui generis*, i.e. are of a different quality and can therefore not easily be interpreted as the result of individual delegation, even if several of these individual and private delegations are summed up. The coming into existence of a corporate body creates a new space among the individuals so constituted, and the new rights and duties belonging to this corporate body cannot be said to consist of individual rights that have been delegated. Corporate law speaks in this context of the "corporate veil", that cannot be lifted unless, and until, the corporate body no longer exists.[1] This seems to suggest that at least one of the reasons Rousseau tried to distinguish the *volonté des tous* from the *volonté général* was perhaps to call attention to this new quality that emerges through the constitution of a number of people as a body politic. [. . .]

The peculiarity of this incorporation, and the emergence of the public space is further shown by the intended duration and practical irrevocability of the contract. As Locke put it in his *Second Treatise of Government* (hereafter *STG*):

> . . . he that has once, by any express declaration, given his consent to be of any commonwealth, is perpetually and indispensably obliged to be and remain unalterably subject to it, and can never be again in the liberty of the state of nature; unless by any calamity, the government he was under, comes to be dissolved; or else by some public act cuts him off from being any longer a member of it.

(Locke, 1963, §121, pp. 393–95)

This is all the more important as Locke distinguishes clearly between the implied and explicit consent binding the members of a commonwealth. Implied consent is indicated by the enjoyment of property. But after sale or donation of such possession, this consent dissolves and leaves the individual free to "to go, and incorporate himself into any other Commonwealth, or to agree with others to begin a new one, in *vacuis locis*, in any part of the world, they can find free and unpossessed" (*STG*, §121, pp. 393–95). Thus, while it is only express consent "which makes any one a member of any Commonwealth" (*STG*, §122, p. 394), it is not quite clear within the contractual paradigm why the commitment shall be insoluble, and also not be terminable by an *actus contrarius* if not by the very act of alienating one's property, as Locke himself seems to suggest.

A *fourth* difficulty with a strict consent theory and of its attendant conception of political obligation (both of which are the two sides of the same argument justifying governments and their actions) emerges when we consider the problem of hold-outs which, in private law, simply result in the abortion of transactions, a result that, in the case of a body politic, however, could be fatal. It is here that Locke introduces as a remedy the notion of a "majority" that can oblige even recalcitrant or opposing members (*STG*, §§98, 99). But in that case the notion of "consent" becomes strained as Locke himself realises. While he suggests that the construction of an act backed by a majority as an act of the whole is problematic since "nothing but the consent of every individual can make anything to be the act of the whole", he also admits that "such a consent is next to impossible even to be had" (*STG*, §98, p. 376). This ambivalence, of relying on principles other than consent while wanting to make it appear that "consent" still serves as the foundation, runs through the entire *Second Treatise*. Thus Locke declares on the one hand that "the supreme power cannot take from any man any part of his property without his own consent", but he also states, when faced with the hold-out problem and the need to procure public goods by means of taxation that a

> government cannot be supported without great charge [and] 'tis fit, everyone who enjoys his share of protection, should pay out of his estate his portion for the maintenance of it. But still it must be with his own consent, i.e. the consent of the majority, giving it either by themselves, or their representatives chosen by them.
>
> (*STG*, §140, p. 408)

"Never has an innocent Latin abbreviation (i.e.)", Don Herzog aptly remarks, "done more work in an argument" (Herzog, 1989, p. 185). Locke not only magically transforms the necessary individual consent into one of *the majority*, but he also makes it into one of a *majority in parliament*. Individual consent is, thereby, twice removed as a legitimising force. It also happens that without the silent, or even explicit, reliance on other principles (such as functional necessity), or on practices that have attained some stability and standing, the question of legitimacy would be indeterminate. It has been the merit of Herzog's analysis to have uncovered the fact that the political roots of these particular arguments owe more to the events and political practices of the English revolution and the Stuart Restoration than to their conceptual coherence. Herzog notes:

> Against the practices of loyalty oaths and the virtual blackmail by the King as well as by Cromwell – who extracted "loans" and "benevolent"

contributions from their subjects – parliament as the assembly of power holders had means of refusing such "hold ups" which individuals did not. Parliamentary consent was preferable not because August representatives make better choices, or because Parliament was somehow a "perfect microcosm of all England", a rather problematic construction given the extremely limited franchise and, thus, the "unrepresentative character" of this assembly. But parliament as a "corporate body" had powers that individuals didn't. Locke's hastily changing the individual's own consent to taxation to the consent of a parliamentary majority is then not a gaffe. ... To the contrary, it's perfectly sensible in light of these practices.

(Herzog, 1989, p. 194)

These critical remarks have driven home the fact that, given the special character of the political order, consent theorists have to fall back on other principles in order to deal with these special problems. Two were of particular importance in this context: representation and membership. While the issue of representation has received most of the attention in subsequent treatises and has become one of the mainstays of democratic political theory, the membership question has hardly ever been subjected to scrutiny. This is all the more surprising as the clarification of who "the people" are is obviously of great importance, especially if a majority vote is introduced as one of the reasonable means of dealing with hold-out problems. Locke himself seems to have realised, at least indirectly, the importance of this question by making membership irrevocable. A stable body politic can only be formed if entry and exit options are constrained. Membership in a political community apparently cannot be fashioned analogously to the contractual paradigm of simple exchanges (see Kratochwil, 1994).

Nevertheless, the predominant tendency of liberal theory has been to assume that this membership in particular political societies is either somehow illegitimate, or that the established communities provide the unproblematic units of analysis. The protagonists of these two versions are Locke, on the one hand, and Rawls, on the other.

For Locke it is clearly mankind as a whole that represents the proper subject of the enquiry into the foundations of political order. To that extent, the facts of historical singularity are of no significance since "were it not for the corruption and viciousness of degenerate Men, there would be no need ... that men should separate from this great and natural Community (Mankind), and by positive agreements combine into smaller and divided associations" (*STG*, §128, p. 397). For Rawls, on the other hand, the theory of justice is no longer a universal but a political project (e.g. Rawls, 1985), i.e. an attempt to specify the principles of justice for societies that have been historically constituted. But despite this, Rawls's argument concerning the choice behind the veil of ignorance, his complete rejection of any historically grounded principles of desert, his insistence on the irrelevance of practical experience with these principles and their possible revisions in the light of such lessons, all suggest that he is after something far more ambitious and demanding.

The internal contradiction, at least in the early Rawls, is indicative of the tension between, on the one hand, the universalism of classical liberalism as a foundationalist account of political order – often indebted to some intuitionist version of natural law – and, on the other hand, the recognition of historicity. The latter can no longer invoke some intuitive natural law and has to accept the multiplicity of political societies. Nevertheless, an analytical philosophy à la Rawls must consider the historically constituted separateness of the political units not to be a matter of significant moral import, otherwise the principles of justice lose their obligatory force. But as Hume suggested in his "anti-foundationalist" *History of England* (see Hume, 1872), it might be due to these very historical peculiarities and settled habits, rather than to the coherence of political theories or constitutional principles, that political systems function. Similarly, Weber's argument regarding legitimacy, when properly cleansed of the rather debatable implications of a universal and unidirectional historical trend towards modernity, provides considerable food for thought (Weber, 1978). Indeed, traditional forms of legitimacy share certain common myths embedded in narratives and collective memories. But the claim to rule is always the result of *particular* events and of their later reconstructions in the light of specific political problems a community faces. To that extent, political scientists had better examine these peculiarities instead of treating them merely as contingencies which can be neglected.

Our preliminary enquiry into the logic of consent theory as an explanatory as well as a justificatory device did nothing to encourage our optimism in formulating clear universalist criteria. Since issues of representation and membership loom large on the horizon, it seems clear which direction such a theoretical revision has to take. It is the task of the next section to examine more closely the two concepts of representation and membership and their function in the larger semantic field of legitimacy.

The puzzles of representation and membership

To represent someone or something is, according to the etymology of the term, "to make present" something or someone who is not there. To that extent, the issue appears to be straightforward. Representing "the people" in a political sense seems to provide something akin to a map that informs us about the attitudes, desires or interests of the population at large, in order to make public choices. Two questions arise in this context. First, representation by resemblance attempts to provide information, but not all information is relevant, as even the most accurate maps cannot show everything. The key problem is which characteristics are politically relevant and worthy of reproduction. The "history of representative government and the expansion of the suffrage is one long record of changing demands for representation based on changing concepts of what are the politically relevant features to be represented" (Pitkin, 1972, p. 87). Property requirements or restrictions of political rights to free males belong here, as do the debates about various electoral systems and their respective distortions. But most important, of course, is the question which remains in the background, i.e. who "the people" are; in other words, the universe which requires representation and makes itself "present".

Second, at least in liberal theory, it is necessary to represent not simply amorphous people but specific interests of these people. But how does their representation help in making legitimate public choices? After all, we know from public choice that no common preference ordering can be established by simple methods of aggregation from three or more non-identical individual preference orderings. Here, James Madison provides an interesting answer. Not simply relying on exhortations of public spiritedness, or on the *volonté générale*, he emphasises the ubiquity of factions generated by diverging interests. But he also sees that institutions can play a decisive role by selecting the relevant features of the "will of the people". In this context his argument about the advantages of a republican form of government become crucial. It is this form which is supposed to cure the ills of direct democracy.

Through representation, the business of government is entrusted in a *republic* to a few men rather than to the people at large, and the founding father hopes that through this representation the passions of factionalism will be abated. In other words, representation serves like a filter to

> refine and enlarge the public views, by passing them through the medium of a chosen body of citizens, whose wisdom may best discern the true interests of their country, and whose patriotism and love of justice will be least likely to sacrifice it to temporary or partial considerations.
>
> (Madison, 1961, p. 82)

Like Hobbes, who suggested that through the establishment of a sovereign the expectations of individuals radically change, and that, therefore, the Laws of Nature are no longer obligatory only in *foro interno*, so Madison hopes to produce a refinement of interests by institutional means. Even his second and most famous suggestion – i.e. that through the expansion of space, interests would become more varied and prevent the domination of one group – has a certain institutional ring. Here the danger of tyranny by the majority is abated by the existence of distinct states. "The influence of factious leaders", he writes, "may kindle a flame within their particular States, but will be unable to spread a general conflagration through the other States" (Madison, 1961, p. 84)

With this argument concerning the blessings of the republican form of government, we reach a rather different understanding of representation which transcends or competes with the descriptive meaning of the term. How such an institutional version of representation can mediate the notions of "the people" or their "interests" can easily be seen when we call judges, for example, "representatives" of a political system. It is not "interests", but the notion of the public order itself, whose agent the judge is, that now comes into focus. In this way the judge becomes a representative in two ways: as an elected official, as is done in some countries, or as a representative, standing for the public order symbolically. However, we have to keep in mind that although being a judge involves some symbolic representation – signalled by the special settings, robes and formulaic invocations – a judge is not *merely* a symbol as the following considerations suggest.

First of all, it is important to realise that symbols "represent" by not conveying particular information about the matters for which they stand. To that extent, symbolic representation is radically different from descriptive representation with which we began our discussion. Indeed, we do not perceive or evaluate symbols by their descriptive accuracy, as there are no correct or incorrect symbols. Rather, what is at stake in symbolic representation is that the symbol evokes certain feelings and emotions,[2] and, thus, becomes the "focus of attitudes thought appropriate" (Griffith and Wollheim, 1960, p. 198). Second, purely symbolic representations, e.g. the flag representing the United States, or even the Queen representing England, do not depend for their effectiveness as symbols on actions. Symbols represent largely by their *being*, and not by their ability to make choices on behalf of the people. Indeed, the representative function of a king in a democracy consists precisely in restricting the public choices which he makes on behalf of his subjects.

The similarities and differences of the symbolic representation of a judge now become clearer. When a judge pronounces judgments in the "name of the people" s/he is a representative of the public order by deciding a case and controversy in accordance with the rules that establish the limits of his discretion. To that extent, s/he is the truer representative the less s/he is swayed by public opinion, or by the organised interests of the society. Indeed, legal theorists such as Ronald Dworkin have taken great pains to demonstrate the strict rules to which judges have to submit in order to arrive at decisions and thus to become representatives of the constitutional order (Dworkin, 1978, 1986). Similarly, the limits imposed on the law-making capacity of representative institutions, such as the First Amendment to the US Constitution which enjoins Congress from restricting the freedom of speech, as well as the theoretical possibility of an unconstitutional amendment discussed among American legal scholars (Harris, 1993), demonstrate that we use the term "representation" and "representing" in contexts quite different from the first descriptive and iconic account above.

Our puzzlement concerning the true meaning of representation is still further enhanced when we consider two more cases which are also part of the grammar of representation. Consider in this context the two versions of formalistic theories of representation, one focusing on the initial act of authorisation, the other looking at the problem of accountability for actions performed. Both are formal, as they concern only the conditions which determine the capacity for an agent to act on behalf of others. While Hobbes is particularly interested in the act of authorisation, accountability-theorists stress the importance of holding the representative accountable after s/he has acted on behalf of the community. In the latter case, it is not the right of acting on behalf of others which is at issue, but rather the control of the decisions made by the representative.

It is not difficult to see that Hobbes's account of representation is built on the example of authorisation. Fundamental to Hobbes's paradigm is the distinction between an actor, i.e. the person who acts, and the author, who provides the actor with the right to act. Representation concerns virtually exclusively the issue of how a multitude authorises an agent to act on its behalf.

> A multitude of men, are made *one* person, when they are by one man, or one person represented; so that it be done with the consent of everyone of the multitude in particular. For it is the *unity* of the representer, not the unity of the represented that maketh the person *one*. And it is the representer that beareth the person, and but one person; and unity, cannot otherwise be understood in multitude.
>
> (quoted in Pitkin, 1972, p. 30)

Two things are important here: firstly, the argument that the unity of the people is constituted by the representer, not by some communality of all the people; and secondly, the notion which attributes the actions of the sovereign to everyone. In this sense Hobbes reminds us that someone punished by the sovereign is "the author of his own punishment" (Leviathan, chap. XVIII, p. 229). Thus both notions together explain why the sovereign possesses powers and rights over whose exercise the subjects have no control while these actions can still be ascribed to the individual subjects. Within the bounds of the newly constituted authority, the sovereign alone can judge how to make use of them, as there is no duty owed to the subjects to consult them, or to act according to their instructions or their interests.

It is precisely this latter point which *accountability theorists* of representation stress. For democratic theory based on this idiom of accountability the decisive institutional feature becomes elections. They are not primarily seen as mechanisms for the selection of representatives who are then authorised to make policy, but as an institutional measure for holding the representatives accountable for their actions. Actually, accountability might also be ensured by other means, as for example the appointment of representatives on administrative boards is designed to ensure responsiveness of the administrative officials. Here, the transition of the accountability theory of representation to the descriptive theory of representation becomes visible, even though the emphasis here is more on ensuring the responsible exercise of power, and less on the representation of "the community" or "the people".

Our analysis seems to turn on itself. Puzzled by the problem of consent which relied on representation for much of its persuasive strength, we encounter a new puzzle: there is no clear concept of representation. Instead, a variety of closely related, though quite distinctive, practices and conceptions of making public choices are covered by this term. Even more importantly, it seems that we cannot decide which of the different cases of representation is the accurate one, since all of them seem to exemplify at least one genuine aspect of representation. Each of the different models seems to be derived from one example which quickly loses its plausibility when it is applied to other contexts that are illuminated by a different example. Representation is thus more like a cluster-term for a variety of understandings that might share a certain family resemblance but that do not seem to have a firm core aside from the fact that they serve as a cipher pointing to the importance of "the people".

It is, therefore, to this problem and to the practices of inclusion and exclusion that we have to turn our attention. Making membership and the dichotomy between friend and foe the fundamental categories for "the political" is not only characteristic of Carl Schmitt; it has a long tradition dating back to Aristotle and Plato who focused on participation, ancestry and the land as defining criteria of the political. Thus choosing membership as a critical category for this enquiry does not entail sharing Schmitt's concerns for or criticism of Western democracies. It follows rather cogently from the need to understand the practices by which we decide whether one is "inside" or "outside", whether one is a "member" or an "other". This does not mean that one has to be a foe; here Schmitt's dichotomy appears hasty and unwarranted. True, one *can* be the "foe", the "foreigner", with whom one has little in common even if relations are peaceful and without animosity. But one can also be admitted to sharing a place with a group, but not to being a member of it, even if, or particularly when the group understands itself not simply as a multitude, or as a fortuitous aggregation, but as an ongoing transgenerational enterprise, as a "community of fate".

This community has to be located somewhere, it has to have a place in the world. Thus it is not surprising that the *land* often defines the group or indicates the origins of the group or is invoked in order to evoke a sense of permanence and identity. And it is out if this dynamic between defining the group and locating it in certain places that the drama of politics emerges (Zartman, 1996). After all, the term politics derives from *polis*, which means to build a wall. These walls include and exclude members as well as delineate the space that is home, by setting it apart from the wilderness, the no-man's land, or from the land of others. Locke's argument, quoted above, comes to mind. He speculated about the legitimacy of leaving the political association, provided one had not been part of the social contract, could find others with whom to contract, and also could find *unoccupied land* in order to found a new civil society and then a government.

But if states are membership as well as territorial organisations, and if they are transgenerational rather than purely contractual enterprises, then the drawing of lines has less to do with voluntary undertakings and individual choices, and more with the ascription of *status*. "To be defined as a citizen", writes Roger Brubaker, "is not to qualify as an insider for a particular instance or type of interaction; it is to be defined in a general, abstract, enduring, and context-independent way as a member of that state" (Brubaker, 1992).

This status is difficult to shun. It imposes special duties that are not chosen, and gives members certain rights that others may not claim. This status is usually ascribed at birth because growing into the role will shape the attachments, life plans and interests, and thereby provide the emotional bonds and loyalties that transcend the immediate family, by also tying us to our fellow-citizens. This does not mean that citizenship is necessarily primordial,[3] so fundamental that it cannot be changed, but it *does* mean that such changes are not easy, for individual as well as for political reasons. [. . .] The modern nation-state is the architect of a variety of such exclusions comprising borders, suffrage, military service and far-reaching welfare rights. However, the state's ability to maintain order and manage these tasks in turn pivots on the institution of citizenship. Only as a member can you not be excluded from entering your state's territory, and only as a member can you claim certain entitlements to goods and services from your fellow citizens that are crucial for shaping your life.

The politics of place and origin

The above discussion concerning the language games of consent and representation suggests that the semantic field of our various concepts and their interconnection is powerfully influenced by the drawing of lines between inside and outside and between members and non-members. Furthermore, we found that the spatial and the ascriptive distinctions are interdependent, and thus powerfully shape our solidarities and define the distinct nature of the political game. But despite all of our efforts, we could not provide a contradiction-free theoretical account that assigns a definite place to each concept and systematically includes the important connections between them. Finally, aside from cognitive issues, emotional attachments seem to play a decisive role, and no analysis can hope to be complete unless it pays proper attention to those factors.

But what type of analysis could comprise all of these themes? Obviously, there is a need for the inclusion of some social-psychological approaches to unearth the logic of emotions (see Oksenberg-Rorty, 1980; Solomon, 1994). Here the history of political thought provides us with some clues.

All of the above themes are already paradigmatically woven together in Plato's Republic. Here Socrates speaks of the necessity to tell the members of the *polis*, a "Phoenician tale", i.e. a story that is a "myth". Literally not "true", it conveys a "truth" which is not based on purely cognitive factors but is designed to shape attitudes, and evoke feelings of pride and approval. It is this feeling of identity that allows the individual members of a body politic to act as a community, and to transcend the divisions and differences that are so obvious in everyday life. The *gennaion pseudos* – variously translated as noble lie or pure fiction – that Socrates wants to tell the rulers and ruled alike, is as follows:

> They are to be told that their youth was a dream and that the education and training which they received from us, an appearance only; in reality during all that time they were being formed and fed in the womb of the earth, where they themselves and their arms and appurtenances were manufactured; when they were completed, the earth their mother sent them up; and so, their country being their mother and also their nurse, they are bound to advise for their good, and to defend her against attacks, and her citizens they are to regard as children of the earth and their own brothers.
>
> (*Republic*, book III, p. 105)

What is of interest for us is not Plato's teaching in general, or the specific role this "tale" plays within the *Republic* in particular. For our purposes, it is the symbolic strategy that Plato uses, the form of symbolic representation which he hopes will ground a political community and which induces solidarity and motivates political action. For this purpose the myth of common descent is inculcated. But it is also a descent which is not lost in indeterminate time but rather one in which the land, the earth, serves as the common origin, as the mother of them all. As being a child is not a matter of choice, so being born into a community with all its attendant privileges and obligations is not like being part of a club or network.

It has always been considered odd that Plato, who riled at the poets and their false tales, chose at crucial points in his dialogues to utilise "myths" in order to convey some of his most fundamental messages. Part of the solution to this puzzle might lie in the fact that these existential questions do not concern simple cognitive issues. If they are reduced to such, they quickly end in contradictions. Why, according to the logic of the liberal account, should the contract be insoluble? Why should future generations be bound by some voluntary undertakings that occurred several generations ago? If we were dealing with a genuine contract, such circumstances would in all likelihood allow for the invocation of the *clausula rebus sic stantibus* (changed circumstances which void obligations). Obviously, something more is at issue.

Such incoherence is then often quickly masked by an additional postulate, i.e. that of the inevitable rise of modernity. To that extent it is suggested that the non-cognitive problems to which some classical texts point, such as the Platonic tale above, are either simply denied or treated as overtaken by historical developments. As modern actors, we are supposed to have interests rather than attachments, we are to conceive of politics as an instrumental activity – properly defended as the paragon of rationality itself – and to be committed, if to anything at all, to progress and democracy as the end of history. Was not Plato, after all, a proto-fascist? And is not the call for a return to the classics part of a well-known conservative strategy? Have not the passions engendered by nationalism shown the dangers of admitting emotions into the public space? And, therefore, is not the only hope to push for universal rights and a new conception of cosmopolitanism? Has not the communications revolution, and the processes summarised by the concept of globalisation shown the atavistic nature of the state and traditional concepts of community?

Without examining the prima facie plausibility of these admittedly rather diverse claims, I only want to point out that they prevent us effectively from understanding ourselves and the world around us. This is not an advocacy for a return to a conservative tradition or canon (although "progressives" have obviously similarly holy texts, and engage in precisely the same argumentative gambits), or to subject a political philosopher like Plato to the standards of a sophomoric debating team. It is rather a call for rethinking precisely those conventional wisdoms that served as the background for the above caricature. As a caricature it distorts, but it does so not by falsifying what is there, but by highlighting salient characteristics.

A quick look suggests: that the "end of history" (Fukuyama, 1992) has not arrived; that one of the most distinguished proponents of the rational choice approach warns us not to become "rational fools" by making it appear that political choices are all like consumer choices (Sen, 1990); that a strong advocacy of universal human rights still presupposes the framework of functioning states and societies; that fanaticism and irrationality are (unfortunately) not the exclusive preserve of people who have particularistic attachments (as the terrors waged for universalist goals of the liberation of mankind and the communist deliverance show); that emotions also form the basis of our moral judgements (to paraphrase Hume's argument about the importance of the sentiments of approval and disapproval) (Hume, 1970); that globalisation and modernity have not overcome the old identifications but rather stimulated the search for "roots", for which (like it or not) nationalism still provides the most powerful idiom.

Should we not ponder more carefully Benedict Anderson's astute observation that there is in nearly every country the tomb of the unknown soldier, but none of the unknown Marxist (Anderson, 1983, p. 10)? Apparently, there is an appeal in nationalism that other ideologies have great difficulty in matching, even if it has nothing to do with primordialism as is sometimes suggested. After all, nationalism might be a thoroughly modern concept, although the invocation of a glorious past, the myths of common descent and the particular importance of place utilise themes that have an ancient pedigree indeed, as the above Plato quote demonstrated. Nationalism though, is a phenomenon of modernity and not only in the sense of Gellner (1983), who

emphasised the need for homogenisation of ancient ethnic and status differences in the wake of the Industrial Revolution.

Nationalism not only allowed people to leave their old station in life, to
participate as enfranchised citizens in public affairs, but also made people
more alike by subjecting them to a uniform educational discipline. Through
national curricula and compulsory education, through the inculcation of
national history, people not only acquired a new identity, far removed from
that imposed by the traditional order, but they also became interchangeable
exemplars of the standardised technical skills and know-how needed for
mass production. Nationalism was for Gellner clearly a "stage" in the development of societies, a development driven by the successive modes of production. Given the present circumstances of increasing interdependencies, it
was a rather atavistic form of social and political organisation.

But such characterizations are problematic not only for the reason that
attempting to map entire societies by the mode of production or stage of
development is clearly obsolete as Offe and Preuss (1991, p. 144) correctly
pointed out. Even more important for the purposes of legitimisation is that
after the death of God – the traditional guarantor of order – "the people"
remain the only source of legitimacy. Thus "the people" are not only the
authors of their own lives and social arrangements, they are also, in a strange
twist of the old sophist adage, "the measure of all things". The death of God
made the problems of a theodicy, traditionally part of our religious understanding, part of the political discourse. It is certainly no accident in this
context that Hobbes talked about the Leviathan as "the mortal God". Despite many deep and decisive differences between religion and our secular
understandings formed by the Enlightenment, both presuppose that the

> destiny of mankind requires justification through the will of a creator
> that binds humankind in a good order, whether divine or secular. This
> reference to the concept of political theology (or as it were, to the idea of
> immanent transcendence) may help us to understand the tension between
> the claim of the political order to be good and just, and the omnipotence
> of its sovereign – a tension which can only arise where we cannot resort
> to the authority of any external norms and principles of justice.
>
> (Offe and Preuss, 1991, p. 144)

We have traced some of these tensions in the above discussion concerning
representation. But what needs further elaboration is the connection between
this new understanding and the politics of identity to which it gives rise.
Uncovering this connection will also help to explain why the nationalist call
for a return to the roots resonates with, and is propagated most decisively by,
intellectuals rather than by people who live the embedded life of their traditional communities. It is, therefore, a radical misunderstanding of this phenomenon to interpret it as an atavistic remnant of a time long passed. Rather,
more like the modern revitalisation of religious fundamentalism, it is one

attempt to come to terms with the twin problems of modernity: identity and authenticity. Elie Khedourie (1993) has carefully examined the sources of nationalism and their connection with the specific problems brought about by the crises of modernity.

Only against the background of the modern preoccupation with the autonomy of the individual, does the search for an authentic expression of "the self" make sense. Only against the particular valuation of diversity, and the implicit understanding articulated by Herder that each distinct people had an historical mission, did the principle of "self-determination" develop its explosive potential. Thus nationalism answers to a variety of modern problems in the construction of meaning.

> Autonomy, the key to dignity in the modern world, requires authenticity; freedom depends on identity, and destiny on shared memory. So the desire to participate in a modern world of wide opportunities and technological expertise, requires the forging of separate moral communities with incommensurable and authentic identities. But if the secret of identity is memory, the ethnic past must be salvaged and reappropriated, so as to renew the present and build a common future in a world of competing national communities.
>
> (Smith, 1995)

By joining premodern ties and sentiments, characteristic of traditional *ethnies*, with the modern idea of popular sovereignty, nationalism provides an answer to the crisis of meaning engendered by modernity. Instead of the traditional myth of ethnic election by the deity, modern nations insist on the uniqueness and the value of their historical heritage. The concepts of identity, autonomy, authenticity, unity and fraternity form part of a discourse that not only explains by means of conceptual elaboration and the narratives of myths and histories, but by expressive symbols and ceremonials that evoke the sentiments of self-worth and dignity.

> Symbols and ceremonies have always possessed the emotive qualities described by Durkheim, and nowhere is this more apparent than in the case of nationalist symbols and ceremonies. Indeed, much of what Durkheim attributes to the totemic rites and symbols of the Arunta and other Australian tribes applies with far greater force to nationalist rites and ceremonies, for nationalism dispenses with any mediating referent, be it totem or deity; its deity is the nation itself. By means of the ceremonies, customs and symbols every member of the community participates in the life, emotions and virtues of that community and through them, re-dedicates him or herself to its destiny. By articulating and making tangible . . . the concepts [sic!] or the nation, ceremonial . . . symbolism helps to assure the continuity of an abstract community of history and destiny.
>
> (Smith, 1991, p. 78)

While this passage points to the importance of the symbolic dimension of politics (adumbrated in the discussion of symbolic representation above), we should also realise that the emotions of dignity and self-worth can of course easily derail and lead to the denigration of others, even to hatred, for which we all, unfortunately, can readily cite examples. Nevertheless, without feelings of self-worth and dignity it is hard to imagine that our most basic moral assessments could function. The connection between the lack of feelings and the baseness of character, between the irresponsibility of a person, and his or her lack of self-esteem, are well established by psychology. Even if one has to be particularly careful with inferences from individual to collective behaviour, there is no doubt that the moral discourse treats collectivities analogously to individuals, and that feelings of self-worth and appreciation are constitutive of the definition of individual and collective roles.

Thus, when Robert Kennedy, during the Cuban missile crisis, rejects the option of a surprise air-strike on the basis that "we" are not like Tojo, he not only shows the relevance of these considerations even for "high politics" and for crisis situations, but also demonstrates that decision-makers do make inferences jumping from the individual to the collective level. It is here that political theory most clearly needs help from psychology and social psychology, not only for cognitive issues but also to clarify the role of emotions in shaping thought and perception.[4]

Conclusion

The perspective outlined above may leave us with more questions than answers. It began with an enquiry into the question of legitimacy via the traditional liberal arguments for consent as the basic foundation. It soon had to expand its scope by examining the language game of representation. By enquiring into the meaning of the term "the people", we finally had to give up the hope of finding a fixed referent, but were directed to the activities of drawing conceptual boundaries. It was in this context that the importance of place and origin emerged for filling in the cipher of "the people". But seeing that our theoretical terms are part and parcel of systems of signification, which we construct and deconstruct by tracing the historical developments of various conceptual linkages and mutual referrals, we must not believe that everything is possible.

The modern nation might be an imagined community – and thus a product more of our abilities of symbolic manipulation than of natural facts – but this imagining takes place in an environment which is not empty. In it we find the sediments of former imaginative acts that sometimes occupy central places. Besides, "imagining" a community is not like wishing it into existence. It entails a collective enterprise that has to give rise to particular disciplinary understandings as well as to settled practices. The notion that this activity of imagining is somehow preordained by the course of history is one of the phantasms of modernity. The critical remarks above were not only designed to dispel such private flights of fancy, but also to show that nationalism is a specific response to the strains of modernity. To that extent it is neither atavistic, nor is it likely to be simply overcome. Two of the other major contenders, religion and human rights, can answer some of the existential questions adumbrated above, but neither of them explicitly addresses the social configurations that have attained such prominence in modernity. Even the Islamic revival takes place *within* the organisation of the state system, and if anything can be learned from the fate of universal religions, it is that they are not able to organise "mankind" as an undifferentiated totality.

Similarly, the secular attempt to claim universal status for human rights does not do much better, partly because this discourse is constituted by a rather disparate amalgam of various traditional strands of thought. There is, above all, an uneasy link between the natural law tradition, which relies on some intuition as to what is right, and the notion of subjective *rights*, i.e. claims that have to be respected even if the right-bearer does the "wrong" thing. To that extent, the notion of "right" is a convenient cipher to cover up significantly different meanings. But it is not surprising that conflicts appear when, for example, a group wants to punish a writer who has done the wrong thing in exercising his rights, while others maintain that such a reading not only smacks of fundamentalism but negates the very notion of having a right. Even if we all agreed that the second version is the (politically?) correct one, our troubles are not over. Any subjective right is a socially respected claim which, in turn, presupposes a functioning society. To that extent it seems not only practically difficult, but logically impossible to found a society on the assertion and the exchange of rights. We either slide back to some intuitionist version of the laws of nature and some concomitant notions of what is right, or we have to face the problem of contract theorists, that without "the people" and the establishment of shared conventions of what constitutes a contract, no such undertaking can get off the ground (discussed further in Kratochwil, 1989, chap. 6).

[. . .]

In short, the value of human rights consists neither in the conception that we find some inchoate international authority which enforces them, or that the universalist programme transcends the existing social arrangements of nations and states, but rather in the fact that human rights have become part of the legitimising discourse *within* each state. It is to those rights that people can appeal in appraising and (de)legitimising political acts. To what extent this discourse will be successful in replacing other notions of right and wrong, which have their roots in other intellectual traditions, remains to be seen. Given that increasingly particular political agendas are pursued by Western states under the flag of human rights, it is not surprising that such policies engender resistance from leaders and various strata in non-Western countries, their popularity among certain local groups notwithstanding.

Thus the dream of a world culture, and of the victory of universalism against traditional parochialism seems largely mistaken. If memory is central to identity, then the futuristic fantasies of the technotronic age are unlikely to be able to address this problem of identity formation. The fact remains that the elements that would help us to build new identities are actually largely appropriated by specific cultures and traditions. Nowhere does this become more obvious than in the case of Europe, where even a common cultural awareness is unable to create a viable new political identity. If this is so, then chances for a global revolution of consciousness are dim indeed. As Anthony Smith points out:

> The packaged imagery of the visionary global culture is either trivial or shallow, a matter of mass commodity advertisement, or it is rooted in existing historical cultures, drawing from them whatever meanings and power it may derive. . . . For a time we may be able to get by and invent traditions and manufacture myths. But if myths and traditions are to be sustained, they must resonate among large numbers of people over several generations, and this means they must belong to the collective experience and memory of particular social groups. So new traditions, too, must be culture specific: they must be able to appeal to and mobilize members of particular groups while excluding, by implication, outsiders, if they are to maintain themselves beyond the generation of their founders.
>
> (Smith, 1995, pp. 23–4)

Thus, instead of the ideology of modernity which interprets history as a development of ever more inclusive forms, thereby realizing the cosmopolitan ideals of mankind, the truth of the matter is that patterns of integration as well as assertions of particularity are part of our predicament. No purpose is served when, instead of investigating these two equally important phenomena, one is treated as normal, while the other is relegated to oblivion. As its name suggests (and this paper has argued), *politics* seems thoroughly partial.

Acknowledgements

This paper has appeared previously in M. Ebata and B. Neufeld (eds), Confronting the Political in International Relations (London: Millennium, 2000). The Editor gratefully acknowledges the permission granted by the Millennium Publishing Group to publish this paper.

Notes

1 For an interesting case in international law which had to deal with these issues see Case Concerning the Barcelona Traction Light and Power Co. (Belgium v. Spain), 1970 ICJ 3.
2 For a fundamental discussion of the role of emotions in politics, and the "condensation symbols" that activate these emotions, see Edelman (1967), *passim*.
3 For the argument about the enduring character of ethnic attachments, see the collection of essays by Walker Connor (1994); the term "primordial feelings" was

first used by Edward Shils, though in a context which suggested that there exist a variety of such "primordial" attachments (Shils, 1957).
4 For an important discussion of "subject referring" emotions and their role in identity construction, see Taylor (1985, part I).

References

Anderson, B. (1983) *Imagined Communities*. London: Verso.

Brilmayer, L. (1989) "Consent, contract, and territory", *Minnesota Law Review*, 74, 1–35.

Brubaker, R. (1992) *Citizenship and Nationhood in France and Germany*. Cambridge, MA: Harvard University Press.

Connor, W. (1994) *Ethnonationalism: The Quest for Understanding*. Princeton. NJ: Princeton University Press.

Dworkin, R. (1978) *Taking Rights Seriously*. Cambridge, MA: Harvard University Press.

Dworkin, R. (1986) *Law's Empire*. Cambridge, MA: Harvard University Press.

Edelman, M. (1967) *The Symbolic Uses of Politics*. Chicago, IL: University of Illinois Press.

Fukuyama, F. (1992) *The End of History and the Last Man*. New York: Free Press.

Gellner, E. (1983) *Nations and Nationalism*. Ithaca. NY: Cornell University Press.

Griffith, P.A. and Wollheim, R. (1960) "How can one person represent another?", *Aristotelian Society*, Suppl. Vol.XXXIV, 187–224.

Harris, W. (1993) *The Interpretable Constitution*. Baltimore, MD: Johns Hopkins University Press.

Held, D. (1991) "Democracy, the nation state, and the global system", in D. Held (ed.), *Political Theory Today*, Stanford. CA: Stanford University Press.

Herzog, D. (1989) *Happy Slaves: A Critique of Consent Theory*. Chicago, IL: University of Chicago Press

Hume, D. (1872) *The History of England*, new edn, 6 vols. Boston, MA: Little, Brown.

Hume, D. (1970) *Treatise on Human Nature*, book III "Of morals", in Hume's *Moral and Political Philosophy*, ed. H. Aiken. Arien, CT: Hafner.

Kedourie, E. (1993) *Nationalism*, 4th edn. Oxford: Blackwell.

Kratochwil, F. (1994) "The limits of contract". *European Journal of International Law*, 5, 465–491.

Kratochwil, F.V. (1989) *Rules, Norms, and Decisions*. Cambridge: Cambridge University Press.

Lapid, Y. and Kratochwil, F. (1996) "Revisiting the national: toward an identity agenda in neorealism?", in Y. Lapid and F. Kratochwil (eds), *The Return of Culture and Identity in IR Theory*. Boulder, CO: Lynne Rienner.

Locke, J. (1963) *A Second Treatise of Government*, in P. Laslett (ed.), *Two Treatises of Government*. New York: Mentor.

Madison, J. (1961) "Federalist 10", in *The Federalist Papers*, ed. C. Rossiter. New York: Mentor.

Offe, C. and Preuss, U.K. (1991) "Democratic institutions and moral resources", in D. Held (ed.), *Political Theory Today*. Stanford, CA: Stanford University Press.

Oksenberg-Rorty, A. (ed.) (1980) *Explaining Emotions*. Berkeley, CA: Campus.

Pitkin, H.F. (1972) *The Concept of Representation*. Berkeley, CA: University of California Press.

Plato (1973), *Republic*, trans. B. Jowett. New York: Anchor Books.

Rawls, J. (1985) "Justice as fairness: political not metaphysical", *Philosophy and Public Affairs*, 14, 223–251.

Sen, A. (1990) "Rational fools: a critique of the behavioral foundations of economic theory", in J. Mansbridge (ed.), *Beyond Self Interest*. Chicago, IL: University of Chicago Press.

Shils, E. (1957) "Primordial, personal, sacred, and civil ties", *British Journal of Sociology*, 17, 113–45.

Smith, A.D. (1991) *National Identity*. Reno, NE: University of Nevada Press.

Smith, A.D. (1995) *Nations and Nationalism in a Global Era*. Cambridge: Polity.

Solomon, R. (1994) *The Passions: Emotions and the Meaning of Life*. Indianapolis, IN: Hackett.

Taylor, C. (1985) "Agency and the self", in *Human Agency and Language*. Cambridge: Cambridge University Press.

Weber, M. (1978) *Economy and Society*. Berkeley, CA: University of California Press.

Zartman, W. (1996) "Self and space: negotiating a future from the past", mimeo.

13 Global governance and the emergence of a "world society"

That nations dwell in eternal anarchy has been one of the defining assumptions that have shaped the socialisation of several generations of students of international relations. While political struggle inside the state takes place in the shadow of the law (conceived as the sovereign's command), this mediation was thought to be absent in the international arena. However, the demise of the Soviet Union and the increase in the volume, scope and speed of transnational interactions challenged this traditional assumption of anarchy and non-co-operation. Departing from the presumption that war was now a less plausible defining characteristic of the international arena, and the subsequent subversion of the foundational distinction between "internal" and "external" arenas, it was naturally tempting to conceive of these fundamental changes as constituting a transformation of the international system into a global or "world society". This chapter will consider to what extent this argument is valid.

Several strands of argument converged to produce this new "synthesis" of global change. First, so successful was realism's imposition of its own conception of the world system that, when the premises of anarchy were called into question, it seemed that no other vocabulary was as readily available as that of a "society". Second, the failure of socialism seemed to prove the impossibility of an alternative to the liberal political project and thus suggested the "end of history". Third, the "sociological" vocabulary also pointed to a way out of the conceptual impasses of earlier debates, in which states were conceived of not only as rigid billiard balls but also as "containers" for their respective societies. The focus on complex networks of policy-making, rather than clearly defined central decision-making centres, was thought to provide a more accurate picture of these processes in the internal and the international arenas than when they were observed through the conceptual lenses of sovereignty and the autonomy of the "state". Finally, it seemed possible to distinguish between government and the broader notion of "governance", the former being only one specific historical form of the latter.

However, this sociological vocabulary masks some deeper conceptual problems. Issues of reference and self-reference are crucial in the discourse of "society", since the meaning of terms in political and social discourses is derived from their relationship to other terms – to "the state", for example, or the public, citizenship and participation – rather than from some "correspondence" between a concept and the phenomenon thereby named. Precisely because "constitutive" issues and explanations are thereby raised, their clarification cannot be reduced to empirical observations of the workings of dependent and independent variables in a causal pattern, or to a harder look at the "facts".

Thus a type of critical analysis becomes necessary that rests on conceptual clarification and the satisfaction of historical contextual criteria, rather than on the collection of further "confirming" evidence or instances of refutation. As is the case with any analogy, the validity of the conceptualisation – of the state as a "contract", for example – depends on the similarity of certain relationships among the crucial concepts, and not on the discovery of some similarities through a point by point comparison. In other words, to find a similarity between A and B in two different domains is not enough to establish validation; what is required is to discover a similar *relationship* between A and B: as A:B, so C:D. This logical requirement points to the importance of the historical context. We have to understand the "puzzles", of which the analogy is part, and which issues are thereby brought to the fore and which ones recede into the background. To that extent, the "social contract" (and its distinction between "society" and the "state") arose from the dissolution of the estates society, in which "rule" (*dominium*) was shared and "belonged" to individuals as members of a certain status; now what was emphasised was the impersonal nature of the public order. It is also clear that the shift from the master metaphor of a "body politic" to the metaphor of a contract cannot be understood as having reached greater descriptive "accuracy" or fit with social reality (because a state is neither a "body" nor a simple "contract"). The new metaphor is part of a different political project, in which the nature of the association and the nature of "rule" are fundamentally altered.

One could now argue that exactly the same conceptual moves are now under way when we consider the emergence of a global society. The first conceptual move implies, therefore, the severance of the notion of a "society" from that of a state in order to allow for its reconstruction at a higher level. Here, the forces of globalisation are invoked as having undermined the close connection between the territorial state and the existing political community. This move paves the way for the argument that for (democratic) rule to be effective, a "cosmopolitan community" has to be established.[1] The opposition of state and society is thus transferred from the national to the global scale, whereby a differentiation between the steering or "governing" and society (which has historically occurred through the formation of the state) is awaited: this is the cosmopolitan project. However, the problem with the analogy is that there is neither a world state in the offing, nor is there much evidence that the "local" identifications of historical communities have lost their significance in practical life, as advocates of cosmopolitanism suggest.

As Hobbes pointed out, the "state of nature" at the international level need not give rise to a Super-Leviathan, because the possibility of collective defence by the organised community alleviates the security dilemma considerably and thereby undermines the "necessity" for a global government. But if no world state is necessary or likely to develop, it is unlikely that a world society will emerge. The issue is not only how the "unity" or the horizon within which the interactions of states take place has to be thought of – typically as a "system" or a community of a special kind such as a "republic", or a "society" of states – but also how a "thicker" institutionalisation of this particular common horizon can be achieved, even though its experience is (still) mediated by identifications with more circumscribed communities. After all, the state remains deeply ingrained in most of our political and social practices. It is the ever-present "third person" Hobbes discerned in all bilateral transactions among the members of a society,[2] while no such systematic presence seems accorded in our political life to cosmopolitan concerns.[3] We see instead a variety of trends: the decay of the state and rule by intermediaries, as in many regions of Africa and the former Soviet empire, and a new type of "sub" politics that not only involves a "renaissance of political subjectivity" in the West, but also transforms traditional binding decisions on behalf of a community into "options" for private individuals. This "privatisation" and the pervasive scepticism towards traditional structures and identities makes it difficult to interpret this new politics as the harbinger of a new form of global citizenship.[4] Finally, since even the most principled "advocacy networks" have to pick and choose their fights carefully, their activities give rise to at best a spotty pattern in the pursuit of cosmopolitan concerns. Finally, the nature of public goods seems also relevant in this context. Consumption goods obviously invite transnational activity, and distributive goods might also spawn greater transnational activity, but when "redistributive" public goods are at issue we seem trapped in classical national decision-making structures.

The concept of world society does not usually rely on a "lowest common denominator" argument. Rather, as evinced by Meyer et al. (1997), it is a claim that an ensemble of cultural forms has become universal as part of a modernisation process encompassing the whole globe and virtually all dimensions of social reproduction. However, even if it is true that the form of political associations, the enterprise of knowledge generation, family life, sexual practices and so forth have all been revolutionised, we still have to look at the practices that are informed by these forms but are hardly ever mere performances of a given script. Given the ample local variation and considerable blending of rather heterogeneous cultural forms that characterise the reproduction of the social world, a concept of a world society must identify two things if it is to help in the diagnosis of our present predicament. The first is *the important elements of the ongoing processes*, including the analysis of homogenisation and the emergence of new patterns of differentiation – sometimes described problematically as the re-tribalisation of primordial ties;[5] and the second, *the levers for action*, even if – or rather because – the "projective" character of the term remains a part of its grammar.

The issues of discerning, defining and describing society emerge when we enquire into the understandings and practices of actors and of the "boundaries", inclusions and exclusions that are always part of and form the background to our practices. They are also raised when we examine the increased density in scope and domain of boundary-transcending transactions and try to understand these processes within a larger whole, even if the actors themselves are not (or are only vaguely) aware of these influences. To that extent, the notion of a world society is a "projection" of processes of transformative change that predates its actual emergence in the vocabulary of actors in the closing decades of the last millennium. The term "world society" ought not to be dismissed because of its "fuzziness", because identical or quite similar problems will be encountered after substituting other terms – "system" for "society", for example, as in Wallerstein's approach, or after engaging once more in structural-functional analysis. Ultimately, the idea that the terms of political discourse function like "labels" that more or less describe the elements of the social world rests on a mistaken assumption: that is, that we are dealing here with analogues to "natural kinds" and that it is the "fit" between concept and phenomenon that decides the question of truth and/or utility. However, while the notion of natural kinds is already highly contested and problematic in the sciences, the meaning of concepts in the social world is derived from their "use", that is, what they do and how they function in practice, rather than what they designate. To that extent, these concepts are more like signals, telling us how to "go on", rather than labels for things.

The most interesting question, therefore, is not whether a world society exists, but what the "gap" between the practices and the vocabulary means, and what a critical reflection is able to disclose when we, because of this gap, can *no longer* "go on". To that extent, neither the projective anticipation of "one world" as the last horizon of a common human consciousness, nor the processes of system integration and disintegration, are sufficient. Instead, we have to reflect critically on the links between these practices and their conceptualisations, without privileging either process, that is, viewing one as essentially determined by the other. Admittedly, this might not make for an analysis that satisfies or comes close to the ideal of a social "science" that is concerned with the discovery of universal laws or constant causal mechanisms. Nevertheless, it might be all that we can do to capture the open-ended nature of mankind's "history" and to provide a diagnostic for appraisal.

From these initial remarks the plan for this chapter can be discerned. The next part will be devoted to a discussion of global governance as it has emerged in debates over the claims of movements and international networks to be part of a newly emerging sphere – that is, a global civil society – and from the programmes and practices of international organisations. In the following, third part of the chapter, I attempt to show the paradoxes of global governance as a "practice" that has replaced "development", and to provide a preliminary assessment. The chapter concludes with a brief analysis of the "diagnostic" limitations of this novel liberal universalism.

From globalisation to global governance

If one examines the discourse on globalisation during the last two decades, one notices a decisive shift from a notion of an encompassing process that, like a tidal wave, casts aside anything in its way,[6] to a notion that emphasises again the possibility of choice. For the latter, the rather amorphous notion of "governance" becomes the dominant term of reference. Even in the industrialised world, the events of September 11, 2001, shifted the emphasis away from earlier "atopian" notions[7] of networks and exchanges, of transnationally organised movements and an emerging civil society, to an analysis of the "performance" and (in)efficiency of intergovernmental networks – from courts to routinised police collaboration – and regulatory institutions[8] ensuring "governmentality",[9] transparency and accountability. Instead of the former "resistance" to globalisation by societal groups and NGOs, their changing role as norm creators or service providers is now more often the focus.[10] Nevertheless, there seems to have emerged a substantive agreement on what "globalisation" is.

The most important element of the globalisation discourse has been the nearly overwhelming recognition of change in all areas of social life. In fact, "globalisation" has become a container for various complex processes of transformative change. Although as such it cannot act or cause anything, it does become some "actant", an acting unit, which is adduced to make the observed changes intelligible. Three specific aspects of change are associated with this sense of transformation. First, at the most basic level, there is the communications revolution engendered by digitalisation and telematics (linking computers to new information networks[11]) that has resulted in the compression of time and space to an extent never before imagined. Without such a new way of handling information, the modern forms of "flat" organisational structures, observable in many multinational corporations, just-in-time production and the global diversification of production and of products according to customer demand, could not be imagined.

Second, the development of financial markets and thus of credit creation on a global scale would not have been possible without the continuous and virtually frictionless linking of established financial markets into what is effectively a single institution operating on a twenty-four hour basis. This development, in turn, has raised two further problems. One concerns the explosive growth of financial transactions: for each dollar changing hands on the basis of trade, sixty are exchanged in financial transactions.[12] The other deals with the connection of markets and the rest of the political and social system; here "liberalisation" engendered a debate on the loss of "steering capacity" by state institutions. Hence the fear that the classical welfare state is being undermined *from below* through its shrinking capacity to provide for "redistributive public goods"[13] while it is also being hollowed out *from above*, since globalisation has removed many policy issues from national institutions to international fora or bureaucracies (Zuern 1998).

The more sanguine view is that new forms of control and influence by the various stakeholders result in the internationalisation of the state[14] which, in turn, makes its democratisation necessary. The prospects for such developments are auspicious since the third process lumped together in the container "globalisation", namely, the circulation of ideas, has reached explosive proportions. Notions of individual rights, governmental accountability, minimum standards and so forth have not only been universally diffused, but also have acquired a virtually exclusive legitimacy in all societies.[15] Besides, as cultural optimists have suggested, new public spaces are likely to emerge that are no longer tied to territorially organised societies. Instead, common concerns are now founding new communities (Ekins 1992) existing in virtual space or linked transnationally through a network of "movements".[16] Thus, cosmopolitan ideals – until now limited perhaps to certain elite strata – appear in this interpretation as the logical conclusion of the democratic revolutions that formerly needed nationalism and the territorial state to integrate viable societies. However, nowadays looser but more complex formations typical of a global civil society might do (Falk 1998)[17] or, as James Rosenau has suggested, global civil society might become a "functional equivalent" to the classical territorially defined democracy (Rosenau 1998: 41).

The *political project* associated with the issue of governance arose as the autonomy of these transformative forces was contested and the question of "regulation" was raised. The identification of options for control and the search for levers for action marked the shift in focus from "globalisation" to "governance". Three factors have proved decisive in this shift. First, earlier claims about the inevitability and inexorability of globalisation have been replaced by more fine-grained approaches. As the studies of Hirst and Thompson (1996) and Scharpf and Schmidt (2000) clearly indicate, choices and decisions are still available and they need to be made, even though, interestingly, the arena is no longer restricted to individual nation states alone. A second crucial factor has been the attempt to rescue both the failed states of the South, which experienced mass violence, and the "transition states" of the former Soviet empire. The place for this debate has been the UN and the ever more complex missions of "peacekeeping" and "peacemaking" in which it has become involved. Here, "governance" means, above all, a disciplining of state institutions – as long as they still function – through greater transparency and accountability. If state structures have ceased to work, alternative systems for the delivery of services and certain public goods such as health care, schooling and disaster relief must be established. NGOs have offered themselves as an alternative to the corrupt and inefficient delivery systems of states, and also serve as advocates for local, often silenced voices, which now can be heard because of their links to the internationally organised advocacy networks. As Paris (2002: 638) observes:

> Without exception peace-building missions in the post Cold War world have attempted to transplant the values and institutions of the liberal democratic core into the domestic affairs of peripheral host states ... In this respect, the contemporary practice may be viewed as a modern rendering of the *mission civilisatrice* – the colonial era belief that the European powers had a duty to civilize their overseas possessions. Although modern peace-builders have largely abandoned the archaic language of civilized vs. uncivilized, they nevertheless appear to act upon the belief that one model of domestic governance – liberal market democracy – is superior to all others.

Here, two additional terms that are part of the governance discourse become important. One is the concept of "transition". It differs from earlier notions of political development because its broader scope for transformation includes institutions and practices in the public as well as the private realm. The other is "transparency" (often meaning "accountability" rather than merely the enhancement of visibility), which has become a major issue in social, political and economic realms, and which can also be fitted neatly under the term "governance" when issues of *corporate governance* attain new salience. Thus "governance" is reformist in a much wider sense than earlier attempts at establishing a functioning "developmental state". Its goal is not only the establishment of a viable democracy, but also human rights and a "liberal market-economy", thereby subjecting large swathes of social and economic life to international scrutiny and discipline. Moreover, even though international governance programmes address mainly state institutions, the reforms rely for their legitimacy on arguments about the efficiency gains achieved by a "lean" state, and on the disciplinary control of all aspects of social life through the creation of transparency, benchmarking and reporting. As politics is largely dissolved into *technique*, the problem of "rule" (*dominium, Herrschaft*) is mystified, making it appear that it is all about "rules" that either work by themselves – because they are "clear" and "precise" – or, if there is still the need for some form of "direction" – politics consists in "delegation"[18] to some form of dispute settlement "mechanisms". These range from the WTO to the ICJ, to the global "network of courts"[19] or chambers of arbitration, so that the problem of the rule of law is "operationalised", in a way, as rule by experts.

This "removed" and neutral stance, however, hardly squares with the difficulties engendered by the complex problems of transitions, because the viability of local structures is decisive. Local knowledge therefore seems more important than expertise in, or familiarity with, procedures for "helping" that have been developed in other contexts but are of little use, given local circumstances. Thus, a third factor accounting for the rise of a governance discourse is the result of the demise of development planning. The realisation that projects based on the reigning orthodoxy had done little to achieve the goal of jump-starting economic development was sobering but incontrovertible. Feasibility studies notwithstanding, many grand projects of yesteryear, such as dams, turned out to be of dubious economic value, usually having quite a detrimental *environmental* impact, and leading to increasingly vocal and active local resistance. Likewise, the traditional structural adjustment loans of the IMF, which had already been connected with obtrusive interventionist policies of "conditionality", did not prove effective. Despite the administration of many bitter pills, the IMF encountered again and again the problem of "slippage": a noble circumlocution for the fact that the programme had failed to induce the changes thought to be necessary. Money disappeared into the coffers of local "elites" and loans had to be rescheduled for political reasons. But neither the IMF nor the government could afford to admit failure. The government needed access to funds; the international financial institutions needed recognition of their expertise for legitimising purposes. Mounting criticism of these practices finally led the World Bank to reconsider some of its programmes, introduce poverty reduction as an important objective, and institutionalise some form of "dialogue" with local groups and transnational activist networks. Participation at both *planning* and *implementation* levels seemed to be a necessary, if not a sufficient, condition for success.

These ideas dovetail neatly with the argument that a global civil society is able to provide governance not only by outflanking the increasingly corrupt state structures but also by creating new forms of participatory politics and accountability. "Governance" is seen as a new type of public management that increases accountability through local involvement and through the introduction of managerial and market-based methods into public service provision. Thus "good governance" for the World Bank involves efficiency in public services, the rule of law with regard to contracts, an effective judiciary, respect for human rights, freedom of the press and a pluralistic social and institutional structure. These goals, in turn, require the marketisation of public service, a reduction of public sector staffing, budgetary discipline, the decentralisation of administration and the participation of local and transnational NGOs. The emerging structure is one of a network that straddles not only the classical boundary between the inside and the outside of the state but also the boundary between the public and the private realm.

The paradoxes of "global governance"

Strangely enough, little attention has been paid by the governance discourse to problems that arise from the multiplicity of goals that might work at cross-purposes, such as when an expansion of participation might make greater "efficiency" a hard goal to achieve. Even more significant an oversight is the failure to take account of how the participation of elements from "civil society", such as NGOs, in the governance project is affected by the introduction of "market elements" – competitive tenders and short-term renewable contracts – for providing services in failed states or transitional countries. Competition in these contexts need not be a boon. With a plurality of bidders for the same project, there arises the "multiple principals" problem of serving more than one master, while there can also be races to the bottom affecting the quality of services. Conversely, co-operation should not be treated as a consumption good, as those who are subject to mafia–like cartels of "co-operating" local actors are likely to find out. Finally, having to compete incessantly for funding displaces the time and energy of NGOs, detracting them from their actual goals, for example health care or schooling. Not only will there be a disincentive to report problems with the programmes one administers, but the scramble for funding might also lead to dysfunctional behaviour, such as undermining a competitor, and clientelistic practices (via side payments) towards the recipients of the service.

Thus, a different picture of "civil society" and of the chances for a new and more effective form of governance emerges. Unfortunately, it is not necessarily one of benevolence, burden-sharing and joint commitments to common causes. Arguments that competition among NGOs demonstrates the "vibrancy" of civil society, and that the ever-increasing number of NGOs exemplifies the force of this civic vision and of a new form of cosmopolitan politics, are clearly exaggerated. They simply take no account of possible negative externalities. While it might be considered obscene to charge humanitarian or "principled" organisations or activist frameworks with selfish interests, it would be ideological in the worst sense, not to say foolish, to assume that humanitarian organisations are *toto caelo* to other organisations because they pursue some ideals or goals of which we approve. As Cooley and Ron (2002: 17, 22) suggest, after having examined several aid projects with substantive NGO involvement:

> Calls for IO and INGO coordination are ubiquitous in the humanitarian aid literature, prompting the periodic creation of new UN coordination studies and agencies. Recurring coordination problems are, however, not caused solely by poor communication, lack of professionalism, or the dearth of coordinating bodies. They are also – and perhaps chiefly – produced by a crowded and highly competitive aid market in which multiple organizations compete for contracts from the same donors. Inter-organizational discord is a predictable outcome of existing material incentives . . .
>
> The lack of coordination is not a product of ill will or poor organizational culture. Rather it is increasingly generated by the marketized environment in which IOs and INGOs feel required to demonstrate their ability to spend monies and win influence, regardless of broader project outcomes.

Hegel's inkling that civil society would not lead to integration on either the individual or the systems level, but that for such an integration the "state" was needed, was perhaps not far from the mark, even though the first part of the sentence seems much less controversial than the second. After all, the "mediation" by the state that Hegel himself proposed was largely entrusted to the "bureaucracy", that is, a group with a special ethos and knowledge. Given the different trade-offs between competing policy goals, the differential impact a policy is likely to have on different groups, and the likely disagreements over the timing and implementation of the measures under consideration, the idea of "one best solution" based on technical expertise quickly shows its phantasmagorical quality.

A good illustration of these problems is the example of help to Kyrgyzstan to reform its institutions in accordance with "governance" benchmarks. During the discussion of how to privatise Kyrgyz Energo, the former state-owned energy monopoly, USAID wanted to dismantle the firm completely, whereas the European Bank for Reconstruction and Development wanted to keep it intact, provided a foreign partner could be found who could then initiate gradual reforms. The World Bank, which had sided originally with USAID, shifted later to endorse the European position. Meanwhile, the Kyrgyz officials stalled, as the donors vied for influence and proposed strikingly different strategies. Much of the disagreement among the agencies and contractors, who had developed their strategies essentially by placing different bets on the future, rested on the question of which monitoring and statistical data collection method should be adopted, making it appear that the basic difficulties were only "technical" in nature.

The obvious lesson is, however, that since these problems are not technical in nature the appropriate strategy is to ensure that all stakeholders of a policy are brought together. This shifts the emphasis from expertise to political participation. Sometimes it was on the basis of this strategy – adopted enthusiastically by transnational social movements – that the emergence of new political spaces and participatory structures was expected. Again, the actual record is rather mixed and gives much food for thought. On the one hand, the establishment of the developmental dialogue by the World Bank, and the adoption of the WTO Council's Guidelines for Arrangements with Nongovernmental Organisations (1996), has increased the legitimacy of NGOs by allowing them to attend plenary sessions (but not formal or informal negotiating sessions). The meeting at Seattle (1999), which was attended by 739 accredited NGOs, who – aside from protests – organised a whole programme of workshops and symposia to which the WTO delegates were invited, represents the apogee of NGO activism.[20]

While these numbers are certainly indicative of a changing political landscape and a new agenda, the question remains whether spectacular events and even mass violence translate into political influence, or constitute the emergence of a new particular political space. The numbers alone should make us a little suspicious. How can one speak of a meaningful debate and participation with such numbers? True, many NGOs espoused similar positions, so that the problem of *quot capita tot sententiae* need not arise. However, how can one speak of participation and the emergence of a public if not even the agenda is known, or if access is not granted to the ministerial meetings where the decisions are being made? Given the entrenched position of the WTO and its success in representing issues of far-reaching social and political import as belonging to "trade", one has to wonder whether the democratisation of its procedures – weak as it is – is not bought at a heavy price, that is, by undermining both national and international politics. David Kennedy's laconic remarks about why anyone should be excited and celebrate "the expansion of participation in an emasculated policy process" seem rather apt (Kennedy 1999: 54).

The real question is whether the potential for meaningful democratic politics is merely dependent on an increase in information or even of "transparency", or whether such a strategy has perverse effects. Zizek's (1999: 388) suspicion that "our deepest commitments to equality and participation bind us into practices whereby we submit to a global capital" may be very well founded. In other words, the institutions where the choices are actually made have successfully insulated themselves from public scrutiny and accountability by creating fora for endless debates and "arguing" (Risse 2000)[21] but with no possibility of participation in or influence on decisions, or of exercising effective control over those in power.

Even if we admit that the inclusion of "stakeholders" improves the input and possibly also the output legitimacy of a decision by opening up the process of deliberation and bringing to the negotiation relevant information that otherwise would not have been available, the unresolved issue remains that of how stakeholders are identified in the first place, and thus, whether or not the necessary level of representation has been achieved.[22] Furthermore, we know from the corporatist literature that diffuse interests, though extremely relevant for the viability and the welfare gains derived from negotiated settlements, are difficult to organise. Corporatist "partnerships" are frequently subject to "capture" by narrow but well-organised interests, particularly if one group has an important asset, such as information that others lack, or can provide the necessary *episteme*, which integrates otherwise separate issues and links them to particular strategies. Some studies of the influence of European business on EU trade policy – to the virtual exclusion of other groups of civil society – suggest that these two factors, that is, information provision and *episteme*-definition, are the most important ones in explaining actual policy outcomes.[23] Transplanting such "corporate" arrangements from the national to the international level obviously does not by itself enhance either the quality of the decisions or their legitimacy. As Ottaway (2001: 266) has pointed out:

> Despite the claims that tripartite agreements will introduce greater democracy in the realm of global governance, it is doubtful that

close cooperation between essentially unrepresentative organizations – international organizations, unaccountable NGOs and large transnational corporations – will do much to ensure better protection and better representation of the interests of populations affected by global policies.

It is perhaps no surprise that, despite the high expectations from global policy networks, only very few of them satisfied the original criteria for public/private partnerships. And questions could be raised even in the "satisfactory" cases such as the Apparel Industry Partnership (which was charged with formulating standards for the US apparel industry and its subcontractors), since only the presence of the US government was envisaged, but its participation was practically non-existent during the negotiations (Bobrowski 1999). Two other rather satisfactory projects were the World Commission on Dams (WCD), which resulted from a Workshop sponsored by the World Bank and the World Conservation Union, and the ISO 14000 Project (Clap 1989), tasked with developing standards for environmental management systems (EMS).

Evaluations of the democratic dimension of these projects are rather mixed, although the Dam project apparently fared much better (Dubash et al. 2001). But even here its identification of stakeholders and the confidentiality of its proceedings can be criticised. The ISO 14000 was, in effect, a closed meeting between governmental and industry representatives from the northern hemisphere. Although developing countries had to come on board and held an effective veto position, given the nature of the enterprise they lacked know-how and access to information, and therefore possessed no clout at the bargaining table. For many NGOs and developing countries, the process appeared to them, as Virginia Haufler states, "opaque, expensive and industry led" (Haufler 1999: 25).

The bitter truth for much of the "Third World" is that its traditional fear of exploitation and colonialism is increasingly being replaced by the practical irrelevance of entire parts of the globe for the "global" economy, while they increasingly create problems for the society of states and its public order. This can perhaps best be seen in the privatisation of security and in the development of a new form of predatory state that we encounter in many regions of the world. Marauding militias and mercenaries at the command of subnational actors and warlords who have access to globalized networks of (misused) aid, as well as to international crime, increasingly determine the life of many "failed" or "transitional" states.[24] When, with the failure of the "developmental state", which attempted at least to integrate society and provide the structures for political and economic accumulation, the resources channelled through official structures cease, it is inevitable that the state apparatus decays. More and more officials take bribes and the system of clientelism and patronage, prevalent in many societies, quickly generates new parallel structures for social reproduction. The resulting pattern is that of rule by a variety of intermediaries – "big men", traditional leaders, ethnic entrepreneurs, religious fundamentalists, and so on.

Examples abound, ranging from Pakistan and Uganda to the successor states of the former Soviet empire. Thus, a Ugandan "minister" owned the central train terminal in the capital, had a private security service which protected embassies, TNCs and NGOs and, at the same time, did not hesitate to use his "private" force to disperse and coerce protestors who had taken issue with his licensing practices for "servicing" the railway station. In Pakistan, the military – the only remaining state institution that is still somehow functioning at the price of representing a state within the state – had, in 1999, to use 30,000 soldiers to collect water and electricity bills, restore the networks by capping illegal taps and arrest corrupt officials. When the public education system broke down, nobody even knew how many schools actually existed, as many teachers had jobs in phantom schools. Elements of "civil society", such as the largely fundamentalist brotherhoods, filled the gap, providing their pupils more with indoctrination than education.

These last two examples clearly illustrate the serious problems that the new emphasis on "governance" and "civil society" hides. Attempts at curbing corruption and making the state more efficient by relying on the capacities of private actors and civil society were, of course, quite in tune with Western ideas about liberalisation and a "lean" state. However, the beneficial effects of such a retrenchment of the state could not be realised in most developing or transitional countries. Instead of improving the efficiency of the existing state apparatus, such a "downsizing" contributed to its further decay and to the development of parallel networks of power. It curtails the chances for a politics in which the state as an arbiter can make legitimate and binding decisions. Contrary also to the hopes of anti-statists and the advocates of the democratic potential of civil society, who often insisted on the superiority of private ordering, we notice the re-feudalisation of these societies and the emergence of an entrenched and internationally well-connected kleptocracy. This leads to predatory rule by intermediaries and warlords who have commoditised the main function of the state, namely, security (with all the implications for responsibility, legitimacy and accountability), and who have "communalised" other traditional state functions, such as education and welfare, by transferring these responsibilities to local and international networks of civil society. Even if we put a more optimistic gloss on these rather sobering experiences and assessments, one thing is evident: no general emergence of a "global public sphere", or of a space for cosmopolitan democratic practice, seems to be in the offing. Although we do notice the emergence of new actors and claimants attempting to establish some institutional framework, the appropriateness of the civil society analogy is rather doubtful.

Morals

The above analysis not only explains why homogenisation and differentiation are part and parcel of the same process of transformative change but also suggests that the function of "civil society" in both contexts is rather different. Increasing reliance on these NGOs by Western states and international organisations in the name of "governance" is not likely to have the expected beneficial consequences, particularly if this involves dealing with "big men" and contending with the networks and structures of kleptocratic regimes. Far from creating the conditions for a flourishing global civil society, the result could be the emergence of new para-statal forms of rule in which predatory elites are even less dependent upon their "subjects" than before, precisely because they can link to international networks (criminal ones and legal ones) that provide them with the necessary resources. Similarly, the idea that, through the organisation of all the stakeholders, new political spaces could be opened up, or at least more legitimate and effective regimes could be created, reflects a distorted optimism that ignores the difficulties involved in identifying the appropriate stakeholders and the problems with corporatism writ large.

Thus the question arises as to why the liberal project's promotion of the autonomy and legitimacy of civil society seems powerful and persuasive, despite its obvious flaws. There are several reasons that can, on their own and in conjunction, explain this. One is the inherent abstraction of the perspective that systematically eliminates differences, or declares them unimportant or in need of justification. Unsurprisingly, then, all the problems usually associated with social differentiation do not appear in the model, because they have been ignored in the first place. The most obvious problem is that, for a theory of democracy, the liberal paradigm has no way of providing a coherent account of the role of boundaries in establishing and maintaining existing communities. It either simply assumes that "we, the People" exist, or that it does not matter whether or not people are constituted as "a people".

The shortcomings of this liberal perspective are best illustrated by Rawls' attempt to rely on either the specification of the transcendental conditions of a rational choice (behind the veil of ignorance) in order to derive the criteria for a just society, or on the assumption of an existing community. In the second case, some form of "overlapping" consensus is supposed to provide the grounds for the establishment of an order that assigns precedence to the right over the good. Here, historical contingency enters the picture and the identification of an overlapping consensus means empirically examining which structures prove viable under what circumstances, an enterprise that undermines, however, both universalism and the notion of absolute foundations. Thus, given the contingent historical practice, the existence of societies that resemble those of free associations under the rule of law are extremely rare: they are exceptions rather than the rule. Furthermore, as Habermas (1998: 115) suggests:

Since the voluntariness of the decision to engage in a law giving praxis is a fiction of the contractualist tradition, in the real world who gains power to define the boundaries of a political community is settled by historical chance and the actual course of events – normally, by the arbitrary outcomes of wars and civil wars.

A second and, of course, equally important reason for the success of the liberal project is the concept of the individual that is taken as the ultimate entity for the construction of the social world. Although such a move entails usually a naturalistic fallacy, there is an intuitive, even if mistaken, plausibility to this position. Here I do not want to renew the debate between communitarians and liberals. I simply want to point out that the construction of the individual who "owns" himself, and is, therefore, the bearer of subjective rights, mystifies in the concept of "property" the exercise of power that comes with the granting of subjective rights. In addition, it skews the discussion of a whole host of socially important questions about the nature of property rights, the limits of their exercise and their coercive character, by providing powerful "trumps" in debates. In this way, a comprehensive rights discourse can be constructed in which virtually all problems can be recast as issues of subjective rights. Any interference with them, for instance by regulatory measures, can be "debunked" as improper interference, as the recent controversy about the patents for AIDS medicine in developing countries shows.

The upshot of these remarks about the liberal project is that, by making it appear that certain social arrangements work like natural forces, the project in the end subverts itself and becomes ideological. It projects a universality that is neither normatively nor historically justifiable, as it discounts both the inherent potential for diversity and the existence of several paths to modernity. It also mystifies power and its need for legitimisation and accountability by making it appear that the particular arrangements we have arrived at are somehow the outcome of nature's plan, and thereby deserve to be universally accepted. Furthermore, by selectively focusing on some aspects of global transformation, e.g. the spread of certain cultural forms, or on transactions, such as capital movements, and by not paying attention to the local mediations that occur, a curious narrative is created in which the elements of the Western tradition, from natural law to modernity, are reconfigured. To what extent they can still serve as templates for a world of our making remains to be seen.

Notes

1 In this context, see the arguments by Held (1998) and Linklater (1998).
2 Usually, we restrict this presence of the sovereign to the sanctions that are part of the legal order and that allow not only for the punishment of lawbreakers, but also the prospective ordering of a society in the "shadow of the law". Conceptually even more important is the fact that certain of our moral evaluations are deeply

embedded in the institutional order of the state. Consider in this context the problem of corruption. That we expect from a public official a "neutral" performance of his duties – instead of paying back his family or clan who enabled him to study, for example, and thus gain office – is the outcome of a "conceptual revolution" into which we have all been socialised: that "traditional" loyalties and personal ties have no place in the public realm.

3 It seems that only Martin Albrow suggests this "global presence" by pointing out that all types of people and groups derive their ideas and values, as well as their identity, increasingly from global contexts and problems and no longer from nationally constituted communities. See Albrow (1996).

4 See, for example, the various formulations by Beck (1995, 1997).

5 See, for example, Barber (1995).

6 For an interesting discussion of the imagery of "globalisation", see Mueller (2003).

7 This is the expression used by the German sociologist Willke (2001) in order to describe the non-localisable nature of modern interactions without attributing to them the "non-existing" or imaginary nature that is part of the "utopian" vocabulary.

8 In this context the notion of the "internationalisation of the state" has been used. See, for example, Wendt and Duvall (1989: Chapter 4).

9 I use here the Foucauldian notion that designates a particular form of power that is diffused throughout society but co-ordinated by a government that has disciplined society. Thus, in a way, although governments are no longer seen as an expression of the "sovereign" facing the people or its subjects, but becoming themselves objects of scrutiny and assessment, they nevertheless reconstitute themselves as crucial nodal points for networks of control that transcend classical notions of the "public" order, or of social control (discipline), or "private" maximisation strategies, exerting "capillary control" rather than working on the basis of "sanctions". For a further discussion see, for example, Dean (1999).

10 On the role of private actors in world politics see, for example, the assessment by Hall and Biersteker (2002).

11 See, for example, Drake (1995).

12 See, for example, Strange (1998).

13 See the discussion by Cerny (1995).

14 See, for example, Shaw (2000).

15 See here the importance accorded to norm entrepreneurs and the network in Keck and Sikkink (1998). See also Khagram et al. (2002).

16 See, for example, Tarrow (1998).

17 See also Kaldor (2003), who distinguishes between different types of movements that have emerged and different forms of civil society. Such a perspective contrasts sharply with one that is derived from notions of an empire in which a no longer identified "multitude" takes over the empire from below (Hardt and Negri 2000).

18 Such an essentially misleading approach to law and its function in the (inter)-national arena is exemplified by the work of Goldstein et al. (2000).

19 See, for example, Slaughter (2003).

20 At Doha only 366 had registered.

21 For a more strategically oriented approach, see Schimmelfennig (2001).

22 See the assessment of Nölke (2000).

23 Thus van Appeldoorn (2002) shows that the notion of "competitiveness" provided the European Round Table with an important framework to which further programmes such as job creation could be bolted and which allowed the business association to influence the Commission's policy decisively.

24 For an interesting account of these developments, see Schlichte and Wilke (2000).

References

Albrow, Martin, 1996, *The Global Age: State and Society Beyond Modernity*, Stanford, CA: Stanford University Press.

Barber, Benjamin, 1995, *Jihad v McWorld: How Globalism and Tribalism are Reshaping the World*, New York: Ballantine Books.

Beck, Ulrich, 1995, *Die feindlose Demokratie*, Stuttgart: Reclam.

—— 1997, *Weltrisikogesellschaft, Weltöffentlichkeit und globale Subpolitik*, Vienna: Picas.

Bobrowski, David, 1999, "Creating a Global Public Policy Network in the Apparel Industry: The Apparel Industry Partnership", case study for the UN Vision Project on Global Public Policy Networks, http://www.gppi.net/

Cerny, Philip, 1995, "Globalization and the Changing Logic of Collective Action", *International Organization*, 49, 595–625.

Clap, Jennifer, 1989, "The Privatization of Global Environmental Governance: ISO 14000 and the Developing World", *Global Governance*, 4(3), 295–316.

Cooley, Alexander, and James Ron, 2002, "The NGO Scramble: Organizational Insecurity and the Political Economy of Transnational Action", *International Security*, 27, 5–39.

Dean, Mitchell, 1999, *Governmentality: Power and Rule in Modern Society*, London: Sage.

Drake, Bill (ed.), 1995, *The New Information Infrastructure*, New York: Twentieth Century Fund.

Dubash, Navroz, Mairi Dupar, Smitu Kothari and Tundu Lissu, 2001, *A Watershed in Global Governance? An Independent Assessment of the World Commission on Dams*, Washington DC: Brookings.

Ekins, Paul, 1992, *A New World Order: Grassroot Movements for Global Change*, London: Routledge.

Falk, Richard, 1998, "Global Civil Society: Perspectives, Initiatives, Movements", *Oxford Development Studies*, 26(1), 99–110.

Goldstein, Judith, Miles Kahler, Robert Keohane and Anne Marie Slaughter (eds), 2000, *Legalization and World Politics*, Special Issue of *International Organization*, 54(3).

Habermas, Jürgen, 1998, "The European Nation State: On the Past and Future of Sovereignty and Citizenship", in C. Cronin and P. De Greiff (eds), *Inclusion of the Other: Studies in Political Theory*, Cambridge, MA: MIT Press.

Hall, Rodney, and Thomas Biersteker (eds), 2002, *The Emergence of Private Authority in Global Governance*, Cambridge: Cambridge University Press.

Hardt, Michael, and Antonio Negri, 2000, *Empire*, Cambridge, MA: Harvard University Press.

Haufler, Virginia, 1999, "Negotiating International Standards for Environmental Management Systems: The ISO 14000 Standards", case study for the UN Vision Project on Global Public Policy Networks, http://www.gppi.net/cms/public/

Held, David, 1998, "The Transformation of Political Community: Rethinking Democracy in the Context of Globalization", in I. Shapiro and C. Hacker Cordon (eds), *Democracy's Edges*, Cambridge: Cambridge University Press.

Hirst, Paul, and Grahame Thompson, 1996, *Globalization in Question*, Cambridge: Polity Press.

Kaldor, Mary, 2003, *Global Civil Society: An Answer to War*, Oxford: Polity Press.

Keck, Margaret, and Kathryn Sikkink, 1998, *Activists Beyond Borders: Advocacy Networks in International Politics*, Ithaca NY: Cornell University Press.

Kennedy, David, 1999, "Background Noise? The Underlying Politics of Global Governance", *Harvard International Review*, 3, 52–85.

Khagram, Sanjeez, James Riker and Kathryn Sikkink (eds), 2002, *Restructuring World Politics: Transnational Movements, Networks and Norms*, Minneapolis MN: University of Minnesota Press.

Linklater, Andrew, 1998, *The Transformation of Political Community*, Oxford: Polity Press.

Meyer, John, John Boli, George Thomas and Francisco Ramirez, 1997, "World Society and the Nation State", *American Journal of Sociology*, 103(1), 144–81.

Mueller, Philip, 2003, *Unearthing the Politics of Globalization*, Muenster and New Brunswick: Lit. and Transaction Pub.

Nölke, Andreas, 2000, "Regieren in transnationalen Politiknetzwerken: Kritik post-nationaler Governance-Konzepte aus der Perspektive einer transnationalen, Inter-Organisationssoziologie", *Zeitschrift für Internationale Beziehungen*, 2(2), 331–58.

Ottaway, Marina, 2001, "Corporatism Goes Global: International Organizations, Nongovernmental Organization Networks, and Trans-national Business", *Global Governance*, 7(3), 265–92.

Paris, Roland, 2002, "International Peace Building and the 'Mission Civilisatrice' ", *Review of International Studies*, 28, 637–56.

Reinicke, Wolfgang, 1998, *Global Public Policy: Governing without Government*, Washington DC: Brookings.

Risse, Thomas, 2000, "Let's Argue: Communicative Action in World Politics", *International Organization*, 54(1), 1–39.

Rosenau, James, 1998, "Governance and Democracy in a Globalizing World", in D. Archibugi, D. Held and M. Kohler (eds), *Re-imagining Political Community*, Cambridge: Polity Press.

Scharpf, Fritz, and Vivien Schmidt, 2000, *Welfare and Work in the Open Economy*, 2 vols, New York: Oxford University Press.

Schimmelfennig, Frank, 2001, "Liberal Norms, Rhetorical Action and the Enlargement of the EU", *International Organization*, 55, 47–80.

Schlichte, Klaus, and Boris Wilke, 2000, "Der Staat und einige seiner Zeitgenossen", *Zeitschrift fuer Internationale Beziehungen*, 7(2), 359–84.

Shaw, Martin, 2000, *Theory of the Global State: Globality as an Unfinished Revolution*, Cambridge: Cambridge University Press.

Slaughter, Ann Marie, 2003, "A Global Community of Courts", *Harvard International Law Journal*, 44, 191–220.

Strange, Susan, 1998, *Mad Money*, Manchester: Manchester University Press.

Tarrow, Sidney, 1998, *Power in Movement: Social Movements and Contentious Politics*, Cambridge: Cambridge University Press.

van Appeldoorn, B., 2002, *Transnational Capitalism and the Struggle over European Integration*, London: Routledge.

Wendt, Alexander, and Raymond Duvall, 1989, "Production, the State and Change in World Order", in E. Czempiel and J. Roseanu (eds), *Global Changes and Theoretical Challenges*, Lexington KY: Lexington Books, chap. 4.

Willke, Helmut, 2001, *Atopia: Studien zur atopischen Gesellschaft*, Frankfurt: Suhrkamp.

Zizek, Slavoj, 1999, *The Ticklish Subject: An Essay on Political Ontology*, London: Verso.

Zuern, Michael, 1998, *Regieren jenseits des Nationalstaats: Globalisierung und Denationalisierung als Chance*, Frankfurt: Campus.

Index